# SPIRIT, QI, AND THE MULTITUDE

COMPARATIVE THEOLOGY: THINKING ACROSS TRADITIONS

Loye Ashton and John J. Thatamanil, *Series Editors*

This series invites books that engage in constructive comparative theological reflection that draws from the resources of more than one religious tradition. It offers a venue for constructive thinkers, from a variety of religious traditions (or thinkers belonging to more than one), who seek to advance theology understood as "deep learning" across religious traditions.

# SPIRIT, QI, AND THE MULTITUDE

## A Comparative Theology for the Democracy of Creation

HYO-DONG LEE

*Fordham University Press* NEW YORK 2014

Fordham University Press also publishes its books in a variety of electronic formats. Some content that appears in print may not be available in electronic books.

Library of Congress Cataloging-in-Publication Data
Lee, Hyo-Dong.
Spirit, Qi, and the Multitude : a comparative theology for the democracy of creation / Hyo-Dong Lee.
pages cm — (Comparative theology: thinking across traditions)
Includes bibliographical references and index.
Summary: "A comparative theological and philosophical analysis of the concept of spirit in the West and the concept of qi (ch'i) in East Asia in regard to their respective and mutually illuminating potentials for sustaining a pluralistic and democratic metaphysical vision of the cosmos" — Provided by publisher.
ISBN 978-0-8232-5501-6 (hardback) — ISBN 978-0-8232-5502-3 (paper)
1. Qi (Chinese philosophy) 2. Philosophy, Korean. 3. Philosophy, Chinese. 4. Spirit. 5. Philosophy, Modern. 6. Cosmology. I. Title.
B127.C49L4 2014
181'.11—dc23

2013014386

Printed in the United States of America

16 15 14 5 4 3 2 1

First edition

*for Younhee and Saehan*

# CONTENTS

# PREFACE

This book has been long in coming. The job of Christian theologians is an arduous and often dispiriting one today, unless they are blissfully unaware of either the checkered history of the theological tradition to which they are committed or the confusing and even perilous cultural and religious landscapes, full of discordant voices and diverging paths, which they have to navigate. A case in point is a theologian from a corner of East Asia (Korea) who has been a recipient of the ambiguous legacy of missionary Christianity with all its blessings and woes, and who has migrated to the de facto center of the Western-dominated global order (the United States) and participated in its benefits and hazards, like myself. Although I do not want to be too autobiographical and present this book exclusively as a narrative of my search for religious and cultural identity, my personal background (male, heterosexual, "middle-class," Korean, Christian, post-colonial, Western-educated, diasporic, and so on) has certainly had a lot to do with—and much complicated—my preoccupation in writing this book: to reenvision the trinitarian God in a deep encounter with my East Asian and Korean heritage.

If there is a single running thread—a *cantus firmus*—and a driving concern in this task of comparative-theological reconstruction, it is the idea of *democracy* and what I believe is the pressing need for its theological articulation in the contemporary global context filled with various forms of political oppression, economic exploitation, and cultural marginalization. By democracy I do not mean narrowly the well-known concept in political philosophy that has its historical provenance in the Western political tradition and serves as the animating ideal for the diverse forms of government by the elected representatives of the citizens of the modern nation-states today. I am using the term more broadly as a cipher for the notion that people and ultimately all creatures have the power to rule and to create themselves. My comparative-theological reflection on such a notion of democracy draws its inspiration and impetus primarily from the biblical narrative of the coming of the Holy Spirit on Pentecost on the one hand and the Donghak (Eastern Learning) account of the descent of Ultimate Gi (Qi) on the other. In my assessment, both signal the advent of a new age in which all of the creaturely multitude are empowered to release their spontaneous capacity for self-creativity, self-determination, and self-rule. That is why my focus is on a *pneumatocentric* or Spirit-centered reconstruction of the Trinity that attempts to follow the wild wind of the Spirit, which truly "blows where it will"—East and West, North and South. In this book, I track its movement East and West first. I bring together the Western, Christian theological concept of Spirit (or its philosophical analogues) and the East Asian, Daoist, and Confucian notion of *qi* (which is better known in the West as *ch'i* and read as *gi* in Korean) in order to construct theological and philosophical underpinnings for the idea of democracy—that is, what may be called *a metaphysics of democracy*. In that sense, this book is not a full-blown eco-political theology that would trace the movement of the Spirit North and South, but rather the metaphysical prolegomenon to such a work.

It is a truism to say that writing is never the work of a solitary individual. I have been supported and nurtured along the way by many who put faith in me as a theologian and scholar. I am especially indebted to Peter C. Hodgson, Catherine Keller, and Heup Young Kim—Peter for my continuing fascination with the liberating "winds of the Spirit" and my study of Hegel; Catherine for sparking my interest in Whitehead and Deleuze, not to mention her own tehomic theology; and Heup Young Kim for being a model for my comparative-theological engagement of the East Asian traditions, especially Confucianism and Donghak, with his theology of tao. I also extend my sincere appreciation to my colleagues at Drew University Theological School, especially Robert Corrington, Wesley Ariarajah, and Christopher Boesel, and my students. Their encouragement, support, and thought-provoking questions have been invaluable, particularly when my thinking hit roadblocks.

I am genuinely grateful to Fordham University Press and its editorial staff for their adventurous spirit, excellent leadership, and impeccable attention to detail in publishing this book. My special thanks go to Helen

Tartar, editorial director. Without her enthusiasm shown my book, it may not have seen the light of day.

Above all, Younhee, my spouse, and Saehan, our son, deserve my deepest gratitude. For the last several years, as this book took shape, they put up with my countless hours of sitting with my laptop in front of me. I dedicate this book to them.

# Prologue

## A MEETING OF TWO STORIES

One evening in the spring of 1897 in Korea, in a tiny village of peasants southeast of what is now Seoul, the capital city, a small group of people gathered in a house—a thatched hut—to perform the customary Confucian ritual of honoring the ancestors. When the food and drink offerings were set up on a table to face the wall, where the spirits of the ancestors were supposed to take a seat, the spiritual leader of the group, seventy-one-year-old Choe Si-hyeong (崔時亨 1827–1898 C.E.) whose honorific name was Haewol (海月), asked the group to reverse the table setup: "From now on, when you perform the ritual, set up the offerings to face yourselves."[1]

## The Story of Ultimate Energy in "Eastern Learning"

For centuries if not millennia, the food and drink offerings in the ritual of ancestor veneration had always been made to the higher spiritual powers for their enjoyment, not for the people who served them up. When the people helped themselves to the offering, it was always after they were graciously invited by the spiritual powers to participate in the enjoyment, the invitation being the sign of the pleasure and willingness of the spiritual powers to bless the good folk who had just proven their devotion and loyalty. Such a structure of worshipping or honoring higher spiritual powers seems to be fairly universal, historically speaking. We can discern it from the setup of temples and altars or the sequence of worships and rituals across cultures and religions. It is therefore hard to miss the fact that there was a potent symbolism involved in Haewol's act of reversing or turning upside down what was almost a universally accepted way of relating to higher spiritual powers.

The symbolism becomes even more potent when we understand the timing of Haewol's instruction, as indicated by the way his words began: "*From now on.*" When was the "now"? Haewol gave that speech three years after the first revolutionary attempt at establishing a government of the people, by the people, for the people in Korea was defeated by an imperial, colonial power. In 1894, a largely peasant revolutionary army of one hundred thousand, armed mostly with spears and matchlock muskets, marched to the capital city, Seoul. At the strategically crucial mountain pass of Ugeumchi, it was met by the combined forces of the Imperial Japanese Army and the client Korean government troops, well entrenched in their defensive positions and armed with artillery, Gatling guns, and modern high-powered rifles. There, after four days of bloody battle, their dream of a new world, a new era, died, together with the short-lived democratic self-government which they had established in the most populous southwestern province under their control.[2] Haewol was the spiritual leader who had inspired that dream, while being reluctant to use force to achieve it.

Now on the run and in hiding, in what was probably the darkest hour for himself and his followers, in fact with only a year left before he was to be captured, tried, and executed, Haewol taught his last teaching, which many in the West or North Atlantic world might misinterpret as a secular-humanistic disavowal of higher spiritual powers, but which was in fact the spiritual climax and culmination of the revolutionary dream of his and his followers. To explain what I mean, we need to go back thirty-seven years earlier, to the year 1860. In that year, the British and French expeditionary forces captured Beijing, the capital of the neighboring Chinese Empire, after a series of brutal campaigns, and burned down the summer palace of the emperor, the Son of Heaven. It was an event with earth-shaking repercussions in Korea as China's model client state within the old imperial order. The British and the French, together with their U.S. and Russian allies, forced various humiliating territorial and trade concessions upon the Chinese Qing Dynasty, including—significantly—unimpeded Christian missionary activities, at a time when all of Southern China was wrested from the Qing control by the Taiping Rebellion, the leader of which was a product of Christian missionary activities. The supreme leader of that colossal and bloody struggle, a heterodox Christian convert named Hong Xiuquan, called himself a Son of God and the younger brother of Jesus, and saw it as his God-given mandate to restore China to the forgotten classical Confucian worship of the Lord on High

(上帝 *shangdi*), whom he identified with the Christian God, by setting up an apocalyptic Heavenly Kingdom of Great Peace.[3]

In the other neighboring nation, Japan, the gunboat diplomacy of the United States had forced open its doors to the West several years earlier, and helped it begin a process of rapid modernizing, "enlightening" transformation—in the fashion of the European Enlightenment—which was to enable Japan to "escape" Asia and to join the ranks of the modern imperial powers. Japan was soon to copycat, at the Korean port of Incheon, the same tactics taught it by the U.S. navy, forcing its way into the heart of the Korean peninsula as the first act of its eventually successful colonizing project. Within Korea, the five-hundred-year-old rule of the Confucian literati of the Joseon Dynasty, called *yangban*, had exhausted the socially and culturally reforming impulses of its beginning, and was losing its once firm grip on the people and their everyday way of life, as it faced the widespread corruption in the government and the repeated revolt of the exploited mass of peasants. Roman Catholic Christianity had reached the Korean shores many decades earlier and was spreading its revolutionary message of the equality of all people—men and women, *yangban* aristocrats and peasants, Koreans and "barbarian" foreigners—before one God, called Lord of Heaven (天主 *cheonju*); yet its Vatican-directed condemnation of traditional Confucian rituals and customs such as the ancestor veneration as pagan idolatry, and its repeated appeal to the intervention of the European imperial powers, together put on Catholic Christianity an indelible stamp of being an alien threat, leading to brutal persecutions that drove it underground.[4]

In such a time of external and internal crises, in a remote village located in the southeastern corner of Korea, someone heard a divine voice. That person was Choe Je-u (崔濟愚 1824–1864 C.E.), whose honorific name was Su-un (水雲). Su-un was Haewol's teacher and spiritual predecessor.[5] He was an ex-Confucian scholar, born into the ruling class of Confucian literati, but whose once illustrious family line had fallen to the nadir of poverty and marginalization in his generation. Forced into what was the degrading occupation of trading in everyday items such as cotton cloth, he had traveled all over the country and witnessed the suffering of people in a highly tumultuous, confusing, and oppressive time, under the looming threat of foreign imperial powers and the corrupt and tyrannical hands of the ruling elites. To find an answer to the spiritual and social ills of his time, Su-un had returned to his hometown, secluded himself in a mountain cave, a Buddhist place of retreat, and started to pray fervently to the highest spiritual power yet unknown to him. After a year of spiritual wrestling, praying for forty-nine days at a time like a devout Buddhist, he finally had a life-changing encounter with *haneullim* (하늘님) or Lord Heaven, whose teaching he initially thought was the Christian teaching, only to be immediately corrected by Lord Heaven. In the wake of that encounter, Su-un started to proclaim a new teaching, that is, a new way (道 *do*), which promised a new age of peace and harmony, and which he claimed to encompass the traditional teachings of Confucianism, Buddhism, and Seondo (the Korean form of Daoism). He named the new teaching Donghak (東學), or Eastern Learning, in a self-conscious attempt at providing a revolutionary yet nonalien, indigenous alternative to what he considered was the inadequate, if not entirely false, teachings of Western Learning (Christianity).

Su-un's new teaching consisted in a simple truth: All of us were bearers of Lord Heaven. The core tenet of his teachings that enabled him to make that claim was the notion of 氣 (*gi*/*qi*),[6] which is part of the commonly shared cosmology among Northeast Asian cultures even today, and which I translate here as "psychophysical energy." Psychophysical energy has two modalities—receptive (陰 *eum*/*yin*) and active (陽 *yang*)—whose dynamic combination and constant turning into each other constitute the creative-transformative processes of the universe that give birth to all things. In this worldview there is nothing that is not psychophysical energy, for that energy is both mind and body, ideal and material, and spiritual and natural. Su-un made this notion of psychophysical energy the pivotal connecting link between Lord Heaven and human beings, when he went a step further to speak of Lord Heaven as *jigi* (至氣) or Ultimate Energy.

By Ultimate Energy, he meant psychophysical energy in its primordial and ultimate form, being mysterious, indescribable, ineffable, beyond existence and nonexistence, yet all-encompassing and omnipresent as the ground of being and becoming, as the dynamic creativity at the root of all things, and as the womb filled with chaotic waters from which the myriad creatures were born. Su-un taught his followers a regimen of bodily and meditational practices to cultivate and rectify their psychophysical energy in the attitude of sincerity, reverence, and trust; and at the core of this practice lay the recitation of a devotional incantation:

> Ultimate Energy being all around me here and now, I pray for its great descent. I bear Lord Heaven; and [the Heavenly work of] creative

> becoming is being established in me. If I never forget [the Heavenly presence within], I will know all things.[7]

By earnestly desiring and praying to be united with Ultimate Energy, people could become aware of the intimate connection between their own psychophysical energy and Ultimate Energy, because Ultimate Energy within them would speak to them as a personal deity, as Lord Heaven, and tell them the following earth-shaking truth: "My heart-and-mind is no other than your heart-and-mind."[8] Humanity is Heaven—this short sentence became the principal motto of the Donghak movement.

When one of his disciples asked a question about the difference between his teachings and Western Learning or Christianity, Su-un's answer was telling, because it encapsulated the challenge which his Eastern Learning threw down to Christianity and the entire Western or North Atlantic civilization whose imperial aggression was seen by him to be spearheaded by Christianity: Christians (or Westerners), he remarked, did not have in their bodies "the spirit of the harmonious becoming of psychophysical energy" (氣化之神 *gihwa ji sin*).[9] He explained what he meant as follows: Western Learning, or Christianity, lacked an understanding of the vital and intimate connection between Lord Heaven and humanity, between human beings, and between human and nonhuman creatures. As a result Western Learning excelled in the production of inauspicious death-dealing technologies and violent instruments of domination, as proven by the formidable armaments of the Western imperial powers, while promoting the selfish pursuit of individual salvation from this oppressive world by imagining a heavenly world where Lord Heaven was believed to dwell and to which people needed to go after death in order to be saved.[10]

What Su-un envisioned as his task was to create a community of bearers of Lord Heaven who were all equal to one another, here and now. As one of his first acts after his awakening to the truth, that is, his encounter with Lord Heaven, he emancipated his two female bond servants, and adopted one as his daughter and took the other in as his daughter-in-law—something virtually unthinkable for a person of his lineage. And as a growing number of people of diverse backgrounds gathered around him, he selected Haewol, who was a lowly son of poor peasants and nearly illiterate, as his spiritual successor. When Su-un was arrested and executed for alleged acts of treason after merely three years of propagating his new way, even after his disciples were all scattered to the four winds and the community dissipated, Haewol did not disappoint his teacher.[11] For three decades, as a hunted man constantly on the run, Haewol carried the torch, kept alive Su-un's teaching, rebuilt the community person by person, gathered the manuscripts of Su-un's writings to print the Donghak scriptures, propagated the good news that every human being embodied Lord Heaven, and attracted an ever-increasing multitude of people downtrodden and oppressed for millennia. This he did by giving them a sense of dignity as bearers of Lord Heaven and the hope for a new world in which none was to be treated as a nonperson just because he or she happened to be born as a peasant, a slave, or a woman—a new world in which even an animal, a bird, or a single blade of grass would be honored and respected as an embodiment of the highest spiritual power.

The following passages from *Haewol sinsa beopseol* (The sermons of Haewol the divine teacher)—part of the Donghak scriptures—give us a glimpse of that new world:

> At Seo Taek-sun's house, I [i.e., Haewol] heard the sound of Taek-sun's daughter-in-law weaving on the loom. I asked Taek-sun, "Who is weaving"? Taek-sun answered, "It's my daughter-in law." I asked again, "Is your daughter-in-law weaving truly your daughter-in-law weaving?" Taek-sun did not understand. Would that be the case only with Taek-sun? When someone visits you, do not say so-and-so has come for a visit, but say Lord Heaven has come.[12]
>
> We human beings come into the world by bearing the psychophysical energy of the divine spirit, and we human beings live by bearing the psychophysical energy of the divine spirit. How can it be the case only with human beings? In fact, there's nothing in the world that does not bear Lord Heaven. That bird song you hear is also the sound of a bearer of Lord Heaven.[13]
>
> What fills the entire universe is the one psychophysical energy of chaotic beginning. Refrain, therefore, from taking even a single step lightly. One day as I was resting, a child ran across the yard in front of me wearing a pair of wooden sandals. Alarmed by the tremor of the earth caused by the sound, I stood up, massaging my chest, and said, "My chest hurts, because of the sound of the wooden sandals." Cherish the earth as if it is the flesh of your own mother.[14]
>
> Lord Heaven relies on humans and humans rely on food. To be intimately attuned to all affairs is simply a matter of eating a bowl of rice.[15]

> Feed Lord Heaven by means of Lord Heaven, and serve Lord Heaven by means of Lord Heaven.[16]

If Lord Heaven as Ultimate Energy is embodied in every being, including ourselves and even in the very food which we are consuming to nourish ourselves, then we could even say that we are feeding and nourishing Lord Heaven by means of Lord Heaven in the simple act of sharing a bowl of rice or a loaf of bread. Then, we can perhaps understand why Haewol's last instruction—"From now on, set up the offerings for yourselves"—was the climax and culmination of the subversive dream of the multitude, who had accepted the way of Lord Heaven proclaimed by Su-un and Haewol, and whose vital energy had powerfully irrupted in the revolutionary resistance of 1894. By consecrating the food and drink offerings to themselves, that is, by returning the fruit of the labor of the unholy, ignoble, subjugated, and colonized multitude to the multitude themselves, they were resisting the forces that tried to sever the vital link of cosmic psychophysical energy between heaven and earth, the holy and the unholy, the noble and the base, male and female, the ruler and the ruled, the colonizer and the colonized. They were attempting to reestablish the free circulation of psychophysical energy in the entire *oikoumene*, the whole inhabited earth, without the artificial obstruction and excessive concentration of that cosmic energy in the hands of just a few or even one. By doing so, they were sounding the death knell of God as a perfectly transcendent monarch—the very God whom Su-un criticized as devoid of the harmonious becoming of psychophysical energy.

Su-un's notion of Ultimate Energy as Lord Heaven and vice versa, which I argue represents his subversive and resistant rewriting of the pivotal cosmological concept of psychophysical energy in the hegemonic East Asian traditions of Confucianism and Daoism, thus throws down the gauntlet to Christianity, which has always claimed to be empowered, driven, and guided by the Holy Spirit proceeding from God the Father, who is the lord and king of the universe. Yet the biblical testimonies declare that God is Spirit, whom we need to worship in spirit and truth (Jn 4:24), that we are bodily temples of God's Spirit (1 Cor 3:16), and that the Spirit of God dwells within us in Christ as the sign of our adoption as heirs of the new world, the reign of God, in which the whole creation will obtain the freedom of the glory of the children of God (Rom 8:9–17). In declaring us to be bearers of the Spirit, the biblical testimonies seem to point to a connecting link, that is, a mediation by spirit, between God and creatures, the holy and the unholy, the noble and the base, in the Good News of Jesus Christ, which the apostle Paul proclaims. Is the Holy Spirit then not something analogous to the "spirit of the harmonious becoming of psychophysical energy"?[17] This book is in a major sense a Christian theological attempt to answer this question in the affirmative. But in order to try an answer, we need first to tell the story of the Holy Spirit in Christianity more closely.

## The Story of the Holy Spirit in "Western Learning"

One of the fundamental claims made by the Christian Scriptures about God is that God is Spirit (Jn 4:24; 2 Cor 3:19). As the translation of the original biblical terms *ruach* and *pneuma*, the word "spirit" has rich semiotic connections to natural, biophysical phenomena, such as breath, wind, fire, water, and winged creatures, all of them metaphors for the power of creation, life, and healing that pervades the world. Spirit is the breath or life-force given to creatures to enliven and to empower them (Gen 2:7; 6:3; 7:15; Job 27:3; 33:4; Ps 104:29; Ezek 37:9–10; Jn 20:22). As a fluid and dynamic energy, Spirit permeates the universe like a swift wind or raging fire and carries out powerful acts of creation and salvation, of judgment and renewal (Gen 1:2, Ex 10:13; Matt 3:11–12; Jn 3:8; Acts 2:1–4). Like a gushing spring of water that flows and inundates the field, Spirit feeds and nourishes life (Jn 3:5; 4:13–14; 7:37–39). In the form of a hovering, brooding mother bird or dove (Gen 1:2; 8:11; Matt 3:16; Mk 1:9–11; Lk 3: 22; Jn 1:32), Spirit nurtures life and brings peace and renewal to the world.

At the same time, in close connection with the biblical terms *hochmah/sophia*[18] and *dabar/logos*,[19] the word "spirit" captures what is considered psychic or "spiritual" phenomena, such as consciousness, feeling, thought, speech, understanding, knowledge, intelligence, and wisdom, all of which have something of the divine in them. Spirit refers to human thoughts, feelings, and passions (Gen 41:8; 45:27; 1 Sam 1:15; 1 Kgs 21:5). Spirit is the divine gift of knowledge, understanding, speech, intelligence, and wisdom, which enable humans to act creatively (Ex 31:3) and to discern, proclaim, and carry out God's will (Ezek 36:27; Isa 11:2). Spirit is the power whereby God acts in creation (Gen 1:2; Job 33:4; Ps 104:30) and in human history, particularly through the agency of judges, prophets, apostles, and the Anointed One (Judg 3:10; 6:34; Ezek 11:5; Lk 4:18; Jn 20:22; Rom 1:9).[20]

As the latter—psychic and "spiritual"—phenomena largely presuppose a sense of intentional focus and centered activity premised on rational coherence and purposiveness, the concept of unified, self-integrative, and self-reflexive subject-agency here becomes an indispensable and prominent interpretive category for the notion of spirit. Within the theistic world of the Christian Scriptures, that God is Spirit implies that God is an intentional agent, and that the meaning of being human in the image of God must include the sense of being such an agent. At the same time, the metaphoric connections of the term spirit to the material and the elemental confer upon that unified subject-agency certain earthen qualities that strongly suggest its embodied and cosmic character. In other words, the intentionality, coherence, and unity of spirit as subject-agency, whether divine or creaturely, go hand in hand with the sense of its being the cosmic power and agent of life permeating the ebb and flow of the universe and incarnate in the multitude of different forms of being and life within it. This implies that the notion of spirit as subject-agency has an indelible association with the plethora of reflective, interpretive, passionate, and/or vital responses of embodied selves to one another in the cosmic web of relations. The intentional, coherent, and self-reflexively unified agency of *ruach/pneuma* is firmly anchored in the multiplicity of relational and responsive acts of creation, nurture, guidance, judgment, healing, and renewal that are ubiquitously present in creation. If the biblical affirmation, "God is Spirit," is to be taken seriously, then the biblical idea of God, as encapsulated in the Shema ("Hear, O Israel: The Lord our God is one Lord" [Deut 6:4])[21] or the classic New Testament declaration that God is love (1 Jn 4:8), can be adequately explored only when one never loses sight of the boundary-blurring character of *ruach/pneuma*, occupying the liminal space between one and many, ideal and material, mind and body, divine and creaturely, and metacosmic and cosmic.

It has been the function of the doctrine of the Trinity in Christian theological traditions to serve as a reminder of the boundary-blurring "spiritual" nature of God. In the classical construction of the trinitarian doctrine, which emerges from the patristic tradition, both East and West, and which arguably finds its most historically influential formulation in Aquinas, the Holy Spirit is the gift of the Father's love through which the Father begets the Son as his self-knowledge ("Word") and image, and creates all things in the image of the Son. It is also through this divine gift of love that the Father loves the Son and reconciles the fallen creatures to one another and to himself "in" the Son by "configuring" all things to the

Son—that is, by empowering all things to love and to conform to the Father in the same way that the Son loves and obeys the Father with the very gift of love given him. In the power of the same gift of love given them, the Holy Spirit, all things reach their true end, which is their eternal loving communion with the Father, by participating in the mutual love of the Father and the Son whose image they bear.[22] The portrayal of the Holy Spirit given here, namely, the loving communion of the Father and the Son, is one that attains its true meaning and goal only with the participation of all creation in the divine communion so that "God may be all in all" (1 Cor 15:28). By construing the fulfillment of the creative and reconciling love of God in and through the Spirit-enabled agency of creaturely spirits, the trinitarian doctrine presents a notion of spirit that bridges one and many, ideal and material, and divine and creaturely, in order to bring about a harmonious divine-human-cosmic Whole.

However, this theological tip of the hat to the biblical pneumatological tradition, intimated in the dynamically triadic structure of the Trinity that opens itself up in and through the agency of the Holy Spirit to all of creation, is by and large eclipsed in the dominant monotheistic and monarchical thrust of the trinitarian doctrine, which has exhibited what Laurel Schneider calls the "logic of the One."[23] Under the essentialist-substantialist rubrics of classical Western thought with asymmetrically binary and excessively dualistic constructions of one and many, transcendence and immanence, ideal and material, mind and body, spirit and nature, eternity and time, permanence and change, essence and existence, and substance and phenomena, the ideal unity of God is seen as originary and self-subsistent while the embodied multiplicity of God is regarded as derivative and dependent. The Father as simple, unitary, and immutable substance and singular agency is considered God in the most primordial, absolute, and unqualified sense from whom the Son eternally derives and the Spirit eternally proceeds, notwithstanding the ontological affirmation of the consubstantiality of the divine persons in the orthodox Nicene-Constantinopolitan creedal tradition. The Father is the one Unoriginate Origin, whereas the Son is his eternally—but freely—generated singular and unchanging Word or Image who acquires a body in the contingent and historically unique event of the Incarnation. The Spirit, who eternally proceeds from the Father and the Son as their mutual love, one pole of which is originary and the other derivative, comes to embrace the multitude of creaturely spirits only with the Father's decision to create the material world ex nihilo and send the Son into that world in the "economy" of salvation history.[24]

Granted, insofar as the Father's eternal, "immanent" relations to the Son and the Spirit are concerned (i.e., within the so-called "immanent Trinity"), the classical doctrine has always adamantly affirmed the equality of the divine persons. The three divine persons share a common divine substance or essence equally, because the Father communicates to the Son and the Spirit the totality of the divine essence without any diminishment. This means that the distinctions among the persons are purely relational, denoting relations of origin ("generation" and "spiration") which, unlike those found among creatures, do not imply any difference in quantity, degree, or power, because the relations are not accidental but "subsistent," being identical to the divine substance itself that is one and simple.[25] The Father is the Father only in relation to the Son, just as the Son is the Son only in relation to the Father, without there being any subordination or relation of superiority and inferiority between them. Likewise, the Father as the origin is so only in relation to the one who proceeds from the origin, the Spirit, and vice versa. Hence, the consubstantiality of the divine persons in principle resists monarchical interpretations of the intratrinitarian relations. What is more, as many contemporary trinitarian theologies have pointed out,[26] the classical trinitarian idea of perichoresis, namely, the mutual indwelling of the divine persons or their co-inherence in one another, works against any hierarchical understanding of the intratrinitarian divine life. The relations among the divine persons are characterized by love, other-centeredness, and mutuality, as seen in the Father's self-giving act of generating the Son and "breathing out" the Spirit in love, on the one hand, and the equally self-giving acts of obedience on the part of the Son and the Spirit who do the will of the Father, on the other. In addition, the divine persons glorify one another, never themselves. In their mutual glorification, one might observe that the trinitarian "throne" of God does not seem to be the exclusive possession of a single divine person, not even the Father.

Despite these genuine antimonarchical strains found in the classical doctrine, however, a certain hierarchical structuring seems almost intrinsic to the way the doctrine formulates the trinitarian divine relations. Even with all the caveats and careful qualifications made to dispel the specter of subordinationism, the very fact that the Father is conceived as the single origin of all divinity and divine attributes, and that the Son and the Spirit derive their essence from that origin, can easily open up the slippery slope toward understanding their relations as relations of hierarchical subordination, not merely of voluntary, loving subordination.[27] A prominent case in point is the ontological status of the Son as the Image of the Father. Just as the Son as the Father's self-knowledge and spoken Word mirrors the knower and speaker, the Son as the "visible" Image reflects the invisible Origin, the Father. But however much their equality by way of their identically shared essence is underscored, as seen in the affirmation of the Son as the *perfect* image of the Father,[28] a copy cannot help being always subordinate in rank, authority, and power to the original. Exacerbating the slide toward subordinationism is the tradition's other construal of the unity of the Father and Son in terms of the Son's obedience to the Father in knowledge and will: A copy must conform to the original. The hierarchical structuring intrinsic to the relation of origin reveals itself further in the insistence of the classical tradition that there can be only one perfect image, the only begotten Son, since the origin, the Father, is one.

When it comes to the Father's temporal, "economic" relationship to creation in and through the Son and the Spirit, the picture of the Father as an absolutely self-subsistent and independent sovereign monarch looms even larger. The classical doctrine, especially as articulated by Aquinas, is resolute in its affirmation of God's absolute independence from creation, allowing only God's logical—ideational—relation to creatures, not real relation.[29] In pneumatological terms, this means that the Spirit as the loving communion of the Father and the Son, which fulfills itself by opening itself up to and being incarnate in the communion of all things with one another and with God, has come to represent an ultimately—if not explicitly—derivative mode of being of the essentially immaterial, self-sufficient, unitary, unrelated, impassable, unchanging, omnipotent sovereign Father and his only begotten Son who is the Father's self-reflection.[30] One notable consequence of this "economic"—if not ontological—subordination of the Spirit to the originally disembodied and unrelated singular Father and his equally singular true heir is that the Spirit in the world has largely been understood to be sacramentally confined to the Christ, the only incarnate Son, and the church as his unworldly body, all in the name of the exclusive unity of the City of God transcending the messiness and discord of the City of Man.[31]

Particularly with the beginning of imperial Christianity and the elevation of the Christ of the church to the Christ of empire, his embodied humanity all but forgotten only a few centuries after he was brutally executed as a rebel by an imperial power, the Holy Spirit became the herald and envoy of the imperial Prince of Peace, guarding the *pax imperia* by presiding over and moving the imperial ecumenical councils that enforced unity upon the often fractious imperial domains.[32] Throughout the history of Christendom with its successive empires, from Roman to British (and, one might add, American), the Holy Spirit has remained for all intents and purposes a derivative and secondary name of the one God and Lord, despite the repeated emergence of at times resistant and subversive invocations of the name, from the Montanists and the Franciscan radicals in the mold of Joachim of Fiore to the Shakers and the early Pentecostals. The vivifying, saving, and sanctifying work of the Holy Spirit has been construed as that of "configuring" the dominant, ruling subjects of the empires to the divine imperial Prince of Peace who is the perfect and co-equal image of the self-sufficient, independent, impassable, and omnipotent sovereign Monarch and thus fully human only in name.[33] The flipside of this construal of the work of the Spirit is that the Spirit's mission has been understood, more often than not, to consist in "pacifying"—"civilizing" and "Christianizing"—the earthly and unruly mass of subaltern (female, colored, "native," queer, and laboring) subjects on whose back the illusory autonomy and transcendence of the dominant imperial subjects is founded.

In order to decolonize the Holy Spirit and creaturely spirits from their traditional subjection and subject-ification under totalizing imperial orders of alleged divine origin, we need to bring back into the spotlight the liminal notion of spirit, hovering back and forth between one and many, ideal and material, mind and body, and divine and creaturely, that is found in the biblical intuitions of spirit and retained, however dimly, in the trinitarian doctrine. The question is how to make sense of the biblical claim that God is "one God and Father of all, who is above all and through all and in all" (Eph 4:6) in such a way that the dynamic, liberating, immanent, historical, earthly, fluid, processional, relational, and pluralistic character of spirit's being is affirmed as the intrinsic being of God whom the biblical and doctrinal traditions at the same time have never failed to conceive as one originary and foundational subject-agent. In recent years, there has been a proliferation of pneumatocentric theologies in the North Atlantic world that attempt to answer this question by appealing to a wide range of resources, from the pioneering nondualistic constructions of spirit by Hegel and Tillich to contemporary liberationist, feminist, ecological, process, scientific, postmodern, and postcolonial thoughts.[34] Taking my cue from the Donghak critique of imperial and missionary Christianity for lacking "the spirit of the harmonious becoming of psychophysical energy," I would like to join the chorus of recent pneumatocentric theologies by drawing on the category of psychophysical energy and some of its representative conceptualizations in East Asia, especially in Confucianism, Daoism, and Donghak.

There is, however, a significant methodological issue that I need to address before I can move on. Traditionally those "other" religions of East Asia are not considered part of the legitimate sources of Christian theology. They are viewed as comprising separate religious identities with well-defined boundaries and, thus, seen to carry with them an ever-present danger of syncretism when their ideas are mixed into Christian theological reflections. Nevertheless, during the last half century or so, there has been an emergence of various "indigenizing," "inculturating," and "intercultural" theologies within world Christianity, with their efforts to articulate the Christian gospel in the symbols and conceptualities of local cultures and religions so that the gospel would not always speak in Greek. These newer "contextual" theologies have challenged the facile charges of syncretism for masking the global pretension of the hegemonic Western, Anglo-European Christianity with its provincial Greco-Roman/Germanic cultural and religious heritage taken to be timeless and universal. Such questioning of homogeneous and static understandings of the Christian "tradition" and "identity" goes hand in hand with the recent rise of a postcolonial critique of the universal category of "religion" as a Western colonial construct aimed at creating a rigid hierarchy of "religions" within which Christianity is placed at the top. By launching an assault on the category of religion, the postcolonial critique challenges the neatly drawn boundaries of "religions" as artificial constructs meant to suppress spontaneous and mutually transformative intercourse among cultures. The development of comparative theology in the latest decades contributes significantly to these criticisms of the negative judgments heaped upon the idea of syncretism. It calls for Christian theologians genuinely to honor the dialogical imperative of the religiously pluralistic world today by doing theology interreligiously, that is, not *after* interreligious dialogue but *in and through* interreligious dialogue, with a radical openness to the theologically transformative potential of the truth-claims of one's non-Christian interlocutors. In the next, introductory, chapter, I examine these developments in order to lay out clear steps in which my attempt at a constructive theology of Spirit-Qi will proceed by way of Asian contextual theology and comparative theology, even as I draw on the postcolonial insight into the sociopolitically contested nature of every cultural and religious identity.

# Introduction

## A DECOLONIZING ASIAN THEOLOGY OF SPIRIT AS A COMPARATIVE THEOLOGY OF SPIRIT-QI

Like many of the other tributaries to the ecumenical theology[1] of world Christianity since the beginning of political decolonization in the 1950s, Asian theology has been grappling with the task of critically examining the history of Christian mission in Asia in order to decolonize the theology of the younger churches in the Asian continent from the implicit and explicit hegemonic control historically exercised by the theology of the Anglo-European churches in the North Atlantic world. With this task in view, like its African and Latin American counterparts, Asian theology has tackled the two intertwined issues of cultural indigenization—or "inculturation"—and social liberation in order to respond to the twofold postcolonial-neocolonial context of the cultural hegemony of the West, on the one hand, and the sociopolitical and economic reality of pervasive injustice, oppression, and poverty, on the other.[2] The various inculturating theologies (such as the works of C. S. Song, M. Thomas Thangaraj, and Ryu Dong-sik) and the Asian theologies of liberation (most notably minjung theology in Korea and dalit theology in India) have been the products of this endeavor.

### Asian Theology: Cultural Indigenization and Social Liberation in a Postcolonial-Neocolonial Context

Asian theologies of inculturation start out with the premise, shared with their counterparts in Africa and Latin America, that every theology is a local theology, being a contextual, historical product of a particular time under the influence of a local culture or local cultures.[3] Accordingly, they try to articulate the Christian gospel in the symbols and concepts of local cultures and religions, so that the gospel would not always have to "speak in Greek." In particular, responding to the specificity of the Asian context of religious diversity, many put heavy emphasis on interreligious learning, regarding other religions as the storehouse of cultural symbols, linguistic tools, conceptual frameworks, and spiritual practices that can help Christian theology in Asia be truly Asian Christian theology.[4] They challenge the usual charges of syncretism directed against them for masking the global pretension of hegemonic Anglo-European Christianity with its provincial Greco-Roman and Germanic cultural and religious heritage taken to be universal and timeless.[5]

For these inculturating theologies, the dominant model has been—in the words of Robert J. Schreiter—that of indigenization as adaptation or "sowing" (the gospel being the seed and the local culture being the soil) vis-à-vis the colonial model of indigenization as translation (the gospel being the kernel and the local culture being the husk).[6] Against the essentially homogenous, static, and closed understanding of the gospel assumed in the translation model, which sees the essentially self-identical substance of the gospel merely taking on different linguistic garbs for the sake of more effective communication, the model of indigenization as adaptation accepts the notion of Christian tradition as a living entity that grows and changes by adapting itself to diverse environments. When driven to its logical conclusion, this model can go as far as to reject any attempt to carve out the unchanging transcultural core of biblical revelation from the cultural accretions of the Christian tradition and advocate more dynamic, historical, and relational ways of understanding the very notions of tradition and identity.

The adaptation model, however, has also been criticized for presupposing often an asymmetrical, even unilateral understanding of the gospel-culture relation in which the gospel or the Christian tradition is the theologically creative agent of change and the local culture the largely passive object providing the ore of theological resources to be mined.[7] In many versions of the model, the primary concern still lies in transmitting the received tradition effectively rather than engaging the local context so that the exigencies of the context shape the message of the gospel itself. One of the most radical of the Asian inculturating theologians, the Korean theologian of culture Kim Kyoung-jae, goes a step further to propose the model of "grafting," according to which the gospel is the shoot and the local culture the stock onto which the gospel is grafted.[8] This proposal envisions a more bilateral, dialogical, and context-centered relationship between the Christian tradition and the local culture in which both function as theological subjects taking part in the creative process of theological indigenization that always starts from the questions and issues emerging from within the local context. Kim's "grafting" model resonates with Schreiter's model of "interculturation" that moves beyond the more-or-less unidirectional concept of adaptation—as epitomized by the word "inculturation"—to envisage a process of bidirectional cross-fertilization between the two cultures, that is, the Jewish, Greco-Roman, and Anglo-European culture of the hegemonic missionary Christianity and the local "host" culture.[9] Kim and Schreiter both reject a hard-and-fast distinction between the transcultural core of the gospel and the cultural accretions of the Christian tradition, and view a creative form of syncretism or a "fusion of horizons" as an unavoidable aspect of the historical development of the dominant Christian tradition that emerged from within the Jewish culture and developed in a mutually transformative relationship with the Greco-Roman culture of the Mediterranean world and the Germanic culture of Western Europe.[10]

The strength of the model of grafting or interculturation lies in its recognition of the nonhomogenous and nonstatic nature of both the Christian tradition and the local culture, on the one hand, and of the need to take the cultural configurations of the local context as the starting point of theological reflection, on the other. Nevertheless, as the indigenization-contextualization debate of the 1970s and 1980s has shown, the discourse of indigenization or inculturation as a whole can sometimes be divorced from the dynamic and conflictual social relations underlying the cultural configurations of the local context.[11] It often concerns itself exclusively with the issue of cultural identity to the point of becoming a form of cultural romanticism and nativism unconcerned with resolving social conflicts and in effect ending up representing the interests of the dominant groups. It has been the role of liberation theologies to try to indigenize the gospel primarily in response to the concrete social conditions of systemic poverty, political oppression, and cultural marginalization in a given local context. Within the Asian context, minjung theology and dalit theology have carried the standard for liberationist approaches.[12] Minjung theology in Korea has focused on the poor, oppressed, and marginalized (minjung), namely the mass of exploited workers and farmers that materialized during the period of rapid industrialization in the 1970s and '80s led by a close partnership of military dictatorships with large family-owned business conglomerates.

The message of the gospel emerging in such contexts, minjung theology claims, is that the minjung are the subject-agents of the history and culture of their particular contexts and therefore the subject-agents as well of their salvation understood as liberation.[13] Accordingly, minjung theology has paid close attention to the marginalized symbols, narratives, and ritual practices of the poor and oppressed, including their reading of the Christian scripture, as the privileged loci of divine revelation and the very culture in which the gospel needs to be indigenized.[14]

Such an affirmation of the culture and religion of the poor and oppressed is echoed by dalit theology in India with its emphasis on the experience of the dalits, namely, the so-called "untouchables" historically associated with manual labor that was considered ritually polluting and therefore belonging to the lowest castes of India's traditional caste system, or outside the castes altogether. Criticizing what was known as "Indian Christian theology" in the past as a product of missionary Christianity's encounter with the high-caste—largely Brahmin—culture and religion, dalit theology attempts to base its theological reflection on the dalit experience of oppression, suffering, and exodus, and the stories and symbols that have arisen from that experience.[15]

Those who have advocated the use of the term "contextual theologies" since the indigenization-contextualization debate have done so in the belief that the term does a better job of interrelating the primarily cultural approach of inculturating theologies and the primarily political and economic approach of liberation theologies, minjung theology and dalit theology being good examples of Asian contextual theologies.[16] Contextual theologies, however, have recently been challenged by the rise of postcolonial biblical hermeneutics and postcolonial theologies, which have criticized both the discourse of indigenization and that of liberation with the help of postcolonial theories, notably the leading works of Homi Bhabha and Gayatri Chakravorty Spivak.[17] Attending to the colonial and postcolonial sociohistorical dynamic of both local and global cultural contexts, Homi Bhabha has advanced a nonessentialist concept of culture as a ground of contest in power relations, particularly the relations between the colonizer and the colonized, that serves as a hybrid "third space" of cultural identity between self and other, sameness and difference, collaboration and resistance.[18] There is, therefore, no pure, homogeneous culture, he claims, be it that of the colonizers or the colonized, that can provide the home of stable, secure, and superior identity vis-à-vis the other. Accordingly, there is no basis for the colonial practice of hierarchical recognition—the lining up of the colonizers, the "civilized" natives (forming part of the colonial elites), and the mass of colonized subjects along an essentialistic and supersessionistic developmental path. Neither is there any unmoving ground for the traditionalist, nativist, and nationalist movements of anti-imperial resistance and liberation when they appeal to the glory and pride of indigenous tradition or national culture and in the course of doing so suppress their own internal heterogeneity, including anything that sounds "modern" or "progressive" and therefore "Western" and alien—such as the call for the colonized women's voices to be heard and their right to represent their traditions to be recognized.

Spivak agrees with Bhabha that the grand narrative of Anglo-European colonialism and imperialism has always already inscribed itself within the cultural identities of the colonized and the decolonized peoples of the Two-Thirds World, and that therefore there are no pure, homogeneous "natives" uncontaminated by the culture of imperialism but only hybrid cultures performing acts of both mimicry and mockery of the colonizers—that is, acts of both collaboration and resistance.[19] At the same time, Spivak champions the voices of the "subalterns," namely, those excluded by the hegemonic discourses and practices of colonialism and imperialism, and calls for the creation of a space of ethical responsibility and mutuality (and yes, even *love*) that would allow the subaltern to come out of the space of utter, incommunicable difference to which they have been relegated. By participating in—and in thus becoming "adulterated" and "hybridized" by—hegemonic discourses, the subalterns can finally be heard and gain subjecthood and agency.[20] The subalterns' escape of subalternity is to be nurtured and promoted, she claims, given the postcolonial inescapability and necessity of inhabiting and appropriating the cultural heritage of Western imperialism, such as the essentializing metanarratives of nationhood, constitutionality, citizenship, democracy, and socialism, as an anchor and beachhead for the liberating agency of those at the margins. Nonetheless, this appropriation of essentializing metaphysical structures or metanarratives is only "strategic" in the sense that it is accompanied without ceasing by a critique of the very structure or narrative that one inhabits for the sake of holding ones' liberating oppositional agency together.[21] The deconstructive spirit of strategic essentialism, she avers, is precisely what keeps the subject-agency of the subalterns from being closed to the welling up of difference from within itself—such as the voices of the subaltern women—and prevents it from reincarnating the homogenized other of the colonizers' imaginations and nationalistic or nativistic anticolonial resistance.

Postcolonial biblical hermeneutics and postcolonial theologies have taken to heart postcolonial theory's critique of essentializing discourses of cultural nativism and liberation, as exemplified by R. S. Sugirtharajah's proposal for a postcolonial biblical hermeneutics beyond what he calls "vernacular" (nativist) hermeneutics and liberation hermeneutics.[22] Kwok Pui-lan and Marcella Althaus Reid, among others, call for a complexification of the relationship of theology to the concepts of culture and emancipatory subject-agent within the postcolonial world through the multiple and heterogenizing lenses of gender, race, class, sexuality, religion, and so on, in the name of postcolonial feminist theology and postcolonial queer theology, respectively.[23] Even as many Asian theologians, particularly Asian women theologians, have grappled in their writings with the sociopolitical, economic, and cultural impact of colonialism and imperialism in the lives of Asian men and women, Namsoon Kang criticizes the essentializing colonial (Orientalist and neo-Orientalist) assumptions of the homogenous identity of the Asian subject or the Asian female subject underlying their works, and asks: Who/What is Asian? Who are Asian women? What counts as Asian theology (or Asian feminist theology)? Who does Asian or Asian feminist theology?[24]

These questions and proposals, if earnestly engaged, help Asian theology be a more robust contextual theology in the postcolonial context of Asia. In the work of decolonizing Asian theology, postcolonial theologies help Asian theologians constantly be aware of and vigilant about what Spivak calls *postcoloniality* pervading their work of theological contextualization. Postcoloniality refers to the fact that the indigenous symbols, stories, texts, concepts, intellectual systems, rituals, and practices, which are chosen to serve as the seedbed or host for the gospel, are loci of cultural contestation and negotiation along the interlocking axes of power relations involving gender, race, class, sexuality, religion, and so forth. Further, postcoloniality names the fact that cultural contestation and negotiation taking place in those loci have always already been multiply inscribed by the essentializing metaphysical structures and grand narratives of Western cultural imperialism, whether these loci come primarily from the "high" culture of the precolonial, colonial, and neocolonial elites, or the "low" culture of the oppressed, exploited, and marginalized. This fact of postcoloniality suffusing the global-local or "glocal"[25] cultures makes a simple theological reversal—the proclamation that God is on the side of the (neo)colonized or the oppressed and marginalized groups—not a viable and productive option for decolonizing contextual theologies, as it simply reiterates the essentializing binary logic of the culture of imperialism.[26] What is needed, rather, is a much more complicated work of hearing the speech of the subaltern in Spivak's sense of the term, that is, making room for the hybrid voice and internally heterogeneous subject-agency of the oppressed and marginalized groups that are compromised and at the same time enabled by the hegemonic discourses and practices, both local and global.[27] We need to recognize that speech-agency precisely as the locus of the liberating absent presence of the divine and therefore as the privileged site of contextual-theological reflection. For this work, Asian theologians need to engage the culture and religion of the oppressed, exploited and marginalized groups in various Asian contexts through their symbols, stories, texts, concepts, rituals, and practices. They are to follow the way in which the self-emancipatory speech-agency of those groups has coalesced and come into being by inhabiting intimately and coding itself subversively within the dominant local and global discourses, while being continually destabilized by the perpetually vanishing trace of its internal difference, its own subaltern other.

The postcolonial and decolonizing path of theological contextualization, however, faces a thorny issue perhaps more intensely felt in the Asian context of religious diversity than in the other contexts. The work of contextualization as liberating inculturation needs to engage the global-local cultures with an acute attunement to the postcolonial cultural dynamic operating in them along the interlocking axes of power relations. But should those interlocking axes include *religion*? In other words, while Christian contextualizing theologies are to engage preferentially the symbols, stories, texts, concepts, rituals, and practices of the oppressed, exploited, and marginalized groups within a global-local context, are the *religious* symbols, stories, texts, concepts, rituals, and practices of those groups to be included in that preferential option, even if they are non-Christian? It is true that the intercultural method of theological contextualization affirms religious syncretism as an inevitable and necessary feature of the Christian tradition as a dynamic, historical, and relational entity. However, many of them do so by assuming a more or less clear distinction between religion and culture and by allowing the participation of non-Christian religions in the syncretistic process only as repositories of cultural symbols, linguistic tools, conceptual frameworks, and communal practices, not as well-defined systems of belief and practices concerning matters of ultimate concern, to paraphrase Paul Tillich's famous definition of religion.[28] Is such a clear-cut distinction warranted? This question invites a discussion of comparative theology as a form of contextual theology in today's religiously pluralistic, postcolonial-neocolonial *glocal* context.

## Comparative Theology: A Decolonizing Contextual Theology in a Religiously Pluralistic Context

One of the most prominent features of today's world is religious plurality. The economic, sociopolitical and cultural forces of recent history have all worked to interweave the fate of different religious communities to an unprecedented degree, both globally and in the North Atlantic world. To an extent never before paralleled, different religious communities around the world are pushed by the forces of the postcolonial history to inhabit not merely neighboring spaces but a *common* economic, political, and cultural space and in so doing to become constituents of a larger, more encompassing human community.[29] The dominant theological response to this newfound centrality of the issue of religious plurality, especially in the North Atlantic context but not limited to it, has been what is called theology of religions—or theology of religious pluralism—as a self-conscious thematic focus and subspecialty within Christian theology. The key debate within theology of religions has involved the question of the salvific efficacy of non-Christian religions and has centered on the typology of exclusivism, inclusivism, and pluralism.[30] No matter which type, theology of religion is an attempt to come up with overarching theological theories accounting for the fact of religious plurality in the world by drawing mainly on resources within the Christian tradition. Since 1990, however, there has been a surge of interest in comparative theology, especially in North America, among Christian theologians who are academically trained also in the study of other religious traditions, particularly Hinduism and Buddhism.[31] Criticizing theology of religions as abstract and premature theorizing about religious plurality, comparative theology has demanded that the Christian theologian first learn concretely the wisdom and insights of other religions and take them as his or her primary resource and working context. The leading voices, Francis Clooney and James Fredericks, have argued that comparative theology should consist of limited case studies that interpret specific elements of the Christian tradition in comparison with and in the light of specific elements of another religious tradition.[32] In practice, this means that one reads the Bible or Christian theological texts together with the texts of another religious tradition, and lets one's reading of the Christian texts be informed by the insights garnered from the concomitant reading of the other texts.[33]

This dialogical and textual emphasis of comparative theology has emerged partly in response to another critic of theology of religions, especially in its pluralistic variety—namely, postliberal theology with its emphasis on the incommensurability and untranslatability of religions.[34] Postliberal theology has claimed that, just as each language constitutes a semiotic "world" not reducible to another, religious traditions form culturally and linguistically distinct communities of discourse and practice that are mutually incommensurable and cannot therefore be translated into putatively neutral and universal categories for the sake of gaining plausibility and truth. Nevertheless, although religious traditions are incommensurable and therefore resist being translated into universal categories, each does translate and redescribe the entire world to form a coherent worldview.[35] Religious scriptures and doctrines, postliberal theology contends, function both as the rules shaping and governing the communal life of each religious community and as the "lens" through which everything is interpreted "intratextually" within its semiotic world. Such a grammatical and interpretive function of scriptures and doctrines, it argues, confers the characteristics of centrality and comprehensiveness on the truth claims made by religious communities—the characteristics that render those truth claims very difficult, if not impossible, to reconcile with one another.[36]

Although partly agreeing with the postliberal notion of intratextuality insofar as it concerns the thesis of incommensurability of religions, Clooney and Fredericks have criticized its corollary, the thesis of untranslatability, as one-sided.[37] They have argued that, when one reads the texts of the Christian tradition together with the texts of other religious traditions, and lets the reading of one be informed by the parallel reading of the other, he or she is in fact stepping outside of the Christian intratextual world by inscribing the Christian texts within a larger context formed by the strange and alien texts of other religions and their equally unfamiliar commentarial traditions.[38] Just as all of reality, including the texts of other religions, is translated and redescribed within the semiotic world of the Bible and tradition, as the postliberal thesis of Christian intratextuality argues, the texts of the Christian tradition can also be translated and redescribed within other semiotic worlds. This, they claim, enables the comparative-theological reader to reread and reuse the Christian text "in a way that is strikingly divergent from the intention of its author and from the tradition's habitual handling of it."[39] Such an unconventional strategy of textual retrieval, which resists habitual choices and evaluations as to what constitutes the most important, representative, and original in the tradition, is not merely for the sake of novelty but in order to excavate the forgotten and repressed possibilities of reading the Christian theological tradition.[40] In other words, comparative theology is a form of open, self-critical, nonidolatrous, and relational commitment to one's home tradition.[41]

It is to be noted that neither Fredericks nor Clooney criticizes the postliberal notion of religious intratextuality with a general theory of religion. For Clooney, what makes a comparative reading possible is not a general theory of religion but the *truth* of other religious texts, namely, their transformative power and claim on the reader who reads with openness to being changed by the texts.[42] For Fredericks, comparative theology is an exercise of skills for interreligious friendship, that is, "skills for living responsibly and creatively with non-Christians"[43] who invite Christians to interreligious friendship on the strength of the innate attractiveness of their beliefs and practices.[44] Nonetheless, recent developments in various critical—cultural, postcolonial, feminist, and so on—theories of religion have exposed the power relations woven into the discourses of religious studies, interreligious dialogue, and theology of religions, and have thereby theoretically both clarified and complicated the work of comparative theology. These critical theories ask: Whose tradition? Which texts? Why texts? In what language and symbols? For whose interests? What is "religion," to begin with? What are these different entities called "religions" implied in the adjective "interreligious"?

The postliberal notion of religious intratextuality has been influenced in a large measure by the anthropologist Clifford Geertz's phenomenological and structuralist definition of religion as a cultural system or a system of symbols generating and conveying meanings linked to conceptions of a general order of existence.[45] In his influential critique of Geertz, Talal Asad has argued against Geertz's formalistic and abstract conception of religion as a self-originating and self-contained semiotic system, and instead advanced a material, dynamic, and relational conception of religion as a concrete way of life predicated on sociohistorical practices and subject to forces of social antagonisms.[46] Critically assessing the modern notion of culture as a self-contained, clearly bounded, and internally homogenous unit of meaning with socially integrative functions, Kathryn Tanner has also proposed a material, dynamic, and relational cultural theory of religion that stresses the indeterminate, internally diverse, hybrid, conflictual, and contested character of religious identity formation predicated on historical processes of social interaction.[47] Asad and Tanner are part of the growing chorus of scholars who question the hitherto dominant conception of religion and religious symbols as unique, self-generating entities. They criticize it as an abstraction originating both from the privatizing and universalizing modern Christian theological assumptions and from the modern Western demarcation of the secular public sphere that divorced the domain of religion and religious meaning from concrete sociopolitical, economic, and cultural practices.[48] They have shown that the universal comparative category of "religion" that emerged in the last few centuries in the West, which putatively captured the essence of an independent religious domain based on the unity of human religious experience, was a colonial construct aimed at regulating cultural differences by creating a hierarchy of "religions" or "world religions." Within such a hierarchy, Christianity, which was associated with a firm sense of transcendence of everything earthly (such as geographic, national, ethnic, and cultural boundaries or material and political concerns), ranked at the top as the most consummate "world religion," that is, as the perfect realization of the universal category of religion and a lofty testimony to the superiority and universality of Western civilization.[49]

These scholars differ on their assessment of the viability and usefulness of the category of religion today, ranging from the radical demand made by Timothy Fitzgerald to do away with the category altogether to the more moderate stance of Richard King and Talal Asad calling for religious representations and meanings to be thoroughly intertwined with analyses and explanations of concrete social practices and cultural discourses that generate them.[50] They all, however, agree on the view that religions, like cultures, are not monolithic, fixed, and unique entities consisting of systems of symbols existing by themselves. Religions are, to quote Anselm Min, thoroughly relational "concrete totalities" whose respective boundaries and internal configurations are constantly changing in accordance with alterations in their sociohistorical conditions.[51] If religions are such concrete totalities, religious identity is not a stable and static set of commonly held beliefs, ideas, symbols, and texts deposited in tradition and acting unilaterally as regulative grammar. Rather, religious identity is a site of both regularity *and* contestation in which people as embodied carriers of tradition generate the sense of who they are by skillfully negotiating and contesting various social and cultural identities coursing through the site and being inscribed in their gendered, racialized, sexualized, and laboring bodies.[52] Any neatly drawn boundaries of "religions" or "world religions" are therefore artificial constructs meant to suppress spontaneously and mutually transformative intercourse among cultures based on concrete social interactions.

Inspired by the newly emerging material, dynamic, and relational theories of religion, one of the new generation of comparative theologians, Hugh Nicholson, launches a fresh critique of the unidirectional conception of religious intratextuality advocated by postliberal theology for being blind to the cultural hegemony of the West woven into interreligious relations. What prevents intratextuality from working both ways in interreligious relations—that is, what keeps other religious texts and their worldviews from simultaneously acting back upon the Christian interpretive framework—is not, he argues, some kind of intrinsic inviolability and untranslatability of the Christian semiotic system but the asymmetry in social power relations. In other words, it is Christianity's association with the global hegemony of Western civilization that impedes the reverse interpretive flow and in so doing empirically "proves" the postliberal thesis of the unidirectional intratextuality of the Christian semiotic system.[53] Comparative theology as practiced by Clooney and others, he claims, functions in fact as a strategy of neutralizing the power differences between the Christian intratextuality and the intratextuality of other religious traditions. It functions as a strategy of counteracting what the postcolonial critic Dipesh Chakrabarty calls "asymmetric ignorance"—or, in Spivak's words, "sanctioned ignorance"[54]—which frees the scholars and theologians in the West from the need to refer to non-Western classics while their non-Western counterparts feel the pressure to refer to Western classics for the sake of gaining recognition as legitimate partners in academic and theological discourses.[55] It is precisely this political act of restoring symmetry in power relations, similar to the comparative juxtaposition of religious texts or concepts practiced currently in the comparative study of religion, that enables the Christian semiotic system genuinely to experience the transformative power of non-Christian texts and their worldviews, leading to a new and even unconventional relational-dialectical constitution of Christian identity sought by comparative theology.[56]

How does the experience of the transformative power of non-Christian texts and worldviews arise in the bidirectionally conceived process of intratextuality, concretely speaking? Nicholson puts forward a relational model of metaphorical negotiation and redescription, involving two terms of comparison on an equal footing, à la Paul Ricoeur's theory of metaphoric process and the new paradigm of comparative studies of religion proposed by Jonathan J. Smith. In the identity-forming metaphorical process between two religious relata, one term represents the past formulations of Christian identity in continuity with the notion of the people of God as portrayed in the biblical narrative (championed by the postliberal notion of intratextuality), while the other pole reflects the current encounters with other worldviews borne aloft by the social dynamics of each particular historical and geographic situation.[57] Comparative theology, Nicholson contends, forms an integral part of such a metaphorically redescriptive process leading to destabilization and reformulation of Christian identity. Such a comparative theology stands in contrast to the earlier, liberal-universalist comparative theology of the nineteenth century, which employed metonymies to establish depoliticized and allegedly universal categories of comparison, such as "universal religion" or "world religion," that masked their provincial and political origin in the universalizing and supersessionistic agenda of Anglo-European liberal Protestant Christianity.[58]

Nicholson's work makes a persuasive case for comparative theology being an integral part of the enterprise of Christian theology as such, by pointing out the intrinsically relational constitution of Christian identity predicated on social dynamics that unavoidably include interreligious dynamics in today's global-local context. Moreover, it gestures toward the need for comparative theology to complicate further the concept of religion operating in the adjective "interreligious" and to problematize essentialist notions of interreligious relations and dynamics in a way similar to the anti-essentialist moves made by Richard King and others in the comparative study of religion.[59] Echoing this gesture, John Thatamanil draws a parallel between essentialist notions of interreligious dialogue and the much criticized paradigm of "race relations," which employs the colonial category of race as a biological and ontological reality that is divided up into various races whose mutual relations then need to be theorized. Similar to the paradigm of race relations, the essentialist paradigm of interreligious relations and interreligious dialogue regards religions as quasi-ontological realities with clear and impermeable boundaries and whose external relations are managed by a hierarchical and developmental trajectory in which various world religions lead in tow those religions not yet arisen to the status of world religions.[60] Pointing to the porosity of religious identities and the rich diversity within as well as across religious traditions, Thatamanil urges comparative theologians to take seriously the possibility that differences *within* traditions may prove to be sharper than those *across* religious traditions.[61] If liberated from their captivity to the colonially constructed notions of homogeneous and intrinsically unrelated religious identities, he argues, comparative theologians can then freely engage religious others, such as the Buddhist thinker Nagarjuna, not merely as objects of theorizing or as "native informants" but as normative thinkers whose claims and arguments require comparative theologians to rethink their own, both in the work of theorizing interreligious relations and in the work of reformulating Christian symbols and doctrines.[62]

One of the pioneering works by Clooney, *Hindu God, Christian God*, shows that there exist unexpected interreligious parallels between some of the core tenets of Christian theology and classical Hindu thought (such as the cosmological argument for the existence of God and the concept of divine embodiment); this book has borne out in concrete practice Thatamanil's argument that substantive religious differences do not always coincide with established religious boundaries.[63] Thatamanil's own ground-breaking, interreligiously constructed thesis, that the trinitarian paradigm of ground, contingency, and relation can be discovered in many religions with a similar or even equal degree of internal differences, variations, and hues, also confirms in practice the claim that intrareligious differences may trump interreligious differences.[64] In this light, perhaps comparative theologians might find useful David Chidester's definition of religions as "intrareligious and interreligious networks of cultural relations"[65] Chidester's call for the study of religion to examine "the production of meaning and the contestation of power in situations of cultural contact and change"[66] nudges comparative theology as a political strategy of neutralizing power differences in interreligious relations, as Nicholson defines it, to pay attention also to the power differences in *intrareligious* relations. Spivak's notion of "sanctioned ignorance" needs to be applied not only to the relative Western neglect of the "classics" of the non-Western world religions but also to the

West's overwhelming nonrecognition of the non-Western religious representations of the oppressed, exploited, and marginalized except as objects of ethnography or "area studies." After all, the "core" texts of the "great world religions" representing the locally and traditionally hegemonic yet globally marginalized elite discourses—such as those of India's Brahmins and China's Confucian literati—have in many instances been recognized as "classics" by the West, however grudgingly, because they are deemed to contain the ahistorical and unchanging essence of true religion covertly modeled after modern liberal Christianity. In other words, they are thought to transcend earthly boundaries and material concerns to speak to all people about things spiritual through an authoritative body of tradition encapsulated in written scriptures. Many in the West have often recognized their status as classics even with much enthusiasm because they are imagined, in their premodern traditionality, to retain the religious essence that has been lost in the now secularized modern West—the perspective that is the essence of Orientalism, as Edward Said has so profoundly analyzed and exposed it.[67] The traditionalist and nativist religious nationalism of the colonial and neocolonial elites demands recognition of their core religious texts as classics on a par with the classics of the West precisely on those terms, thereby unwittingly perpetuating Christian theological imperialism and the master-narrative of the fulfillment of the East in the West, as Richard King and others have shown.[68]

In view of this history, the first order of the day for comparative theology, strategically speaking, should be a social and cultural analysis of the non-Western and non-Christian religious representations and discourses—symbols, stories, ideas, and texts—produced by the "outsiders within," to quote Michelle Voss Roberts,[69] within the communities of the world religions, including those in situations of transnational migration, exile, and diaspora in the present postcolonial-neocolonial global context.[70] This is to be followed by a political act of neutralizing power differences, both intra- and interreligiously, by including those religious representations and discourses in the extrabiblical theological canon of comparative theology. Such an act of inclusion is analogous to the discourses of multiculturalism and politics of difference widely practiced today, especially in the metropolitan centers of the global order, such as the demand made by women and minority communities that their history and tradition be included in the curriculums of public education.[71] It amounts to what is called the recognition of the "participatory parity" of all—that is, the recognition of the free subject-agency of the members of oppressed and marginalized groups to participate equally and fully in social interaction.[72]

In calling for comparative theology as a political strategy of neutralizing power differences to apply itself not only to interreligious relations but also to intrareligious relations, I partly share the concerns articulated in Kwok Pui-lan's plea for a postcolonial theology of religious difference: that academic theology go beyond the preoccupation of theologies of religious pluralism with religious truth and meaning conveyed by the different religious symbols of world religions and that it first and foremost examine "religious difference as it is constituted and produced in concrete situations, often with significant power differentials" along the intersecting identity markers of gender, race, sexuality, class, and so on.[73] Although I appreciate Kwok's pointing to the traditional neglect of the second task in theologies of religious pluralism, I do not think that the two modes of theological operation constitute an either/or for comparative theology. Once comparative theology recognizes the participatory agency of the "outsiders within" and gives them space to speak, there should not be any artificial barriers to a heartfelt recognition of the value or worth of their group-specific cultural and religious identity as expressed and conveyed in their religious representations. Otherwise, the political act of inclusion is blocked from going beyond a mere "tolerance" of the oppressed and marginalized that may actually be a thinly veiled contempt of who and what they are.

A classic diagnosis of this phenomenon of recognition in bad faith is found in the Martinican-French psychiatrist and philosopher Frantz Fanon's famous postcolonial reading of Hegel's "master-slave dialectic," where he points out the essential separability of the master's manumission of the slave from his heartfelt recognition of the slave as an equal.[74] The master, argues Fanon, may free the slave out of fear of rebellion, and in doing so recognize the slave's free and self-determining agency, yet at the same time can still regard the slave as quite inferior to him. Such a condescending recognition of free agency is precisely what Fanon finds prevalent in the postcolonial situation in which the former colonizers who have recognized and let go of the colonized as free beings still refuse to acknowledge the latter, including their culture and way of life, as on a par with themselves and their own values. In such a situation as Fanon describes, although there may exist a mutual recognition of free participatory agency, social solidarity is out of the question.[75]

Nevertheless, despite the need for comparative theology's recognition of the oppressed and marginalized to be in good faith, there is something self-contradictory about the notion of recognition of worth given to certain values and practices *solely* because of their uniqueness and difference. Recognition, as *re-cognition*, implies the seeing, remembering, and rediscovering of oneself in another, and therefore involves by definition some assessment and evaluation of another from one's perspective and criteria, for both individuals and communities. Charles Taylor's pioneering essay on the politics of recognition shows how a suppression of this fact actually results in nonrecognition. If one's recognition of the worth of another is produced purely by the force of will following a sense of moral imperative to respect difference as such, it can easily become patronizing if not downright condescending: I do not know why or on what grounds I should recognize you, but I will grant you recognition anyway because you need it.[76] Furthermore, as long as one cannot do away with some criteria of evaluation, such a patronizing recognition degenerates into hypocrisy in case the object of recognition does not meet the criteria: I know deep down in my heart that you do not really deserve it, but . . . .

The political and psychological analyses of Fanon and Taylor show that, if comparative theology is to include religious representations of the oppressed, exploited, and marginalized in its extrabiblical theological canon as a political act of restoring symmetry in social power relations, then such an act must be open to a genuine positive assessment of them as religious "classics" worthy of inclusion, and such a positive evaluation has to involve the question of their meaning and truth. But here a thorny question lingers: meaningful and true on whose terms? As Kwok points out, the question of religious meaning and truth is contingent on one's epistemological and theological viewpoints.[77] In the absence of a truly global culture with a horizon or perspective more comprehensive than and inclusive of the perspectives of the individual communities and traditions, here a hermeneutic of suspicion creeps back in, reminding comparative theologians of the colonial history of their own discipline which earlier appealed to the allegedly universal category of religion as alibi for Christian theological imperialism when settling on the rule of recognition for religious meaning and truth.

Although such a hermeneutic of suspicion is legitimate, Thatamanil has a point in arguing that comparative theology, as the work of evaluating and reformulating the religious symbols of one's home tradition in dialogue with religious others, is not decisively foreclosed by the fear of reenacting Christian theological imperialism as long as it is not beholden to the idea of pure and homogeneous religious identity with fixed boundaries.[78] Insofar as the first step of comparative theology consists in a political act of neutralizing power differences in social relations, it pries open the door through which interpreted meanings can flow back and act on the existing rule of recognition, enabling the bidirectional process of intratextuality that underlies an experience of the transformative power, the *truth*, of the religious other. To quote Nicholson, "To recognize certain works as classics is to allow one's perception of the world to be transformed by the vision of reality that such works disclose."[79] The relational model of metaphorical negotiation and redescription of religious symbols, which Nicholson proposes for comparative theology, reminds us that the process of recognition, as *re-cognition*, involves not only the seeing, remembering, and rediscovering of *oneself in another* but also the seeing, remembering, and rediscovering of *another in oneself*, insofar as a mechanism is in place to secure the terms of comparison on an equal footing. Across the porous boundaries and shifting internal configurations of religious identities, comparative theology as a practice of political theology may enable one to encounter the representations and discourses of the "outsiders within" the religious other and recognize them as the different voices of truth, power, and authority that have been sounding for long, unheard, within oneself. The recent works of Michelle Voss Roberts and Tracy Sayuki Tiemeier, both engaging marginalized female representations of the Hindu tradition in comparison with similar voices within the Christian tradition, present examples of how comparative theologians can challenge the hegemony of gender, race, class, and so on in comparative theology, even as they are at the same time driven to the work of reimagining the religious symbols of their home traditions in the wake of their encounter with the transformative power—yes, even *truth*—of the suppressed voices not merely *of* but *within* other religious traditions.[80]

Comparative theology, thus conceived, legitimates the theological work of preferentially engaging the *religious* symbols, stories, texts, concepts, rituals, and practices of the silenced groups within the religious others for the sake of liberating theological contextualization, not only for Asian theology but also for any theology done within a postcolonial-neocolonial context of religious plurality and difference, including the North Atlantic cosmopolitan metropole of the global order. As a form of contextual-political theology, it acutely attunes itself to the interreligious and intercultural dynamic operating along the interlocking axes of power relations within a postcolonial-neocolonial *glocal* context. More concretely, it strategically privileges the internally heterogeneous speech-agency of the oppressed, exploited, and marginalized within the religious others, as inscribed in their suppressed religious representations and discourses, as the locus of the liberating absent presence of the divine. First of all, it follows the way the subject-agency of the "outsiders within" the religious others has coalesced in and through their religious representations and discourses that intimately inhabit and subversively rewrite both the locally hegemonic and the globally hegemonic religious representations and discourses. Second, out of its intrinsic responsiveness to what is other—the so-called ethical responsibility—that is constitutive of its own relational-dialectical identity, comparative theology opens itself up to what Spivak calls a "secret encounter."[81] In other words, it embraces the "impossible experience" of the radical alterity and singularity of the "outsiders within" whose metaphorically redescriptive and transformative power can be experienced as they escape from their subalternity via their subversive recoding of the dominant religious representations and discourses.[82] Such a "deconstructive embrace"[83] of the transformative truth of the religious representations and discourses of the oppressed and marginalized within the religious others disagrees with Spivak's rather pessimistic verdict on the enabling capacity of the hegemonic religious discourses of the great world religions when compared to the emancipatory potential of the hegemonic secular discourses of the modern West (such as "citizenship" and "democracy").[84] It refuses the notion that the legacy of Western colonialism has wholeheartedly eradicated precolonial, non-Western forms of institutionalized knowledge and agency to the extent that they have entirely lost even their ambiguous capacity to provide their subaltern mass truly alternative paths to arrive at subversive and emancipatory forms of speech-agency.[85] Such alternative paths to the speech-agency of the subaltern may even provide a glimpse of the dialogically plural, sociohistorically liberating, and ecologically just and harmonious vision of the world, which Spivak has named "planetarity" vis-à-vis the "globality" of today's neocolonial world.[86]

## A Decolonizing Asian Theology of Spirit as a Comparative Theology of Spirit-Qi

The Donghak notion of Ultimate Energy (*jigi*) and the related notion of "the spirit of the harmonious becoming of psychophysical energy" (*gihwa ji sin*), which I argue represent a subversive and resistant subaltern rewriting of the pivotal metaphysical and cosmological idea of psychophysical energy (*gi*/*qi*) in the hegemonic East Asian traditions of Confucianism and Daoism, constitute a challenge for Asian contextual theology and comparative theology. They present a challenge to Asian theology because it was precisely for the lack of them that Su-un criticized the then dominant forms of missionary Christianity—which are continuous with its dominant forms today—that claimed to be driven and guided by a divine spirit, the Holy Spirit. The same notions present a challenge also for comparative theology because they epitomize exactly the kind of decolonizing religious other with which comparative theology needs to perform its interreligious theological reflection if it is to root itself squarely within the violent postcolonial-neocolonial contexts of today's globalizing world.

As an attempt at a constructive theology of Spirit that seeks to proceed by way of Asian contextual theology and comparative theology, I focus on the idea of psychophysical energy and trace the historical path of textual tradition through which that idea has traveled. The idea of psychophysical energy initially emerged out of the pre-Axial Age symbol of primeval creative chaos. It then became a pivotal metaphysical and cosmological concept in Confucian and Daoist thoughts, only to be devalued in both traditions as the mere physical-cosmic vessel of the metaphysical ultimate, the Way (道 *do*/*dao*) or pattern (理 *li*), until it finally clawed its way out of its status as a metaphysically subordinate concept, most subversively in the Donghak notion of Ultimate Energy. Throughout the course of this historical-textual inquiry into the "adventures" of the idea of psychophysical energy, to paraphrase Whitehead, I compare the idea of psychophysical energy with the Christian theological idea of Spirit. I particularly zoom in on the various ways in which the hegemonic classical—quasi-dualistic—theological formulations of Spirit have been challenged by their modern and postmodern (or late-modern) critics, ranging from the pioneering nondualistic construction of Spirit as *Geist* by Hegel to the work of some contemporary philosophers and theologians who have advanced analogous nondualistic conceptualizations of the ultimate creative/spiritual power, mainly Whitehead's creativity, Deleuze's *chaosmos*, and Catherine Keller's *tehom* (the deep).

The process of comparative theological reflections that I undertake in this book may be construed more concretely in terms of Robert Schreiter's "intercultural hermeneutics," particularly his semiotic understanding of cultural interaction as a triadic structure of communication: *sign* (the signifier) as the material dimension of culture, consisting in texts, symbols, and artifacts; *code* (the pathway) as the performative dimension of culture, such as rituals and commentarial traditions; *message* (the signified) as the ideational dimension of culture, including ideas, beliefs, and values.[87] According to his intercultural hermeneutics, the pivotal question for any intercultural communication is: "How does the same *message* get communicated via different *codes*, using a mixture of *signs* from two different cultures?"[88] The Christian gospel as a message has a considerable degree of indeterminateness, as the different cultural codes through which one of its core signs (e.g., the cross) travels will highlight the different aspects of the message.[89] Paul encoded the sign of the cross variously in the legal codes of justification and reconciliation, the social codes of manumission from slavery, and the ritual codes of atonement. Anselm encoded the same sign in the Germanic military code of honor, highlighting the meaning of the message as vicarious satisfaction. Luther encoded the cross in what has become the central code of modernity, resulting in the gospel of an individual alone before God and saved through his or her faith.[90] This means that crossing cultural boundaries and reencoding the message bring out hitherto unnoticed or suppressed aspects of the message.[91]

Intercultural communication takes place, Schreiter argues, when a sign taken from one culture gets translated into what translation theorists call its "dynamic equivalent" (or "functional equivalent") in another culture—namely, a sign playing more or less similar roles in that culture. Because of the different codifications of its dynamic equivalent, the original sign from the home culture becomes imaginatively reencoded as a result of the translation process and starts to highlight new, hitherto obscured aspects of the message it carries.[92] One could say that the dynamic equivalents function as the terms of metaphorical negotiation and redescription, and that the interaction and "mutual fecundation"[93] of the different codifications of the dynamic equivalents are precisely what gives rise to the metaphoric insight and new meaning. The hermeneutical underpinnings of my comparative-theological exercise may be put precisely in those terms. First I take the word "gi" (or "qi") to be the functional equivalent of the word "spirit," which, as a direct translation of the biblical words *ruach* and *pneuma* and sometimes a code word for the related biblical terms *hochmah* and *sophia*, has rich root-metaphorical connections to the physical, biological, and psychic phenomena of wind, fire, water, energy, breath, life-force, consciousness, and mind.[94] *Gi* is the functional equivalent of spirit because in both its etymology and its function within East Asian cultures it is a root metaphor for the same kind of physical, biological, and psychic phenomena, as implied by the term "psychophysical energy"—which in my view implies the more cumbersome phrase "psycho-bio-physical energy"—being used to translate the word.[95] Second, I follow the way in which the idea of psychophysical energy is codified differently in its textual history, tracing its various conceptualizations within different intellectual—epistemic and philosophical—frameworks, which reflect the cultural contestation between the hegemonic Confucian and Daoist discourses and the marginalized, subversive discourses within those traditions, including the teachings of Donghak. I then try to envision how the various codifications of psychophysical energy as they are conceptualized within different intellectual frameworks, particularly the subversive ones, may highlight and liberate the hitherto suppressed codifications of the word "spirit" for Christian theology, in ways both similar to and different from the various reencodings of the same word being carried out by some of the modern and postmodern Christian theologies.

In chapter 1, I examine the idea of psychophysical energy and trace its development in Daoist thought. As a metaphor referring to the constantly changing creative processes of the universe that constitute whatever exists, both mind and body, ideal and material, living and nonliving, and organic and inorganic, psychophysical energy resists any overtures toward an excessively dualistic construal of transcendence. Yet within its conceptual development and refinement within Confucian and Daoist thoughts, there have been tendencies to place the creative-transformative power of psychophysical energy in the derivative and dependent position within a hierarchically structured binary relationship with some form of metaphysical transcendence. In Daoist thought, the foundational text of the *Laozi* (*Daodejing*) and its dominant commentarial traditions place psychophysical energy midway between the Way (*dao*) as the metaphysical ultimate, on the one hand, and the concrete things of the world, on the other. In other words, Daoist thought envisions psychophysical energy as a kind of primal matter-energy whose cosmic creativity is seen as derived from and dependent on the Way, even as the Way is presented in the tradition "apophatically" and "an-archically" as chaos-like Nothing (*wu*).

In Daoist thought, then, one can see looming large what may be called a totalizing metaphysics of one empty Nothingness.

In chapter 2, I follow the development of the idea of psychophysical energy in the dominant stream of Neo-Confucian thought represented by Zhu Xi. Zhu Xi shares in the Daoist subordination of psychophysical energy when he posits "pattern" (*li*) or "the Great Ultimate" (*taiji*) as the metaphysical ultimate that is logically and ontologically prior to psychophysical energy even as it depends on the latter for physical dynamism. Further, Zhu Xi construes the dynamism of psychophysical energy only as a chaotic and random activity, even as he locates the source of all order and harmony in the metaphysical ultimate, the Great Ultimate. One of the most significant consequences of these developments is that oneness, unity, and harmony associated with the metaphysical ultimate are valorized at the expense of the manyness and divergent multiplicity of the world of concrete things and their self-creative freedom. Zhu Xi's Neo-Confucian thought is shadowed by a totalizing metaphysics of one Heavenly Pattern.

In chapter 3, in order to highlight the problematic nature of Zhu Xi's "qualified dualism," I introduce Whitehead's notion of creativity and the vision of "a democracy of fellow creatures," which his notion of creativity points to. In Whitehead's account of the cosmos, every concrete entity consists in a creative process—called "concrescence"—in which a multiplicity of past entities are constantly brought into a new unity, which is that concrete entity. What drives this unending creative process, according to Whitehead, is creativity. But creativity is a notion of pure activity and merely a descriptive term for what is taking place constantly in the cosmos, not some kind of ultimate ontological ground. Creativity, in that sense, is the creativity of every concrete entity, every "creature," that creates itself. Whitehead does have a place for God in his cosmology, but his God is a concrete entity like any other, even as it is the locus of eternal, pure possibilities of order and harmony. The creative process takes place when these pure possibilities are "felt" by concrete entities to become the initial map or the "DNA" of their self-creative becomings. Since God is a concrete entity and therefore a self-creating "creature" of creativity, the eternal pure possibilities in God are also products of creativity. What this means is that, for both concrete actualities and pure possibilities, manyness or multiplicity is as ultimate as oneness or unity. Whitehead's radical ontological pluralism of eternal pure possibilities and temporal concrete actualities goes together with a thoroughly desubstantialized notion of creativity sustaining their multiple self-creative becomings. If we take creativity as a comparative analogue to psychophysical energy, then Whitehead's radical ontological pluralism challenges Zhu Xi's de-valorizing conception of the spontaneous dynamism of psychophysical energy manifest in the seemingly chaotic interrelated becoming of the myriad creatures.

In chapter 4, I engage the Neo-Confucian Toegye, who points to an "idealistic" solution to the problem of the totalizing metaphysics of one Heavenly Pattern by allowing pattern or the Great Ultimate an independent dynamism of its own. The pivotal implication of Toegye's independently dynamic interpretation of the Great Ultimate is that change, difference, and multiplicity can be seen to belong to the ontological ultimate originarily and primordially, not secondarily and derivatively. In principle, this could open the path toward a genuine affirmation of the multiple self-creative becomings of the myriad creatures, since they could be seen as the embodied realizations of the primordial multiplicity of ideal potential harmonies within the Great Ultimate. Nevertheless, Toegye does not challenge Zhu Xi's refusal to recognize the existence of an intrinsically unifying and harmonizing dynamic in psychophysical energy. This results in a continuation of Zhu Xi's tendency to devalue creaturely agency's dependence on the spontaneous dynamism of psychophysical energy.

In chapter 5, I compare Toegye's dynamic Great Ultimate with Hegel's ontological ultimate, the logical Idea. Hegel's Idea is an "idealistic" comparative analogue to Toegye's Great Ultimate in the sense that it marries a recognition of the ontological ultimacy of multiplicity with a devalued understanding of nature's multiply concrete agencies. Hegel's Idea consists in an unceasing dialectical movement of the universal One positing the other of itself, namely, the particular Many, and reuniting itself with the other to produce the singular or individual as internally differentiated unities of multiplicity (i.e., concrete unities). Even with this recognition of the ontological ultimacy of multiplicity, however, because Hegel defines Nature as the other of the logical Idea, that is, as the principle of mutually indifferent particularity and dispersion into chaotic nothingness, he exhibits a tendency to devalue the embodied self-creativity of the multitude of finite spirits emerging from and inhabiting nature—a tendency shared by Toegye. Their shared affirmation of the primordiality and ontological ultimacy of multiplicity receives an injurious blow when the logical Idea and the Great Ultimate are not considered in abstract but as immanent in nature or in union with psychophysical energy, respectively.

In chapter 6, I discuss the Neo-Confucian Nongmun, who represents a more "naturalistic" solution to the Daoist and Neo-Confucian problem of totalizing metaphysics, as he confers upon psychophysical energy an intrinsically unifying, harmonizing, and creative power. Nongmun's core thesis is that "pattern and psychophysical energy are equally actual," meaning that they are totally parallel to each other in all aspects, in all their modes of being and operation, including their creatively harmonizing capacity and function. In fact the complete correspondence of pattern and psychophysical energy is to such an extent that they may be seen as different aspects of one and the same ontologically creative ground that is both metaphysical and physical, both one and many, both indeterminate and determinate—the Great Ultimate. For Nongmun, psychophysical energy is right there at the heart of the Great Ultimate, constituting both its primordial, ontologically ultimate plurisingularity and its creatively harmonizing power. This means that, due to the materiality and physicality thus assigned to the Great Ultimate as primordial Manyone, its creatively harmonizing power can be construed as the *affective* power of mutual openness and attraction—that is, *empathy*—that exists among the primordial many within the Great Ultimate.

In chapter 7, I put Nongmun's understanding of the Great Ultimate in dialogue with Deleuze's concept of the chaosmos. Nongmun's fundamentally affective construal of the ontologically ultimate creative power of the Great Ultimate means that, first of all, his conception of the Great Ultimate can be compared with Whitehead's construal of the primordial nature of God as *unconscious*. But more significantly, Nongmun's Great Ultimate resonates with Deleuze's concept of the chaosmos and the "trinity" of *complicatio-explicatio-implicatio* that undergirds that concept. At the core of the "chaosmotic" trinitarian structure is the power of connection that directly relates differences to one another without any conceptual mediation. This power of conceptually unmediated, "apophatic," relation, which enables the power of pure difference to be a *creative* power, can be the "lens" through which Nongmun's Great Ultimate can be interpreted. In other words, the power to put differences in direct, unmediated, and creative relation to one another is like the *affective* power of mutual openness and attraction that exists among the primordial "many" within the Great Ultimate and forms a "chaotic" unity that gives birth to the orderly, patterned cosmos of the "ten thousand things." This fundamentally affective, nonconceptual construal of the ontologically ultimate plurisingularity of the Great Ultimate prevents it from being interpreted as a predetermined imperious order—a Heavenly Pattern—at the root of things, that is, as that to which the self-creative journeys of myriad creatures need to conform to and to submit themselves to. Furthermore, the Deleuzian inflection given to the Nongmunian Great Ultimate leads me to take up the well-known Neo-Confucian interpretation of the Great Ultimate as the "trinity" of Change (*yeok/yi*), Way (*do/dao*), and Spirit (*sin/shen*), and develop it into a triad of (a) Change as a chaotically enfolded actuality with an apophatic, "virtual" ontological depth, (b) divergent series of constantly changing Ways unfolding from Change and folding back into it, and (c) Spirit as the direct empathetic connection among the divergent Ways forming the fields of individuation from which the "ten thousand things" are born. With a hint from Catherine Keller's tehomic trinity of Tehom, Elohim, and Ruach, all deities, including a personal creator God, can be seen as part of the patterns or Ways unfolding from Change. Deities, in other words, are different interpreted patterns imposed on Change by creatures divergently emerging from it, including human beings.

In chapter 8, I propose that my reconstruction of the Neo-Confucian trinity of Change, Way, and Spirit in dialogue with Nongmun, Deleuze, and Keller, which I call "the panentheism of transcendent body," has a great potential for what Keller calls, following Whitehead, "the democracy of creation." I argue this by connecting the panentheism of the transcendent body with the theology of Donghak. Donghak helps us overcome the primary obstacle in constructing a full-blown theology of Spirit while drawing on the East Asian religious heritages—that is, the fact that, largely speaking, Confucianism and Daoism are philosophically nontheistic. With a striking similarity to Nongmun's conception of psychophysical energy, the Donghak teaching speaks of the Lord Heaven as *jigi* (Ultimate Energy), which is precisely psychophysical energy brimming with harmonizing and unifying creativity. At the same time, incorporating the religiosity of the "heterodox" Neo-Confucian school of Toegye, the ancient indigenous tradition of worship of *haneul* (Heaven) and possibly the theism of Catholic Christianity, the Donghak teaching avers that one can have an intimate, personal encounter with Ultimate Energy in the form of a personal deity, Lord Heaven. The experience of the personal encounter with Ultimate Energy as Lord Heaven makes one a "bearer of Lord Heaven" who has become one with the rest of the universe and whose entire psychophysical being shares in the cosmic creative-transformative agency of Ultimate Energy. Through its monistic yet explicitly panentheistic reformulation of the Neo-Confucian "qualified dualism" of pattern and psychophysical energy, Donghak liberates the latter's largely suppressed "democratic" potential. By conferring a clear sense of creative subject-agency to the spontaneous and pluriform creativity of psychophysical energy whose harmonizing power is not predicated on some kind of transcendental metaphysical unity, Donghak develops a view of the divine that is both one and many, divine and creaturely, and works toward the creation of a free, egalitarian, inclusive, empathetic, and harmonious society of "the bearers of Lord Heaven."

In the concluding chapter (epilogue), I provide a brief sketch of a possible constructive development of the panentheism of transcendent body in response to the present postcolonial-neocolonial global context. A theology of Spirit-Gi (or Spirit-Qi) emerging from the chaotic Change provides ontological-cosmological underpinnings for a pneumatology of the multitude. Drawing on the theorists of empire, Michael Hardt and Antonio Negri, postcolonial critics such as Spivak, theological critics of empire such as Néstor Miguez, Joerg Rieger, and Jung Mo Sung, and Korean minjung theologians, I attempt a merger of the notion of *minjung* as subjects of history with the concept of the migrant multitude as the planetary outcasts of the globalizing world. In the pneumatology of the multitude thus developed, the Spirit-Gi is none other than the spirit of the displaced and wandering multitude whose somatic and relational self-cultivation leads to their awakening and rebirth as the emancipatory and solidary divine-human subjects of history at kairotic moments. My theological sketch of the spiritual agency of the uprooted and wandering multitude is ultimately aimed at envisioning their rooting themselves again within a planetary web of life characterized by the interdependent flourishing of all, that is, the democracy of creation. This sketch, however, will remain a sketch. The scope of this book remains that of constructing a liberating pneumatocentric metaphysics of the Trinity on East Asian and contemporary Western philosophical bases. I leave to a future work a full-blown attempt at interpreting the contemporary global reality on the basis of such a theological metaphysics.

# 1 The Psychophysical Energy of the Way in Daoist Thought

What is psychophysical energy (氣 *gi/qi*)? Etymologically rooted in the words "steam," "breath," and "wind," and variously translated as "material force," "vital energy," or "psychophysical stuff,"[1] *gi/qi* is an idea for world-explanation ubiquitously found in East Asian cultures and religions and philosophically developed in the two great traditions of Daoism and Confucianism.[2] Perhaps owing to its metaphoric roots in the animistic indigenous cultures of preclassical East Asia,[3] *gi/qi* in its original meaning encompasses both nonphysical and physical, mind and body, macrocosmic and microcosmic, and sacred and secular. In that sense, it is similar to the Semitic *ruach* and the Greek *pneuma* with their own roots in the polytheistic and/or pantheistic myths of the pre-Axial Age cultures of West Asia.[4]

## Psychophysical Energy as Nature and Spirit

Psychophysical energy is the primordial energy of the universe that constitutes whatever exists—visible and invisible, with form and without form, nonliving and living, and material and ideal. The entities that appear to be solid and unchanging are in fact temporary coalescences or harmonies of psychophysical energy's own bifurcated and mutually complementary modalities of the receptive force (陰氣 *eum gi/yin qi*) and the active force (陽氣 *yang gi/yang qi*), which are themselves in a constant process of following and turning into each other. The creatively harmonizing operations of the two modalities of psychophysical energy is captured by the symbol of the Great Ultimate (太極 *taegeuk/taiji*) that depicts a ceaseless dynamic union of complementary opposites.[5]

The binary of receptive and active forces (which represents and includes the binaries of soft and hard, cold and hot, dark and light, rest and movement, female and male, earth and heaven) constitutes complementary opposites, because each pole of the binary always includes the other within itself and depends on the other for its own coming into being. The receptive force harbors and grows the seed of the other within itself until it is itself "taken over" and turned into the other, the active force, which in turn nurtures the seed of the receptive force within itself until it becomes its opposite. Furthermore, this relation of mutually dependent coming into being has a "fractal" structure in which each pole of the binary reproduces within itself the polarity of the whole: The receptive force always carries within itself the seed of the active force, which always carries within itself the seed of the receptive force, which always carries within itself the seed of active force . . . and so on and on.[6] In other words, the Great Ultimate has a dynamically fractal structure of constantly self-differentiating opposites that come into being and cease to be in and through an unending process of one differentiating itself from itself by having the other within to negate itself.

Because the "logic" of psychophysical energy's movement as symbolized by the Great Ultimate configures all coalescences or harmonies of psychophysical energy, any construal of them as unchanging essences or permanent substances is to be seen as a product of optical illusion and wishful thinking. As confirmed by the universal phenomena of birth, growth, decay, and death, one particular configuration of psychophysical energy continuously transforms itself into another as its balance of the receptive and the active within shifts in response to and in communication with other similarly dynamic and changing coalescences of psychophysical energy.[7] The fact that all things—or rather, thing-events[8]—in the universe are various configurations of the same shared psychophysical energy does not mean that the latter functions as some kind of immutable substance underlying mutable phenomena. Rather, it serves as the field (場 *jang/chang*) and medium of interaction among all thing-events, enabling their synchronic "correlativity" prior to and beyond their diachronic causal relations.[9] Furthermore, as a continuous movement it constitutes the essence of time, its incessantly changing combinations of the active and the receptive being the qualitatively different, "kairotic" markers of time.[10]

In this vision of the cosmos there is little space for the kind of metacosmic/cosmic distinction, based on the binaries of one and many, ideal and material, and substance and phenomena, that characterizes many predominant cultures of West Asia or South Asia. Admittedly, the creative and transformative operations of psychophysical energy can be extraordinarily subtle, mysterious, and marvelous—as, for example, in the operations of human consciousness such as deliberation and imagination—to the point of appearing almost "otherworldly" and thereby attaining a measure of numinous transcendence. In such occasions, psychophysical energy is said to have become 神 (*sin/shen*), usually translated as "spiritual" or "divine."[11] Nevertheless, even as sacrifices have been offered and homage paid in East Asian cultures to anthropomorphically envisaged spirits and deities, ranging from the Lord on High (上帝 *sangje/shangdi*) and Heaven (天 *cheon/tian*)[12] to the spirits of ancestors, natural features, and various locales, they are all understood to be especially fine, ethereal, and invisible coalescences of psychophysical energy, not "supernatural" and metacosmic entities totally independent of the exigencies of the temporal and physical.[13] Even the revered Lord on High or Heaven is regarded as the wisest and most powerful member of the one shared cosmos, not an outsider.[14] In sum, psychophysical energy is what underlies and constitutes the dynamic, creative becoming that is the universe, encompassing both one and many, transcendent and immanent, object and event, organic and inorganic, ideal and material, mind and body, spirit and nature, and *natura naturans* and *natura naturata*.[15]

Whereas the category of psychophysical energy thus captures an essentially and ultimately nondualistic worldview shaping the cultures of East Asia, its conceptual and philosophical developments have by and large taken place within intellectual frameworks that affirm the existence of a fundamental *duality* characterizing the overarching structure of all that is and becomes. One of the earliest and historically most influential formulations of this duality is found in the Appended Remarks (繫辭傳 *xicizhuan*) of the Classic of Change (易經 *yijing*), a Warring States period (475–221 B.C.E.) text allegedly of a Confucian lineage but containing a classical paradigm of thought shared by the Confucian and Daoist traditions: "That which is above physical form—it is called the Way [道 *dao*]; that which is with physical form—it is called the vessel [器 *qi*]."[16] The saying makes a distinction between what is above or without physical form and what has physical form, naming them, respectively, "the Way" and "the vessel." The vessel points to the myriad thing-events of the universe that have determinate shapes and concrete physical existence, such as the sun, moon, and stars in heaven and mountains, rivers, plants, animals, and humans on earth. The Way, by contrast, has no concrete existence of its own, having no determinate physical form, yet at the same time is "contained" in the myriad "vessels" of the visible universe.

What is the Way, then? The Appended Remarks of the Classic of Change has its own answer: "The successive movement of the receptive and the active is called the Way" (一陰一陽之謂道 *yiyin yiyang zhiweidao*).[17] Although psychophysical energy and the binary of the receptive and the active are explicitly mentioned rather sparsely in the Appended Remarks, this remark provides a clear and succinct articulation of the implied understanding of the Way: The Way is none other than the regularity or order observed in the creative and transformative operations of the two modes of psychophysical energy, as it is captured by the symbol of the Great Ultimate.[18] When the Appended Remarks says, "Giving birth again and again is called Change [易 *yi*]," and "Change has the Great Ultimate; the Great Ultimate generates two Modes [兩儀 *liangyi*]; two Modes generate four Figures [四象 *sixiang*]; four Figures generate eight Trigrams [八卦 *bagua*],"[19] it is symbolically describing the observed pattern of the creative Becoming or Change in terms of the constantly shifting combinations of the active and receptive forces which produce the myriad formed "vessels" of the visible universe. If the Way is merely the orderliness of the creatively harmonizing operations of psychophysical energy, then the duality of the formless Way and the formed vessel in fact means the duality of the abstract "logic" of psychophysical energy's movement apart from its concrete coalescing, on the one hand, and the particular configurations of the two modes of psychophysical energy, on the other. In other words, psychophysical energy functions here as a third, mediating term between the formless Way and the formed vessel, preventing their duality from becoming a dualism of two independent principles.

The rendition of the Way in the Appended Remarks thus interprets the classical dyadic paradigm of the Way and the vessel as an articulation of the fundamentally nondualistic worldview of East Asian cultures centered on the boundary-transcending category of psychophysical energy. At the same time, the history of its interpretive traditions, including both Confucian and Daoist, has exhibited tendencies either to drive the poles of the duality further apart or bring them closer to each other. The Daoist tradition is significant in that it could be read as doing both at the same time. Its predominant classical interpretation of the duality of the formless Way and the formed vessel in terms of the triad of the Way (道)—psychophysical energy (氣)—the myriad thing-events (萬物) can be viewed in such a manner that the Way acquires an ontological depth verging on the classical Western conception of the metaphysical transcending the physical. At the same time, the classical Daoist construal of the Way has enough of what in the vocabulary of Christian theology may be called an "apophatic" tendency to make the ontological depth given to the Way *an-archic* (i.e., without origin and rule) and *chaophilic* (i.e., chaos-loving). Given the wide-ranging historical influence exerted by the Daoist triadic articulation of the duality of the Way and the vessel, it is imperative that the classical Daoist understanding of the Way be examined.

## The Psychophysical Energy of the Way: An Anarchic and Chaophilic Development in Daoist Thought

To understand the Daoist understanding of the Way, it is apropos to examine the *Laozi* (老子), alternatively called the *Daodejing* (道德經), which is the earliest and foundational text of the Daoist tradition, either predating the above passage from the Classic of Change by about a century or two, or roughly contemporaneous with it.[20] Its understanding of the Way has been extremely influential not only in the Daoist tradition but also in the cultures of East Asia in general. In chapter 25, the *Laozi* gives a poetic description of the Way:[21]

> There is a thing confusedly formed,
> Born before heaven and earth.
> Silent and void
> It stands alone and does not change,
> Goes round and does not weary.
> It is capable of being the mother of the world.
> I know not its name

So I style it "the way." (25.56)
If forced to make up a name for it
I call it "the great."[22]
Being great, it is further described as moving on,[23]
Moving on, it is described as far away,
Being far away, it is described as turning back. (25.56a)

There are a couple of things to be noted about the Way as described in this passage. First of all, the Way is like a chaos. It is "confusedly formed," "silent," and "void." This indeterminate, ineffable, and empty nature of the Way is repeatedly expressed by the *Laozi*: "indistinct and shadowy" (14.33; 21.49); "dim and dark" (21.49); "deep" (4.11); "empty" (4.11; 5.3); "evanescent (or invisible)," "rarefied (or inaudible)," "minute (or imperceptible)" (14.32); "darkly visible, it only seems as if it were there" (4.13); "a shape that is of no-shape, an image that is of no-thing" (14.33).[24] All of these terms and phrases point to the idea that the Way is dark and chaos-like without form, without any kind of order that would allow the light of the human mind to penetrate it and to discern the contours of its features as a concretely existing thing. The *Laozi* also calls the Way "the One [一 *yi*]" and "Uncarved Block [朴 *fu*]" precisely because of its utter simplicity, that is, its lack of inner distinctions, shape, and order.[25] Moreover, due to its chaos-like lack of form and order, the Way is completely nameless and unnameable, as the famous beginning verse of chapter 1 paradoxically states: "The Way that can be spoken of is not the constant Way; the name that can be named is not the constant name" (1.1).[26] That is why, as the *Laozi* explains in chapter 25, even the term "Way" is only a metaphor or symbol: "I know not its name, so I style [字 *zi*] it 'the Way'" (25.56). Perhaps it is due to the "nonexistent" and no-thing-like character of the nameless and unnameable Way that the *Laozi* even uses the term "nothing [無 *wu*]" to designate it (40.89).

Nonetheless, the Way as chaos-like nothing is not synonymous with the *nihil* (nothingness) of the Western metaphysical tradition whose definition as utter disorder and annihilating void is the source of dread and existential angst. The second notable characteristic of the Way is that it is what may be called ultimate reality, that is, the ultimate origin and source of all that is.[27] As something "born before heaven and earth," the Way "stands alone and does not change"—for the Way is not dependent on or conditioned by anything—and precisely on that account is the constant Way of which the first verse of chapter 1 speaks. Being "the beginning of heaven and earth" (1.2), the nameless and constant Way is prior to and more ultimate than what is customarily worshiped as the highest spiritual power of the universe: "I know not whose son it is. It images the ancestor of Lord on High [帝 *di*]" (4.13).[28] At the same time, the Way is "capable of being the mother of the world" from whom the myriad thing-events (萬物 *wanwu*) are born. In fact, as something already named "the Way" and thereby become part of the cosmos and an object of human linguistic discourse (as all named things are), the Way "*is* the mother of myriad creatures" (1.2, italics mine), serving as the origin and source of all thing-events.[29] The Way as the one, simple, and nameless "uncarved block" shatters and becomes many vessels (器) with names and distinctions (28.64). In other words, the Way as vacuous, ineffable, and nothing-like ultimate reality is a chaos pregnant with the possibility of an infinite variety of nameable orders that are made constantly emergent by the power of being and life inherent in it.[30] This generative power of the Way is underscored by the names such as "the gateway of the mysterious female" and "the spirit of the valley" (6.17), with female reproductive connotations. As the mother of all thing-events, the Way "gives them life and rears them, brings them up and nurses them, brings them to fruition and maturity, feeds and shelters them" (51.115). The Way can be the mother of the entire world because it is omnipresent as the origin, source, and power of all being and life: "The Way overflows, reaching left as well as right" (34.76).[31] Not only does the Way so permeate the myriad thing-events that it produces and brings to completion, but it also never wearies of or fails in its role as mother—the Way "goes round and does not weary" (25.56)—as befitting the designation of "the constant Way."[32] Insofar as the Way as the universal and unfailing power of being and life pervades the myriad thing-events as their own power of being and life, it is called their "virtue [德 *de*]": "The way gives them life; virtue rears them" (51.114).[33]

The third notable characteristic of the Way is that its constant activity is characterized by "turning back" (反 *fan*) (25.56a) or reversal: "Turning back is how the Way moves [反者道之動 *fanzhe daozhidong*]" (40.88). The power of the Way, which permeates the world as the virtue of the myriad thing-events, generates and brings them to completion. Once the myriad thing-events reach the zenith of their power of being and life, however, the movement of the Way is revealed in their gradual waning, as the universal phenomena of birth, growth, decay, and death give witness to. As the *Laozi* puts it, "After a period of vigor there is old age" (30.70);[34]

and "a sudden downpour cannot last all day" (23.51a). This movement of reversal toward non-being and death is tantamount to the myriad thing-events' return to their origin and source, i.e., to the chaotic and empty "nothing" of the Way.

The return of all thing-events to the Way is not "arche-ological" in the sense that the origin (*archē*) to which they return is "not there" or "only seems as if it were there" (4.13). Given this absence of graspable and definable origin, one could call the Way's movement of reversal "an-archic (*an-archē*)."[35] The implication is that, insofar as the Way pervades the myriad thing-events as their virtue or power, what one observes in the latter is "an-archy." Because the Way's movement of reversal lacks a definable origin that could function as the legitimizing foundation of an existing creaturely order, the power of being and life that is the virtue of the myriad thing-events does not found any particular order of beings in order to claim possession of it and to exercise authority over it: "It gives them life yet claims no possession; it benefits them yet exacts no gratitude; it is the steward yet exercises no authority; such is called the mysterious virtue" (51.116). In the absence of a founding authority, the presently existing orders of the world at the height of their power and opulence cannot lay claim to absoluteness or immunity from challenges leveled by new and emergent alternative orders. In other words, what results from the anarchic movement of the Way is a radical openness to the spontaneously emerging new orders. The Way constantly makes the myriad thing events return to the dark chaos pregnant with an infinite variety of possible new orders that emerge spontaneously from the ashes of the older orders in ways that are not entirely conditioned by the latter.[36]

The anarchic movement of the Way is what the famous Daoist notion of "being so of itself" (自然 *ziran*) captures (25.58).[37] Like the empty space within the hub of the wheel that receives the spokes and thereby enables the cart to move (11.27), the chaotic nothing as the empty and "self-less" mother of the myriad thing-events receives and accommodates them without contending with them or asserting itself to impose its own authority and designs on them, and precisely in doing so enables them to rise and flourish according their own respective natures. As the second-century commentator Wang Bi (王弼) insightfully observes in his commentary on chapter 45, the Way seems empty, chipped, bent, awkward, and tongue-tied (45.101), because its great generative and nurturing power constantly adapts itself to the myriad thing-events and does not assert and implement its own coherent, orderly, and tidy scheme of things.[38] This virtue of "responding [應 *ying*]" (73.179) to the different conditions, circumstances, needs, and exigencies of the myriad thing-events is what enables the Way to be their "refuge" where they are allowed to be what they are of themselves (*ziran*) without being subject to judgments and discriminations based on some preset criteria (62.143, 145).[39]

"Being so of itself," or spontaneity, is characteristic of the workings of the world of myriad thing-events which receives its power of being and life from the Way. Heaven and earth—i.e., the cosmos—do not live for their own interests (7.18).[40] Heaven excels in responding while not asserting itself and contending with the myriad thing-events (73.179). Heaven is the Great Equalizer in the sense that, because it unvaryingly follows the Way's anarchic movement of reversal and does not practice favoritism in accordance with its own designs and likings, no excesses or deficiencies—that is, what are not "so of themselves"—are found in the myriad thing-events (77.184). When it comes to human beings, however, deviations from the virtue of the Way seem to be more of a norm than an exception. Instead of ordering human life in manners that avoid excesses and deficiencies, the way of human beings "takes from those who are in want in order to offer this to those who already have more than enough" (77.184a). Far from giving the myriad thing-events what is properly their due—each according to its nature—so that they could thrive of themselves, human beings create an order in which humans contend with one another and the rest of the myriad thing-events in order to impose their own, self-interested understandings of due proportion that are characterized by an excessive and limitless drive toward self-preservation, self-assertion, and self-aggrandizement. This trend in the human world toward self-interested excesses is illustrated by metaphoric allusions in the text, such as "adding to one's vitality," "egging on the breath [氣]" (55.126), "filling it to the brim," and "hammering it to a point" (9.23)—all of which are "ill-omened" and "violent" (55.126). The point is that, of all creatures, human beings are uniquely capable of deviating from the Way by being fixated on the "male" terms of the binary opposites, such as activity, knowledge, fullness, height, priority, strength, hardness, straightness, sharpness, and distinctiveness, and by trying to egg themselves on toward the conditions corresponding to those terms and to perpetuate their stay in those conditions in obstinate denial of the inevitable reversal. The result of this is the propensities toward ever-more increase and refinement of knowledge, wealth, and power in human civilization, which the *Laozi* calls "going against the Way" (55.127).

For the *Laozi*, the culprit here is desire (欲*yu*). To be sure, there is nothing wrong with desire as such. Human desire in its most simple, instinctive, and biophysical level, such as the need for food, sex, and shelter, is not condemned as the source of all that has gone wrong with the human world. When the *Laozi* says, "The sage is for the belly, not for the eye" (12.29), it is endorsing the simplest satisfaction of the basic needs—all the instinctive, "programmed" aspects of a human being's biological life—as "being so of itself," while warning against the human capacity for fine discrimination of outward features and qualities of things necessary for sophisticated pleasures, on the one hand, and the deliberative, purposeful, and evaluative consciousness behind such capacity, on the other.[41] As an excited state of the heart-mind (心 *xin*) full of diverse and pleasurable sensory stimulations (3.9;12.28), the deliberative, purposeful, and evaluative consciousness tends to isolate things, patterns, trends, and forces in the world—especially the "male" terms of the binary opposites—from their location in the flow of the Way as contingently and provisionally achieved harmonies. In other words, it becomes fixated on them as enduring absolutes capable of serving as the objects of artificially invented desires and aspirations. Through this consciousness, human beings themselves become estranged from the virtue of the Way and, unlike heaven and earth, come to live for themselves (自生 *zi sheng*) in isolation from and opposition to the movement of the Way.[42] This leads human beings to create an entire new world of conscious goals, such as refined pleasures, wealth, honor, the power of domination, technical and manipulative knowledge (technology), and even ideals for individual moral perfection and harmonious social order, insofar as they are predicated on a hierarchy of artificially created goods. This brave new world of human civilization is against the Way in the sense that its "enlightening" and "civilizing" enterprises do not accommodate and let the myriad thing-events be so of themselves, but rather order, control, and manipulate them in ways designed to maximize human self-assertion and self-gratification. In the *Laozi*'s reckoning, the history of human civilization is one of devolution and decline from an earlier state of unadorned simplicity and still harmony (14.34; 65.157) to the present state of contentious self-assertion and self-aggrandizement, both individually and collectively speaking. The rise of increasingly complex human institutions and practices, on the one hand, and the concomitant production of ever-more refined hierarchies of values that function to buttress them, on the other, are together seen to constitute the "great artifice [大僞 *dawei*]" (18.42) of the present age.[43]

To cure the human world of its present ills, then, it is necessary first and foremost to counter the tendencies created by humanity's wayward desire that pursues the goods of the world as enduring and independent absolutes. In order to do so, the *Laozi* calls upon the rulers or leaders of the human world to become "sages" (聖人 *shengren*)[44] who "know when to stop" (32.72) and not to fill a jar to the brim or hammer the tip of a spear to a point (9.23)—that is, not to prod the things, patterns, trends, and forces of the world which one finds desirable on to their maximum reach and to attempt to perpetuate that state. Such an act of self-restraint is tantamount to a refusal to isolate the objects of desire from their proper places in the flow of the Way, that is, their emergence from and eventual return to the (non-) origin to make way for and to contribute to the new. By means of this refusal, any absolute evaluative distinctions imposed on thing-events by the analytic, deliberative, and purposeful consciousness are relativized and rendered contingent. Just as the Way is a refuge for all myriad thing-events, the sage accepts and accommodates both what is regarded as "good" and what is regarded as "bad" by artificially created hierarchies of values (2.4; 62.143–45; 49.111).

The *Laozi*'s exhortation to the rulers to relativize humanly created schemes of things, and to restrain the unruly human desire that constantly attempts to absolutize such schemes, is encapsulated in one of the key notions of the *Laozi*'s religious, ethical, and sociopolitical thought, namely, "no-action" (無爲 *wuwei*): "Therefore in governing the people, the sage . . . always keeps them innocent of knowledge [無知 *wuzhi*] and free from desire [無欲 *wuyu*], and ensures that the clever never dare to act (3.9). Do that which consists in taking no action and order will prevail" (3.10). No-action does not imply complete passivity for the *Laozi,* since the claim is that "when one does nothing at all there is nothing that is undone [無爲而無不爲 *wuwei er wubuwei*]" (48.108). What it means, rather, is that "the sage benefits them [the myriad thing-events] yet exacts no gratitude, accomplishes his task yet lays claim to no merit" (77.185). Put otherwise, no-action is a form of action that relinquishes self-asserting knowledge and desire, and in that sense can be translated as "nonassertive action."[45] It designates the kind of receptive, responsive, and accommodating posture toward the world that lets the myriad thing-events be and flourish spontaneously according to their own nature—i.e., "be so of themselves"—and does not attempt to dominate and to control them. Thus, "no-knowledge" (無知 *wuzhi*)—or "unprincipled knowing"[46]—exhibited by no-action is like a polished mirror that reflects the myriad thing-events just the way they are without self-interested, subjective distortions (10.24);[47] and "no-desire" (無欲 *wuyu*)—or "objectless desire"—achieved by no-action is like an uncarved block or the state of infancy in its utter simplicity and self-lessness (28.63). The sage who has attained no-action is without thought of self (7.19a) and, being thus without a constant heart-mind of his own, "takes the heart-mind of the people as his own" (49.110).[48] The sage-rulers who practice no-action defer to the myriad thing-events, as the following exhortation makes clear: "Hence look at the person through the person; look at the family through the family; look at the hamlet through the hamlet; look at the state through the state; look at the world through the world" (54.124).[49] The sages defer to the world as a sacred vessel and dare not do something about it (29.66). Precisely because of this receptive, responsive, accommodating, and self-effacing relation of theirs to the world, the sages can be said to "keep to the role of the female" and to become "a ravine to the world" (28.63).[50]

In holding fast to the "female" terms of the binary opposites—emptiness, stillness, simplicity, receptiveness, responsiveness, deference, and self-lessness—by means of no-action, the sage as polished mirror, infant, uncarved block, and ravine provides a countervailing force to the fixation of the "great artifice" of human civilization on the "male" terms of the binary opposites.[51] When the *Laozi* says, "Do that which consists in taking no action, and order will prevail" (3.10), it is pointing to the sage's no-action functioning for the world as a channel of the Way's power to let the myriad things be so of themselves and thrive, so that there could emerge a contingent and nonfoundational order characterized by simplicity and maximum openness to spontaneity and novelty. Of the charismatic power of the sage's no-action to transform the world into such "an-archic" order, the *Laozi* says: "I [the sage] take no action and the people are transformed of themselves; I prefer stillness and the people are rectified of themselves; I am not meddlesome and the people prosper of themselves; I am free from desire and the people of themselves become simple like the uncarved block" (57.133).[52]

What then would the restoration of the human world, via the sages' no-action, to the an-archic movement of the Way and the state of "being so of themselves" actually look like in concrete economic, sociopolitical, and cultural terms? In contrast to the so-called rulers of the world, that is, "those dressed in fineries, with swords at their sides, filled with food and drink, and possessed of too much wealth," who leave the fields overgrown with weeds and the granaries empty, and who are no different from robbers in eating up too much in taxes (53.121; 75.181), the *Laozi*'s sages cherish the "three treasures" of compassion, frugality, and self-effacement (67.164). In governing, they do not honor men of worth (*xian*),[53] do not value luxuries, and do not display what is desirable, all in order to keep the people from contention, theft, and being unsettled of mind (3.8). They do not keep a tight control over the people by means of laws, edicts, and close surveillance, which only make the people more cunning in evading them (57.132; 58.134). They refrain from intimidating the world by show of arms (30.69) that are "instruments of ill-omen" (31.71), engage in wars only when there is no other choice (30.69), and observe the rites of mourning when victorious (31.71). Like the an-archic mother of the world that is "not there," their rule is so inconspicuous and perfectly accommodating that the people flourish of themselves without realizing that they have been empowered to do so: "The best of all rulers is but a shadowy presence to his subjects. . . . When his task is accomplished and his work done, the people all say, 'It is just the way we are [我自然 *wuziran*]'" (17.41).[54]

## Amor Chai: A Totalizing Metaphysics of One Empty Nothingness?

I have shown that the Daoist understanding of the Way, the paradigm of which was historically set by the *Laozi*, is that the Way is a chaos-like, formless nothing, which is at the same time the ultimate origin and source of the myriad concrete thing-events of the world. From this perspective on the Way, the Daoist tradition has by and large placed psychophysical energy in the role of the mediating principle or force between the two poles of the duality, namely, the formless Way and the formed "vessels" of the physical universe. Pioneering this understanding is again the *Laozi*, although the text has only a few explicit references to psychophysical energy, as that concept is part of the text's implicit and assumed cosmology. In a celebrated passage in chapter 42, the *Laozi* says:

> The Way begets one;
> One begets two;
> Two begets three;
> Three begets the myriad creatures.
> The myriad creatures carry on their backs the shade [陰 *yin*]
> And embrace in their arms the light [陽 *yang*][55]

And become harmonies by the dynamic blending of the [two] psychophysical energies.[56]

As can be inferred from the use of the binary of the receptive and the active in describing the myriad creatures on the one hand and the explicit reference to psychophysical energy on the other, the *Laozi* assumes a cosmology in which psychophysical energy plays a constitutive role in the coming to be of all thing-events. Corroborating this reading is the *Laozi*'s allusions to the practical—i.e., self-cultivative—basis of its theoretical-philosophical ideas, which presupposes precisely such a cosmology, particularly in the verses such as: "Can you embrace in your arms the One and not let go? In concentrating your breath [氣 *qi*] can you become as supple as a babe? Can you polish your mysterious mirror [the heart-mind] and leave no blemish?" (10.24). The practical regimen of self-cultivation for attaining sagehood, as intimated here, consists in a technique of guiding, concentrating, and refining the flow of psychophysical energy—represented here by the metaphor of breath—within the human body by means of a sitting meditation. The meditational practice involves regularized natural breathing aimed at emptying out the normal, ossified contents of the heart-mind in order to produce a profound experience of utter receptivity and "letting be"—the experience that is explained in terms of merging with the Way and of obtaining the charismatic power to govern by no-action.[57] In other words, the path back to the origin and source of all thing-events lies in recovering the "original condition" of psychophysical energy perfectly in sync with the movement of the Way, that is, as empty and wholly accommodating of spontaneity as the Way itself.

A more explicit affirmation of the mediating role of psychophysical energy between the Way and all thing-events is found in the *Zhuangzi*, the other founding document of the Daoist tradition, roughly contemporary with or postdating the *Laozi*. In chapter 22, the *Zhuangzi* explains life and death in terms of the gathering and dispersing of psychophysical energy: "Humans are born when their psychophysical energy [氣] comes together. There is birth when psychophysical energy comes together; there is death when psychophysical energy disperses. . . . It is, therefore, said: 'Throughout the world there is one psychophysical energy [一氣], that's all.'"[58] Furthermore, psychophysical energy, which has two modalities of active and receptive,[59] is construed as having come from the Way that is poetically depicted as a sort of primal chaos: "In all the mixed-up bustle and confusion [芒芴之間 *wangwu zhijian*], something changed and there was psychophysical energy [氣]. The psychophysical energy changed and there was form [形]. The form changed and she [Zhuang Zhou's wife] had life. Today there was another change and she died. It's just like the round of the four seasons: spring, summer, fall, and winter."[60] Not only does Zhuang Zhou, the alleged author of the text, construe psychophysical energy as being born of the chaos-like Way, but also as the source of all thing-events with physical form, and thus as occupying the mediating position between the formless Way and the formed thing-events of the world. Moreover, in a manner similar to the *Laozi*, the *Zhuangzi* prescribes a regimen of self-cultivation called the "fasting of the heart-mind" (心齋 *xinzhai*), which involves a meditational practice of "sitting and forgetting" (坐忘 *zuowang*) and in which psychophysical energy, again, plays a crucial mediating role. The "fasting of the heart-mind" concentrates and refines one's bodily psychophysical energy until the heart-mind is able to communicate with the world directly via psychophysical energy without relying on the sense-organs. Such an intuitive connection with the world, at which point the sense of self-other distinction disappears, implies that one's psychophysical energy has become as empty and perfectly reflective of the myriad thing-events of the world (虛而待物 *xu er daiwu*) as the Way itself is, and that one has achieved what the *Zhuangzi* calls the Great Communication (大通 *datong*) with the Way.[61]

The Daoist tradition, which emerged in large part as a tradition of commentaries on the *Laozi* and the *Zhuangzi*, has established as its paradigm of world-explanation and self-cultivation a triadic formulation of the duality of the Way and the vessel: the Way (道)—psychophysical energy (氣)—the myriad thing-events (萬物).[62] Although this ontological-cosmological paradigm is certainly present in other ancient Daoist classics such as the *Huainanzi* (淮南子) and the *Liezi* (列子),[63] its most succinct articulation is arguably found in one of the earliest and most influential commentaries on the *Laozi*, the *Heshang Gong* (河上公) that zooms in on the beginning verses of chapter 42 of the *Laozi* quoted earlier: "The Way begets one; one begets two; two begets three; three begets the myriad creatures."[64] According to the commentary, the "one," which is the firstborn of the Way, is the one psychophysical energy (一氣 *yiqi*), called the Quintessential Psychophysical Energy of the Supreme Harmony (太和之精氣 *taihe zhi jingqi*), or the Primordial Psychophysical Energy (元氣 *yuanqi*).[65] The one psychophysical energy differentiates itself into the "two," that is, the active and receptive psychophysical energies, which in turn produce the "three," namely the three configurations of the active and receptive psychophysical energies named harmonious (和氣 *heqi*), clear (清氣 *qingqi*), and turbid (濁氣 *zhuoqi*). It is the various combinations of the three that give birth to the triad of heaven, earth, and humanity, and ultimately, to the myriad thing-events of the world.[66] Like the Way, the one psychophysical energy is without form, yet it is physical and takes on physical forms to become the myriad vessels of the Way. Although its defining characteristic is that of an indeterminate muddle and jumble, it nonetheless moves in perfect sync with the Way to generate its own two modalities and ultimately the myriad thing-events of the world.[67] Furthermore, it is precisely the mediating position of the one psychophysical energy that makes its attainment the primary goal of self-cultivation: As it is the "essential pattern" (紀綱 *jigang*) or "kernel" (要 *yao*) of the Way, people's cultivation of their bodily psychophysical energy in order to obtain—or recover—the one psychophysical energy is the key to bringing about both individual well-being and the ideal social order characterized by no-action and spontaneous freedom, that is, the so-called era of the "Great Peace" (太平 *taiping*).[68]

In sum, the Daoist tradition firmly establishes the classical duality of the formless Way and the formed vessel by creating a triad. It accomplishes this feat first of all by "deepening" the Way's ontological plane and interpreting the Way as the chaotic nothing that lies at the ultimate origin of the universe and the firstborn of which is the one psychophysical energy. Second, it does so by accounting for the Way's generation of the myriad vessels in terms of the creative and transformative operation of the one psychophysical energy, whose two mutually produced opposite modalities and their shifting combinations offer a conceptually more rigorous explanation of the Way's movement of "turning back" or reversal. The development of this triadic interpretation within the Daoist tradition is significant for the comparative purpose of this book, in the sense that the triadic interpretation introduces an ontological hierarchy into the relationship between what might be called ultimate reality and the concrete thing-events of the world by putting psychophysical energy in a position subordinate to the Way within the triad. For the claim that this book makes—that the East Asian category of psychophysical energy offers an inspiring resource for countering the subordinate construction of the Spirit's place and role within the divine trinitarian hierarchy of classical Christian theology—the Daoist rendition of the relationship between the Way and psychophysical energy may not seem particularly helpful.

If there is a redeeming factor, it lies in the definition of the Way as chaotic nothing whose endless an-archic movement is reflected in and responsible for the transitoriness of the myriad thing-events as provisional configurations of constantly self-differentiating and mutually dependent opposites. Such a definition makes the ontological depth given to the Way by the Daoist tradition a far cry from the kinds of ontotheological grounding of God the Father and his creation in classical Western theism that have been the target of contemporary postmodern philosophical criticisms, from Heidegger's *destruktion* ("destruction") of Western metaphysics to Derrida's deconstruction of the transcendental signified.[69] As David Hall points out, the leitmotif of the Western intellectual and religious tradition has been the *chaoskampf*, namely, "the struggle to win cosmos from chaos."[70] This motif is represented by the various ancient Near Eastern and Greek myths all depicting a battle of a culture-hero deity with a chaos monster, often in the shape of a serpent or sea dragon (e.g., the Babylonian Marduk versus Tiamat or the Greek Perseus versus Medusa) and the faint echoes of which still remain in the biblical accounts of creation around the symbol of *tehom* (the deep) and the figures of sea monsters, Leviathan and Rahab.[71] The Christian doctrine of *creatio ex nihilo* epitomizes the culmination of this Western fear of chaos, as it completely does away with the last trace of the creative power of chaos by turning it into a literal nothingness. At the same time, the Christian theological tradition covers up the arbitrariness at the heart of the founding of the cosmic order—a divine will or command—by identifying God with the Divine Mind full of eternal, unchanging, and perfect ideas or forms à la the Platonic account of creation found in *Timaeus*.[72]

By contrast, the an-archic cosmogonic and cosmological paradigm established by the Daoist tradition is *chaophilic*, as it boldly and affirmatively posits, behind the visible and physical order of the cosmos, the invisible flow of chaotic Change. The Way as Change, while being the source out of which all orders arise, is not itself ordered, and in that sense cannot be said even to "exist" separately from the existing orders of which it is the source. Because of that, there has always been an internal debate within the Daoist tradition as to whether the Way is just a name for the spontaneous self-generation of all things.[73] Furthermore, because the Way has no preestablished order of its own to impose on or at the least to propose as an arch-paradigm to the myriad emergent orders of the world, the latter are freed to be "so of themselves." In other words, in contrast to the *chaophobia* of classical Western theism that has led to the logic of empire, the logic of the One, the anarchic *chaophilia* of the Daoist tradition points to a *democracy of creation* undergirded by a radical ontological pluralism,[74] as David Hall has well articulated: "The actual world presumed by Taoism [*sic*] is an anarchy in the sense that it is without *archai*, or *principia*, serving as determining sources of order and value distinct from the order they determine. The units of existence constituting the nature of things are thus *self-determining* [italics mine]."[75] The Way in this "anti-imperial" and "democratic" reading is "the sum of all possible orders resulting from the self-creativity of each event."[76] The point is communicated even more clearly if one adds the word "nonordered" to rephrase it as "the nonordered sum of all possible orders."[77]

It is precisely the anarchic, chaophilic, and radically pluralistic manner in which an ontological depth is given to the Way that has enabled the Daoist tradition to serve as a perennial gadfly at the side of the ruling Confucian elite of the successive dynasties and empires in East Asia. For the classical Confucians, human culture or civilization consisted primarily of patterns (文 *wen*) of ritualized behavior[78] that were based originally on the patterns of Heaven, instituted by the sage-rulers and civilizational heroes such as Huangdi, Yao, Shun, and the Duke of Zhou, and to be imitated by the ruling elites through many years of learning the accumulated ritual tradition (禮 *li*) of the past generations.[79] When the classical Confucians spoke of the Way, they meant the way of human beings represented precisely by such an accumulated tradition consisting in "civilized" patterns of ritualized behavior. The classical Daoist attack on the Confucian way—the cherished Confucian values of benevolence, rectitude, filial devotion, and loyalty, on the one hand, and the ritual tradition embodying those values, on the other[80]—was based on the belief that all systems and hierarchies of values institutionalized in social relations as cures for the ills of human society were merely symptoms pointing to humanity's deviation from the Way: they are part of the disease, not the cure.[81] In the words of Norman Girardot, what classical Daoism rejected was the Confucian tendency to locate the golden age *after* the creation of the world from the primordial chaos *at* the moment of the aristocratic ordering of human civilization—represented by the aforementioned sage rulers and culture heroes—and to seek to go back to that moment to find models of action for the present. Unlike the earlier forms of cultural life, classical Daoism claimed, civilizations sought to suppress and control the "primitive," disorderly, and yet creative presence of the chaos in individual and social life by insisting that the hierarchical ritual order of the ruling class was the one and only right order. By contrast, classical Daoism attempted to return to an experience of deeper, more primitive life-order covered over by the accreted layers of language and culture, that is, an order that "embraced both chaos and cosmos, non-being and being, nature and culture."[82] What it sought, namely, the primitive "chaos-order" clearly manifest in the spontaneously emergent order of nature, was an idealized version of the neolithic culture before the emergence of writing, metallurgy, cities, monarchs, and priests, and characterized by "great equality" (大同 *datong*).[83] It attempted to rediscover this order by means of a self-cultivative and internalized mystical reversal of the civilizational "fall" from the chaos.[84] As Roger Ames points out, for the "anarchism" of classical Daoism, the contrast is not so much between order and disorder as between natural or spontaneous order emergent from below and artificial order consisting of laws and regulations imposed from above.[85]

Nonetheless, despite the anti-imperial and democratic impulse found in the an-archism and *chaophilia* of classical Daoism, the history of the Daoist tradition as a whole has testified to some real ambiguities within its original promise. Even as there have been Daoist secret societies regarded as subversive by the authorities and occasional outbursts of Daoist-inspired peasant rebellions,[86] the tradition has become better known either for its prescription of various techniques for procuring health, long life, and even immortality—a gamut of dietary regulations, gymnastics, breathing and meditative exercises, elixirs of immortality, and a life of quiet withdrawal in the mountains—or for its establishment of organized religious bodies with clergy largely preoccupied with the issues of individual and communal well-being and therefore often patronized by emperors and monarchs.[87] Although both may have been legitimate developments in line with the spirit of the classical tradition, they have often led either to hostile interpretations of its an-archism and *chaophilia* as mere indifference to matters of ethical and social order—as evident in the Confucian condemnation of the Daoist tradition for its alleged nihilism, antinomianism, and individualism—or to an easy co-optation by the ruling elites as useful instruments for pacifying the subject population. Is there something intrinsic to the triadic Daoist paradigm—the ontologico-cosmological and "salvific" paradigm of the Way, psychophysical energy, and the myriad thing-events—that has been a major contributing factor to what is seemingly too facile a capitulation to the logic of empire, to the logic of the One, despite its an-archism and *chaophilia*? Is there perhaps a perennial danger of undercutting the unique value of each self-determining and self-organizing order if it is viewed as ultimately dependent on and returning to a single chaotic, indeterminate nonorder, however "empty"—and therefore accommodating and freeing—the latter is construed to be? Does the Daoist paradigm end up evacuating the nonordered multiplicity of all spontaneously emergent orders into a totalizing metaphysics of one indiscriminate emptiness?[88] Does the pitfall lie in too radical an "apophatic" move made by the tradition to make the nothingness of the unnameable Way more ultimate than the generative power of the Way named as the mother of all things, as most famously declared in the beginning verse of the *Laozi*: "The Way that can be spoken of is not the constant Way"?

These questions go to the root of the Daoist tradition, as the *Laozi* itself could be seen as presenting conflicting pictures of the ultimate Way as the One in some instances—where it speaks of the sages "embracing the One"[89]—but also as that which gives rise to the One.[90] Although many commentarial traditions have interpreted the One as the one psychophysical energy, the scripture's emphasis on the Way's simplicity—symbolized by the metaphors of Nothing and Uncarved Block, among others—has created enough ambiguity about the ultimate Way's genuine difference from some kind of totalizing and annihilating nothingness, thereby courting the Confucian criticisms of Daoist nihilism. To answer these questions in earnest, it would be vital then to examine how the Confucian tradition—both under the influence of the Daoist tradition and in critical reaction to it—has interpreted the classical duality of the Way and the vessel in various manners, all less *chaophilic* than the Daoist paradigm in their shared preoccupation with issues of ethical and social order but not all *chaophobic*. In this work of critical examination, the pivotal question would be how the category of psychophysical energy has figured in the Confucian conceptualizations of the duality of the Way and the vessel for the purposes of world-explanation and self-cultivation.

# 2 The Psychophysical Energy of the Great Ultimate

## A NEO-CONFUCIAN ADVENTURE OF THE IDEA IN ZHU XI

For the classical Confucians, the Way (道 *dao*) was always the "way of," such as the way of the human world or the way of Heaven, in contrast to the Daoist conception of the Way as the origin and supreme principle of all that is.[1] The classical Confucian tradition arose in what is now North China in response to the breakdown of the sociopolitical and moral order that had been claimed to be patterned after the way of Heaven, namely the order of the Zhou dynasty (1046–256 B.C.E.).[2] The Zhou dynasty had replaced the high god of the preceding Shang dynasty, Lord on High, with Heaven (a semipersonal higher power), claiming that the Shang had forfeited the mandate of Heaven (天命 *tianming*). With the gradual deterioration of the Zhou feudal order, the sense that the way of the human order had become estranged from the way of Heaven became widespread. The founder of the Confucian tradition, Kongzi, or "Confucius" (孔子 551–479 B.C.E.), remembered the early Zhou era as the Golden Age in which the empire (天下 *tianxia*)—literally, "all under Heaven"—was united in harmony under the "Son of Heaven" (天子 *tianzi*), and aimed his program of governance at a renewal of that era's institutions, rites, customs, and mores.[3] What was innovative about his program, however, was the envisioned path through which the estranged way of the human order was to be brought back in alignment with the way of Heaven.

### The Confucian Way of Heaven

One of the earliest religiopolitical ideas in China, going all the way back to the Shang oracle bones and the Zhou bronze inscriptions, was the virtue (德 *de*) of the "superior man" (君子 *junzi*) as a charismatic power accruing to the ruler who was ritually correct and therefore in accord with the will of Lord on High or of Heaven.[4] While the ruler was originally regarded as obtaining his virtue or charismatic, numinous power to govern from the highest spiritual power by means of correct rituals, above all sacrifices properly offered and divinations rightly performed, what was innovative about Kongzi was his emphasis on learning and self-cultivation rather than sacrifices and divinations as the primary and more direct means of aligning oneself to the way of Heaven.[5] The notion of "superior man," which had originally meant men of noble birth, was broadened by Kongzi to embrace, in principle, anyone who applied himself to learning and practically embodying the accumulated ritual tradition of the Zhou culture which he saw as having been instituted by the sage-rulers and civilizational heroes of old, such as Huangdi, Yao, Shun, King Wen, and the Duke of Zhou.[6]

Another crucial innovation of Kongzi's involved a redefinition of what constituted the essence of the ritualistic Zhou culture allegedly patterned after the way of Heaven. For Kongzi, the way of Heaven at the heart of the Zhou culture was to be found in the spirit of mutuality and reciprocity permeating its rituals. Accordingly, when Kongzi declares that the way of human beings patterned after the way of Heaven consists in their becoming fully human, that is, becoming persons of "humanity" (仁 *ren*),[7] he defines humanity as the integrity of a guileless self with a capacity for empathetic response to (or sympathetic understanding of) others.[8] In other words, Kongzi puts at the heart of his understanding of the way of human beings an ideal of selfhood that is open, empathetic, relational, and all-embracing—ultimately embracing of the entire cosmos.[9] He views such an ideal selfhood and its bodily enactment in rituals of divine-human and interhuman interactions as constituting the foundation of a harmonious social order.

This idea of a radically open, empathetic, and relational selfhood at the core of the way of human beings finds its concrete anthropocosmic mooring in Mengzi, or "Mencius" (孟子), arguably the second most important figure within the Confucian tradition, about a century removed from the revered founder. His idea of "vast, flood-like psychophysical energy [浩然之氣 *haoran zhiqi*]"[10] anchors Kongzi's concept of humanity as the way of humans firmly in the category of psychophysical energy and in so doing imbues what is understood to be the primordial energy of the universe with a moral teleology. According to Mengzi, humanity (仁 *ren*) is none other than the human nature with which everyone is born—"nature" (性 *xing*) here being the spontaneous course in which a life-form completes its development when nurtured and not obstructed [11]—and which has a close connection to the way of Heaven to such an extent that it could be said to have been decreed or endowed by Heaven.[12] The way of the human order patterned after the way of Heaven means in this context the "seed" of a radically open, empathetic, and relational selfhood that is in all of us humans as the core human potential to be developed fully if we are to be genuinely human. Mengzi speaks of the "sprouts" of humanity within every human being, namely, the four good "heart-minds" (i.e., feelings) of sympathy and benevolence, shame and dislike, deference and compliance, and approval and disapproval, all of which are diverse relational articulations of human nature as empathy that culminate in the Four Virtues of benevolence, righteousness, propriety, and wisdom (仁義禮智).[13] The crucial point is that he describes the growth of these so-called Four Sprouts (四端 *siduan*) in terms of the bodily cultivation of one's "vast, flood-like psychophysical energy" that progressively expands the boundaries of one's embodied self until it comes to encompass the entire universe in empathy, that is, until it becomes united and fully resonating with the cosmic psychophysical energy filling heaven and earth.[14] One carries out the bodily self-cultivation by accumulating right—that is, empathetic and measured—moral responses to others in diverse relational contexts,[15] relying on both the spontaneous issuing forth of the core human feelings of empathy, on the one hand, and the deliberative capacity (思 *si*) of one's heart-mind as the faculty of reflecting on and judging the relative importance of our various feelings, appetites, and inclinations, on the other.[16]

Although Mengzi's interpretation of the Confucian Way thus affirms the critical role of psychophysical energy in the path of self-cultivation and thus reveals a significant overlap between the classical Confucian tradition and the classical Daoist tradition, neither he nor his revered hero, Kongzi, dwells on cosmological or metaphysical speculations, preoccupied as they are with the question of creating and sustaining a harmonious moral order. Although the classical Confucians of the later times, notably Dong Zhongshu (董仲舒 179–104 B.C.E.), contributed to the establishment of the widely influential cosmology of Primordial Psychophysical Energy (元氣 *yuanqi*), which integrated the cosmology of the receptive and active forces with the theory of the Five Processes (五行 *wuxing*),[17] it was not until the rise of so-called Neo-Confucianism or the School of the Way (道學 *daoxue*) in the eleventh century C.E. that the Confucian tradition came to acquire a metaphysical and cosmological sophistication rivaling or surpassing that of the Daoist tradition. As the dominant school in the history of the Confucian tradition from the eleventh century to the nineteenth century C.E. in East Asia, Neo-Confucianism was highly critical of both Daoism and Buddhism while at the same time being influenced by them in one way or another, especially in the way it interpreted the classical duality of the Way and the vessel in terms of the dyad of pattern (理 *li*) and psychophysical energy.

## Pattern, Psychophysical Energy, and the Great Ultimate in Zhu Xi's "Moral Metaphysics"

Neo-Confucianism starts from a high regard of Mengzi as the one who began the "orthodox" line of transmission of the Confucian Way established by Kongzi, and embraces his affirmation of the intrinsically empathetic character—"goodness"—of human nature as evidenced by the Four Sprouts. Nonetheless, while acknowledging the pivotal role played by the bodily cultivation of one's "vast, flood-like psychophysical energy" in growing the sprouts of humanity within, the dominant trends within Neo-Confucianism do not locate the origin of the sprouts in psychophysical energy, with the consequence that the latter's creatively transformative power is deprived of an intrinsic moral teleology. Most notably, Zhu Xi (朱熹 1130–1200 C.E.) of the Chinese Southern Song Dynasty, who represents the historically most influential "orthodox" Cheng-Zhu School within Neo-Confucianism, places the creative-transformative power of psychophysical energy in the derivative and dependent position within a hierarchically structured binary relationship with pattern (理 *li*),[18] resulting in what might be called a "qualified dualism" with a sense of metaphysical or metacosmic transcendence. For Zhu Xi, pattern—also called "Way"—is the metaphysical ultimate, which is logically, ontologically, and normatively prior to psychophysical energy and upon which the cosmic creativity of the latter is dependent. Following the Daoist bestowal of an ontological depth upon the Way, he interprets the classical duality of the Way and the vessel of the Appended Remarks in such a manner that the duality comes to resemble the Western distinction between the metaphysical and the physical, as can be seen from the following well-known remark: "Pattern is the Way above physical form [形而上之道] and the root from which all things are born. Psychophysical energy, by contrast, is the vessel with physical form [形而下之器] and the instrument by which all things are produced."[19]

Nonetheless, in contrast to the substantialistic portrayals of the metaphysical ultimate as unchanging divine substance found in the dominant strains of classical Western theism and Hinduism, Zhu Xi explains pattern as a kind of dynamic ontological creativity—that is, as an incessant activity of patterning, structuring, and harmonizing at the very root of the cosmos, including the production and reproduction of psychophysical energy itself.[20] For him, pattern is the Change of which the Classic of Change speaks, but now located in a deeper ontological context than the one that the Classic itself may have envisioned. At the same time, over against the an-archic and *chaophilic* construals of the metaphysical ultimate as vacuity, emptiness, and nothing found in the Daoist tradition (and in certain strands of East Asian Buddhism), Zhu Xi assigns ultimate rational determinability and orderliness to the intrinsic being of pattern. In other words, while there is an "apophatic" aspect to the manner in which the Daoist tradition depicts the creatively harmonizing movement of the Way—its movement of reversal—as originating ultimately from the chaos of the indeterminate and unnameable Way, Zhu Xi construes the very being of pattern "kataphatically" as consisting in none other than the harmonizing "logic" of its creatively harmonizing movement.

Probably nothing is more indicative of Zhu Xi's kataphatic conception of pattern than his use of the symbol of the Great Ultimate to illustrate pattern's dynamically and rationally creative operations.[21] As shown in chapter 1, the Great Ultimate is a cosmological symbol depicting the ever-shifting dynamic union of the constantly self-differentiating and mutually dependent opposites of the receptive and active psychophysical energies. One of Zhu Xi's Neo-Confucian predecessors, Zhou Dunyi (周敦頤1017–1073 C.E.), makes an innovative move ostensibly to make the Great Ultimate a symbol of the metaphysical ultimate in his enormously influential *Explanation of the Diagram of the Great Ultimate* (太極圖說 *Taiji tushou*).[22] In that treatise, however, Zhou Dunyi places the term "the Non-Ultimate [無極 *wuji*],"[23] which originally appears in chapter 28 of the *Laozi*, alongside the word "Great Ultimate" in such as way that the Non-Ultimate appears to come before the Great Ultimate as the origin of all things: "The Non-Ultimate, therefore, the Great Ultimate [無極而太極 *wuji er taiji*]." Having been influenced by the Daoist tradition to a considerable degree, he probably intends a hierarchical relationship between the two Ultimates in which the structuring cosmic power of the Great Ultimate is rooted in the vacuity of the Non-Ultimate, just as the generative power of the Way named as the mother of the world is subordinated to the chaotic nothingness of the unnameable Way in the *Laozi*.[24] In other words, Zhou Dunyi's Great Ultimate remains a cosmological symbol pointing to the creatively harmonizing movement of psychophysical energy and therefore does not represent a truly innovative advance beyond the triadic Daoist paradigm of the Way, psychophysical energy, and many vessels.[25]

Although highly respectful of Zhou Dunyi's pioneering attempt, Zhu Xi shows his originality in his rejection of a hierarchical reading of the relationship between the two Ultimates suggested by his predecessor. Reading the character 而 (*er*) as meaning juxtaposition ("and") instead of sequence ("therefore"), Zhu Xi argues that the Non-Ultimate merely names the indeterminacy of the Great Ultimate abstracted from its actual, determinately harmonizing operations and imaginatively and logically inferred as existing "prior" to the latter. In other words, the Non-Ultimate is a symbol pointing to the transcendence of the Great Ultimate, being beyond ordinary conceptions characterized by dualities such as being and nothingness.[26] For him, therefore, there is literally nothing beyond and more ultimate than the Great Ultimate.[27] As the metaphysical and ontological symbol pointing to pattern, the Great Ultimate gives witness to the fact that, far from being utterly undifferentiated, chaos-like, and ineffable no-thing, pattern is essentially a repetitive series of creatively harmonizing movements of the interdependently self-differentiating binary principles of the receptive and the active, which captures the "logic" of the movements of psychophysical energy's two modalities.[28] To put this another way, the Great Ultimate as the symbol of pattern points to the latter's very being as the ground and "logic" of the movements of psychophysical energy, that is, that which makes psychophysical energy move the way it moves.[29] The claim that the Non-Ultimate is not more ultimate than the Great Ultimate means precisely that, underneath the determinable "logic" of the creatively harmonizing operations of psychophysical energy, there lies no arbitrary and irrational power or activity independent of and more ultimate than that "logic."

Zhu Xi's essentially kataphatic construal of the metaphysical ultimate, however, faces a problem. If pattern is none other than the creatively harmonizing logic of psychophysical energy's movement, in what sense is it a creative *activity* of patterning, structuring, and harmonizing at the very root of the cosmos—namely, a kind of dynamic ontological creativity? How is the primordial ontological creativity of pattern to be differentiated, if at all, from the cosmic creativity of psychophysical energy supposedly dependent on and derived from the former? In resolving this problem, Zhu Xi utilizes one of the key concepts in East Asian thought, namely, the substance-function (體用 *ti-yong*) distinction, and applies it to the pattern–psychophysical energy relation. The substance-function distinction refers to the distinction made between the original state of a thing, that is, its nature or potential to act, and the state after it has been activated or put into use in response to another within a relational context.[30] An important point to note here is that, for Zhu Xi, substance and function are interrelated and interdependent concepts, inseparable from each other and, strictly speaking, without one having either logical or temporal priority over the other.[31] For the sake of analysis they can be isolated from one another and examined as abstractions, but in concrete reality they are indivisible.

What is notable in relation to the substance-function distinction as applied to the relationship between pattern and psychophysical energy is that, although Zhu Xi posits pattern as the metaphysical ultimate in the sense of dynamic ontological creativity or ground, he denies pattern its own creative dynamism independent of that of psychophysical energy.[32] Pattern is here allowed only an ontologically conceived abstract status of formal and final cause, to borrow Aristotelian terminology, which needs to be activated by the dynamism of psychophysical energy to be effective. That is how Zhu Xi structures the pattern-psychophysical energy relation in a thoroughly interdependent fashion: assign to pattern the status of substance, that is, the potential to act, minus the "potency" of that potential, and give that potency over to the other, that is, psychophysical energy, by whose power pattern becomes functional. In this interdependent relation pattern functions as the ultimate ideal horizon of becoming for the cosmic creativity of psychophysical energy without itself actually being an agency in its own right. Furthermore, it is even the case that pattern can be called dynamic ontological creativity only insofar as it is inseparably united with psychophysical energy in concrete reality.[33] Because of the interdependent substance-function construction of the pattern–psychophysical energy relation, pattern as the creative *activity* of "patterning," "structuring," or "harmonizing" at the root of the universe refers to pattern as function, not to pattern as substance. This implies that, while pattern is transcendent of the physical universe in the sense of being the latter's creative ground, it remains in a sense dependent on the latter to be the creative ground in the concrete sense of the term. What this in turn means is that pattern's incessant production and reproduction of psychophysical energy can even be construed as psychophysical energy's *self-generation*, provided that the coming to be of psychophysical energy as raw dynamism is viewed as always already guided by the harmonizing mandate of pattern and thereby always already given a value-orientation toward order.[34] In sum, although Zhu Xi insists on the logical, ontological, and normative priority of pattern over psychophysical energy and the need to distinguish the two from each other firmly, he also emphasizes their inseparability in concrete reality.[35]

Zhu Xi's nondualistic and nonreductionistic construal of the pattern–psychophysical energy relation on the basis of the substance-function distinction lies behind his affirmation of the Great Ultimate's universal presence in every single being or process in the world to endow it with its individual nature (性 *xing*).[36] On the one hand, individual thing-events are what they are because they are each endowed with their patterns, that is to say, their individually unique patternings of the receptive and active forces in relation to one another, which enable them to be harmonies (和 *he*) and constitute their respective natures, more precisely their embodied and concretized "physical natures" (氣質之性 *qizhi zhi xing*). In this sense, each of them can be said to possess its own individual Great Ultimate, which is precisely pattern as function. On the other hand, the Great Ultimate represents the one Pattern or Harmony, namely, pattern as substance, which is no other than the shared "logic" of such diversely harmonious patternings of the receptive and active forces that give rise to the myriad thing-events of the world.[37] From the perspective of the individual thing-events, the one Pattern could be called their "original nature" (本然之性 *benran zhi xing*) in abstraction from its dynamic concretization into being their respective physical natures.[38] It is in that sense somewhat similar to Plato's Idea of the Good, that is, the Idea of perfection in which all the individually perfect ideas participate, though without the dualistic separation of the ideal and the material.[39] Zhu Xi employs the Buddhist metaphor of the moon and its many reflections to make the point: Although there is only one moon in the sky, when its light is scattered on rivers and lakes, it can be seen in many places. That, however, does not mean the moon has been split, as what is seen on the surface of rivers and lakes is the moon in its entirety.[40]

Nonetheless, a question remains regarding the precise relationship between the one substantial Pattern and many functional individual patterns. Although the images of the moon on the surfaces of rivers and lakes are identical to one another, reflecting the same moon in the sky, the individual patterns in the ten thousand thing-events of the world are not identical to one another, even though there may be degrees of similarity among them. The "original nature" of human beings may be one, but the "physical nature," namely, its concrete embodiment in the diverse bodily coalescences of psychophysical energy found among humans, emerges as many. Precisely what happens when pattern is activated by the dynamism of psychophysical energy for the one Pattern as substance to become many individual patterns as function—that is, for the one abstract Harmony to become many concretely and creatively harmonizing acts? Zhu Xi answers this question in his highly consequential reading of the famous dictum of one of his Neo-Confucian precursors, Cheng Yi (程頤 1033–1107 C.E.): "Empty and tranquil, and without any sign, and yet all figures are already luxuriantly present [沖漠無朕, 萬象森然已具 *chongmo wuzhen, wanxiang senran yiju*]."[41]

The saying is meant by Cheng Yi to capture the gist of another famous saying of his, expressing the thorny ontological problem of one and many: "Pattern is one, but its manifestations are many [理一而分殊 *liyi er fenshu*]."[42] Zhu Xi reads Cheng Yi's sayings as referring to the Great Ultimate[43] and renders an original interpretation of the Great Ultimate in terms of substance and function:

> The receptive psychophysical energy and the active psychophysical energy, [the relationship between] the ruler and the minister, the father and the son—these are all concrete things and affairs, what people do. They are with physical form, i.e., they constitute the differentiated assembly of the ten thousand figures of the world. All of these [things and affairs] have a pattern according to which they ought to be, the so-called "way" or path upon which they ought to travel. It [pattern] is what is above physical form; it is what is "empty and tranquil, and without any sign." *If we are to speak in terms of what exists above physical form, then that which is "empty and tranquil" is in essence substance; and its activation among concrete affairs and things is function.* If we are to speak in terms of what exists with physical form, then concrete things and events constitute substance, and the manifestation of their patterns is function. (Italics mine)[44]

According to Zhu Xi's interpretation of the saying through the prism of the substance-function distinction, the phrase "empty and tranquil, and without any sign" points to the Great Ultimate as substance. When taken by itself totally in abstraction from its operation in the world, that is, as pattern without psychophysical energy, the Great Ultimate may be seen as the indeterminate and quiescent One, namely, the so-called Non-Ultimate (無極 *wuji*), interpreted by Zhu Xi not as pure emptiness or chaotic nothingness but as representing the transcendent and nonconcrete aspect of the one Pattern as pure potentiality for harmony. As activated "among concrete things and affairs," that is, as function or united with psychophysical energy in concrete reality, however, the Great Ultimate is in the world, differentiated into and encompassing an infinite number of dynamically coalescing patterns of receptive and active psychophysical energies, as captured by the phrase, "All figures are already luxuriantly present."[45] This means that it is none other than psychophysical energy that provides the concrete link between one and many, that is, between the one Pattern as substance and the many individual patterns as function. In other words, psychophysical energy is the very reason for there being multiplicity and difference in the world. With its bifurcated modalities of receptive and active forces that represent the primordial existence of difference in the world, psychophysical energy serves as the principle of concretization in accordance with which one indeterminate and abstract potential of dynamic patterning, which is the one Pattern (or the Great Ultimate as substance), becomes delimited into many actual creative patternings of psychophysical energy that constitute the ten thousand thing-events of the world.[46] Psychophysical energy is the one responsible for the concretization of the single "original nature" into the multiplicity of the "physical nature" unique to each human individual.

Thus accompanied by his answer to the problem of the relationship between the one abstract metaphysical Harmony and the many concrete physical harmonies of the world, Zhu Xi's nondualistic and nonreductionistic account of the pattern–psychophysical energy relation lays the basis of his "moral metaphysics."[47] His moral metaphysics takes the Neo-Confucian avowal of the Mencian affirmation of the intrinsically empathetic character of human nature and reconciles it with the Neo-Confucian denial of an intrinsic moral teleology to the "vast, flood-like psychophysical energy" so central to the Confucian project of becoming fully human. As mentioned before, because Zhu Xi identifies the Great Ultimate—or pattern—with the overarching structure or "logic" of everything that is and becomes, he affirms the Great Ultimate's universal presence in every single being or process in the world to endow it with its individual nature. As it is present in human beings, the Great Ultimate is none other than the very humanity shared by all human beings as their inborn original nature, namely, the capacity for a radically open, empathetic, and relational selfhood that manifests itself in the Four Sprouts of creatively harmonizing feelings.[48] The moral agency that cultivates and nurtures that innate capacity resides in the human heart-mind (人心 *renxin*), which, as the most clear and responsive coalescence of psychophysical energy, possesses the marvelously "awakened" and therefore extraordinarily creative quality of "spirit" (神 *shen*) and which, as such, is the seat of consciousness and the somatic vessel of the Great Ultimate.[49]

In Zhu Xi's picture of moral self-cultivation, the most fundamental and initial activity of the human heart-mind consists in feelings and desires that are activations of human nature by one's bodily psychophysical energy in response to concrete relational contexts. Those initial, embodied affective responses to others may follow without deviation the "mandate" of the human nature within, retain as a consequence the heart-mind's original state of "equilibrium" (中 *zhong*) that perfectly mirrors the harmonizing potential of the Great Ultimate as substance or as indeterminate and quiescent One, and thereby become fitting and harmonious (和 *he*) to the particular relational contexts (i.e., empathetic, other-oriented, and therefore conducive to harmonious relations). They may, however, deviate from the dictates of human nature, lose the original equilibrium of the heart-mind, and become inappropriate and discordant to the relational contexts (i.e., excessive or deficient, being self-oriented and unempathetic). The role of the heart-mind's moral agency is to follow up on its initial affective responses to others in the form of intentional deliberation and judgment in order to nurture the relationally harmonious feelings while bringing under control the nonharmonious ones.[50] When the human heart-mind fulfills this role by following without deviation the promptings of the human nature within, it is identical to what is called "the heart-mind of the Way [道心 *daoxin*]."[51] A continued exercise of the human heart-mind's moral agency as the heart-mind of the Way over the long haul accumulates relationally correct psychosomatic responses and judgments to such an extent that one's psychophysical energy is habitually conditioned to respond to others in proper measures spontaneously while one's judgment is perfected always to favor such spontaneous responses. It is in this way that the human heart-mind progressively transforms one's individual coalescence of psychophysical energy into a clearer, more open, balanced, and responsive condition and in so doing expands the boundaries of one's psychophysical energy beyond the self-other distinction to encompass heaven and earth—that is, the condition Mencius has called "vast, flood-like psychophysical energy." When such a condition is reached, the perfect equilibrium of psychophysical energy would make the human heart-mind completely resonant with the "pulsation" of human nature vibrating from within to harmonize the self creatively with the rest of the world, enabling one to join the ranks of the fulfilled human beings, namely, the "superior persons" (君子 *junzi*) and the sages (聖人 *shengren*), who have an enduring and unwavering possession of the heart-mind of the Way.

Hence, the Neo-Confucian project of becoming fully human as outlined by Zhu Xi has a cosmic dimension, since the full realization of the Great Ultimate as humanity (仁 *ren*) within the context of interhuman and social relations resonates with the creatively harmonizing operations of the Great Ultimate in the entire universe. Zhu Xi explicitly identifies humanity in the sense of generous and empathetic self-giving with the other pattern-endowed natures of the myriad thing-events of the world, which are understood to be no other than their ceaseless and harmonious creativity (literally "life-giving intention [生意 *shengyi*]").[52] Their harmonious creativity expresses itself in the heart-mind, which they are all seen to possess individually; and their heart-minds mirror the "fecund heart-mind of heaven and earth [天地生物之心 *tiandi shengwu zhi xin*]," which is the name for the creativity of the cosmos reflecting the universal presence of the Great Ultimate.[53] Given this cosmic context, the ultimate goal of human life, human fulfillment, can therefore be said to lie in achieving the heart-mind of the Way, which perfectly mirrors the fecund heart-mind of heaven and earth, and thereby participating fully in the universally and harmoniously transformative creativity of pattern that is found everywhere and represented by the symbol of the Great Ultimate.

## "Pattern Unites; Psychophysical Energy Differentiates": A Totalizing Metaphysics of One Heavenly Pattern?

Zhu Xi's moral metaphysics, the outline of which is sketched in the preceding section, represents the dominant Neo-Confucian reading of the classical duality of the Way and the vessel. Similarly to the Daoist tradition, it confers an ontological depth to the Way and in so doing affirms the hierarchical interpretation of the classical duality expressed by the triad of the Way, psychophysical energy, and the myriad thing-events.

It creates an ontological hierarchy between ultimate reality and the concrete thing-events of the world by subordinating psychophysical energy to the Way as pattern, or the Great Ultimate. As such, it shares part of the ambiguity that the Daoist tradition presents when it comes to offering an inspiring resource for the comparative task of employing the category of psychophysical energy to counter the subordinate construction of the Spirit's place and role within the divine trinitarian hierarchy of classical Christian theology.

At the same time, however, Zhu Xi's moral metaphysics construes the ontological depth of the Way differently from the Daoist tradition in rejecting the Daoist an-archic and *chaophilic* interpretation of the Way in favor of a more kataphatic rendition of it, in which there is nothing more ultimate than the discernible order and "logic" of the Way's creatively harmonizing movement in union with psychophysical energy. The Way, as the pattern of the Great Ultimate, is not dependent on and subordinate to the Non-Ultimate as the chaotic and indeterminate nothingness of the unnameable Way. Accordingly, Zhu Xi's conception of the Way as the ontological ultimate appears at least to be capable of laying to rest the concern about the seeming tendency of the Daoist paradigm to absorb the concrete ethical and social orders into a totalizing metaphysics of one indiscriminate emptiness, as pointed out in the previous chapter.

But there is another, different risk lurking in the ontological hierarchy created by Zhu Xi's metaphysical account. Because it lacks the kind of internal critical principle found in the Daoist apophatic account, it seems to have difficulty preventing any humanly discerned, determined, and instituted Way from claiming to have a lock on ultimacy. It assumes no invisible flow of chaotic Change underneath the existing visible and physical order of human society and the cosmos ("what is") declared to be ultimate—in other words, the kind of ontological depth required to relativize the allegedly ultimate order of the present and to provide again and again openings of spontaneous freedom and novelty ("what could be"). The Way as pattern, the Great Ultimate, or the original human nature appears to be in danger of being ossified and even hypostatized into a preexisting ideal order that is imposed on or at the least presented as an arch-paradigm to the myriad emergent orders of the world to the extent that the latter are not freed to become "so of themselves." The duality of the Way and the vessel seems here to be on the verge of turning into a dualism, despite Zhu Xi's dynamic construction of the pattern–psychophysical energy relation in terms of the nondualistic and nonreductionistic substance-function relation.

Zhu Xi's moral metaphysics, however, may be read in such a way that the logical and ontological ultimacy it assigns to the kataphatically conceived pattern could avoid being likened to the ontotheological grounding of a self-subsistent and immutable God in classical Western theism, harboring the chaophobic and imperialistic "logic of the One." The Way, or pattern, as the ontological ultimate is symbolized by the Great Ultimate because the successive movement of the receptive and the active constitutes its very being as becoming. In other words, the ontological ultimate is conceived dynamically as a repetitive series of creatively harmonizing movements of the interdependently self-differentiating binary principles of the receptive and the active. This means that within the incessant creative activity of patterning, structuring, and harmonizing at the root of the cosmos, there is always a receptive moment, the phase of *yin*, in which the dynamic ontological creativity "contracts," or pulls back into itself, after having "extended," or pushed beyond itself, in the active moment or the *yang* phase.[54] Given the substance-function construction of the relationship between pattern and psychophysical energy, this dipolar movement of the ontological creativity of the one Pattern is not to be treated as other to the dipolar movement of the cosmic creativity of the individual patterns riding on the dynamic of psychophysical energy, but always to be seen as interpenetrated and "in concert with" the latter. In other words, the receptive moment in the creative harmonizing operation of the Great Ultimate can be conceived as the phase in which the myriad achieved patterns or harmonies of the world "wane" and "flow back" into the one abstract Pattern, and in so doing provide the factual basis of old spent orders in response to which the one Pattern embarks on a new stage of creative issuing forth into many novel emergent orders of the world.[55]

Such a "spiral"—progressively cyclical—understanding of the Great Ultimate's creative movement is reflected in Zhu Xi's conception of the process of moral self-cultivation. Within this process, there is a kind of "feedback loop" between the moral agency of the heart-mind of the Way and that of the human heart-mind. It is only by following the mandate or "promptings" of the original nature or the Great Ultimate within, which can be named the moral agency of the heart-mind of the Way, that the human heart-mind can act on its initial affective responses to others in a manner that intentionally nurtures relationally harmonious feelings. At the same time, it is precisely the accumulated experience of relationally harmonious psychosomatic responses and judgments exercised by the human heart-mind over the long haul that enables the heart-mind of the Way to "come into being" in the fullest and most concrete sense of the term, as seen in the unimpeded realization of the mandate of the original nature achieved by the heart-minds of superior persons and sages whose bodily psychophysical energy has attained the perfect clarity and equilibrium of the "vast, flood-like psychophysical energy." One could say that there is a receptive moment, the *yin* phase, within the "fecund heart-mind of heaven and earth"—that is, within the universal and cosmic operation of the heart-mind of the Way carried out in and through the myriad human or creaturely heart-minds. In this receptive phase, the relationally correct psychosomatic experience of the myriad human or creaturely heart-minds, which has enabled them to become more resonant bodies, "flow back" into the heart-mind of the Way to "inform," "nurture," and "develop" it further. As a consequence, in its active or *yang* phase, the heart-mind of the Way can better guide the myriad human or creaturely heart-minds with the harmonizing impulse of the original nature, for it is now capable of issuing forth into the Four Sprouts of creatively harmonizing feelings in them with less obstruction and distortion than previously, due to their now more resonant bodies. In sum, the human or creaturely heart-mind on the one hand and the heart-mind of the Way on the other, which are both "spiritual" (*shen*-like) embodiments of the metaphysical ultimate (the Way, pattern, or the Great Ultimate) in psychophysical energy, are related to each other in a nondualistic and nonreductionistic relationship of mutual influence even as the latter functions as the transcendently normative ground and immanent *telos* of the former.

Nevertheless, I find conceptual weakness in the way Zhu Xi structures the pattern–psychophysical energy relation as a hierarchically binary construction of unity over multiplicity, which lays a considerable roadblock to the spiral conception of the Great Ultimate's creatively harmonizing movement just suggested as germane to his theory of self-cultivation. It undermines the nondualistic and nonreductionist intent of his overall thought and potentially poses a threat to the pivotal role of the heart-mind of the Way in the Neo-Confucian project of becoming fully human. The locus classicus of the problem is found in his well-known statement, "Pattern unites, [whereas] psychophysical energy differentiates

[理同氣異 *litong qiyi*]."[56] Here the crux of the matter is that, although it is conceivable for Zhu Xi to attribute whatever unity found in the world to one psychophysical energy shared by all, he nonetheless denies psychophysical energy any unifying and harmonizing function of its own.[57] According to his account, the unavoidable excesses and deficiencies in psychophysical energy's differentiating and coalescing movements continually give rise to the kinds of psychophysical energy that are opaque, impure, turbid, coarse, indolent, and therefore less open and communicative. Zhu Xi locates the source of evil, which is understood as selfishness, in these nonresonating and uncommunicative kinds of psychophysical energy—the kinds of psychophysical energy that would obstruct the full realization of humanity as empathy.[58] By contrast, he regards pattern as never losing its original condition as one abstract unifying potential (one Pattern) even in the midst of its concretizations into myriad actual patternings of psychophysical energy (many individual patterns). Zhu Xi's statement, "Pattern unites; psychophysical energy differentiates," captures this contrast in a succinct fashion.

Such an asymmetrical treatment of pattern vis-à-vis psychophysical energy in regard to their respective unifying and harmonizing power gives rise to two thorny issues, one ontological and the other ethical. First, as shown in the earlier quote and in line with his inordinate emphasis on pattern's unity, Zhu Xi construes pattern "by itself" (i.e., the Great Ultimate as substance) as the indeterminate and quiescent One standing for the transcendent and nonconcrete aspect of the pure potentiality for harmony. It is only when pattern becomes functional, that is, as it is united with and activated by psychophysical energy, that he depicts pattern as being multiple. If multiplicity is introduced into pattern only insofar as pattern is united with and activated by psychophysical energy, for which manyness is intrinsic, then is that not a testament to the fact that pattern is originarily and primarily one, and only derivatively and dependently many? There is an added force to this question, as long as Zhu Xi posits pattern as the metaphysical ultimate in the sense of dynamic ontological creativity or ground that has logical, ontological, and normative priority over psychophysical energy. Despite his use of the symmetrically construed substance-function relation, an undercurrent of ontological asymmetry is undeniable. Although Zhu Xi argues firmly against speaking of pattern alone in abstraction, insofar as pattern is the metaphysical ultimate, it is hard to dispel the suspicion that multiplicity belongs to pattern only penultimately and derivatively, only by virtue of its inevitable association with psychophysical energy. Given the presence of ontological asymmetry that makes psychophysical energy—and its inherent delimiting dynamic—depend for its being on pattern, the possibility that pattern's multiplicity may not be ultimate threatens the ontological ultimacy and primordiality of multiplicity as such.

This in turn puts into question the spiral conception of the Great Ultimate's creatively harmonizing movement, which Zhu Xi appears to offer. The ontologically penultimate and derivative multiplicity of the concretely achieved orders of the world are here in danger of being "brought in line with" and, for all intents and purposes, disappearing into the one ultimate Order or Harmony of their ontological ground when they "flow back" into the one abstract Pattern in its receptive phase, notwithstanding Zhu Xi's dynamic and nonsubstantialistic conception of the latter. If the multiply achieved patterns of the world—the ten thousand thing-events—are assimilated into the one overarching primordial Pattern, with no internal differences or contrasts between the factual old and the hypothetical new remaining in it to generate creative tensions, then there would be no novelty introduced in the one Pattern's active or extensive stage of creative unfolding into many concrete patterns. The process of generation and regeneration would be purely cyclical, tantamount to an "eternal return of the Same" that dynamically completes the logic of the One.

It needs to be said at this juncture that Zhu Xi does make allusions that seem to draw a picture of the Great Ultimate as multiple in and of itself, referring to it sometimes as the *sum or totality* of all the individual patterns rather than the one Pattern.[59] The most prominent reference of this kind goes as follows:

> In general, the Great Ultimate is the unfathomable wonder of the original state; and activity and tranquility constitute the mechanism of its riding [psychophysical energy]. The Great Ultimate is the Way above physical form; and the receptive and active psychophysical energies are the vessels with physical form. When looked at from the perspective of its [the Great Ultimate's] manifestation, therefore, activity and tranquility are not co-present at the same time, and the receptive and the active do not occupy the same place, yet the Great Ultimate itself is present everywhere. *When looked at from the perspective of its concealment*, it is "empty and tranquil, and without any sign," but *the patterns of activity and tranquility, of receptive and active, are all already furnished within it.* (Italics mine)[60]

In other words, from the perspective of the Great Ultimate in its "manifestation" in the world (i.e., as function), while each concrete thing-event has its own individual pattern that cannot be mixed or confused with another, the Great Ultimate as the one Pattern is always copresent with each individual pattern in each thing-event, because it transcends the determinate concreteness of individual patterns. At the same time, however, from the perspective of its "concealment" (i.e., as substance), the Great Ultimate is undifferentiated and without movement, yet it nonetheless contains within itself the sum or totality of all individual patterns. In essence, what Zhu Xi seems to be saying is that the Great Ultimate is plurisingular, that is, *both* one indeterminate Pattern *and* the totality of individually differentiated patterns, even when it is taken in abstraction from its concrete existence in union with psychophysical energy. This provocative statement, which seems to contradict his valorizing emphasis on the unifying role of pattern over against psychophysical energy as the exclusive principle of differentiation, is however not really explained in any further detail. Although Zhu Xi makes quite a few references to the plurisingular nature of the Great Ultimate as it is present to the concrete thing-events of the world, no clarification is given as to how the Great Ultimate can be primordially and ultimately multiple in any way different from its derivative and penultimate multiplicity among the ten thousand thing-events.[61] The above quote, therefore, sits in uneasy tension with the statement, "Pattern unites, whereas psychophysical energy differentiates," and fails to provide a sufficient ground to dismiss the question about the ontological ultimacy of multiplicity in Zhu Xi's thought.

Second, Zhu Xi's denial of an independent unifying power to psychophysical energy, when coupled with his relegation of multiplicity to penultimacy, presents a challenge to the moral agency of the heart-mind required for the project of self-cultivation. The problem lies in the fact that the heart-mind itself is a coalescence of psychophysical energy, albeit the clearest and most responsive—"spiritual"—kind. The human nature or pattern within the heart-mind cannot be activated without the dynamism provided by the very thing that it is supposed to guide and control, namely, the spontaneous dynamism of psychophysical energy. Since pattern is only the a priori, abstract, and general value of "unity" and "harmony" made determinate in diverse ways by the differentiating dynamism of psychophysical energy, and not an independent agency with its own dynamism to shape harmonious patternings of relations, human moral agency is in fact completely dependent on the power of psychophysical energy in order to be active. But since Zhu Xi takes psychophysical energy solely to be the principle of difference and denies it any spontaneously unifying and harmonizing function, it raises a critical question about the effectiveness and reliability of human moral agency. If the moral agency of the human subject is supposed to be driven solely by a morally neutral dynamism of ever-proliferating random differentiation, having only a passive map or guide that merely prescribes possible forms of order and their ultimate harmony,[62] it is then definitely conceivable that the human heart-mind more often than not caves in to its own relentlessly differentiating dynamism and creates forms of self-other opposition consisting in self-centered, relationally indifferent, and nonharmonious psychosomatic responses to others. Especially strengthening the doubt is the common Neo-Confucian observation that the vast majority of people are born with opaque, turbid, and indolent—that is, unbalanced, nonresonating, uncommunicative, and therefore involuted—kinds of psychophysical energy to begin with, which makes the guiding beacon of pattern in them all the dimmer.[63] When this observation is coupled with Zhu Xi's assignment of ontological penultimacy to the multiplicity of local patterns derived from the delimitation of the one abstract Pattern by the morally ambiguous, relationally indifferent differentiating dynamism of psychophysical energy, then a devaluation of the moral agency of the vast majority of people becomes inexorable. Their heart-minds are seen to fall largely under the sway of their spontaneously self-centered psychosomatic responses and to fail to achieve the self-transcendent, empathetic, relational, and harmonizing moral agency, namely, the heart-mind of the Way, that is characteristic of fulfilled human beings.

Such doubt about the effectiveness and reliability of human moral agency results in a tendency to distrust spontaneously emerging human feelings and desires. The so-called Seven Feelings (七情 *qiqing*)[64]—pleasure, anger, sorrow, fear, love, hatred, and desire—representing ordinary, everyday feelings come under a cloud of suspicion, because they are perceived as prone to lose the middle and to become either excessive or deficient, unbefitting particular relational contexts, and therefore not capable of readily serving as the vehicle of the Four Sprouts of creatively harmonizing feelings and of facilitating an effective presence of the heart-mind of the Way. This wariness is abundantly evident in the Neo-Confucian opposition of "Heavenly Pattern" (天理 *tianli*), which is "public" (公 *gong*), to "human desire" (人欲 *renyu*), which is "private" (私 *si*), and the hierarchical social ordering in which the ruling class of cultured male gentry, who are versed in the classics and thus trained in the way of the sages to exercise public leadership, stand as "superior persons" (君子 *junzi*) over women, the working mass of commoners, and nomadic "barbarians" as "inferior persons" (小人 *xiaoren*) unfit to participate fully in the work of creatively harmonizing the world.[65] What is thereby considerably weakened is the thought that the heart-mind of the Way as human-transhuman moral agency may be understood as emerging "in concert with"—in a mutually constitutive spiral dialectic with—many self-creative practices of somatic cultivation in various relationally embodied (racialized, gendered, sexualized, class-located, etc.) contexts. The heart-mind of the Way is here in danger of turning into an abstract, blank tablet upon which a dominant group can inscribe its own parochial patterns and claim for itself the false universality of representing the Heavenly Pattern allegedly discovered by the ancient sages and preserved in the classics.[66] The vast multitude of human and creaturely heart-minds are to submit themselves to the concretely—for example, ritually—patterned inscriptions of the Heavenly Pattern found in the classics and taught by their guardians, namely, the ruling class of male literati and ritual masters.

The consequences of Zhu Xi's failure to provide a sympathetic carrier or vehicle of pattern's creatively harmonizing mandate, which is called for by his interdependent construction of the pattern–psychophysical energy relationship, makes one search for an alternative conception of the ontological status of the multiplicity of patterns accompanied by a different way of envisioning the dynamism of psychophysical energy. Before I move on to some of the options that have emerged within the Confucian tradition, I think it is an opportune time to engage in a comparative reflection involving the critique of Western theism, both classical and modern, launched by Alfred North Whitehead (1861–1947 C.E.) and his "philosophy of organism," propounding a dipolar process conception of God. His philosophy, which assigns categorial ultimacy to both one and many, envisages within God a primordial presence of infinite multiplicity of "forms of definiteness" as pure potentialities, and in so doing presents a challenging counterexample to the derivative multiplicity of patterns in Zhu Xi's thought. What is more, precisely due to the primordiality of the multiplicity of pure potentialities within God, Whitehead's dipolar process conception of God coupled with its linear trajectory provides helpful conceptual remedies to the deficiencies in Zhu Xi's construal of the spiral movement of the Great Ultimate as reflected in the workings of the heart-mind of the Way in self-cultivation. Last and not least, Whitehead's notion of creativity, to which he also assigns categorial ultimacy, points to a fruitful way of reconceiving the dynamism of psychophysical energy so that it would be equipped with a creatively unifying and harmonizing function of its own.

# 3 Creativity and a Democracy of Fellow Creatures

## THE CHALLENGE OF WHITEHEAD'S RADICAL ONTOLOGICAL PLURALISM

In his magnum opus, *Process and Reality*, Alfred North Whitehead names three major images of God as having come, in various combinations, to dominate the development of theistic philosophy: God as an imperial ruler, associated with the Roman Empire and its divine Caesars, and also with Islam; God as a personification of moral energy—"the ruthless moralist"—as with the Hebrew prophets; and God as an ultimate philosophical principle, as found in Aristotle with his notion of the Unmoved Mover, and also in Indian thought.[1] Regardless of whether this threefold scheme of historical interpretation does justice to all the religious and philosophical traditions implicated, it is clear in *Process and Reality* that Whitehead uses this interpretive framework to criticize classical Christian theism in favor of a notion of God, found in "the Galilean origin of Christianity," that "dwells upon the tender elements in the world" and "slowly and in quietness operate[s] by love" (343). An interesting fact to note here is that Whitehead sees his notion of God, which he developed from its Galilean origin into an integral part of his "philosophy of organism," approximating more to "some strains of Indian, or Chinese thought" than to "western Asiatic, or European, thought" (7). In order to follow this suggestive allusion to a comparative theological reflection, we need to examine Whitehead's philosophy of organism, especially as it is presented in its mature form in *Process and Reality*, so as to situate his "dipolar" conception of God as Love within its proper systematic and interpretive context.

### Creativity, Actual Occasions, and Eternal Objects: Reality as the Process of "Concrescence"

According to one of his metaphysical first principles, that is, the "ontological principle," what Whitehead calls "actual entities" or "actual occasions" are "the final real things of which the world is made up" (18).[2] Because there is "no going behind actual entities to find anything more real," God is an actual entity also, as is "the most trivial puff of existence in far-off empty space" (18). What is an actual entity, then? An actual entity or occasion, he explains, is an instance of "concrescence" (211), which is "the name for the process in which the universe of many things acquires an individual unity in a determinate relegation of each item of the 'many' to its subordination in the constitution of the novel 'one'" (211). In other words, an actual entity is none other than the very *process* of the *creation* of a new "one" out of the "many." On the one hand, the very "being" of an actual entity is constituted by its "becoming"—the thesis encapsulated in another one of Whitehead's metaphysical first principles, namely, the "principle of process" (23). On the other hand, the becoming of an actual entity is never a mere random movement or change but always a "creative advance into novelty."[3] The concrescence of an actual entity is tantamount to the creation or production of a new unity, which is "the universe conjunctively," out of the existing disjointed multiplicity, which is "the universe disjunctively," in such a way that the new unity participates in and adds to the past multiplicity: "The many become one, and are increased by one" (21).

The "many" here does not, however, refer to elements more fundamental and ultimate than actual entities but to actual entities themselves. Actual entities are the atomic units of reality and the basic building blocks of the universe, though conceived as units of becoming rather than of being (35). In terms of modern particle physics with which Whitehead was familiar, actual entities may be seen to correspond, with some qualifications, to subatomic elementary particles such as quarks. They "atomize" what Whitehead calls "the extensive continuum," that is, the actual world conceived in terms of its most general features of unbounded extension and indefinite divisibility, both spatially and temporally speaking. Many actual entities come into being in an instant as the indivisible atomic units of one extensive space-time continuum, "perish" in the same instant, and in their moment of perishing contribute to the concrescence of a novel actual entity.[4] It is by forming "nexūs" (Whitehead, *Process and Reality*, 20)[5]—sets of spatiotemporally interrelated and mutually immanent actual entities—that actual entities come to constitute more ordinary and seemingly enduring objects of perception, from protons and atoms to plants and animals, which are all "societies" of actual entities with defining characteristic or "common form" (Whitehead, *Process and Reality,* 34).

Here it is important to note that, for Whitehead, there is no transcendent creator God in the classical sense of the term behind the incessant process of the creation of a new actual entity out of many past actual entities. Rather, underneath the process of concrescence of the world of actual entities lies "creativity," which is "that ultimate notion of the highest generality at the base of actuality" (31). Creativity is another rendering of the Aristotelian notion of "matter" and the modern notion of "neutral stuff," neither of which has a character of its own because all characters are more specific than they are, and which become actual only by being conditioned and characterized (31). In contrast to these two notions, however, which are more or less synonymous with the pure notion of passive receptivity set over against "form" or external relations, Whitehead's notion of creativity stands for the notion of pure *activity* underlying the process of becoming of actual entities (7, 31). As the notion of pure activity, creativity is an abstract principle rather than a concrete agency or agent—"that ultimate principle by which the many, which are the universe disjunctively, become the one actual occasion, which is the universe conjunctively" (21). Creativity, in that sense, is actual only insofar as it is conditioned and qualified by its creatures, that is, only when characterized *as* the process of concrescence of actual entities that are agents in the real and factual sense of the term (20).

Since creativity is no actual agency, actual entities or occasions are creatures without a creator—they are *causa sui.* The process of their concrescence, in other words, is none other than the process of their self-creation or self-causation (88).[6] That is why Whitehead calls actual entities "subjects"—beings functioning in regard to themselves or determining themselves in the self-constituting process of concrescence by being immediately present to themselves and not losing self-identity in the midst of self-diversity:

> An actual entity functions in respect to its own determination. . . . An actual entity by functioning in respect to itself plays diverse roles in self-formation without losing its self identity. It is *self-creative.* . . . This self-functioning is the real internal constitution of an actual entity. It is the "immediacy" of the actual entity. An actual entity is called the "subject" of its own immediacy. (Whitehead, *Process and Reality,* 25; italics mine)

As a subject, an actual entity is the agent of its own becoming, actively receiving and appropriating the world in its manyness to constitute the unity of what it becomes. This is the meaning of Whitehead's "reformist subjectivist principle," namely, the claim that actual entities "experience," that they are "drops of experience, complex and interdependent" (18), and that "apart from the experiences of subjects there is nothing, nothing, nothing, bare nothingness" (167).

As a "drop of experience," an actual entity has a threefold character corresponding to the three phases of its concrescence (87). First, it has the character "given" to it by the past, which is none other than the many and diverse objectifications of the past actual entities of the world functioning as its "efficient cause." This first, "given," and deterministic character or phase of an actual entity, which conditions and characterizes creativity primordially as a "ground of obligation" (29) insofar as actual entities are concerned, is what Whitehead calls the "objective immortality" of the actual world (31). It is none other than the "inflow of the actual world"[7] whose teeming multitude of already concresced and now objectified entities are "felt" or positively "prehended"[8]—included in a subject's internal constitution—and reenacted severally by the novel concrescent subject in and through a process of selective elimination and abstraction (65, 245). It is the "datum from the past" whose disjointed multiplicity accounts for the self-diversity within the initial phase of a novel concrescence (164).

Second, an actual entity has a subjective character or phase that consists of "subjective form" and "subjective aim." The "subjective form" is *how* an actual entity experiences, that is, actively becomes what it determinately comes to be by responding to the objectified data of the past, valuing them and selectively either rejecting them from or admitting them into the self-creative process (23, 85–86). The "subjective aim," in contrast, is an actual entity's "final cause," "lure," or "appetition" (87, 33)—namely, its ideal of itself as a determinate individual that guides the valuation of its subjective form so that through the process of its concrescence it makes the "decision" to come to be what it comes to be (85–87). While being conditioned by its first character, that is, the deterministic efficient causation, an actual entity in the second, subjective character not merely reenacts the disjointed objective data from the past but selectively brings them into a novel harmony in order to determine itself to be this or that entity. The freedom and spontaneity manifest in this process of creative advance into novel orders speak for the character of actual entities as autonomous subjects that are conditioned but not wholly determined by the past objective immortality of the world.

Last but not least, an actual entity as a subject has a "superjective" character or phase, which is "the pragmatic value of its specific satisfaction qualifying the transcendent creativity" (87). Following another one of his metaphysical principles, namely, the "principle of relativity," according to which every "being" is a potential for every "becoming" (22), Whitehead conceives of an actual entity as losing its subjective immediacy—that is, "perishing" as a subject—and turning into an object for other concrescing actual entities,[9] becoming part of the "datum from the past" for them, as soon as it has achieved full subjectivity or the "satisfaction" (26) of being definitively this or that entity: "An actual entity is to be conceived both as a subject presiding over its own immediacy of becoming and a superject which is the atomic creature exercising its function of objective immortality" (45). The term "subject" as applied to actual entities, in that sense, is always an abbreviation of "subject-superject" (29).

The self-creative autonomy of actual entities as subjects, however, is not only conditioned by the inflow of the actual world from the past. It is also partially dependent, even in the immediacy of the present, on something other than itself, at least in the initial stage of concrescence. The subjective freedom of an actual entity to determine itself definitively into being this or that actual entity presupposes a form of definiteness functioning as its telos (its "lure" or "final cause") (20); and Whitehead conceives of forms of definiteness as the other kind of entities, that is, potential entities, which, together with actual entities, make up the world. He names the potential entities "eternal objects" (158),[10] which include patterned combinations of them called "complex eternal objects."[11] A complex eternal object is precisely that specific interrelation of eternal objects that provides the defining characteristic or common form—and functions as the "conceptual lure for feeling" (86)—for the correspondingly ordered society of mutually immanent actual entities. Eternal objects, be they simple or complex, are "pure potentials" (23) for the process of becoming in the sense that an analysis of their nature discloses only other eternal objects and does not reveal in what determinate actual entities they are to be realized (23, 29). In other words, eternal objects represent the "general" and "absolute" potentialities (65) of the universe that are indeterminate in regard to their relevance to particular actual entities and therefore are not yet part of concrescence (29). They may in that sense be envisaged as connoting a kind of "cosmic geometrical/genetic code"[12] harboring many divergent possibilities of concrete and determinate actualization. It is only with their "ingression"[13] in the process of becoming, in which they are conditioned and limited by the data provided by the actual world, that they come to form "real" potentialities relative and relevant to some actual entities (Whitehead, *Process and Reality,* 65), expressing their definiteness and thus determining the concrete shapes of their respective self-creative concrescence. As real potentialities, therefore, eternal objects point in fact to the actual world itself in its character as a "datum for creativeness" given to itself as it forges ahead beyond a given standpoint in cosmic space-time toward a radically novel future (65).

In sum, Whitehead's "philosophy of organism" presents a thoroughly processual picture of reality as intrinsic to the cosmos in which we find ourselves. The three notions of creativity, actual occasions, and eternal objects make up the conceptual scheme by which reality as the process of concrescence is explained. If so, is there a place for any deity within this picture? Whitehead's answer is yes, although his understanding of God is a far cry from the transcendent creator of classical Western theism.

## God as the Poet of the World: The Dipolar God and Creative Freedom

If we are to understand Whitehead's notion of God, we need to take note of his claim that the ingression of eternal objects in the concrescence of actual entities requires mediation. By his ontological principle, everything, including the general potentiality of the universe (i.e., eternal objects), must be "somewhere." Here "somewhere" means "in some actual entity" (46). Because there is "no going behind actual entities to find anything more real" (18), eternal objects as pure potentialities are not to be relegated to a transcendent realm beyond the world of actual entities. At the same time, however, because actual entities are finite, they cannot contain the infinite general potentialities of the universe represented by all eternal objects. Eternal objects, therefore, must be found within the formal—not physical—constitution of an actual entity that is itself also eternal, nontemporal, absolute, and unbounded. By the principle of relativity, according to which every being is a potential for every becoming, there can, however, be only one such nontemporal actual entity unconditioned and unbounded by the inflow of the past of the actual world, because more than one such actual entity would imply an eternal relation between them of mutual prehension, conditioning, and limitation.[14] Whitehead names that single nontemporal actual entity "God."

Furthermore, the relevance of eternal objects to actual entities, insofar as it is "effective relevance" (31), consists in "the ultimate, basic adjustment of the togetherness of eternal objects," implying "the conceptual adjustment of all appetites in the form of aversions and adversions" (32). In other words, in order for eternal objects to function as the forms of definiteness for actual entities and the *teloi* of their becoming, their togetherness must be envisaged in such a manner that the mutually compatible or compossible eternal objects—"diversities in contrast"—from the perspective of a possible instance of concrescence are positively valued and affirmed over the mutually incompatible or incompossible ones—"diversities in opposition"—from the same perspective.[15] Such an act of valuation makes eternal objects effectively relevant to actual entities, because it is precisely the eternal objects that are mutually compatible from the standpoint of a potential definiteness that provide a standard of comparison for a novel actual entity as it prehends objectified past actual entities, selectively admitting those compatible with its own particular conceptual lure (i.e., "appetite") toward self-determination while relegating the rest to the background.

God carries out the primordial act of valuing eternal objects with a preference for mutually compatible eternal objects from the standpoint of a potential definiteness, since "what is inexorable in God, is a valuation as an aim towards 'order,'"—especially complex and open-ended kinds of order.[16] Precisely because God as a creature of creativity is its "aboriginal instance" and "chief exemplification" (225, 343), God shares with all actual entities an intrinsic "appetite"—a subjective aim—for "transforming disjointed multiplicity, with its diversities in opposition, into concrescent unity, with its diversities in contrast" (348). That is why God's valuation of eternal objects is carried out in a way that valorizes the beauty of harmonious multiplicity at the expense of the ugliness of merely discordant multiplicity. In that sense, God is "the divine element in the world, by which the barren inefficient disjunction of abstract potentialities obtains primordially the efficient conjunction of ideal realization" (40). In other words, by virtue of God's "complete conceptual valuation" of them (32), eternal objects are in God not as a random, disjointed, and disjunctive multitude suffering the futility of their mutual indifference, but as a multiperspectival and multicentered set of interrelated "circles of convergence"[17] shimmering with creative allure. This ideal realization of pure potentialities in God provides "the *metaphysical stability* whereby the actual process exemplifies general principles of metaphysics, and attains the ends proper to specific types of emergent order" (Whitehead, *Process and Reality,* 40; italics mine).[18] The very subjectivity of God as an actual entity, albeit a unique—primordial and nontemporal—one, is preliminarily constituted by this "non-temporal act of all-inclusive unfettered valuation" (31) in which all eternal objects in their disjunctive multiplicity are ideally realized as an all-encompassing set of disparate yet interrelated conjunctive unities.[19] Whitehead calls this preliminary subjectivity of God—that is, God's achievement of an eternally concrescent unity of all-inclusive conceptual prehension—"the primordial nature of God" (32).[20]

The mediation between the eternal and the temporal or between the potential and the actual is made possible by the fact that, because God is an actual entity, the primordial nature of God, which consists of God's eternal, free, unbounded, unconditioned, complete, and infinite conceptual experience, is at the same time temporally related to other concrescent actual entities and prehended by them, just as all actual entities are by one another: "The things which are temporal arise by their participation in the things which are eternal. The two sets are mediated by a thing which combines the actuality of what is temporal with the timelessness of what is potential. This final entity is the divine element in the world" (Whitehead, *Process and Reality,* 40). By being ideally ordered into effectively relevant conjunctions in God's primordial nature, eternal objects are able to have ingression in the process of becoming in accordance with their graded relevance to each concrescent actual entity, their ingression being tantamount to their "conceptual prehension" by—that is, their incorporation into the conceptual constitution of—the actual entity in question. Owing to their graded relevance, only a selection of mutually converging eternal objects are prehended by each actual entity to make a positive contribution to its internal conceptual constitution ("positive conceptual prehension") while the rest are relegated to the background and excluded from making any real contribution ("negative conceptual prehension") (41).

More concretely speaking, the ingression of eternal objects in concrescence, through which they shed the status of being *pure* potentialities and become *real* potentialities, takes place within the context of the extensive space-time continuum, which, as "one relational complex in which all potential objectifications find their niche" (66), expresses "the solidarity of all possible standpoints throughout the whole process of the world" (66). The becoming of any actual entity means that "what was previously potential in the space-time continuum is now the primary real phase in something actual" (67). Although "the real potentialities relative to all [possible] standpoints are coordinated as diverse determinations of one extensive continuum" (66), due to the graded relevance of those real potentialities, the concrescence of a specific actual entity within the continuum means that "a regional standpoint in the world, defining a limited potentiality for objectifications, has been adopted" (67). In other words, because only a selection of mutually converging *pure* potentials are conceptually prehended by the concrescent actual entity in question to form its initial subjective aim, its *real* potentiality implies a corresponding selectiveness in its conceptual and physical prehension of the objective immortality of the past actual world from a particular standpoint within the extensive continuum.

The fact that this selectiveness is a result of God's primordial valuation—God's "transcendent decision" (164)—is the reason for the initial dependence of the self-creativity of actual entities. The subjective freedom of an actual entity to determine itself definitively into being this or that actual entity is shaped in the initial phase of its concrescence by "an *endowment* which the subject inherits from the inevitable ordering of things, conceptually realized in the nature of God" (244; italics mine). The endowment is none other than the selection of mutually compatible eternal objects that contribute to the "subjective aim" or "living aim" of the concrescent actual entity, that is, its form of definiteness that functions as the "lure" or "final cause" for its own becoming. This is why the self-creativity of actual entities as creatures of creativity is initially dependent on God, who is "the principle of concretion":

> God is the principle of concretion; namely, he is that actual entity from which each temporal concrescence receives that initial aim from which its self-causation starts. That aim determines the initial gradations of relevance of eternal objects for conceptual feeling; and constitutes the autonomous subject in its primary phase of feelings with its initial conceptual valuations, and with its initial physical purposes. (244)

In other words, God is the source of the initial subjectivity—namely, the subjective aim and form—of a concrescing actual entity; and the latter's initial subjectivity consists in its initial conceptual valuations of a selection of relevant eternal objects in God's primordial nature. Its initial conceptual valuations of pure potentiality condition both its physical prehensions of the energy or "power"(58) of objectified past actual entities and its conceptual prehensions of the already realized eternal objects exhibited in the formal constitution of those past actual entities being physically prehended by it (236–43).[21] Such conditioning leads the concrescing actual entity in question to include certain data from the past of the actual world in its internal conceptual and physical constitution while excluding others. Thanks to God, in concrescence "the vivifying novelty of subjective form selected from the multiplicity of pure potentiality" meets the "dead datum" from the past of the actual world and "constitutes the satisfaction of an immediate particular individual" (Whitehead, *Process and Reality,* 164). In this meeting, eternal objects as general or pure potentiality are transformed into real potentiality productive of concrete actual entities (65–66).

Nonetheless, the dependence of the concrescence of actual entities on God is only initial. Although the endowment of initial aim from God is the very reason for there being a novel and original concrescence, the process of concrescence is only conditioned, not wholly determined, by that initial endowment.[22] The eternal objects in ingression, which constitute the endowment of the initial aim, are "cosmic genetic codes" harboring many divergent possibilities of concrete actualization more than they are some kind of predetermined cosmic archetypes. This implies that, having acquired the initial subjective aim and thereby having been constituted as a subject, the concrescent actual entity has the freedom to modify its subjective forms throughout the whole range of its prehensions in that particular instance of concrescence and to guide its own integrative becoming (245). Whereas God and the actual world "jointly constitute the character of the creativity for the initial phase of the novel concrescence," the subject, thus constituted, "is the autonomous master of its own concrescence into subject-superject,"[23] passing "from a subjective aim in concrescence into a superject with objective immortality" (245). Thus, Whitehead avers, "the initial stage of the aim is rooted in the nature of God, and its completion depends on the self-causation of the subject-superject" (244). This conditioned autonomy of actual entities as subject-superjects is the reason for Whitehead's naming God's mode of creative activity in the world a "lure" for concrescence, devoid of any sense of unidirectional determination, imposition, and coercion (25).[24]

The fact that concrescent actual entities are not merely subjects but subject-superjects implies, by the principle of relativity, that the relationship between actual entities and God, who is also an actual entity, must involve prehensions in both directions: not only the conceptual prehension of the eternal objects in the primordial nature of God by concrescent actual entities—which is the same as the ingression of eternal objects in them—but also the physical prehension of the already concresced and objectified actual entities of the past by God. This "objectification of the world in God" (345) is carried out in such a way that God's prehension of actual entities "is directed with the subjective aim, and clothed with the subjective form, [both of which are] wholly derivative from his all-inclusive primordial valuation" (345). In other words, just like any actual entity, God concresces or becomes physically: God's subjectivity prehends the past actual world, "weaving . . . God's physical feelings upon his primordial concepts" (345), and in so doing brings the disjointed multiplicity of objective data from the past into the concrescent harmony of divine life, that is, the temporally achieved actual unity of God's own being as becoming. Whereas actual entities receive their initial subjective aim and form from God's primordial nature,[25] in God's case it is God's primordial nature itself, in its eternally concrescent conceptual unity, that constitutes God's initial, preliminary subjectivity and guides the physical process of divine concrescence as its final cause or "lure." Lured by the conceptual vision of unity and harmony offered by God's own primordial nature, God brings about what Whitehead calls "the consequent nature of God," namely, God's own actual, physical unity in and through the objectification of the world in God (88, 345, 347). In the consequent nature of God, all of the past actual entities achieve their objective immortality in the form of "everlasting" (346) unities by being transmuted into "living ever-present facts"[26] and are retained in their "mutual immediacy."[27] In other words, in the consequent nature of God no individual identity or completeness of unity ever achieved is lost by abstraction and elimination, even as the discordant and destructive failures are purged by being "dismissed into their triviality of merely individual facts" (Whitehead, *Process and Reality,* 346).

God in Whitehead's conception, then, is *dipolar* (345). The primordial nature of God, which constitutes God's "conceptual pole," represents the primordial, eternal, free, complete, and infinite side of God. It is eternal and infinite in the sense that God's primordial conceptual experience, being conditioned and limited by no actuality in time, "is devoid of all negative prehensions" (345). That is why God is "the actual entity in virtue of which the *entire* multiplicity of eternal objects obtains its graded relevance to each stage of concrescence" (164). Being without negative prehensions, God's primordial nature entertains "the unlimited conceptual realization of the absolute wealth of potentiality" (343). In other words, God's primordial nature "envisages" (34) *all* possible harmonies by unconditionally valuing the entire multiplicity of eternal objects from the perspective of each of all possible worlds and ordering the eternal objects into an infinite number of circles of convergence that proposes an infinite number of potential concrescent unities. Since God's subjective aim is toward order ("diversities in contrast"), God's all-encompassing and unconditional primordial valuation includes the qualifying principle that the infinitely multiple circles of convergent eternal objects cannot all be actualized at the same time. For all possible harmonies include mutually incompatible or incompossible ones among them ("diversities in opposition"). Thus, God's primordial valuation implies a conceptual limitation of some possible harmonies by God's "transcendent decision" (164) but only from the perspective of the present cosmic "epoch"—that is, "that widest society of actual entities whose immediate relevance to ourselves is traceable" (91)—constituting the type of cosmic order that includes the principles with which we are familiar, such as the four dimensions of space-time or the formula "$E = MC^2$."[28] Although the present cosmic epoch is set against the spatiotemporally distant and seemingly chaotic background of other epochs representing different or even incompatible types of order (97), that does not mean that God has chosen the best among all possible worlds like Leibniz's God. Rather, as "the foundation of order" (88), God merely provides metaphysical stability for *all* possible worlds conceptually realized in "the primordial mind of God" (46), including the one that has in fact happened to be realized physically as the present cosmic epoch in the actual course of nature driven from within by the creative advance toward novelty. This means that, insofar as God's conceptual experience consists of the complete conceptual realization of *all* possible orders, God as primordial is not "conscious" (343), since consciousness involves negation in the form of an imaginative contrast between what is actually given as a determinate fact, on the one hand, and a conceptual novelty illustrating a yet-to-be-realized alternative, on the other (161). Further, it implies that, insofar as God's primordial nature is concerned, God is "deficiently actual" (343), or "actually deficient" (345), lacking physical factuality, since the unlimited realization of all eternal objects is only conceptual and nonphysical. The primordial nature of God is "God in abstraction, alone with himself" (34).

By contrast, the consequent nature of God, which constitutes God's "physical pole," stands for the consequent, temporal, determined, incomplete, and finite side of God. It is temporal, finite, and incomplete in the sense that God's consequent physical experience is conditioned and bounded by the objectification of the past actual entities in the present cosmic epoch that has in fact come into being at the expense of some other possible worlds.[29] Moreover, because of the self-creative freedom of actual entities, the actual world that has come to be is, at all times, fraught with the creatures' failed attempts at following the initial aim—the lure of order and harmony—endowed them by God's primordial nature, resulting in a "deficiency in the solidarity of individuals with each other" (Whitehead, *Process and Reality,* 350). God's consequent nature "weaves" the wreckage left by these failed attempts, namely the disjointed, dissonant, and finite multiplicity of the past actual occasions, upon God's primordial concepts. In this way it brings about their nonsubjective, objectified harmonies in God—that is, "their everlasting union with their transformed selves, purged into conformation with the eternal order" (347). In other words, God's consequent nature represents God's salvaging and mending of the always incomplete physical realizations of God's primordial nature in the actual world via God's "judgment of the world." By this judgment Whitehead means both "the judgment of tenderness which loses nothing that can be saved" and "the judgment of a wisdom which uses what in the temporal world is mere wreckage" (346). God can be called fully actual only when God has thus achieved a concrete, determinate, physical, temporal, and finite unity of divine life in and through the "saved" and "everlasting" harmonies of the physical world in God.[30] Furthermore, since God's attainment of such physical and temporal unity presupposes the always limited physical realizations of eternal objects in the actual world, always involving negative prehensions of at least some eternal objects, God's full actuality includes consciousness, namely, the very capacity to imagine conceptual novelties "otherwise" than what is given in the actual world. God is conscious to the extent that God can always envision possible worlds in which the excluded—negatively prehended—eternal objects are realized, and present those possible worlds as creative lures to the self-creating creatures of creativity, including Godself.

Thus, when both natures of God are considered together, the creative act in the universe can be seen to consist in three phases: (1) "the one infinite conceptual realization" in the primordial nature of God; (2) "the multiple solidarity of free physical realizations" in the temporal world of actual entities; and (3) "the ultimate unity of the multiplicity of actual fact with the primordial conceptual fact" in the consequent nature of God (346). The threefold creative act, Whitehead avers, gives witness to the "tender patience" of God, diametrically opposed to any exercise of dominating power, to bring creation in line with God's purpose for the world. As he says in the climactic passage within the final chapter of *Process and Reality*, God achieves the "completion of his own nature," that is, the everlasting satisfaction of God's actual and physical concrescence, in and through the co-creative acts of other actual entities led by God's vision or lure:

> If we conceive the first term and the last term in their unity over against the intermediate multiple freedom of physical realizations in the temporal world, we conceive of the patience of God, tenderly saving the turmoil of the intermediate world by the completion of his own nature. . . . God's role is not the combat of productive force with productive force, of destructive force with destructive force; it lies in the patient operation of the overpowering rationality of his conceptual harmonization. *He does not create the world, he saves it: or more accurately, he is the poet of the world, with tender patience leading it by his vision of truth, beauty, and goodness.* (346; italics mine)

By the principle of relativity, however, the everlasting satisfaction of God's concrescence in the consequent nature of God implies at the same time that God turns into a physical object to be prehended both conceptually and physically by the concrescing actual entities of the world, although, unlike other actual entities, God never "perishes"—loses subjective immediacy—thanks to God's primordial nature with its eternally concrescent conceptual unity (346).[31] The consequent nature of God "itself passes into the temporal world according to its gradation of relevance to the various concrescent occasions" (Whitehead, *Process and Reality*, 351). Put otherwise, there is in fact a third pole in the divine nature, that is, what Whitehead calls "the superjective nature of God" (88), in and through which "the perfected actuality passes back into the temporal world, and qualifies this world so that each temporal actuality includes it as an immediate fact of relevant experience" (351). Whitehead invokes the religious symbolism of "heaven" or "kingdom of heaven" to illustrate the superjective nature of God through which God's consequent nature is objectified for prehension and appropriation by actual entities in their novel creative acts: "For the kingdom of heaven is with us today. . . . What is done in the world is transformed into a reality in heaven, and the reality in heaven passes back into the world. By reason of this reciprocal relation, the love in the world passes into the love in heaven, and floods back again into the world" (350–51).

If God has a superjective nature, it means that the conceptual prehension of the eternal objects in the primordial nature of God by the concrescent actual entities of the world—that is, the ingression of the eternal objects in concrescence—is always mediated by the same actual entities' physical and conceptual prehension of the "everlastingly" perfected actuality in the consequent nature of God.[32] When God's consequent nature weaves the dissonant multiplicity of the past actual entities of the world upon the ideally realized harmonies of eternal objects in God's primordial nature, the integrative act gives rise to "the transformation of his wisdom" (Whitehead, *Process and Reality,* 345). In other words, God's integrative act produces what Whitehead calls "propositions" or "theories," namely, potential facts or states of affairs capable of being either true or false, in which the actual entities in question function as the logical subjects and selections of mutually convergent eternal objects as the predicates proposing hypothetical, ideal alternatives.[33] God's consequent nature realizes the propositions, or "makes them true," by transforming the prehended actual world into the everlastingly perfected actuality within itself. God's unconscious, primordial, and infinite conceptual valuation of all eternal objects, which orders them into an infinite number of ideally realized harmonies, is precisely mirrored in God's conscious, everlasting physical realizations of the predicates of those propositions in the perfected actuality of the world.[34] That is why the prehension of the primordial nature of God by novel actual entities can be seen to be mediated by the superjective nature of God in which the perfected actuality "passes back" into the actual world "so that each temporal actuality includes it as an immediate fact of relevant experience." The ingression of eternal objects in novel concrescent actual entities takes the form of the latter's prehension of the alternative forms of definiteness or states of affairs imaginatively proposed for the past actual entities by those propositions and realized everlastingly within God's consequent nature. Given that God as superject implies novel actual entities' prehension of God as a completed actual entity everlastingly "enjoying" both conceptual and physical satisfaction without ever subjectively perishing, their reception of their initial subjective aim from God includes the subjective emotional state of enjoying the perfected actuality while suffering its imperfect past, that is, the subjective form of God who is "the great companion—the fellow-sufferer who understands" (Whitehead, *Process and Reality,* 351).

When the three phases of actual entities' concrescence and the dipolar nature of God are considered together in the light of the threefold creative act in the universe, the meaning of Whitehead's well-known statement about God and the world, that "both are in the grip of the ultimate metaphysical ground, the creative advance into novelty" (340), becomes clear. God and the world are "in the grip of the ultimate metaphysical ground" in the sense that they are "the contrasted opposites in terms of which Creativity achieves its supreme task of transforming disjointed multiplicity, with its diversities in opposition, into concrescent unity, with its diversities in contrast" (348). They are contrasted opposites because, for God, the conceptual pole, standing for "the unity of vision seeking physical multiplicity," is prior to the physical pole, representing "the multiplicity of finites, [of] actualities seeking a perfected unity" (349), whereas for the world the opposite is the case (348). In other words, while it is "as true to say that God is one and the World many, as that the World is one and God many" (348), on a more analytical level God is primordially one and consequently many while the world is primordially many and consequently one:

> God is primordially one, namely, he is the primordial unity of relevance of the many potential forms; in the process he acquires a consequent multiplicity, which the primordial character absorbs into its own unity. The World is primordially many, namely, the many actual occasions with their physical finitude; in the process it acquires a consequent unity, which is a novel occasion and is absorbed into the multiplicity of the primordial character. . . . The theme of Cosmology, which is the basis of all religions, is the story of the dynamic effort of the World passing into everlasting unity, and of the static majesty of God's vision, accomplishing its purpose of completion by absorption of the World's multiplicity of effort. (349)

Nonetheless, although they thus form a contrast, as exemplifications and characterizations of the same "ultimate matter of fact" (i.e., the creative advance into novelty), the two actualities share the status of being "at once a creature of creativity and a condition for creativity" (31), or, to put it another way, "a creature transcended by the creativity which it qualifies" (88). Since creativity as the pure notion of activity is no actual agency by itself, God may be called the "creator" of temporal actual entities in the sense of being "the foundation of order" and "the goad towards novelty" for them, but not in the sense that the creativity of the universe can be ascribed to God's volition (88). That is why Whitehead declares that God "is not *before* all creation, but *with* all creation" (343). Even though God is creativity's "primordial, non-temporal accident" (7) and in that sense more important and even ultimate in a way the temporal world can never be, God and the world are co-creators not capable of being "torn apart" from each other, for they are two actualities belonging to one and the same ontological plane of becoming and "in the grip" of the same "ultimate metaphysical ground" that is creativity. Since "each temporal occasion embodies God, and is embodied in God" (349) by virtue of their mutual prehension, it is "as true to say the World is immanent in God, as that God is immanent in the World" (348). At the same time, since "every actual entity, in virtue of its novelty, transcends its universe, God included" (94), it is "as true to say that God transcends the World, as that the World transcends God" (348). When Whitehead adds that "it is as true to say that God creates the World, as that the World creates God" (348), he is adding a coda to his insistent stance on the *equal actuality* of God and the world of actual entities as the two contrasting yet interrelated creative agencies providing the reason for the becoming of all that is.

## Whitehead and Zhu Xi: A Radical Ontological Pluralism versus a Dualism of One and Many?

Having sketched the major contours of Whitehead's philosophy of organism, I would like to ask at this point the following question: What are the mutually illuminating features of Whitehead's thought and Zhu Xi's that could help Christian theology reconceive its notion of the Spirit? As indicated at the end of the previous chapter, the threefold point of comparison revolves around Zhu Xi's problematic conception of psychophysical energy solely as the principle of differentiation with no share—other than in a derivative sense—in the creatively harmonizing function assigned to pattern as the metaphysical ultimate. When used to explain the relationship between the one abstract and transcendent Pattern—the Great Ultimate as substance—on the one hand, and many concrete and determinate patterns immanent in the world of the ten thousand thing-events—the Great Ultimate as function—on the other, such a conception of psychophysical energy threatens the primordiality and ontological ultimacy of multiplicity. As a consequence, with his Neo-Confucian project of "moral metaphysics" Zhu Xi undermines the vision of radical ontological and ethicopolitical pluralism advocated by the Daoist philosophical tradition, and he does so by banishing the specter of its possibly totalizing metaphysics of one chaotic Nothing and putting in its place—with an unintended twist of irony—another, potentially more totalizing metaphysics of one Heavenly Pattern.

I suggest that the best strategy of engaging this whole *problematique* with Whitehead's philosophy of organism is to compare Zhu Xi's core notions of pattern, the Great Ultimate, psychophysical energy, and the myriad thing-events with the corresponding core notions of eternal objects, God, creativity, and actual entities in Whitehead's system. Let us, first of all, consider the myriad thing-events and actual entities. They are rough equivalents because both define what is the most concrete and factual in the world thoroughly and comprehensively in terms of process and becoming. At the same time, they differ from each other to the extent that the myriad thing-events do not share the "relational atomism" of actual entities. Rather than being analytically specified and grouped into the atomic units of becoming, on the one hand, and their more complex societies, on the other, as in the case of actual entities, the concept of myriad thing-events is a comprehensive notion covering a wide range of concrete facts, from a single grain of sand all the way to complex ethical and political "states of affairs," all viewed as different coalescences of the same psychophysical energy in its binary modes. The myriad thing-events presuppose psychophysical energy as the field of emergence and the medium of interaction for them, enabling their synchronic "correlativity" prior to and beyond their diachronic causal relations. By contrast, not only does the concept of actual entities reject the notion of noncausal relations in general, but it also denies the existence of direct synchronic causal relations among contemporaneous actual entities in allegiance to the relativity theories of modern physics.[35] Here an interesting debate may be possible in regard to the coherence of the atomic or "quantum"[36] understanding of actual entities that assumes the existence of the basic building blocks of the universe, however much relationally or in process terms they are conceived. Although Whitehead's atomism may be able to serve as a strong advocate for the existence of genuine freedom in the world in addition to providing analytic specificity and detail to his cosmological picture,[37] does it not perhaps lessen the sticky organic interrelatedness of all thing-events befitting a philosophy of organism by confining such interrelatedness to diachronic, linear causality?

Second, psychophysical energy is comparable to creativity in the sense that both are notions of pure activity accounting for the power and dynamism observed in coming into being of the myriad thing-events or in the concrescence of actual entities. At the same time, they are different from each other in the sense that, whereas creativity's activity refers to the production of a new harmonious unity out of the past disjointed multiplicity, psychophysical energy's activity, when considered apart from pattern, consists purely in random movements of relationally indifferent differentiation. One can argue that creativity is also a notion of pure activity without any unifying teleology when taken apart from eternal objects, but creativity, unlike psychophysical energy, is the ultimate metaphysical—albeit desubstantialized—"ground" out of which eternal objects themselves emerge. In that sense, it is itself the very creative urge toward unity and harmony represented by eternal objects and concretely manifest in the concrescence of actual entities. By contrast, psychophysical energy cannot claim to be the very ground of the incessant process of creative harmonization symbolized by the Great Ultimate and observed in and among the myriad thing-events, since it is subordinate to pattern as the ultimate metaphysical ground, at least in Zhu Xi's conception of it.

Third, pattern and eternal objects can be taken as analogues, as they both point to the universe seen from its formal aspects. They both refer to the forms of definiteness without which the world would dissolve into random, disjunctive, and mutually indifferent many, and which in that sense constitute the ground of order. Pattern, however, is different from eternal objects, for it is assigned the status of the ultimate metaphysical ground, while eternal objects as potential entities are creatures of creativity which at the same time qualify creativity by giving it definite forms. Another crucial difference is that, whereas eternal objects are primordially many, pattern is only derivatively so because of its concretization in union with psychophysical energy. Even though eternal objects subsist in the eternally concrescent conceptual unity of God's primordial nature, that is, God's nontemporal act of all-inclusive conceptual valuation of them, their multiplicity is in no way harmed or diminished, whereas many patterns, when abstracted from psychophysical energy, for all intents and purposes disappear into the Great Ultimate as one overarching Pattern.

Last, we must contemplate the Great Ultimate and God together. The two notions can be compared because of their similar "dipolar" constitutions that enable them to serve as chief examples of the metaphysical principles of the respective systems to which they belong. Just as the primordial nature of God constitutes God's conceptual or abstract pole representing the eternal, unconditioned, and infinite general potentialities of the universe conceptually realized in God's eternally concrescent unity, the Non-Ultimate makes up the Great Ultimate's transcendent pole, standing for the indeterminate and nonconcrete unity of the one Pattern as the abstract potentiality of there being a world. Similarly, just as the consequent nature of God forms God's physical pole prehending the temporal, conditioned, and finite real potentialities of the universe physically realized in the multitude of actual entities, the Great Ultimate constitutes the Non-Ultimate's immanent pole embodying the determinate and concrete multiplicity of patterns realized in the ten thousand thing-events of the world. The two natures of God constitute the primordial and principal exemplification of the ultimate metaphysical principle of Whitehead's system, namely, creativity or the creative advance into novelty, in the sense that they mediate the eternal, potential unity of eternal objects and the temporal, actual multiplicity of past actual entities, so that many could become one and be increased by one. Likewise, the Non-Ultimate and the Great Ultimate epitomize the ultimate metaphysical principle of Zhu Xi's system, namely, pattern or the incessant process of patterning as creative harmonization, as they form the two poles of the substance-function relation in which the one abstract movement of Patterning rides on the concretizing dynamic of psychophysical energy to give birth to the myriad creative harmonizations of the receptive and the active. Nonetheless, Zhu Xi's Great Ultimate and Whitehead's God diverge from each other insofar as the former is the chief symbol of pattern and in that sense itself the ultimate metaphysical ground and principle of unity and harmony, not an individual entity and agent-unit of becoming like the latter, albeit a primordial, exemplary, and exceptionally unique one.[38]

With the four sets of interrelated core concepts thus identified as comparable, and their main differences acknowledged, let us proceed to the locus of the maximum creative tension between the two systems. By the words "maximum creative tension," I am referring to the contrast between Zhu Xi's qualified ontological dualism of pattern and psychophysical energy with an asymmetrical tilt toward the logico-ontological primacy of the one abstractly unifying Pattern, on the one hand, and Whitehead's radical ontological pluralism of eternal objects and actual entities with a thoroughly desubstantialized notion of creativity sustaining their multiple self-creative becoming, on the other. If Zhu Xi's kataphatic rejection of the totalizing metaphysics of one chaotic Nothing allegedly advocated by the Daoist philosophical tradition has a tendency to lead to an even more totalizing metaphysics of one Heavenly Pattern, due to his inadequate formulation of the relationship between the one Pattern and many individual patterns, can Whitehead's radical ontological pluralism be of help here? The answer to this question hinges on the applicability to Zhu Xi's system of the manner in which Whitehead provides a particular kind of unity-in-multiplicity to the infinitely many general potentialities of the universe, that is, the unity of many eternal objects in God's primordial nature. For Whitehead, the general potentialities of the universe represented by eternal objects are primordially and intrinsically many, because God's eternally concrescent conceptual unity achieved by God's all-inclusive valuation or infinite conceptual realization of them presupposes their infinite multiplicity. Given that the achievement of God's eternally concrescent conceptual unity out of the multiplicity of eternal objects is itself "the primordial exemplification"[39] of the ultimate metaphysical ground, that is, the creative advance into novelty, one can see that multiplicity is as ontologically primordial and ultimate as unity, if not more, in Whitehead's scheme. Can this be a potentially salutary medicine for Zhu Xi's predicament?

I will give a cautiously affirmative answer to this question, since the Great Ultimate's creatively harmonizing movement can be reconceived in such a way that it is "in sync with" the movement between the two natures of Whitehead's God in relation to the world. As I have suggested in the previous chapter, it is possible to envision the Great Ultimate's movement not merely as forming a cycle but a spiral—a progressive cycle—in order to ward off the threat of a totalizing metaphysics of one Heavenly Pattern. A dialogue with Whitehead's notion of a dipolar God would significantly enrich such work of reimagination. The reimagined version would look like this: When the concretely achieved multiple patterns of the world "wane"—that is, decline in their subjective immediacy or subjective intensity, eventually losing it—and flow back into the Non-Ultimate in the receptive phase of the Great Ultimate's movement, they are met not by the one Heavenly Pattern as some kind of voracious, all-assimilating, and all-conquering metaphysical arch-paradigm. Instead, they are met by the one Heavenly Pattern as an inexhaustible reservoir of alternative, more harmonious patterns presented to them as hypothetical "propositions" pointing to novel orderings of the world in the Great Ultimate's new active phase. Thus reenvisioned, Zhu Xi's conception of the Great Ultimate's movement of generation and regeneration could truly be spiral, always retaining internal differences and contrasts—and therefore creative tensions—between the factual old and the hypothetical new. Such a genuinely spiral reconstruction of the Great Ultimate's movement would provide the requisite metaphysical context for a more liberating account of the process of self-cultivation in which the heart-mind of the sage is produced in a truly mutually reinforcing relationship between the heart-mind of the Way and the human heart-mind without a unilateral and unbalanced subjugation of the "human desire" to the "Heavenly Pattern."

Still, given the real differences between Zhu Xi and Whitehead, as evident in my comparative reflections on the four pairs of core concepts, in order for this revisionary work of conferring ontological primordiality and ultimacy on multiplicity to be possible, either of the following two things would have to happen first: (1) Pattern would need to be reconceptualized in such a manner that its multiplicity would be intrinsic to its own being as becoming and no longer dependent on and derived from the concretizing dynamism of the penultimate and subordinate creative principle of psychophysical energy; (2) psychophysical energy would need to be recast so that, while retaining its function as the differentiating dynamism productive of multiplicity, it would at the same time acquire ontological ultimacy similar to the one given to pattern. The first option would preserve the one abstract and ideal Pattern's status as the ontological ultimate and the ground of unity and wholeness in the world, yet at the same time allow it not only the logical possibility but also an inexorable drive to generate multiplicity on its own. By contrast, the second option would depose pattern from its status as the sole ontological ultimate by reenvisioning psychophysical energy's differentiating dynamism as a creatively harmonizing dynamism capable of being the ground of order in the universe. As I will show, whereas the first option tacks closer to a vision of the ontological ultimate that is in some ways similar to the God of classical Western theism minus its substantialistic baggage, the second option has a greater affinity with Whitehead's conception of creativity as the ultimate metaphysical ground even as it refuses to entertain the idea of the principle of order being a special kind of thing-event, like Whitehead's notion of God. In the following chapters I examine two figures in the history of Confucian thought, Yi Hwang (honorific name Toegye) and Im Seong-ju (honorific name Nongmun), who represent the first option and the second option, respectively, and bring them into dialogue with Hegel (in Toegye's case) and with Whitehead, Deleuze, and Keller (in Nongmun's case).

# 4 The Great Ultimate as Primordial Manyone

## THE PROMISE AND PERIL OF TOEGYE'S NEO-CONFUCIAN "HETERODOXY"

Throughout his long life, Yi Hwang (李滉 1501–1570 C.E.) of the Korean Joseon Dynasty—who is better known by his honorific name Toegye (退溪)—thought of himself as a faithful follower of Zhu Xi, whom he regarded as his intellectual and spiritual master and whose true intention he believed he followed. But even as one of the greatest and most influential figures within the dominant Cheng-Zhu school of Neo-Confucianism, he had an idiosyncratic way of reading Zhu Xi that made him deviate considerably from his master's thought. His primary concern revolved around the issue of self-cultivation, particularly the question of the effectiveness and reliability of human moral agency. Although other Neo-Confucians, including Zhu Xi himself, certainly shared that "soteriological" concern,[1] it was found in Toegye with a much more "religious" tone, that is, in an attitude of reverence and even worship. Toegye's preoccupation with securing the effectiveness of human moral agency, on which the ultimate dependability of the project of self-cultivation was premised, drove him to a much more dynamic interpretation of the Great Ultimate, which—perhaps coincidentally—opened up a path toward affirming multiplicity as originary and truly intrinsic to the Great Ultimate.

### Pattern Moves, Issues, and Arrives: Toegye's Conception of Pattern's Intrinsic Dynamism

At the heart of Toegye's novel interpretation of the Great Ultimate is his assignment of an independent dynamism of its own to pattern as the ultimate metaphysical principle of creative harmonization. He confers on what is merely a map and guide, when abstracted from psychophysical energy, the actual power to implement its directives, despite a consequent problem in systematic coherence.[2] The practical implication of this move is that, when human moral agency fails, the project of self-cultivation is not lost, because the transhuman moral agency of pattern is efficacious apart from human moral agency dependent on the morally neutral dynamism of psychophysical energy. In arguing for this move, Toegye makes the same appeal as Zhu Xi's to Cheng Yi's saying, employing the same substance-function distinction but applied in a variant manner at one crucial point. Unlike Zhu Xi, who sees pattern's function only in its union with and activation by psychophysical energy, Toegye envisions pattern's "own" function without psychophysical energy's involvement:

> Pattern has movement [動 *dong*] and rest. Substance refers to its rest; and function designates its movement. . . . There are two levels of substance and function. *If we speak on the level of pattern, the substance-function distinction is parallel to "Empty and tranquil, and without any sign, yet all figures are already luxuriantly present."* If we speak on the level of concrete things and events, the analogy would be the capacity of ships and carriages to travel across water and land, on the one hand, and their actual travels, on the other. (Italics mine)[3]

Toegye agrees with Zhu Xi's reading to the extent that he also claims that the phrase "empty and tranquil, and without any sign" points to pattern as substance in abstraction from concrete reality. He adds, however, that the latter half of the saying, "all figures are already luxuriantly present," which refers to pattern as function, also points to pattern "before" its operation in the world. In other words, Toegye argues that Cheng Yi's saying is meant primarily to describe both pattern's substance *and* function on the same ontological, metacosmic level, apart from its involvement in the world via its union with psychophysical energy. On the level of concrete cosmic reality, by contrast, he explains pattern's substance and function in reference to pattern's union with psychophysical energy, that is, in terms of a concrete thing-event's potential and its actualization.

The substance-function distinction in the Great Ultimate, as it is employed to account for the workings of pattern and psychophysical energy, therefore has two levels for Toegye.[4] On the level of concrete cosmic reality, substance and function both point to the operation of pattern united with psychophysical energy. Here substance designates the nature or capacity of thing-events to be the way they should or aim to be, which refers to individual patterns as "incarnate," while function names the actualization of that capacity in the unfolding of differentiating and coalescing movements of the receptive and active psychophysical energies in accordance with the individual patterns. On the ontological, metacosmic level, by contrast, substance and function both refer to pattern in abstraction from the world. The Great Ultimate as substance names pattern as the indeterminate and quiescent One "before" it has aroused itself, that is, a kind of indeterminate pure potential for unity and harmony called by the name of the Non-Ultimate, while the Great Ultimate as function designates pattern in its active state, namely, pattern as the Whole differentiated into and encompassing within itself an infinite number of abstract potential harmonies.[5] This implies that pattern has the capacity to act on its own, to introduce movement, difference, and multiplicity without having to depend on the dynamism of psychophysical energy.

Furthermore, pattern's capacity to act is such that pattern could even be envisaged as actually "producing" psychophysical energy, as implied in the following written exchange of Toegye's with a student discussing Zhu Xi and another Neo-Confucian, Huang Mianzhai:

> [Question:] Master Zhu [Zhu Xi] says, "Pattern is without feeling, intention, and productive activity." If pattern is without feeling, intention, and productive activity, then I am afraid that it would not be able to produce *eum* and *yang*. . . . [Huang] Mianzhai says, "To speak of the Great Ultimate producing *yang* and *eum* is like saying that *yang* and *eum* arise." Does this not reflect his profound dislike of attributing productive activity to the Great Ultimate?
>
> [Toegye's answer:] In general, *Master Zhu's reference to pattern being without feeling and intention points to pattern's original state of substance; its capacity to activate itself and produce, by contrast, is its extremely wondrous function*. Mianzhai need not have explained it like that, because *pattern has function in and of itself, and therefore spontaneously produces yang and eum*. (Italics mine)[6]

As is evident in his ambivalence toward Huang Mianzhai's "intransitive" interpretation of the Great Ultimate's production of psychophysical energy as psychophysical energy's self-production, Toegye appears to interpret the productive activity of the Great Ultimate in a much more "transitive" sense on the strength of what he calls the "extremely wondrous function" of pattern.[7] In other words, to borrow Aristotelian terminology, pattern is envisaged here as even exercising efficient causality of an ontological kind in addition to its formal and final causality. This has the effect of downplaying the sense of psychophysical energy's self-origination and self-production, which the Cheng-Zhu school has always retained despite the subordination of psychophysical energy to the ontological creativity of pattern, thanks to pattern's conception as being without its own dynamism.[8]

An argument can be made that, in recognizing pattern's own capacity to move independent of psychophysical energy, Toegye is not so much concerned about securing the ontological ultimacy and primordiality of multiplicity as about pattern's capacity to be an active and effective source of unity and harmony in the world. A continuing preoccupation with pattern as the source of unity may explain Toegye's seemingly more "orthodox" comment like this one:

> Pattern is pattern in such a way that its substance is originally vacuous, and being vacuous, without internal contrasts or opposites. Because it is without inner contrasts or opposites, when pattern is immanent in people and thing-events, it is one, truly without anything added to or taken away from it. When it comes to psychophysical energy, however, from its very beginning there appears the image of the opposition of the receptive [*eum*] and the active [*yang*]. . . . In the myriad transformations of the receptive and active forces, each is never without its opposite. In general, therefore, when thing-events are endowed with pattern and psychophysical energy, there is no gap between them insofar as their respective natures [i.e., their individual patterns] are concerned; but their psychophysical constitutions cannot be without the distinctions of balanced and unbalanced.[9]

In this comment Toegye describes the substance of pattern as vacuous and one, and contrasts it directly with the primordial presence of complementary opposites in psychophysical energy and the consequent introduction of an incessant proliferation of difference and opposition into the world of the myriad thing-events—all without mentioning the pluralizing function of pattern in and of itself. But this should be seen as reflecting Toegye's desire to emphasize the unity of the one Pattern that is unharmed by its concretizations into the diverse specific natures of thing-events, not as contradicting his use of the substance-function distinction for pattern even in abstraction from psychophysical energy. Toegye's concern with safeguarding the unity of the one Pattern (or the Great Ultimate), while acknowledging its intrinsic multiplicity as the totality of all patterns, is evident in the following conversation with his students:

> [Question:] The expressions, "the total sum of all patterns" and "the fundamental origin of all transformations," refer to the Great Ultimate. Regarding the claim that the ten thousand thing-events each have the one Great Ultimate, then, is it also possible to say that they each have the total sum of all patterns and the fundamental origin of all transformations? Humans are indeed endowed with all patterns, but when it comes to thing-events, each of them merely has the single pattern relevant to it. How can they each be endowed with all patterns?
>
> [Toegye said:] It looks like what is present in a single thing-event could not be called the total sum of all patterns. Nonetheless, what a thing-event is endowed with is the pattern of the Great Ultimate. How is it therefore not possible to say that each thing-event has the one Great Ultimate? How could one say that the Great Ultimate carves a single pattern out of the total sum of all patterns, and assigns it to a single thing-event? It is like a single ray of moonlight that illumines all around. Whether the great expanse of rivers and seas or a small cup of water, there is no place in which it does not shine. How can one say that the moonlight reflected in a cup of water is not the [entire] moon shining, because of the small amount of water in the cup?[10]

Toegye's answer reveals that what he rejects is actually a one-sidedly plural conception of the Great Ultimate and the consequent denial of its *integral* omnipresence in the world of thing-events. In other words, what he opposes is the idea that the Great Ultimate is *merely* a collection of all patterns that is "split" up by individual entities. That the Great Ultimate is the total sum of all patterns means, for Toegye, that it is not merely an aggregate but the one Pattern with an intrinsic capacity to move and to pluralize itself in active response to diverse situations without losing its identity as the one Pattern and consequently disappearing into the multiplicity of individual patterns.

In sum, the implication of Toegye's dynamic interpretation of Cheng Yi's saying is that change, difference, and multiplicity can be seen to belong to pattern originarily and primordially, not secondarily and derivatively. By a repetitive series of self-transformative and self-creative movements, the one Pattern spontaneously multiplies itself into many patterns without relying on the differentiating dynamic of psychophysical energy that is devoid of harmonizing power and therefore morally ambiguous. This enables the symbol of the Great Ultimate to represent the whole of reality without reserve, since the metaphysical ultimate, the creative ground of all, is itself both one and many, both a unifying and a pluralizing force. One can even argue from this that, for Toegye, when each individual thing-event partakes of the omnipresent Great Ultimate because its pattern participates in the one Pattern, all the other individual patterns in their potentiality are co-present to each thing-event—the insight alluded to by Zhu Xi rather ambiguously because of his denial of a substance-function distinction that is based on pattern's own dynamism. From among the infinite number of harmonizing possibilities presented to it by the plurisingular Great Ultimate, each thing-event actualizes a finite and determinate number of them that makes it uniquely what it is in each moment.

By conferring an independent dynamism to pattern, Toegye assuages the doubt about the feasibility and ultimate effectiveness of the Confucian project of being fully human in face of the seemingly insurmountable human predilection toward selfishness and discord. The human heart-mind, whose moral agency comes under suspicion because of its constitution by psychophysical energy, becomes assuredly more than human in Toegye's account, as the original human nature embodied within the heart-mind acquires it own power to implement its telos, namely, the value of humanity as empathy. Apart from any involvement of the dynamism of psychophysical energy, human nature within the heart-mind activates itself and issues (發 *bal*) in the Four Sprouts (四端 *sadan*) of sympathy and benevolence, shame and dislike, deference and compliance, and approval and disapproval, all of which are diverse relational articulations of humanity as empathy. Given that the so-called Four Sprouts of humanity issue in response to relational contexts (for instance seeing a child about to fall into a well), they are always mixed in with and hard to distinguish from those other feelings issued and carried by psychophysical energy within the same relational contexts, such as the Seven Feelings (七情 *chiljeong*) of pleasure, anger, sorrow, fear, love, hatred, and desire. Nonetheless, the Four Sprouts are always distinct from the Seven Feelings in terms of their origination:

> If we contrast the Seven Feelings with the Four Sprouts and discuss each in terms of its distinctiveness, then the Seven Feelings are connected to psychophysical energy just as the Four Sprouts are connected to pattern.

> Their issuances each have their own systematic framework; and their names each have their respective points of reference. It is possible, therefore, to follow their respective predominant factors and classify them accordingly, that's all. . . . And the Four Sprouts move in response to thing-events, and in that sense are definitely no different from the Seven Feelings. It's only that, as for the Four, pattern issues them and psychophysical energy follows; as for the Seven, psychophysical energy issues and pattern mounts them.[11]

Pattern issuing and psychophysical energy following, in contrast to psychophysical energy issuing and pattern mounting—that is the famous thesis of "mutual issuance" advanced by Toegye in regard to the question of the precise relationship between the two within the operation of human moral agency. Toegye sees pattern and psychophysical energy respectively each having a separate yet interdependent issuing function, with one taking the predominant role over the other depending on whether the feelings issued are the Four Sprouts or the Seven Feelings.[12]

Since the human heart-mind relies solely on the incarnate pattern's power to issue in feelings in the case of the Four Sprouts, they are in effect offspring of a *transhuman* moral agency, that is, the so-called heart-mind of the Way.[13] Because it is the human heart-mind that must deliberate on and either oppose or act on these feelings of transhuman origin, the heart-mind of the Way or transhuman moral agency is not an entity separate from the human heart-mind or human moral agency—the two are nondual, strictly speaking. It is just that the psychosomatic responses of the human heart-mind to relational contexts have a more-than-human origin when those responses, as in the case of the Four Sprouts, are conducive to empathetic and harmonious patternings of social and cosmic relations despite the human penchant for conflict and discord. Toegye goes so far as to speak religiously—in a worshipful, reverent tone—of "Lord on High" (上帝 *sangje*) in reference to the transhuman agency of pattern or the Great Ultimate within the human heart-mind,[14] which in his view one can encounter via the practice of cultivation of "mindfulness" or "reverence" (敬 *gyeong*).[15]

Going even further, Toegye asserts that pattern does not sit passively for the human heart-mind to reach it through the practice of mindfulness or reverence; rather, pattern reaches out to where the heart-mind goes and meets up with it, so to speak. Discussing the self-cultivative practice of "the investigation of things" (格物 *gyeongmul*) to reach the patterns of thing-events, Toegye says:

> Hence, although pattern's function is not outside of the human heart-mind, the reason for the marvelousness of pattern's function actually lies in pattern's manifestation of itself, which follows the human heart-mind's reach and arrives [到 *do*] without fail, exhaustively. I am merely to fear that there may be places where my investigation of things does not reach; I am not to worry that pattern may not be able of itself to arrive. When therefore it [the Great Learning] speaks of "the investigation of things," it definitely means that I completely reach the ultimate point of the patterns of things. But when it comes to the phrase, "things investigate [物格 mulgyeok]," why would it not be possible to say that the ultimate point of the patterns of things follows my investigation to arrive without fail? From this I know that what does not have feelings, intentions, and productive activity is pattern's original substance; that which follows the ten thousand manifestations [of things] and arrives inexorably is pattern's utterly spirit-like function. Earlier I only saw that its original substance had no activity, and did not know that its marvelous function could manifest itself and act. I was close to regarding pattern as a dead thing. Was that not also very far from the Way?[16]

Here Toegye makes a crucial point: when we speak of pattern as having no feeling, intention, and productive activity, we are referring only to pattern as substance. Pattern's most "spiritual" function is to "arrive" (到 *do*) at "ten thousand manifestations." If we deny this, he avers, we are in fact treating pattern as a dead thing.

One can see here that Toegye has taken Zhu Xi's Great Ultimate and turned it into a transhuman moral agent in a qualified nondualistic—neither dualistic nor mutually reductionistic—relationship with the human moral agent. The human moral subject finds itself in concrete relational contexts, having always already responded to others spontaneously and psychosomatically in and through a welter of heterogeneous feelings that may or may not help guide its action toward social and cosmic harmony. Many of those feelings have issued from psychophysical energy's activation of human nature incarnate within the human heart-mind, and are deliberated and acted on by the same heart-mind. Some others, however, have issued directly from human nature's activating itself, which is the transhuman moral agency of the Great Ultimate as the pluralizing and unifying power of empathy within the human heart-mind, although these feelings are also empowered and carried by the same psychophysical energy of the human heart-mind as the other feelings. These feelings of transhuman origin are empathetic, other-oriented, and relationally appropriate psychosomatic responses to a variety of concrete situations. They emerge when pattern's self-activation into a multiplicity of potential patternings of harmonious relations, which happens on the abstract, metacosmic plane, becomes actualized without distortion in the concrete cosmic reality of the human heart-mind.[17] Because they are various articulations of empathetic understanding, when deliberated and acted on by the human heart-mind, they are all conducive to harmonious patternings of relations in specific local contexts. Moreover, precisely because these feelings articulate empathetic understanding, despite the amazing plurality and diversity of their situational appropriateness, they can all be viewed as contributing to a creatively harmonious configuration of local harmonies into an overarching sociocosmic whole. This is all the more the case, given the prevalent Neo-Confucian tendency to associate humanity as empathy with ontological and cosmic creativity (the "life-giving intention") and, accordingly, to identify the heart-mind of the Way with the "fecund heart-mind of heaven and earth," thereby giving the transhuman moral agency a truly cosmic reach and a universally generative function.

All in all, one can argue that Toegye's affirmation of pattern's own dynamism stands for an important path one could travel in order to resolve the conundrum presented by Zhu Xi's ambiguous formulation of the relationship between the one Pattern and many individual patterns and the attendant menace of a totalizing metaphysics of one Heavenly Pattern. Toegye points to a way to formulate the relationship between the Non-Ultimate and the Great Ultimate so that a genuinely spiral conception of the Great Ultimate's movement could be achieved. The crucial point lies in this: Although pattern is a dynamic ontological creativity with an independent dynamism of its own, this creativity is never active outside of what it has given birth to. As seen from the issuance of the Four Sprouts, although pattern has the capacity to move without relying on the dynamism of psychophysical energy, when it moves, it moves always in response to concrete relational situations. Pattern as function on the metacosmic level, captured by the phrase "all figures are already luxuriantly present" in Toegye's interpretation of it, refers to pattern's natural capacity to move and to become many, that is, its originary and potential multiplicity, not to the concrete actualization of that capacity or potential. Its actualization always comes in union with psychophysical energy, in the form of the unfolding of the natural capacity of concrete thing-events in a web of relation, for example the human heart-mind's issuance of the creative harmonizing feelings of empathy—the Four Sprouts—in response to others. It is on account of this that the creative agency of pattern, the heart-mind of the Way, is always found within the human and creaturely heart-minds, and is in that sense always related and embodied.

When coupled with his conferral of a primordial and intrinsic potentiality for manyness on pattern, Toegye's thoroughly relational and embodied conception of pattern's own creative harmonizing dynamic could be the key to a genuinely spiral conception of the Great Ultimate's movement. When the myriad achieved patterns of the world wane and flow back into the Non-Ultimate in the receptive phase of the Great Ultimate, insofar as they are embodied realizations of the ontologically ultimate and primordial multiplicity of potential patterns, they are not simply assimilated back into a logically, ontologically, and normatively more ultimate and primordial one Pattern. Instead, they are retained in their multiplicity to form the factual basis in response to which the one Pattern activates itself anew and issues forth into a novel multiplicity of creatively harmonizing potential patterns, all suggestive of the correct and better paths for the myriad thing-events to follow. The most prominent case in point is the issuance of the Four Sprouts from the heart-mind of the Way within the human heart-mind, which takes place always in reaction to both the presence of others and one's accumulated past responses to them in concrete relational situations. It illustrates the potential of Toegye's thought for an unambiguously spiral conception of the Great Ultimate and a clear explanation of the mutually reinforcing and evolving relationship between the heart-mind of the Way and the human heart-mind in the process of learning to be a sage. It could ensure that the way of the sages is always conceived as being realized in and through the genuinely effective moral agency of human and creaturely heart-minds and their diverse achievements of ethicopolitical and cosmic harmonies, never as an abstract, blank tablet on which a dominant group can inscribe its own parochial way and claim for itself the false universality of representing the Heavenly Pattern.

## A Trinitarian Panentheism of the Plurisingular Spirit

What can the spiral conception of the Great Ultimate, as proposed above on the basis of the "debate" between Zhu Xi and Toegye, suggest for the Christian comparative theological task of employing the category of psychophysical energy to counter the subordinate construction of the

Spirit's place and role within the divine trinitarian hierarchy of classical Christian theology? Toegye's non-self-consciously diverging interpretation of the Great Ultimate from Zhu Xi's opens up a path toward something akin to a pneumatocentric panentheism within the rubrics of the Neo-Confucian worldview, if the name "Spirit" may be given to the transhumanly "spiritual" (*sin/shen* [神]-like)—wondrous, subtle, and mysterious—workings of the heart-mind of the Way testifying to the creative agency of the Great Ultimate. The Spirit envisaged here is both one and many, human and transhuman, ideational and somatic, just as the Great Ultimate is both one and many and embraces both the cosmic and metacosmic planes of reality. Such a Neo-Confucian conception of the divine Spirit is panentheistic in the sense that the human or creaturely heart-mind and the heart-mind of the Way, which are both "spiritual" embodiments of the metaphysical ultimate (i.e., the Great Ultimate) in psychophysical energy, are related to each other in a nondualistic and nonreductionistic manner even as the latter functions as the creative source, normative ground, and telos of the former. This resonates with a Christian panentheistic construal of the relationship between God and creatures in which the two are viewed as mutually indwelling and interdependent while God retains the logical, ontological, and normative priority of being the creative ground and goal of the creatures.

Due to his failure to provide a sympathetic carrier or vehicle of pattern's creatively harmonizing mandate, which is called for by his interdependent construction of the pattern–psychophysical energy relationship, Zhu Xi's interpretation of the Great Ultimate is not as conducive to such a panentheistic imagination as Toegye's. For all his high regard for pattern's mandate, Zhu Xi's conception of psychophysical energy purely as the principle of random differentiation sows doubts regarding pattern's efficacy in the world and thus calls into question the very existence and possibility of the heart-mind of the Way (or the fecund heart-mind of heaven and earth). Panentheistically speaking, it would be virtually impossible in Zhu Xi's case to speak of "divine action" in a meaningful sense of the term, as God would be a mere blueprint of creation and moral map, which, even when in possession of a body, is not assured of harmonizing agency and subjectivity—namely, God's being as Spirit—due to the unruliness of the body. The envisioned interdependent and mutually indwelling relationship between God and creatures would be replaced by a dualistic conflict similar to the classical Western one between ideal harmony and material chaos.

In contrast, the Neo-Confucian conception of the Spirit inspired by Toegye could help us deconstruct the monarchical formulation of the Trinity dominant from classical times up to now. If we use the symbol of the Great Ultimate to represent the divine life of the "immanent" or preworldly Trinity,[18] the Father as the unoriginate origin can be thought of as the Great Ultimate as substance (or the Non-Ultimate), while the Spirit as the loving power and efficacy of the Father can be reenvisaged as the Great Ultimate as function. A subtle shift takes place in such a reconception, for the Great Ultimate as substance, namely, the indeterminate One, is not logically, ontologically, and normatively prior to the Great Ultimate as function, because of the interdependent and symmetrical construction of the substance-function relation.[19] In other words, the Spirit can be conceptualized as itself the unoriginate origin, the fountain and wellspring of all thing-events that is fully alive and active in the present, and whose transcendence of the determinate past or whose creative openness to novelty is captured by the notion of the indeterminate One.[20] In its active or *yang* phase, the Spirit's creative activity consists in issuing, out of the One's indeterminate pure potentiality for harmony—which is Spirit's own capacity for transcendence and novelty—into an infinite multiplicity of potentially harmonious or empathetic orders (patterns or Ways [道 *do*/*dao*]), to which the traditional doctrine of the Son as the eternally derived Word or Logos corresponds, albeit now genuinely pluralized. In its receptive or *eum*/*yin* phase, the direction of Spirit's movement is reversed, with the Spirit gathering and receiving the multiplicity of patterns back into the indeterminate One. Of course, this conception of preworldly Trinity (i.e., the indeterminate One, the plurisingular Spirit, many Ways)[21] is still an abstract, though real, notion; in concrete reality, as pattern is always already found united with psychophysical energy, there is only the "economic" or worldly Trinity (i.e., the One, the heart-mind of the Way (or the fecund heart-mind of heaven and earth), human/creaturely heart-minds). The Spirit's creative activity, which issues into and encompasses infinite potential harmonies or "ways," actualizes or concretizes them always in union or in concert with the dynamism of psychophysical energy, within the process of the unfolding of the natural creative capacity of concrete thing-events to be harmonies. The omnipresent Spirit co-presents an infinite number of harmonizing possibilities to each thing-event, which, in turn, responds (or fails to respond) by actualizing a determinate number of them relevant to it as its own potential creatively to become in a harmonious web of relation. As patterns thus concretely realized as thing-events of the world start to decline and wane, they are gathered and received back into the One by the heart-mind of the Way or the fecund heart-mind of heaven and earth to serve as the basis of a new responsive activity of creative harmonization.

There is another significant contribution that can be made by the Toegyean conception of the panentheistic Spirit proposed above to the Christian theological task of constructing a Spirit-centered trinitarian panentheism. It suggests a promising nondualistic approach to explicating the precise relationship between creaturely agency and the agency of the Spirit, that is, the problem of so-called divine action. Within the abstract, metacosmic plane of reality, the Toegyean conception allows to pattern an independent dynamism that is to become efficacious only within the concrete context of pattern's union with psychophysical energy. In the realm of human agency, this means that the transhuman agency of the Spirit acts only "in and through" human agency. The Toegyean conception explains this "in and through" by emphasizing what has been more or less sidelined in the classical Western, Christian tradition, namely the centrality of feelings in embodied, relational contexts for a theory of moral agency, be it human or transhuman. Although pattern is metaphysical and human nature ideal, both consisting in the idea of harmony, that idea is active first and foremost as feelings in and among human agents. In other words, the transhuman agency of the Spirit influences human moral agency by presenting not primarily the idea of unity to assent to or the value of harmony to espouse, but feelings of empathy to enact in relations. Precisely because these feelings articulate empathetic understanding, despite the amazing plurality and diversity of their situational appropriateness, they can all contribute to a wondrously harmonious configuration of local harmonies into an overarching sociocosmic whole. The plurisingular Spirit as Harmony of many harmonies is thus achieved in concrete reality. The "logic" of the pluralizing and unifying operation of the Spirit, that is, the very thing on which the differentiated unity of the Whole is premised, is first and foremost affective before it is nomological, as it unfolds in and through human agencies. And precisely because it is first and foremost affective, the circle of creaturely agencies in which the "logic" of the Spirit can be present in the full sense of the term becomes much more expanded beyond the human realm.

There is, however, one unresolved issue in the Neo-Confucian conception of the Spirit proposed above. It derives from Zhu Xi's problematic conception of psychophysical energy solely as the principle of differentiation with no share—other than in a derivative sense—in the creatively harmonizing function assigned to pattern as the metaphysical ultimate. Toegye does not challenge Zhu Xi's refusal to recognize the existence of an intrinsically unifying and harmonizing dynamic in psychophysical energy. This results in his continuation of Zhu Xi's tendency to abject creaturely agency's dependence on the spontaneous dynamism of psychophysical energy as much as possible through the latter's devaluation. To be sure, the embodied realizations of the ontologically ultimate and primordial multiplicity of potential harmonies, which are represented by the Four Sprouts, are never devalued, leading to an affirmation of the genuinely effective moral agency of human and creaturely heart-minds and their diverse achievements of ethicopolitical and cosmic harmonies. Nonetheless, a hierarchy is created between what are straightforwardly Heavenly orders growing out of the Four Sprouts and reflective of the transhuman moral agency of the heart-mind of the Way, on the one hand, and what are dubious human orders growing out of the Seven Feelings and belonging primarily to the agency of the human or creaturely heart-minds, on the other. Such a hierarchy of valuation significantly narrows the range and scope of those orders considered to be reflective of ontologically ultimate, primordial, and normative patterns. Consequently, Toegye's dynamic conception of pattern does not really counter the tendency to distrust spontaneously emerging human feelings and desires evident in the prevalent Neo-Confucian opposition of the public "Heavenly Pattern" to the private "human desire" and the attendant social ordering in which the ruling class of cultured male gentry exercise public leadership as "superior persons" over the rest.[22] This considerably weakens the thought that the Spirit as human-transhuman agency may be understood as emerging in a mutually constitutive spiral dialectic with many self-creative practices of somatic cultivation in diverse relational contexts. The Spirit's creative activity that issues into and encompasses infinite potential harmonies is here in danger of turning into a dominating power rather than being an "inspiration" (i.e., a "spiritualizing" lure and guide) for creaturely agencies.

What is at stake here is the existence of genuine freedom in the world. The value of the diverse achievements of ethicopolitical and cosmic harmonies in the world is truly affirmed, thanks to Toegye's dynamic conception of the Great Ultimate that recognizes the primordiality and ontological ultimacy of the multiplicity of potential harmonies. But when it comes to recognizing the extent of the independent contribution made by the agency of the human or creaturely heart-minds in achieving those harmonies compared to the agency of the heart-mind of the Way, a shadow of doubt is cast. A more interdependent and symmetrical construction of the relationship between pattern and psychophysical energy, akin to the substance-function distinction, would give us a conception of the Spirit that readily affirms the real plurality of harmonious sociocosmic configurations emerging from our embodied—racialized, gendered, sexualized, class-located, etc.—and therefore multiple agencies.

What is needed, therefore, is a different conception of psychophysical energy, that is, one that recognizes psychophysical energy's own contribution to the creatively harmonizing processes of the universe represented by the symbol of the Great Ultimate. Before I move on to the discussion of a figure within the Neo-Confucian tradition—namely, Im Seong-ju (honorific name Nongmun), the eighteenth-century Korean Neo-Confucian thinker—who has advanced such a theory of psychophysical energy, it is apropos at this point to present a comparative theological reflection involving Toegye and G. W. F. Hegel (1770–1831), the late eighteenth- to early nineteenth-century German philosopher who has been called the "theologian of the Spirit."[23] Hegel's concept of God features the "immanent" Trinity as the divine logical Idea that, when taken by itself in abstraction from the world, is the universal One that is always active. This One consists in an infinitely repetitive series of unceasing dialectical movement to posit the other of itself (the particular), and reunite itself with the other—that is, reunite the universal with the particular—to produce the singular or individual as internally differentiated unities of multiplicity, namely, "concrete unities" or harmonies. The Idea, in other words, is in fact plurisingular, as an incessant activity of becoming Harmony of harmonies. This resonates with Toegye's dynamic conception of the Great Ultimate that is neither merely one homogeneous Pattern nor simply the total sum of all patterns but a mediating agency between the two, issuing from the one Pattern's indeterminate pure potentiality for harmony into an infinite multiplicity of potentially harmonious or empathetic patterns and holding the latter together in an overarching plurisingular Harmony.

Hegel and Toegye are further comparable in the sense that both construe the process of the concretization of the ontological ultimate in relation to what may be called a corollary "material" principle that, though not conceived identically by each, manifests the characteristic of being solely the principle of differentiation devoid of any unifying function. Hegel's logical Idea achieves the concrete actuality of the absolute Spirit in and through a mutually constitutive dialectical relationship with many finite spirits emerging out of a struggle against nature, here conceived as the principle of inertia, mutually indifferent particularity, and dispersion into chaos. Similarly, Toegye's Great Ultimate achieves the concrete creative harmonizing agency of the heart-mind of the Way in and through a mutually constitutive spiral dialectic with many human and creaturely heart-minds carried by the dynamism of psychophysical energy that is devoid of any unifying role. Although the concepts of nature and psychophysical energy differ from each other insofar as their possession of dynamism is concerned, they share the status of being the "material" or physical principle of differentiation and concretion without any unitive function. In that sense, Hegel's conception of nature is faced with a problem similar to the one facing Toegye's conception of psychophysical energy, namely, the doubt about the truly universal scope of the overarching Harmony of harmonies represented, respectively, by the absolute Spirit and the heart-mind of the Way. All in all, Hegel's dynamic trinitarian conception of God as Spirit, which is one of the most influential reworkings of the classical doctrine of Trinity, suggests many points of highly productive resonance and creative tension with Toegye's dynamic conception of the Great Ultimate and the Neo-Confucian pneumatocentric panentheism proposed in this chapter. To a discussion of this, we now turn.

# 5 From the Divine Idea to the Concrete Unity of the Spirit

## HEGEL'S SHAPES OF FREEDOM AND THE DOMINATION OF NATURE

Hegel's philosophical reading of the Christian narrative, or "salvation history," as articulated in the *Lectures on the Philosophy of Religion*, advances the thesis that the trinitarian logic of the divine Idea, which grounds the history of God and brings it to its consummation in the community of the Spirit, permeates nature as the ontological condition of possibility for all that exists and gives rise in history to a communal pattern of human life characterized by its universal reach and the freedom in unity of its members as knowing and willing subjects. The key to understanding this reading of the Christian narrative is Hegel's claim that his philosophical reading *thinks* in the most proper sense of term, that is, it grasps an identifiable logic or pattern in the object of thinking by overreaching or "overgrasping" (*übergreifen*)[1] the otherness of the object afflicted with difference, mutual externality, and dispersion into chaos, which would otherwise lead to irrationality and incomprehensibility.[2] His reading identifies in the Christian narrative, which narrates the trinitarian history of God in the world, the divine logical Idea—namely, the logical pattern of the self-diremption of the abstract universal into the particular and its self-reunification in the concrete universal. It is precisely this discernment of the logical Idea that makes it possible to think God and to have a rational knowledge (cognition) or science (*Wissenschaft*) of God, which is theology.[3]

### Hegel's Reading of the Christian Narrative: The Trinitarian Community of the Spirit

Hegel's definition of thinking and rational knowledge reveals his desire to reconcile two opposing trends within his intellectual context, which was defined, on the one hand, by the predominant epistemological concern of the European Enlightenment—culminating in Kant's transformation of metaphysical theses into moral postulates—and, on the other hand, by the aspiration of Romanticism to the Whole and Infinite.[4] As an act of grasping by means of overgrasping, thinking is for Hegel not the thinking subject's imposition of an alien pattern on the object thought, for thinking is "thinking-over" (*Nachdenken*) that follows the object's self-constitution into an identifiable pattern in and through the object's own overreaching of the mutual externality and difference plaguing it.[5] In other words, thinking as an activity of overgrasping finds the essential nature or concept of the object to be constituted by the same activity of overgrasping that it itself is. This is why philosophy as genuine thinking establishes rational knowledge or science as the subject's *reconciliation* with the object; for philosophy, in disclosing the essential nature or concept of the object, reveals at the same time the essential identity of the subject and the object that is predicated on the object's own repudiation of the externality and difference afflicting it and its self-elevation to the rationality of a thinkable, identifiable pattern.

The Christian narrative, which is the object of Hegel's philosophical reading, is itself also a form of "thinking-over" in the sense that it represents, on the one hand, the religious subject's knowledge of the religious object's (i.e., God's) own overreaching of creation and humanity in and through the divine-human unity of the God-man, and, on the other hand, the religious subject's reconciliation with the religious object by means of that knowledge. In fact, without the kind of subject-object and human divine reconciliation actually achieved "objectively" in and through God and witnessed to by the Christian narrative, philosophy as overreaching "thinking-over" is itself not possible.[6] But this reconciling insight of the Christian narrative is couched in sensible figures, images, and stories (what Hegel calls "representation" [*Vorstellung*]) which mirror or represent mutually external and indifferent finite particulars constituting a web of happenings in spatial juxtaposition and temporal succession, without there being any demonstration of the necessity or logic by which the things or events narrated are the way they are.[7] The task of Hegel's philosophical reading of the Christian narrative, therefore, is to overreach, or overgrasp, the latter's representational mode of thinking—the so-called Understanding (*Verstand*)—by translating it into a logical, "conceptual" mode of thinking—Reason (*Vernunft*)—that leaves its content or essential insight intact while eliminating the vestiges of externality and otherness remaining in it. Such a reading would elevate the content to the level of rational knowledge, or cognition, which is the knowledge of the necessity of things.[8] Hegel's construal of the essence of the Christian insight in terms of the trinitarian logic of the divine Idea, which constitutes the ontological condition of possibility for nature and history, is meant precisely as such a translation. The entire system of Hegel's philosophy, from logic to history of philosophy, is an effort to make the whole range of reality intelligible precisely in terms of the trinitarian logic thus "read off" the pattern discerned in the narrative unfolding of Christian salvation history. It is an attempt to "think over" reality as such, both intelligible and sensible, by following the movement of the divine logical Idea through the various stages of reality, from the realm of pure thought to nature and history, as the Idea progressively overreaches the otherness in reality to manifest itself as the intelligible truth, condition of possibility, and ultimate telos of the latter.

At the center of Hegel's philosophical reading of the Christian narrative stands his christology, which provides a decisive "turning point [*Wendungspunkt*]"[9] for the narrated drama recounting God's salvation of the world afflicted with its "naturalness"—namely, the character of mutual externality, indifference, and dispersion into chaos.[10] Hegel sees Jesus Christ as the one who has decisively overcome the naturalness of the world in the sense that the consummate religious consciousness to which he elevates human beings offers universal, divine, and absolute reconciliation. Hegel explains this consummate religious consciousness in reference to the way it is expressed in Jesus' teaching of "the kingdom of God" as a state of affairs or a reality embodying the universal reconciliation of humanity in God.[11] According to Hegel's reading, Jesus' teaching of the kingdom of God denotes not God alone as the universal essence but a "divine community" permeated by a "living, spiritual life," that is, a community of God and humanity in which humanity is freed from its selfishness in and through its true self-knowledge.[12] In the kingdom of God humanity knows itself to be determined for universal reconciliation, and in and through that knowledge is elevated "out of its natural will, out of evil, out of the willing of singular selfishness, out of every type of restriction" and accordingly also "elevated above all locality, nationality, condition, life-situation, etc."[13] This universalizing drive of the kingdom of God, transcending all conditions and exigencies of individual, familial, tribal, regional, and national life and the various parochial and exclusive attachments, loyalties, and allegiances arising therein, is articulated by

Jesus in terms of *love*—more precisely, the mutual love of the community of disciples. Jesus makes the love of one another in a divine community the principal commandment, and enjoins his disciples to renounce all particular purposes of their own and "to make only this unity, this community in and for itself as their goal."[14] Hence, his teaching of the kingdom of God is opposed to all other—partially and inadequately reconciled—forms of life still afflicted with a persistence of mutual externality and self-seeking.[15] His Sermon on the Mount, breaking of the Sabbath laws, and rejection of the established familial bonds together constitute a "revolutionary attitude toward all the determinate aspects of that outer world, [all the settled attitudes] of human consciousness and belief," which "partly leaves all standing institutions aside and partly destroys and overthrows them."[16]

Nevertheless, although the kingdom of God is taught as a state of affairs or a reality embodying the universal reconciliation of humanity in God, it is still merely a teaching, idea, and vision. It consists of abstract images depicting the state of humanity's universal reconciliation, and as such exists only in inwardness, in thought. It says nothing about how such a state could be concretely realized in the world.[17] The significance of the life and death of Jesus lies initially in the fact that in him as a single individual the kingdom is actualized and made tangible, that is, brought down from the abstract universalism of his teaching to the concrete reality of the sensible, intuitable world, so that it could be accessible to all who have eyes to see: "The kingdom is the universal idea still presented in representational form; it enters into actuality through this individual, and the history of spirit, the concrete content of the kingdom of God, has to portray itself in this divine actuality."[18] Despite the fact that his life is a natural existence imprisoned in the needs of ordinary human life, it is in conformity with his teachings to such an extent that he courts a martyr's death. He dies on account of the stark opposition of what he enacts, namely, the kingdom of God, to the existing forms of unreconciled or partially reconciled life.[19]

Yet if being a martyr to the truth were the sole meaning of his life and death, then although his enactment of the kingdom would be morally grand, he would merely be yet another addition to the long list of failed visionaries. We may attempt to follow his example and try through our subjectivity and agency to overcome our estrangement from one another and from God and to enact his vision of universal reconciliation in God, but there is really no way of knowing whether the condition of "naturalness"—the state of mutual difference and indifference—in which we find ourselves is not the way things are supposed to be. This means that, if the human subject's desire for overcoming its estrangement is not to be a subjective illusion and wishful thinking, then it must be presupposed that the undoing of our estrangement from one another and from God is achieved not only subjectively but objectively also.[20] In other words, the universal reconciliation of the kingdom of God must be something brought about in principle by the universal essence and telos of humanity itself, namely, God, as the condition of possibility for its achievement by human beings.

The genuine significance of the life and death of Jesus, Hegel argues, lies in the fact that his story is an appearance in a single human being of the history of God who realizes in and through humanity God's own concept or telos, which is to be a divine community or a universally reconciled community of God and humanity. Jesus is the one who unites divine and human nature in the sense that his enactment of the universal reconciliation of the kingdom of God and his death on account of it constitute a dramatic witness to God realizing God's concept in human beings in the entire range of their natural existence afflicted with finitude, contingency, frailty, and weakness.[21] What happens in Jesus as a single human being, therefore, "has a significance not only for the definition of human nature but just as much for that of the divine. . . . All differentiation, all finitude . . . is a moment of the process of the divine nature . . . grounded within the divine nature itself."[22] Just as Jesus' life testifies to God's enactment of universal reconciliation in accordance with God's own telos, the true significance of Jesus' death is not merely that it is the inevitable fate of a martyr to the truth, but that "*God* has died, that God *himself is dead*." In other words, the death of Jesus is a moment within the very nature of God that enacts universal reconciliation.[23]

This death of God is for Hegel "a monstrous, fearful picture [*Vorstellung*]," insofar as death is the "highest pinnacle of finitude."[24] As "the greatest dependence, the ultimate weakness, the utmost fragility," death is "the furthest extreme to which humanity as natural existence is exposed."[25] The meaning of the death of God in Jesus is that God in and through humanity experiences and suffers this extreme finitude in the "deepest abyss of cleavage."[26] Yet the death of God is at the same time "the means of salvation, the focal point of reconciliation,"[27] because it gives witness to the fact that, right in the middle of the abyss of cleavage within humanity between its natural will and freedom, God has willed to die to the natural will of humanity. The reversal implied here, that is, that death as the extreme limit of natural existence is precisely what enables God to overcome the natural will, constitutes the salvific significance of the death of the "God-man" that is in continuity with his teaching of the kingdom and his enactment of it in his life:

> Natural will [is] surrendered. All distinctiveness, all traits of personality, all interests and purposes toward which the natural will might direct itself, [are] as nothing. [This is] a revolutionary element to the extent that it gives the world another shape. All things great and of worldly value [are] as nothing; [all these things are] buried in the grave of spirit.[28]

Furthermore, the revolutionary implication of this surrender of the natural will in death is augmented by the fact that the God-man's death is the most degrading death of a criminal executed on the cross, which implies "a complete revolution against all that is established and regarded as valuable" and which leaves "all the bonds of human corporate life . . . fundamentally assaulted, shaken, and dissolved."[29] It is also in this sense, that is, as the divine surrender of the self-seeking natural will of humanity and the accompanying transcendence of all unreconciled forms of life, that Hegel calls the death of God in Jesus "the highest love" or "the absolute love," because love consists in "the supreme surrender [of one-self] in the other, even in this most extrinsic other-being of death."[30] Given that love is to be the sole relational and animating principle of the kingdom of God, the death of God signifies God's ultimate divestment of Godself in order to realize the divine telos of creating a universally reconciled community of God and humanity.[31]

When the death of Jesus is seen in this light, the point of his resurrection is also made properly *theological*: It means that God's death for the sake of love is not in vain, that God "maintains" Godself (*erhält sich*) in the process of surrendering the natural will and existence in and through Jesus' death.[32] By maintaining Godself in the supreme self-surrender of death, God preserves human nature in its subjectivity and spirituality, while purging it of its natural will and elevating ("glorifying") it to the state of universal reconciliation in God, namely, the kingdom of God.[33] This reconciled community of God and humanity is at first perceived as embodied in a single human being (the resurrected Jesus), but soon felt to be present in the community of Jesus' followers as the Spirit that unites them in love, after the ascension of Jesus and the outpouring of the Holy Spirit.[34]

Hegel's construal of the life, death, and resurrection of Jesus as a dramatic witness to the divine history of redemption—God's own experiencing and overcoming of the naturalness of the world—brings into focus the *trinitarian* thesis at the heart of the *theological* premise of his account. What is disclosed and verified by the life and death of the God-man is that, far from being an abstract identity with Godself or "the Father," God has God's other or "the Son"—that is, divine self-negation or the positing of Godself otherwise—as God's own essential determination, and that God subsists therefore as the unity in difference of the infinite and the finite insofar as the other of God is finitude.[35] At the same time, the resurrection of the God-man and his transfiguration into the divinely reconciled community of the Spirit together verify that otherness—the finitude, weakness, and frailty of creation—does not harm the concrete, differentiated unity within which God subsists, and that God as the Spirit is "the absolute power to endure this anguish, i.e. to unite the two and to be in this way, in this oneness."[36] In other words, what is revealed and verified by the history of Jesus Christ is the trinitarian "logic" at the core of God's own being:

> The reconciliation in Christ, in which one believes, makes no sense if God is not known as the triune God, [if it is not recognized] that God *is*, but also is as the other, as self-distinguishing, so that this other is God himself, having implicitly the divine nature in it, and that the sublation of this difference, this otherness, and the return of love, are the Spirit.[37]

When God whose history is witnessed to by the history of Jesus Christ is thought in abstraction from creation and history as the "eternal idea" existing in thought, the internal logical determination of God—which is what Hegel means by "Trinity"—turns out to be a movement or process of self-differentiation and self-reintegration that provides the ontological condition of possibility for the history of God in creation.[38] Logically speaking, God is the all-encompassing universal that posits a distinction within itself, that is, posits the particular as the other of itself, in such a way that the distinguished aspect, the particular, constitutes an internally differentiated unity with the universal rather than being external and alien to it: "In the absolute idea, in the element of thinking, God is this *utterly concrete universal* [*schlechthin konkrete Allgemeine*], the positing of self as other, but in such a way that the other is immediately defined to be himself . . . and does not take on the shape of externality" (italics mine).[39] In this understanding of God as the logical Idea lies the true meaning of the proposition that God is love, for love, according to Hegel's definition, consists in a unity the internal distinctions of which are mutually inclusive of each other.[40] The traditional trinitarian claim that God exists in three persons can be affirmed without destroying God's unity, because it is in the nature of personhood—which for Hegel is identical to subjecthood—to surrender one's particularity, isolation, and separation in order to constitute a concrete unity in friendship and love: "In friendship and love I give up my abstract personality and thereby win it back as concrete. The truth of personality is found precisely in winning it back through this immersion, this being immersed in the other."[41] It is with this understanding of personality or subjectivity in the background that Hegel names God "infinite personality" or "infinite subjectivity," which is what he means by "Spirit." Whereas the Father designates the universal and the Son the particular set over against the universal, the Spirit means the concrete unity between the two that renders the universal boundless and thus truly universal, all-encompassing, and therefore infinite.[42] For Hegel, the most proper name of God is therefore the Spirit, for "the Holy Spirit is eternal love."[43]

Although the internal movement of self-differentiation and self-reintegration which constitutes the divine life of love thus makes God boundless, free, and infinite vis-à-vis God's other, it is still "a relationship of God, of the idea, merely to himself."[44] In abstraction from creation and history, God in the element of thought or the logical Idea is merely "a play of love with itself, which does not arrive at the seriousness of other-being, of separation and rupture."[45] Yet because the freedom of the divine Idea is not threatened by the independence of its other due to its concrete unity with the latter, it can afford to let the other go into the truly serious freedom of genuine other-being. In other words, the trinitarian "logic" of God's inner being creates a division within Godself in such a way that the distinguished aspect or the particular—"the Son"—makes it possible for creation or the world, existing independently and freely, to be posited:

> Only the absolute idea determines itself and is certain of itself as absolutely free within itself because of this self-determination. For this reason its self-determination involves letting this determinate [entity] exist as something free, something independent, or as an independent object. It is only for the being that is free that freedom *is*; it is only for the free human being that an other has freedom too. It belongs to the absolute freedom of the idea that, in its act of determining and dividing, it releases

> the other to exist as a free and independent being. This other, released as something free and independent, is *the world* as such.[46]

Because God is the Trinity, not an abstract, internally homogeneous universal, it belongs to the essence of God to be the creator, that is to say, to posit nature or the world of difference, multiplicity, and finitude as God's other and to be reconciled with it, out of the infinite plenitude of God's creative power and love.[47] Hegel writes that God is "the absolute womb or the infinite fountainhead out of which everything emerges, into which everything returns, and in which it is eternally maintained."[48] The history of God, to which the history of Jesus Christ gives witness, is no other than this "narrative" or drama from its Alpha in the Trinity of the eternal divine Idea to its Omega in the consummation of the Spirit as the concretely reconciled community of God and creation.[49]

A crucial point that Hegel makes in his interpretation of this divine narrative is that, although creation, or nature, has been "let go" by God to be a free and independent subsistence, it does not possess genuine actuality by itself precisely because it is the other of God.[50] Whereas the life of God consists in the concretely uniting love of the Trinity, nature as the other of God is defined by separation and dispersion into mutually indifferent particulars. Put otherwise, nature by definition is the abyss of nothingness in which nothing can maintain its identity and subsist.[51] Insofar as nature is what is posited by the second "moment" of divine self-differentiation within the logical Idea, one could say that it is the extreme end of divine self-divestment. Yet the second moment of divine self-diremption cannot be considered in abstraction from the third and final moment of divine self-reintegration that completes and consummates the trinitarian logic. Concretely speaking, nature is actually a realm pulsating with the divine Idea or the trinitarian life of God that brings together the mutually indifferent particulars and reconciles them in concrete unities, thus enabling a multitude of beings and entities to emerge, sustain their identity, and subsist.[52] The organic realm of life—especially animal life—is for Hegel the highest manifestation of the divine Idea in nature, insofar as the phenomenon of life consists in the concrete unity of the parts in the whole.[53] The emergence of human being as finite subjectivity or spirit bases itself on the phenomenon of life, while recapitulating and transfiguring the concrete unity embodied in the latter on the higher plane of knowledge and will.[54]

Given that the concrete unity in love of the divine life is a knowingly and willingly sustained unity, the human being or finite spirit can be said to actualize the trinitarian logic in the most consummate fashion within the realm of finitude or creation, and can in that sense be seen as the concept or telos of nature toward which the latter is driven by the divine Idea animating it. Yet ironically and tragically, by that very power of knowledge and will conferred on it by the divine idea, the finite spirit can refuse—and in fact does refuse—to complete the trinitarian logic and thereby to fulfill its own concept. Unlike natural entities whose inadequate realization of the trinitarian logic is due merely to their "slumber,"[55] as a knowing and willing rejection of concrete unity, humanity's "fall" into selfishness, division, and conflict represents the highest degree of self-contradiction. Thus, in humanity the divine history arrives at "the most extreme estrangement [*Entfremdung*] and pinnacle of divestment [*Entäußerung*]."[56]

The appearance of the idea of divine-human unity in a single individual, namely, the life, death, and resurrection of Jesus Christ, is a disclosure to human beings in the anguish and misery of their estrangement that the divine Idea within them can, does, and will complete its trinitarian logic in spite of their resistance, and that the nadir of estrangement in which they find themselves is in fact the "turning point" (*Wendungspunkt*) of the divine history, namely, the beginning of the divine history of reconciliation.[57] Appearing in the life and death of a single individual who could be seen, heard, and touched by all without regard for their locality, culture, language, and level of education, the divine idea makes universally available the certainty of its presence and efficacy in the world despite all the historical and existential evidences to the contrary. The passing-away of the God-man and the outpouring of the Holy Spirit transform this sensibly intuited certainty into faith, which is the knowledge that the observed efficacious presence of the divine Idea in the God-man is in truth its implicitly efficacious presence in humanity as such.[58] By means of this knowledge, human beings identify themselves with the "example" of the God-man and, in so doing, convict and divest themselves of their natural will and actualize the concretely universal reconciliation of the kingdom of God. In this explicit and actual completion of the trinitarian logic within themselves, human beings experience the presence and efficacy of the divine Idea within and recognize themselves as united with it.[59] This is the elevation to the consummate religious consciousness, that is, the consciousness of God as the concrete unity of God and humanity, on which the life of the community of the Spirit is predicated. In the life of the community of the Spirit, "religion has become objective to itself"[60]—that is, the object of religious consciousness, namely, God, has turned out to be the fulfillment of the concept (or essence and telos) of religion itself, which is the concrete unity of God and worshiping human beings acknowledged by means of teaching or doctrine and sustained by means of cultic practice.[61]

To the extent that the knowing and willing achievement of the concrete divine-human unity in the life of the community of the Spirit represents the completion of the trinitarian logic of the divine Idea in and through its efficacious presence in humanity, the divine-human unity constitutes the third and final moment of self-reintegration in God's own history. It means that God as the divine Idea in human beings has become objective to Godself in and through the community of the Spirit, that God reveals Godself as infinite subjectivity or infinite self-consciousness (i.e., "Spirit") which returns to itself in and through the self-negation and self-elevation of the multitude of finite subjectivities or finite consciousnesses:

> God is self-consciousness; he knows himself in a consciousness that is distinct from him, which is implicitly the consciousness of God, but is also the divine consciousness explicitly since it knows its identity with God, an identity that is mediated, however, by the negation of finitude. . . . Finite consciousness knows God only to the extent that God knows himself in it; this God is spirit, indeed the Spirit of his community, i.e., of those who worship him. This is the consummate religion, the concept that has become objective to itself.[62]

The infinite subjectivity of God, in other words, means God's "overreaching [*übergreifend*]"[63] relationship with finite subjectivity, in which God encompasses the latter as an essential moment of the constitution of God's own self rather than opposing and negating it altogether as something alien and external, while transcending it precisely by means of its self-negation and self-elevation.[64] It is in this sense that God as "spirit in its community" or "absolute spirit" consists in the "affirmative relationship of [finite] spirit to absolute spirit" that is at the same time "the self-consciousness of absolute spirit."[65] This is also why faith, which completes the movement of the trinitarian logic within humanity, is both "the witness of the spirit concerning absolute spirit" and the "witness of the Spirit to spirit," and why the Spirit is "not a spirit beyond the stars or beyond the world" but "a living God who is effective, active, and present in spirit."[66] God is "absolutely self-sufficient, unconditioned, independent, free, as well as being the supreme end unto itself,"[67] precisely because God constitutes Godself as the Spirit of the community in and through the knowingly and willingly executed self-negation and self-elevation of God's other, namely, finite spirit, which render God boundless and thus truly infinite and free.

The consummation of the trinitarian history of God, which takes place in the life of the community of the Spirit, consists, therefore, in the affirmative relationship of finite subjectivity with infinite subjectivity or the latter's overreaching relationship with the former. To the extent that the divine overreaching enacts itself in and through the self-negation and self-elevation of finite spirits, finite spirits are enabled to overreach one another symmetrically and reciprocally by virtue of God's primary freedom and power to overreach what is other. In the life of the community of the Spirit human beings as finite subjects divest themselves of their self-centered natural will and existence and, thus "belonging to self without seeking for self," elevate themselves to the infinite subjectivity of the community that is concretely universal—all-encompassing yet internally differentiated—subjectivity or universal intersubjectivity.[68] As infinite love that is mediated by the infinite anguish of dying to everything fraught with natural, subjective particularity and to every kind of relation or form of life dependent on such, the concretely universal subjectivity of the community of the Spirit "has given up all external distinctions of . . . mastery, power, position, even of sex and wealth" and affirms the equality of all human beings in their infinite worth as free spirits, thereby leaving no alien human other to remain.[69] In the life of the community, human beings prove themselves to possess, on account of the Spirit dwelling in and working in and through their finite subjectivity, the absolute freedom to transcend their natural will, ties, and allegiances and yet still to exist in a concrete, trinitarian unity with one another, that is, the freedom that is "the infinite power to maintain oneself in this other pure and simple."[70]

## The Ambiguity of Divine Freedom in the Other and the Domination of Nature

For all its emphasis on concrete unity or harmony, however, Hegel's notion of the logical Idea realizing itself as the Spirit encompassing creation exhibits a significant limitation in its harmonizing potential because of the way it conceives of nature as merely implicit or immediate (*an sich*) spirituality. Although nature as it actually exists is a realm permeated and animated by the divine Idea whose concretely uniting power enables entities to emerge and sustain their identity, owing to nature's logical definition as a realm of particularity and mutual externality, which constitutes the logical contrary of the concrete unity of the divine Idea, the divine Idea is seen as particularly opposed and hampered in nature by forces of contingency and conflict. In other words, because nature is defined as a realm of mutually indifferent and chaotically interacting particulars, the trinitarian pulse or logic that permeates nature, namely, the movement of self-diremption and overreaching self-reintegration that enables every concretely existing thing to exist within the totality of its relations, has to be conceived in a mode of struggle against what resists concrete unity, order, and harmony. Although actually existing natural entities are not themselves defined as that which resist order and harmony, they are still conceived as more or less satisfactory outcomes of the divine *agon* against God's other, here defined as nature, as if actually existing entities of nature were trophies of war wrested by God from nature as from a destructive chaos of nothingness.[71]

The main problem with Hegel's consignment of nature to the extreme other of the logical Idea is that it easily leads to setting up an evaluative hierarchy of concretely reconciled unities across the entire range of creation, with nature sitting at the bottom and finite spirit (humanity) at the top.[72] Nature's reconciled harmonies, such as rocks, plants, and animals are assigned lower degrees of self-presence than the unities achieved in the human realm as and by means of knowledge and will. Precisely because nature is defined as a realm of contingent and arbitrary play of difference at the farthest opposing end from the self-reintegrating pulse of the divine Idea, the lower degrees of self-presence achieved in nature are viewed as products of nature's intransigence vis-à-vis the divine Idea. In other words, harmonies of nature are regarded not merely as different but as incomplete and inadequate realizations of the divine Idea, being devoid of the capacity for the knowing and willing exercise of self-negation and self-transcendence that is the sine qua non of the overreaching, affirmatively reconciling, and genuinely free relationship between the infinite Spirit and finite spirits. Moreover, although the human achievement of concretely universal reconciliation by means of knowledge and will is valorized as the consummate realization of the trinitarian divine Idea, the most vicious expression of mutual indifference and self-seeking fragmentation, which is actually found in knowingly and willfully enacted acts of selfishness and conflicts among human beings, is defined as humanity's living "according to nature" or following its "natural will." It is for this reason that Hegel's christology puts the divine-human achievement of concretely uniting freedom in terms of dying to and overcoming the *natural* will. Also, it is for this reason that his account of the logical Idea's becoming Spirit—as seen in his philosophy of nature and spirit (and in the order of his system as a whole)—is one that casts the Idea's reconciling movement in creation as a developmental narrative in which the Idea progressively subdues, disciplines, and overcomes the contingent and arbitrary character of nature's immediate, *an sich* spirituality in order to arrive at the complexity of humanity's self-present attainment of concretely uniting freedom.[73]

A baleful consequence of Hegel's construction of a developmental narrative expressing the teleology of Spirit is that the evaluative hierarchy that it establishes becomes a rule of recognition by which not only entities and communities of entities in nature but also certain categories of human beings and human communities are unfavorably judged as to the extent and manner of their participation in the network of mutual recognition that makes up the universally reconciled community of all entities. Just as there is a hierarchical gradation of natural entities and their communities, more value is conferred on those human beings and human communities that demonstrate, in and through their knowing and willing—free—recognition of one another as free subjects, their adequate mastery of the natural will and their consequent possession of a higher level of self-presence and self-determining subjectivity.[74] Hegel's attempt to construct a developmental narrative of cultures and religions, as worked out in his *Lectures on the Philosophy of World History* and in the *Determinate Religion* part of his *Lectures on the Philosophy of Religion*, for instance, consigns the cultures of the "Oriental World" such as China and India,[75] and various non-Western religions ranging from Confucianism to Zoroastrianism ("religions of nature"), to the dawn of human history where humanity has not yet fully emerged from the *an sich* spirituality of nature.[76] Although these cultures and religions are spiritual to the extent that they are forms of the community of Spirit achieved by the divine Idea in struggle against nature's mutually externalizing tendencies, the presence of the concretely reconciling power of the Idea in them is supposedly too weak and inadequate either to allow the wayward, "natural" play of difference within them to attain the self-presence and self-determining power of knowing and willing subjectivity, or to subdue, discipline, and overcome that subjectivity if it becomes the privatizing, selfish natural will. Consequently, unlike the political and cultural institutions of freedom achieved by the modern West and Christianity, which stand at the apex of Hegel's developmental and supersessionist narrative, the non-Western, "natural" forms of communal life are seen to maintain social unity by various patterns of domination—master-slave relations—in both their internal organization and external relations, and to regard themselves as sanctioned by some arbitrary divine powers appearing and working through the things and forces of nature to evoke fear.[77]

The irony of Hegel's attempt at a developmental narrative of freedom is that, owing to the dependence of its rules of recognition on the human capacity to master the natural will, the self-present and self-determining subjects of the modern West that stand at the end and culmination of that narrative are in danger of being captive to the very logic of domination on account of which Hegel denies full recognition to non-Western cultures and religions. As seen in Hegel's exclusion of women and the poor—and by implication the mentally challenged and demented—from the mutual recognition within the state's public sphere, which is the sociopolitical expression of the universal reconciliation achieved by the community of the Spirit,[78] categories and groups of human beings who are deemed to demonstrate inadequate mastery of the natural will, and therefore to lack a sufficient level of self-presence and self-determination, are admitted into the network of mutual recognition only in a qualified sense, either only in principle—as *an sich* spirits—or at most in the spirit of patronage and tutelage. In the end, Hegel's developmental narrative comes close, perhaps unwittingly, to defining human freedom as the freedom of healthy, educated, and either propertied or working male Christian Westerners who have allegedly overcome their natural will fully by recognizing one another as free subjects and who in doing so mistake the exclusive peer group of slave-masters thus created as the universally reconciled community of Spirit.[79]

Nonetheless, this criticism is not a total repudiation of Hegel's effort to formulate a vision of universal reconciliation in terms of concretely uniting freedom, namely, the freedom to be at home with oneself in the other.[80] As has been observed, the main reason for Hegel's conception of the community of Spirit being unsatisfactory is that it assigns to nature the status of the logical other of the Idea and then construes the concrete unity of the Spirit as attained agonistically in and through the divine Idea's conquest of nature's pull toward mutually indifferent differentiation and singularization. Yet insofar as mutually externalizing singularization constitutes a tendency toward chaos—entropy—that is present in the cosmos as a creative precondition of the emergence of novelty, I wonder if it is really necessary to formulate the trinitarian logic of the divine Idea in nature in a mode of struggle against such a "natural" and in principle benign cosmic tendency. If the spontaneous and chaotic play of difference in nature can be recognized more readily as ultimately creative rather than destructive of concrete unity, then the divine Idea in nature does not have to be weighed down so much by the "archeoteleological"[81] and agonistic motif of self-presence as to find its adequate incarnation only in reconciled unities achieved via the self-clarity and self-determination of knowledge and will in and among finite spirits. In other words, the divine Idea has no need to regard the opacity and unpredictableness of nature's contingency and spontaneity as a threat to itself that needs to be penetrated and overcome by the daylight of full self-presence and self-clarity. Despite the wayward, unpredictable spontaneity with which they emerge, nature's less self-present and less self-transparent—that is, more immediate—harmonies can then be considered as fully legitimate and recognizable forms of the freedom to be at home with oneself in the other, to the effect that the divine Idea's achievement of concretely reconciling freedom by way of self-determining subjectivity is freed from its anthropocentric and logocentric logic of domination.[82] Hegel's unsuccessful developmental narrative of freedom can then be rearranged into a typology of freedom,[83] in which different forms of concretely reconciled unities, both communities of natural entities and human cultures, are compared and contrasted in regard to their respective strengths and weaknesses, and not subjected to a disciplining gaze of asymmetrical recognition that views another as a less developed or failed version of oneself rather than as a genuine other.

## Hegel and Toegye: The Ontological Ultimacy of Multiplicity and the Devaluation of Nature and Psychophysical Energy

At the end of the preceding chapter I claimed that Hegel's dynamic trinitarian conception of God as Spirit suggests many points of highly productive resonance and creative tension with Toegye's dynamic conception of the Great Ultimate and with my sketch of a Neo-Confucian pneumatocentric and panentheistic Trinity inspired by Toegye. In order to expand on this claim, I would like to take what I regard as the core concepts of Hegel's system, that is, the logical Idea, nature, and spirit, and compare them with the corresponding core notions of the Great Ultimate, psychophysical energy, and the heart-mind found in Toegye's thought.

Let us begin by considering the logical Idea and the Great Ultimate. The two are comparable notions in the sense that they designate, each in its own way, both the ultimate formal feature of the universe and the dynamic ontological creativity seen to lie at the root of the cosmic creativity of the same universe. Hegel's logical Idea refers to the ultimate formal structure or "logic" of everything that is, which consists in the overreaching dialectical relationship between universality and particularity that leads to the creation of individuality or singularity as concrete—internally differentiated—unity. What is more, the logical Idea is not merely a formal structure; it has a dynamism of its own. The Idea consists in an infinitely repetitive series of unceasing dialectical movement of the universal One positing the other of itself, that is, the particular Many, and reuniting itself with the other to produce the singular or individual as internally differentiated unities of multiplicity, namely, "concrete unities" or harmonies, which ultimately come to constitute the Concrete Unity of concrete unities or the Harmony of harmonies. Similarly, Toegye's Great Ultimate refers to the ultimate formal pattern underlying the universe of myriad thing-events, which is the spiral-dialectical relationship between the interpenetrating complementary opposites of receptive unity and active multiplicity that is productive of myriad harmonies-in-process. Furthermore, the Toegyean Great Ultimate is dynamic in and of itself: In its active phase, it issues from the Non-Ultimate's (i.e., the one Pattern's) indeterminate pure potentiality for harmony into an infinite multiplicity of potentially harmonious or empathetic patterns; in its receptive phase, it gathers the multiple patterns back into the Non-Ultimate and holds them together in an overarching plurisingular Harmony of harmonies full of creative contrasts between the old and the new. If logical Idea has a "trinitarian" structure in which the universal One and the particular Many are mediated by the individual or singular Harmony that best articulates the "logic" of the logical Idea, the Great Ultimate possesses a similar triadic logic in which the indeterminate and quiescent one Pattern (i.e., the Non-Ultimate or the Great Ultimate as substance) and many potential individual patterns are mediated by the Great Ultimate as function that best captures the dynamic sense of pattern as "patterning."

The mediating trinitarian or triadic logic of their respective conceptions of the ontological ultimate enables Hegel and Toegye in principle to affirm the primordiality and ontological ultimacy of multiplicity.

They agree that that the ultimate is neither simple One nor mere Nothingness but the plurisingular Whole or Harmony that precedes and grounds the universe as a dynamic activity of creating harmonies out of multiplicities. Insofar as Hegel construes the universal One within the trinitarian structure of the logical Idea as indeterminate pure potentiality for concrete—that is, internally differentiated—unity and harmony, the particular Many is intrinsic to the universal One. This ontological symmetry between one and many makes the logical Idea's openness to difference, multiplicity, and novelty as primordial and ultimate as its self-presence and self-identity. It is precisely this ontological symmetry that grounds the absolute—"absolving" and affirmatively reconciling—receptivity of the universal One toward the particular Many and enables the overreaching capacity and genuine infinity of the Idea. Similarly, Toegye's strict adherence to Zhu Xi's symmetrical and interdependent construction of the substance/function relation enables the relationship between the one Pattern and many potential individual patterns within the triadic inner structure of the Great Ultimate to be more or less ontologically symmetrical, insofar as the Great Ultimate is spoken "logically" in abstraction from psychophysical energy. To speak in terms of my sketch of a Neo-Confucian Trinity inspired by Toegye, an ontological symmetry exists between the One and many Ways within the plurisingular Spirit. This symmetry allows the One (i.e., the Non-Ultimate or the one Pattern) to be genuinely receptive to many potential patterns (many Ways) and makes possible a spiral dialectical movement between the receptive phase and the active phase of the plurisingular Spirit (the Great Ultimate as function).

Nevertheless, their shared affirmation of the primordiality and ontological ultimacy of multiplicity receives an injurious blow when the logical Idea and the Great Ultimate are not considered in abstract but as immanent in nature or in union with psychophysical energy, respectively speaking. Although nature and psychophysical energy differ from each other insofar as their possession of their own dynamism is concerned, they are comparable notions because they share the status of being the "material" and physical principle of differentiation and concretion which is without any unitive function and in relation to which the ontological ultimate becomes concretized. Hegel's logical Idea achieves the concrete actuality of the absolute Spirit—the Concrete Unity of concrete unities—in and through a mutually constitutive dialectical relationship with many finite spirits—concrete unities—emerging out of struggles against nature, here defined as the principle of inertia, mutually indifferent particularity, and dispersion into chaotic nothingness. Similarly, Toegye's Great Ultimate achieves the concrete creatively harmonizing agency of the heart-mind of the Way—the plurisingular Spirit—in and through a mutually constitutive spiral dialectic with many human and creaturely heart-minds, which are many potential Ways embodied in myriad coalescences of psychophysical energy and carried by its dynamism devoid of any unifying and harmonizing function.

It is to be admitted that Toegye's conception of the creatively harmonizing agency of the heart-mind of the Way is articulated primarily in affective terms—that is, in terms of the relational efficacy of creatively harmonizing feelings—and in that sense it is notably different from Hegel's primarily logical, cognitive, and volitional conception of the overreaching agency of the absolute Spirit. Nonetheless, precisely because psychophysical energy is given no creatively harmonizing dynamic of its own except the indirect kind it acquires when it is "mounted" by many potential Ways, the independent harmonizing agency of the human and creaturely heart-minds apart from that of the heart-mind of the Way—epitomized by spontaneously emerging human feelings and desires—is devalued, just as the overreaching and infinitizing agency of finite spirits is devalued vis-à-vis that of the absolute Spirit. The evaluative hierarchy created between the heart-mind of the Way and the multitude of human and creaturely heart-minds ends up being similar to the Hegelian asymmetry between the Absolute Spirit and finite spirits regarded as more or less plagued by the exigencies of their embodiement, that is, their varying degrees of closeness to the *an sich* spirituality of nature. What ultimately results from this is a serious impairment of the mutually constitutive dialectic between the unity of ontological creativity and the multiplicity of cosmic creativity, on the one hand, and a significant narrowing of the universal scope of the cosmic immanence of the Harmony of harmonies represented, respectively, by the Absolute Spirit and the heart-mind of the Way, on the other.

All in all, even with the salutary possibility of an affective articulation of the mutually constitutive dialectic between the Absolute Spirit and finite spirits that would balance Hegel's overly logical, cognitive, and volitional conception of it, Toegye ends up not really ahead of Hegel when it comes to dispelling completely the haunting shadow of a totalizing metaphysics of one Heavenly Pattern or one Master Spirit. In order to move beyond this impasse, what is needed is a different conception of psychophysical energy, one that constructs a more interdependent and symmetrical relationship between pattern and psychophysical energy by recognizing psychophysical energy's own contribution to the creatively harmonizing processes of the universe represented by the symbol of the Great Ultimate. Likewise, a different conception of nature is called for—one in which the spontaneous and seemingly chaotic play of difference in nature is recognized more readily as ultimately creative rather than destructive of the concrete unity of spirit, leading to a convincing affirmation of Spirit's open infinity, as declared by Hegel at the end of his *Phenomenology of Spirit*,[84] not Spirit's closed totality. For such a conception, which would be more open to affirming a real plurality of harmonious sociocosmic configurations emerging from our embodied—racialized, gendered, sexualized, class-located, etc.—and therefore multiple agencies, we turn to Im Seong-ju (honorific name Nongmun), the eighteenth-century Korean Neo-Confucian thinker, and examine him in conversation with Whitehead, Deleuze, and Keller.

# 6 Pattern and Psychophysical Energy Are Equally Actual

## THE EMPATHETIC PLURISINGULARITY OF THE GREAT ULTIMATE IN NONGMUN'S THOUGHT

Im Seong-ju (任聖周 1711–1788 C.E.), the eighteenth-century Korean thinker known by his honorific name Nongmun (鹿門) and widely regarded as one of the six "greats" of Korean Neo-Confucianism, is famous for his thesis, "Pattern and psychophysical energy are equally actual [理氣同實 *ligi dongsil*]." Nongmun developed this symmetrical conception of the pattern-psychophysical energy relation within the context of the early eighteenth-century debate among Korean Neo-Confucians, called the *horak* (湖洛) debate, which centered on the issue of whether human nature was identical to the natures of other thing-events and the related question of whether the heart-mind in its original state was purely good or a mixture of good and evil. The root of the *horak* debate can be traced back to Yi I (李珥 1536–1584 C.E.), the sixteenth-century Korean Neo-Confucian thinker and statesman known by his honorific name Yulgok (栗谷). Yulgok had disagreed vigorously with Toegye's "unorthodox" conferral of an independent dynamism to pattern and developed Zhu Xi's interdependent, substance-function construction of the pattern–psychophysical energy relation to the pinnacle of logical and systematic coherence.

### "Pattern Pervades; Psychophysical Energy Delimits": Yulgok and the Horak Debate

Yulgok takes Zhu Xi's core premise, that "Pattern unites, [whereas] psychophysical energy differentiates," and translates it into the statement, "Pattern pervades, [whereas] psychophysical energy delimits [理通氣局 *itong giguk*]."[1] The key to the meaning of this transposition lies in his innovative introduction of a contrasting pair of phrases, "pattern in its original condition [本然之理 *bonyeon ji ri*]" and "psychophysical energy in its original condition [本然之氣 *bonyeon ji gi*]."[2] Following and developing Zhu Xi's interdependent, substance-function construction of the pattern–psychophysical energy relation, Yulgok claims that pattern as substance, that is, the one Pattern, is pattern in its original condition "prior" to its concrete determination into many individual patterns by virtue of its being "mounted" on psychophysical energy.[3] Furthermore, he argues that pattern's concrete differentiation into individual patterns by being mounted on psychophysical energy does not harm or diminish its original condition as a universally harmonizing mandate.[4] This is so, he contends, because pattern in its original condition has no concrete existence of its own as a thing, being the one abstract unifying "logic" common to the myriad individual patterns.[5] As such, pattern in its original condition "pervades" myriad individual patterns as their universal common ground, making them similar to one another insofar as they are all patterns.[6] Because its original condition remains unaffected in the midst of the world of multiple concrete actualities, so to speak, one can say that pattern is determinately indeterminate or concretely universal.

When it comes to psychophysical energy in its original condition, by contrast, the story is different. Yulgok develops his notion of psychophysical energy in its original condition in a critical debate with the followers of Seo Gyeong-deok (徐敬德 1489–1546 C.E.), the contemporary Korean Neo-Confucian thinker known by his honorific name Hwadam (花潭), who advances what may be called a monism of psychophysical energy. Hwadam argues that at the ultimate ground of the world lies the One Psychophysical Energy (一氣 *ilgi*) which is in a state of utter clarity, stillness, oneness, purity, and emptiness (湛一淸虛 *damil cheongheo*),[7] and whose spontaneous differentiating movement gives rise to the binary of receptive and active psychophysical energies and eventually to the myriad thing-events of the world.[8] Yulgok takes the notion of One Psychophysical Energy and names it "the psychophysical energy in its original condition," with one crucial proviso: Unlike Hwadam's One Psychophysical Energy that is universally present in the world as its dynamic and creative ontological ground, Yulgok's psychological energy in its original condition has many places where it is not present.[9] Put otherwise, in a marked contrast to pattern in its original condition, once psychophysical energy in its original condition moves, producing dynamic differences and giving rise to diverse concrete coalescences of psychophysical energy, its original condition of "translucent unity and clear emptiness" (湛一淸虛 *damil cheongheo*) is readily lost.[10] This is the case because psychophysical energy in its original condition has its own concrete existence as a thing, its translucent unity and clear emptiness being one particular state of being among many. Having merely temporal priority, not ontological and logical priority, psychophysical energy in its original condition cannot be simultaneously co-present with individual coalescences of psychophysical energy that are no longer in a state of utter clarity, stillness, oneness, purity, and emptiness.[11] That is why Yulgok criticizes Hwadam for confusing psychophysical energy with pattern in the latter's conception of the omnipresent One Psychophysical Energy.[12] Being itself a concrete physical reality, psychophysical energy in its original condition of translucent unity and clear emptiness cannot "pervade" the myriad individual forms of psychophysical energy and thus play the role of the unifying common ground the way pattern in its original condition does. Consequently, owing to its lack of determinate indeterminateness or concrete universality, psychophysical energy can only differentiate, concretize, and make determinate—the view summarily captured by his statement, "Pattern pervades, psychophysical energy delimits."

Yulgok's bifurcation of a concretely unifying mandate and a concretely delimiting dynamism along the pattern/psychophysical energy division has implications that are relevant to my discussion of Nongmun's thought. First of all, it amplifies rather than resolves the problem within Zhu Xi's thought regarding the ontological status of multiplicity. Since Yulgok does not deviate from Zhu Xi's affirmation of the ontological ultimacy of pattern vis-à-vis psychophysical energy, that pattern acquires concretely differentiating power only derivatively in Yulgok's thought, by virtue of its being mounted on psychophysical energy, merely further reinforces the apparent ontological penultimacy of multiplicity in Zhu Xi's metaphysical paradigm.[13] That, in turn, makes the doubts raised against Zhu Xi, namely, the doubts about the possibility of a truly spiral conception of the Great Ultimate's creative movement that precludes a totalizing metaphysics of one Heavenly Pattern, applicable to Yulgok's thought also. Second, the bifurcation does not remedy the ethically baleful consequences of Zhu Xi's ambiguity regarding psychophysical energy's capacity to be the sympathetic vehicle of pattern's creatively harmonizing mandate—the capacity required by his interdependent construction of the pattern–psychophysical energy relation.

Certainly Yulgok's idea of psychophysical energy in its original condition is a decisive step in the right direction, as the balance, resonating power, and communicative capacity inherent in its condition of translucent unity and clear emptiness can in principle supply pattern in its original condition with a cooperative mount, so to speak, making pattern's concretely unifying mandate truly efficacious in the world. In fact, as Yulgok claims, the heart-mind of the Way is none other than pattern in its original condition mounted on psychophysical energy in its original condition.[14] The problem is that, for Yulgok, psychophysical energy in its original condition is merely one among many individual forms of psychophysical energy, and as such cannot be universally present to be a readily available and reliable carrier of pattern's concretely harmonizing mandate. This fact turns what is supposed to be the concretely unifying power of pattern in its original condition into a merely abstractly unifying power in most cases without a firm possession of effective dynamism to implement its telos. As a result, psychophysical energy in its original condition, as Yulgok conceives of it, cannot really assuage the doubts raised regarding the feasibility and efficacy of the heart-mind of the Way in and among human and creaturely heart-minds. It renders the creatively harmonizing agency of human and creaturely heart-minds devalued and casts a shadow of doubt on the mutually constitutive spiral dialectic between the heart-mind of the Way and many self-creative practices of somatic cultivation in various relationally embodied contexts.

Ultimately, Yulgok ends up with a scheme in which pattern with only abstractly unifying power stands over against psychophysical energy with only concretely delimiting dynamism. This ontological and ethical bifurcation lies at the heart of the *horak* debate conducted among the followers of Yulgok.[15] Those who belonged to one of the two main parties in this debate, the party that was called *hohak* (湖學), claimed that human nature was different from other nonhuman natures because the concept of nature primarily referred to the individually unique nature of a concretely existing thing-event, namely, the so-called physical nature (氣質之性 *gijil ji seong*). The physical nature of each thing-event was none other than the particular empathetic and harmonious patterning distinctive to that thing-event's constitution. It was a product of the one Pattern's concretization into many individual patterns by the delimiting power of psychophysical energy whose movement unceasingly produced the individual "vessels" of pattern in diverse mixtures of clear and turbid, pure and impure, and fine and coarse. The proponents of *hohak* averred further that the human heart-mind was a mixture of good and evil even in its original state, that is, before the human nature within it was aroused to issuing in either empathetic or nonempathetic feelings in response to its embodied interactions in the world. This was the case, they claimed, since the heart-minds of humans—like all coalescences of psychophysical energy—were diverse mixtures of clear and turbid, pure and impure, and so on, with varying degrees of impediment already in place toward a full resonance with the empathetic and harmonious promptings of the human nature within. Consequently, the difference between the heart-mind of the sages and that of the ordinary people lay in the very fact of the human heart-mind's variant constitution by psychophysical energy.

In contrast, the champions of the other party, which was called *nakhak* (洛學), proposed that the human nature was in principle the same as the natures of other thing-events, because the concept of nature properly meant the single original nature (本然之性 *bonyeon ji seong*), namely, pattern as it was universally present in all thing-events as the one Pattern, not its actual, concretized, and delimited existence as the physical nature in union with psychophysical energy. If there was a difference between humans and other thing-events, nonetheless, that was due chiefly to the fact that only humans possessed the clearest, most responsive, "awakened," and therefore "spiritual" coalescence of psychophysical energy in the form of the human heart-mind, which, at least in its unactivated original state, was without any turbidity or impurity blocking the manifestation of the universal Pattern as the capacity for a fully empathetic selfhood. They argued, therefore, that the human heart-mind in its original state was purely good, and that the difference between the heart-mind of the sages and that of the ordinary people was not rooted in the heart-mind's very constitution by psychophysical energy but in external influences that soiled and muddied the original clarity and purity of the heart-mind's psychophysical energy. Everyone, they insisted, initially possessed the same and equal potential to be a sage with an enduring possession of the heart-mind of the Way that was fully in accord with human nature's mandate of empathy and harmony.

As can be seen, the *horak* debate takes up the thesis that pattern pervades while psychophysical energy delimits, and parses out its theoretical and practical consequences. The *hohak* school zooms in on the second half of the thesis, that psychophysical energy delimits, and consequently emphasizes the concretely delimited reality of pattern as it actually exists in the world as different individual natures, while denying the possibility that the human heart-mind as a particular coalescence of psychophysical energy could wholly retain the translucent unity and clear emptiness of its original condition. By contrast, the *nakhak* school latches itself onto the first half of the thesis that pattern pervades, and in so doing puts an exclusive focus on the unifying omnipresence of pattern in its original condition, while affirming a rather severely limited concrete efficacy of that omnipresence by insisting that, only in the case of the human heart-mind in its unactivated state, psychophysical energy does not lose its original condition. What underlies the entire debate but does not explicitly surface, however, is the question: Can it also be said that pattern in its original condition delimits (and thereby differentiates), while psychophysical energy in its original condition pervades (and thereby unifies)?

## "Pattern and Psychophysical Energy Are Equally Actual": A Nonreductionistic Nondualism of Nongmun's Thought

It is Nongmun who provides a daring yet systematically coherent answer in the affirmative to the above question, and thereby secures the ontological ultimacy of multiplicity, on the one hand, and the universally efficacious moral agency of the heart-mind of the Way, on the other. His answer is encapsulated in the dictum, "Pattern and psychophysical energy are equally actual (理氣同實 *igi dongsil*)," which he regards as the guiding principle of his thought.[16] What he means by their being "equally actual" is made clear in his alternative phrasing of the dictum, "Pattern and psychophysical energy completely correspond [to each other] [理氣一致 *igi ilchi*]."[17] In other words, his core claim is that pattern and psychophysical energy are both "actual to the same extent"—that is, they are totally parallel to each other in all respects, in all their modes of being and operation.[18] Nongmun derives this claim from the conviction that, despite his ground-breaking introduction of the notion of psychophysical energy in its original condition, Yulgok was wrong to deny the universal presence of its unifying and harmonizing power, thereby consigning psychophysical energy to being a principle of delimitation only.[19]

Psychophysical energy in its original condition of translucent unity and clear emptiness, Nongmun argues, truly fills heaven and earth and spans the past and present, for it is no other than its differentiating and coalescing movements that give rise to varying forms of psychophysical energy—whole and partial, clear and turbid, pure and impure, and so on—and ultimately to the myriad thing-events of the world, all the way from heaven and earth down to a piece of excrement.[20] Contra Yulgok, however, he rejects the notion that psychophysical energy in its original condition is wholly transformed into and in effect replaced by those specific forms of itself, completely losing its original condition in the process on countless occasions. Although psychophysical energy loses its original physical form of unity, clarity, and purity as it acquires the myriad distinctions of clear and turbid, pure and impure and becomes thoroughly differentiated in the process of constituting the psychophysical endowments of numerous thing-events, it nonetheless retains the all-pervasive presence of the creatively harmonizing capacity of its initial condition:

> In general, the so-called psychophysical energy of translucent unity and clear emptiness does not have its own existence apart from [the concrete coalescences of] the receptive and active forces and the Five Phases [of Wood, Water, etc.]. It is only that, as this psychophysical energy moves to become the active force and comes to rest to become the receptive force, becomes Wood as its operation reaches the springtime and becomes Water as its operation reaches the summertime . . . it [at the same time] runs through the receptive and active forces and the Five Phases, and is not delimited or restricted by them.[21]

In his novel conception of psychophysical energy in its original condition, Nongmun is indebted to Zhang Zai (張載 1020–1077 C.E.) of the Chinese Northern Song Dynasty, who, like Hwadam, advances a monism of psychophysical energy. Zhang Zai argues that at the ultimate ground of the world lies the Great Void (太虛 *taixu*), which he identifies with the One Psychophysical Energy (一氣 *yiqi*) in a state of utter stillness, purity, and translucent unity, and which he calls "the original substance of psychophysical energy" (氣之本體 *qi zhi benti*). The Great Void moves spontaneously to create internal differences and to give rise to the binary of receptive and active psychophysical energies. The emergence and passing away of the myriad thing-events of the world is explained in terms of the coalescence and diffusion of the One Psychophysical Energy that is universally present in the world as its dynamic and creative ground.[22]

While having been inspired by Zhang Zai's notion of the original substance of psychophysical energy in a state of all-pervasive translucent unity, as a Neo-Confucian standing in the line of the Cheng-Zhu school's qualified dualism, Nongmun takes that notion further to relate it to the Mencian notion of "vast, flood-like psychophysical energy" harboring an intrinsic moral teleology traditionally associated with pattern.[23] Nongmun argues that, although the original substance of psychophysical energy may lose the physical appearance of utter clarity, stillness, and emptiness in the process of its concrete differentiation into myriad individual coalescences of psychophysical energy, the balance, resonating power, and communicative capacity characteristic of its original condition remain unaffected and continue to provide pattern in its original condition with a ubiquitously available and fully cooperative carrier of its unifying and creatively harmonizing mandate. For evidence, Nongmun points to the all-pervasive phenomenon of the "life-giving intention" (生意 *saengui/shengyi*) championed by Cheng Hao[24] and Zhu Xi, namely, the ontological and cosmic creativity manifest in and through the very being of the individual thing-events and their power either to flourish according to their respective natures or to support one another in doing so.[25] For example, one cannot find any trace of the original physical state of translucent unity and clear emptiness in the particular coalescence of psychophysical energy that is a heap of dung. Nevertheless, when it is given to a crop as fertilizer, the latter's hundredfold growth and yield give witness to the efficacious presence of the creatively harmonizing mandate of pattern as it is mounted on psychophysical energy in its original condition:

> If [the numbers] one and two are added up to form three, as soon as three appears, one and two pass away. When the [Great] Void congeals to become thing-events, as soon as thing-events are completed, the Void is no longer visible. Nevertheless, although not even a shadow of the translucent unity and clear emptiness [of the psychophysical energy in its original condition] is found in the midst of the stench, filth, and impurity of manure, when manure is given to the rice-field, sprouts shoot up rapidly, thereby revealing the original substance of the incessant generativity of heaven and earth in its full vigor, as of old. From this, one can see that there is no place which this psychophysical energy does not penetrate. The [psychophysical energy of] translucent unity is the original substance of psychophysical energy.[26]

The life-giving power of manure is but one among the countless—yet all individually unique—instances of the omnipresent life-giving intention of psychophysical energy in its original condition. Water flowing downstream, flame shooting upward, kites flying on their wings, fish leaping in and out of the water, horses galloping, and oxen plowing the field—all these are individually unique realizations of the same life-giving intention corresponding to the particular physical forms with which the myriad thing-events are respectively endowed. The psychophysical energy of translucent unity and clear emptiness pervades the myriad differentiated forms of itself without having a separate physical existence of its own, and universally provides them with the genuine and effective presence of the creatively harmonizing mandate of pattern, although the concrete shapes of that mandate's realization—the individual natures of the thing-events—are delimited and determined by their physical endowments:

> Even though people say each [thing-event] consists of an individual psychophysical energy, the so-called original substance of psychophysical energy is definitely present in each, manifesting itself in accordance with the manner in which each congeals. If what congeals is water, then its flow downward is none other than this [original] psychophysical energy manifesting itself and constituting the nature of water. If what congeals is fire, then its flames shooting upward is none other than this psychophysical energy manifesting itself and constituting the nature of fire. If we extrapolate from this the way the myriad thing-events are on the whole, [we can say that] although the natures of thing-events are different from one another due to the variations in the strength and weakness of their respective coming together, not a single one of them is not a product of the life-giving intention of this psychophysical energy.[27]

Nongmun's firm belief in the determinate indeterminateness or concrete universality of psychophysical energy, which is similar to that of pattern, leads him to make a string of paired and contrasting claims all pointing to the coextensive and equal actuality of pattern and psychophysical energy: "Pattern is both one and many [理一而萬 *i il-i-man*]" and "Psychophysical energy is both one and many [氣一而萬 *gi il-i-man*]"; "Pattern unites, pattern differentiates [理同理異 *idong i-i*]" and "Psychophysical energy unites, psychophysical energy differentiates [氣同氣異 *gidong gi-i*]"; "Pattern pervades, pattern delimits [理通理局 *itong iguk*]" and "Psychophysical energy pervades, psychophysical energy delimits [氣通氣局 *gitong gi-guk*]."[28] In making these assertions, he is refusing to read one of the cardinal theses of Neo-Confucianism, that pattern is one, but its manifestations are many (理一分殊 *i-il bunsu/liyi fenshu*), as meaning either that pattern unites whereas psychophysical energy differentiates, per Zhu Xi, or that pattern pervades whereas psychophysical energy delimits, per Yulgok. Instead, Nongmun assigns to pattern a differentiating and delimiting function paralleling that of psychophysical energy, even as he recognizes in psychophysical energy the same universally and creatively harmonizing power as that of pattern. He ultimately comes up with what he thinks is the missing counterpart to the celebrated Neo-Confucian thesis cited above: "Psychophysical energy is one, but its manifestations are many [氣一分殊 *gi-il bunsu*]."[29]

Nongmun's argument for the complete correspondence of pattern and psychophysical energy in all their modes of being and function steers him toward a significant restructuring of the qualified dualism of Zhu Xi. The more thoroughly nondualistic yet nonreductionistic conception of the pattern–psychophysical energy relation that results from this restructuring is encapsulated in the following well-known and often-recited passage from his major work, *Miscellaneous Writings from the Deer Hut* (鹿廬雜識 *Nongryeo japji*):

> There exists on its own one transparently all-encompassing and overflowingly large thing-event, which is so without anything making it be so.[30] It is infinite and vast, having no distinction of inside and outside, no partitions and divisions, no borders and boundaries, and no beginning and end. And what luminously reverberates throughout its entire body is altogether the life-giving intention, which goes around without ceasing and gives birth to myriad thing-events without being grasped. Its substance is called Heaven, original psychophysical energy, "vast, flood-like psychophysical energy" or Great Void; its life-giving intention is called virtue, origination [元 *won*],[31] or the heart-mind of heaven and earth; its constant circulation is called the Way or founding [建 *geon*];[32] its mysteriousness is called spirit; its being so without anything forcing it to be so is called the mandate [of Heaven], lord, or Great Ultimate. Essentially, all these are but names derived analytically from the various aspects of the transparently all-encompassing and overflowingly large thing-event; in reality, they are all one.[33]

For Nongmun, there is one ultimate reality, namely, what he calls "one transparently all-encompassing and overflowingly large thing-event [一箇虛圓盛大底物事 *ilgae heowon seongdae jeo mulsa*]" that is infinite and spontaneously self-existing without beginning or end. Various names are given to it, depending on the perspective from which it is approached. Heaven, the Way, the Great Ultimate, original psychophysical energy, the heart-mind of heaven and earth, spirit, and so on—all these designate the same ultimate reality looked at from different respects. This means that, when pattern and psychophysical energy are said to be coextensively and equally actual, what is implied is that they are different yet intertwined characterizations of the same ultimate reality, psychophysical energy being its characterization from the perspective of its simply being the way it is, while pattern being its characterization from the perspective of the reason why it is or must be the way it is: "Its being so refers to psychophysical energy, while its reason for being so corresponds to pattern [其然者氣也; 所以然者理也]."[34] In other words, if psychophysical energy characterizes the ultimate reality from its aspect of being the dynamic substance-in-process of all that is, pattern characterizes the same ultimate reality from its aspect of being the rational ground and normative governor of all that is.

In fact, the key to understanding Nongmun's nondualistic yet nonmonistic (i.e., nonreductionistic) construction of the pattern–psychophysical energy relation lies in the precise manner in which he understands the ultimate reality's grounding and governing operation identified by the name of pattern. He claims that the ultimate reality's rationally grounding and normatively governing operation is none other than what is manifest in and through the spontaneous movements of the same reality as dynamic substance-in-process, called by the name of psychophysical energy. The following passages from his writings articulate this claim:

> According to my earlier reflections on the meaning of the character "pattern," the two characters, "self" [自 *ja*] and "so" [然 *yeon*], should exhaust its import. As for the words "ought-to-be-so [當然 *dang-yeon*]" and "the reason-it-is-so [所以然 *so-i-yeon*]," their meanings all derive from "self-so." In general, that sons are filial and fathers loving, or that rulers are benevolent and subjects reverent—these correspond to the so-called "ought-to-be-so," which altogether stems from the spontaneity of Heaven's mandate and the human heart-mind, and does not come to an end. This [ought-to-be-so] is none other than the so-called "reason-it-is-so [所以然之故 *so-i-yeon ji go*]." . . . It is only by following what is self-so and cannot be stopped that one comes to observe what ought to be and cannot be changed.[35]
>
> This psychophysical energy exists in and of itself, and spontaneously divides itself to become the receptive and active forces, on the one hand,

> and the Five Phases, on the other, and again spontaneously produces human beings and thing-events. The spontaneity [of psychophysical energy] is precisely where pattern has its seat of government.[36]

What Nongmun articulates in these passages is the idea that, as what is "above" physicality and therefore intrinsically incapable of being grasped directly by our senses, pattern can only be accessed and known in and through the operation of psychophysical energy, which is physical and to which pattern is inseparably united. It is precisely in the unfettered, independent, indomitable, and incontrovertible spontaneity of psychophysical energy's creatively harmonizing operation that Nongmun finds the defining characteristics of pattern, that is, its originary creativity, sovereignty, and normativity.[37] Metaphysical pattern and physical psychophysical energy are two distinct yet intertwined, mutually irreducible, coextensive, and equally actual aspects of the "one transparently all-encompassing and overflowingly large thing-event." The two aspects together give expression to its visible and spontaneous movement of creative harmonization that constitutes the world, on the one hand, and its invisible function of rationally grounding and normatively governing the same world, on the other.

Nongmun's nondualistic stance sometimes appears to advance something like a monism of psychophysical energy, regarding psychophysical energy as the one dynamic substance of the world and pattern as a mere name given to the way it moves, as some of his critics charge him.[38] Arguably the most controversial statement of all is found in the following long passage from his *Miscellaneous Writings*, quoted in full:

> That which fills and spreads out through the entire expanse of the universe from top to bottom, without inside and outside and without beginning or end; that which produces countless creative harmonizations and, in so doing, gives birth to myriad humans and thing-events—it is but a single thing, that is, psychophysical energy. There is, therefore, not a slightest gap in space to accommodate the character "pattern." It is only that, in the light of the overflowingly great capacity of psychophysical energy and the way it operates as observed, when faced with the question of who or what commands psychophysical energy, one can only say that it is so of itself. *The Way or pattern is the name given to it by the sages in the situations in which its self-so character [spontaneity] is manifest.* Moreover, this psychophysical energy is originally no empty thing, for what luminously resonates throughout its entire body, inside and out,

> is altogether the life-giving intention. Accordingly, by its movement it gives birth to myriad thing-events, and by its coming to rest it gathers myriad thing-events back into itself. . . . Such is the intrinsic nature of psychophysical energy, which originates from its spontaneity to become the normative laws [of its operation]. *Faced with situations in which the normativity [ought-to-be-so] of its operation is revealed, the sages have given it the name of the Way or pattern.* Nonetheless, the so-called spontaneity [self-so 自然] and normativity [ought-to-be-so 當然] do not have their own separate domains, for they merely represent the same method of discussing it [pattern] in reference to psychophysical energy [就氣上言之]. While the character "so" [然] certainly designates psychophysical energy, the characters "self" [自] and "ought" [當] belong to mere figures of speech that illustrate the meaning of "so," that is all. If one is indeed capable of understanding what is intended [by these figures of speech], then even if one points to psychophysical energy and calls it pattern, that is also permissible. (Italics mine)[39]

By directly calling the dynamic substance-in-process of the universe filled with the life-giving intention psychophysical energy, which allegedly has no space to accommodate pattern, Nongmun appears to assign to psychophysical energy the status of the ultimate reality to which pattern is subordinated as a mere attribute or characterization, just as the words "self" and "ought" in his interpretation are reduced to mere linguistic illustrations of the meaning of "so." But it is crucial here to make a note of his self-declared method of inquiring after pattern, namely, the method of always "discussing it in reference to psychophysical energy" (就氣上言之 *chwi gisang eonji*).[40] The only way to access and speak of pattern is to discuss it in connection with psychophysical energy, "as if" the former were a function of the latter. There is "not a slightest gap in space to accommodate the character 'pattern,'" not because pattern is a mere attribute subordinate to psychophysical energy, but because pattern has no concrete physical existence of its own apart from psychophysical energy. That's why he speaks of the dynamic substance-in-process of the world as one, not two, and calls it by the name of psychophysical energy in this particular passage. Precisely because pattern is not a mere attribute of psychophysical energy, the one dynamic substance-in-process can be called either psychophysical energy or pattern depending on the perspective from which it is approached: "In general, that which fills the empty space, pervades all creatures, human and nonhuman, and goes around from the ancient times to the present, is altogether one psychophysical energy, and altogether one pattern."[41]

Hence, if one keeps to Nongmun's epistemological premise, then one can parse the above quoted passage as follows: if the "transparently all-encompassing and overflowingly large thing-event" is taken to be the dynamic substance-in-process of all that is, it may be labeled psychophysical energy. The dynamic substance-in-process is not an empty thing, however, but one filled through and through with the "life-giving-intention." The manifestation of the life-giving intention of the dynamic substance-in-process, namely, its generation of myriad thing-events in its active phase and gathering them back into itself in its receptive phase, is a spontaneous operation that never ceases or deviates from its course.[42] Put otherwise, the operation of the life-giving-intention is no other than the intrinsic nature of the dynamic substance-in-process—the very nature that derives from the unfettered spontaneity of the dynamic substance and manifests itself as the rationally grounding and normatively governing operation of the same substance. The sages have given the name of the Way, pattern, or the Great Ultimate to the spontaneity-become-reason or spontaneity-become-normativity of the dynamic substance-in-process, which is clearly demonstrated in the life-giving intention and yet, being itself without physicality, cannot be juxtaposed spatiotemporally next to psychophysical energy as if it were a concrete thing.

The fact that the life-giving-intention derives from the unfettered spontaneity of the dynamic substance (called by the name of psychophysical energy), and manifests itself as the rationally grounding and normatively governing operation of the same substance (called by the name of pattern), implies that the life-giving intention is a joint manifestation of both psychophysical energy and pattern. In other words, the intrinsically creative nature of the dynamic substance-in-process gives witness to the fact that the ultimate reality consists of both psychophysical energy and pattern, one physical and the other metaphysical. To put it another way, the ultimate reality is both physical and metaphysical, both "with form" and "above form." Pattern is the name given to the metaphysical transcendence of the dynamic substance-in-process in its capacity as the rational ground and governing norm underneath, above, and beyond the world of myriad thing-events. At the same time, the fact that pattern can be accessed only in and through the spontaneously generative operation of psychophysical energy means that the metaphysical transcendence of the dynamic substance-in-process is made concretely meaningful only in and through its physical immanence in the world, as manifest in the seemingly self-creative, self-grounding, and self-governing operations of the countless coalescences of psychophysical energy, namely, the ten thousand thing-events.

Hence, Nongmun's conception of "one transparently all-encompassing and overflowingly large thing-event" may be called internally dipolar: Its two constitutive aspects, pattern and psychophysical energy, are neither one nor two. They are conceptually different, but in concrete reality inseparable from each other. The relationship between the two cannot therefore be construed dialectically, in terms of *sic et non*, of affirmation and negation, assuming the independent existence of the poles first and then asking how they are related to each other. The distinction between pattern and psychophysical energy is a strictly relational distinction located within the same dynamic substance-in-process and based on the relationship between its function as the structural/normative ground of the world, on the one hand, and its function as the dynamic ground of the world, on the other. Being nondual—neither one nor two—these "two" grounds are given coextensively and equally constitutive roles in producing the myriad unities or harmonies of the world.

Nongmun's internally dipolar construction of the "one transparently all-encompassing and overflowingly large thing-event" leads to a parallel conception of the relationship between pattern in its original condition and psychophysical energy in its original condition as they operate jointly as the life-giving intention. He identifies Heaven, which is traditionally a symbol of pattern, with the psychophysical energy of translucent unity and clear emptiness, which he in turn associates with the wide-open expanse of the blue sky.[43] At the same time, he refuses to posit pattern as the metaphysical reason and ground of being above and beyond that physically wide-open expanse of blue sky, citing the classical reference in the Classic of Change, "The successive movement of the receptive and active forces is called the Way" (一陰一陽之謂道), and interpreting it through the lens of Cheng Hao's famous dictum, "The vessel is also the Way; the Way is also the vessel" (器亦道道亦器).[44] Taken as the supreme reality and the highest good, on the one hand, and the wide-open expanse of the blue sky, on the other, Heaven encompasses both pattern and psychophysical energy in their original condition, the latter being its substance and the former being its virtue.[45] His firm conviction regarding the thoroughly interdependent and mutually irreducible presence of both pattern and psychophysical energy in their original condition within one ultimate reality, which is evident in the creatively harmonizing operation of the dynamic substance-in-process symbolized by Heaven, is captured in the following passage from his letter to a friend and critic:

> If we speak from the perspective of pattern, then because pattern is originally pure, psychophysical energy is pure in and of itself. . . . If we speak from the perspective of psychophysical energy, then once there is the purity of psychophysical energy, there is the purity of pattern. . . . If pattern is not pure, then psychophysical energy is certainly not pure in and of itself (that is to say, if there is no pattern of ceaseless generativity and pure unity, then there is no psychophysical energy of ceaseless generativity and pure unity to begin with, and nothing exists at all).[46] If psychophysical energy is not pure, then can pattern alone be pure, hanging in empty space (that is to say, if psychophysical energy were not ceaselessly generative and purely one, then where else could we observe the ceaseless generativity and pure unity of pattern)? These few words, root and branch, are completely satisfactory on their own and cannot be refuted. Even if the sages were to appear again, they would not be able to alter what I have said.[47]

What is articulated in these carefully crafted yet forceful statements is the precise manner in which the psychophysical energy of translucent unity and clear emptiness is coextensively and equally actual with the one Pattern. Although the bottomlessly generative mandate of pattern in its original condition is the very ground and fountain of the unlimited spontaneously generative power of psychophysical energy in its original condition, without the latter the former is nowhere to be found—it is as if the former did not exist. In other words, within the dipolar constitution of the dynamic substance-in-process of all that is, the life-giving intention of the psychophysical energy of translucent unity and clear emptiness has its roots in the one Pattern's life-giving mandate while providing the latter with a wholly sympathetic dynamism in the form of its own unfettered and irresistibly harmonizing spontaneity—that is, the very spontaneity that allows the life-giving mandate to be fully efficacious in and among myriad thing-events as their self-creative and self-governing power.[48]

One can see here that Nongmun's nondualistic and nonreductionistic thesis, namely, the coextensive and equal actuality of pattern and psychophysical energy, compels him to deviate noticeably from the dominant

Neo-Confucian recognition of a kind of ontological causality between pattern and psychophysical energy. To be sure, on rare occasions—in fact, just once in his entire corpus—he does gesture toward conferring on pattern a sense of ontological and normative priority over psychophysical energy when he includes even the psychophysical energy of translucent unity and clear emptiness itself, which corresponds to the self-so or unfettered spontaneity of the dynamic substance-in-process, in the category of all that is rooted in pattern as the name for the rationally grounding and governing function of the same dynamic substance-in-process. This can be seen in the following, fairly traditional, statement of his, partially quoting Zhu Xi: "The original substance of psychophysical energy is that which roots itself in pattern to emerge daily [氣本體, 根於理而日生者]."[49] Nonetheless, his pivotal claim, that pattern's grounding and governing function is none other than what is manifest in and through psychophysical energy's spontaneous movements, effectively cuts off any possibility of interpreting the relationship between pattern and psychophysical energy as an external relation of causation, influence, and control. In keeping with the overall thrust of his construction of the pattern-psychophysical energy relation, one should read the statement as pointing to the fact that the self-so or spontaneity of the dynamic substance-in-process *follows and keeps to* the rationally grounding and normative governing function of the same dynamic substance-in-process. Indeed, the statement is another way of saying that the unfettered spontaneity of the dynamic substance-in-process reveals itself as the life-giving intention—in other words, that it tends fundamentally toward the production of valuable and meaningful harmonies that are myriad thing-events. That is why the statement does not contradict his pivotal claim that the rationally grounding and normatively governing operation of pattern in its original condition is what is manifest in the spontaneous movements of psychophysical energy in its original condition. Given the prevailing Neo-Confucian view that pattern lacks its own spontaneous dynamism, and that therefore pattern and psychophysical energy must always be seen as bound together in a relation of interdependence, his symmetrically dipolar construction of the pattern–psychophysical energy relation achieves the status of being one of the most systematically coherent and phenomenologically persuasive articulations within the parameters of the Neo-Confucian nonreductionistic nondualism.

## "All Figures Are Luxuriantly Present": The Empathetic Plurisingularity of the Great Ultimate

Nongmun's thesis of the coextensive and equal actuality of pattern and psychophysical energy ultimately enables him to arrive at an innovative conception of the substance-function relation as it concerns the Great Ultimate. True to his thesis, he neither discusses the Great Ultimate as substance only in terms of unity by abstracting pattern from psychophysical energy nor introduces multiplicity into the Great Ultimate as function by appealing to pattern's actual union with psychophysical energy. He sees no need to abstract pattern in its original condition from psychophysical energy—and then call it the substance of the Great Ultimate—in order to safeguard what is supposed to be the primordial unity of the world, because psychophysical energy in its original condition is not only a differentiating and delimiting power but a unifying and harmonizing power also. Furthermore, since pattern and psychophysical energy are not to be considered in abstraction from each other, in accounting for the actual multiplicity of the world he does not isolate psychophysical energy alone as the one responsible and accordingly attribute the beginning of multiplicity to pattern's concrete union with psychophysical energy, calling their union the function of the Great Ultimate. In other words, true to his core claim of the complete correspondence of pattern and psychophysical energy, Nongmun's conception of the Great Ultimate's substance/function polarity does not follow the dominant Neo-Confucian paradigm that is structured along a quasi-dualistic divide between primordial metaphysical unity—represented by pattern—on the one hand, and actual physical multiplicity represented by psychophysical energy—on the other.

This innovative stance is captured well in the following statements of Nongmun's, commenting on Cheng Yi's well-known sayings to discuss the intrinsic unity *and* multiplicity of the original nature, that is, the Great Ultimate as the one Pattern universally present in all thing-events, which is traditionally conceived primarily in terms of unity:

> If we take only the one origin to be the original nature, and regard the myriad differentiations as having been affected by the physicality of psychophysical energy and therefore not capable of being the original nature, then we are especially being ignorant of the fact that the so-called myriad differentiations have emerged from the one origin as well, not

> from empty space as if they were things without any root. The one origin is the substance of the original nature, and the myriad differentiations constitute the function of the original nature. . . . Cheng Yi said, "The myriad thing-events each have a single pattern, and the myriad patterns together emerge from the one origin." Given what he said about their emerging together from the one origin, how can the myriad patterns not be the original nature? He also said, "Empty and tranquil, and without any sign, yet all figures are already luxuriantly present in it. . . . [Like a hundred-foot tree], from roots and stem to branches and leaves, all of it forms a single thread." Given what he said about it altogether forming a single thread, how can the so-called "all figures" not be the original nature?[50]

As is evident in these statements, Nongmun rejects the Cheng-Zhu school's traditional bifurcation of the single "original nature" and the many individually differentiated "physical natures"—the bifurcation that views the latter as less-than-wholesome versions of the former, having been affected by psychophysical energy conceived solely as chaotically differentiating power. We cannot, he argues, consider the multitude of individual natures to have lost the status and creatively harmonizing power of the one original nature, because the work of concretization through which they have arisen owes itself to the very act of the original nature, not to psychophysical energy thought to be a power wholly external to the original nature. To speak otherwise is tantamount to saying that the multitude of individual natures have appeared out of nowhere. The myriad individual natures have their condition of possibility in the original nature itself, not in an external factor such as the dynamism of psychophysical energy conceived as a chaotically differentiating power set over against the creatively harmonizing mandate of pattern. While the one origin constitutes the quiescent substance of the original nature, the myriad differentiations make up the dynamic function of the same original nature, here envisioned as the united operation in the world of the creatively harmonizing mandate of pattern in its original condition, on the one hand, and the creatively harmonizing power of psychophysical energy in its original condition, on the other.

If the one origin thus harbors within itself the condition of possibility for the myriad differentiations, what precisely is that condition? If the one origin constitutes the substance of the Great Ultimate as the original nature, what is in it to make the function of the Great Ultimate as the original nature profusely many? Nongmun has already advanced the claim that the luxuriant presence of "all figures" is part of the very constitution of the original nature. He appears to make that claim primarily in reference to the *function* of the Great Ultimate, when his assignment of many differentiations to the *function* of the original nature is taken into account. The following quote, however, speaks otherwise:

> "Empty and tranquil, and without any sign, yet all figures are luxuriantly present"—this is the *substance* of Heavenly pattern's original condition. The movements in succession of the two forces [*eum* and *yang*] and the Five Phases, endowing all thing-events each with their proper nature—this is the *function* of Heavenly pattern's original condition. Having no particular leaning or predisposition, allowing myriad patterns to be present in all their glorious luster—that is the substance of the original human nature. Four Sprouts and Seven Feelings mutually functioning to enable each human affair to obtain due proportion—that is the function of the original human nature. (Italics mine)[51]

The critical point here is Nongmun's argument that the dictum, "Empty and tranquil, and without any sign, yet all figures are already luxuriantly present," can be applied in its entirety to the *substance* of pattern in its original condition, just as the phrase, "Having no particular leaning or predisposition, allowing myriad patterns to be present in all their glorious luster," can be seen as a whole to describe the *substance* of the original human nature. To put it another way, multiplicity is as intrinsic to the substance of the Great Ultimate as it is to its function, whether the Great Ultimate is considered generally as pattern in its original condition as such or more specifically as the original human nature endowed in human beings. This is so, because the complete correspondence of pattern and psychophysical energy in all their modes of being and function leaves no room for a metaphysical or metacosmic transcendence of the primordial unity of the world, which is customarily represented by pattern and assigned to the Great Ultimate as substance, above and beyond the actual multiplicity of the world, which is traditionally accredited to psychophysical energy and allocated to the Great Ultimate as function. For Nongmun, one cannot understand the relationship between one and many only or even primarily in terms of a distinction drawn between the primordial unity of the world and its actual multiplicity, especially when such a distinction is made on the basis of the substance-function distinction interpreted as expressing a metaphysical-physical split. Instead, he sees intrinsic to the substance of the Great Ultimate not only the primordial unity of the world but also what may be called the *primordial multiplicity* of the world. Since it belongs to the substance of the Great Ultimate, the primordial multiplicity of "all figures" is in union with the primordial unity that is "empty and tranquil, and without any sign," and therefore yet without concrete actualization. In other words, the primordial multiplicity should be envisioned as a kind of *indeterminate* multiplicity and, further, even as a *chaotic* multiplicity that echoes the sense of being an impenetrably dense, bushy, and chaotically entangled overgrowth carried by the phrase "luxuriantly present [森然 *samyeon*]."

Insofar as the Great Ultimate as substance or the Non-Ultimate is an abstraction from the Great Ultimate as function, the primordial unity and multiplicity intrinsic to the Non-Ultimate also constitute an abstraction from the actual unity and multiplicity of the world. Yet it is one that is not metaphysical or metacosmic in a dualistic sense, because it is an abstraction of *both* pattern in its original condition *and* psychophysical energy in its original condition from their all-pervasive, active, and concretely—that is, determinately—harmonizing presence in the world. It is the kind of abstraction that may be described, with qualifications, in terms of "nascence" or what R. C. Neville has called "incipience." By nascence or incipience I mean—following Neville—a latent or germinal state ontologically more basic than the determinate unity and multiplicity of the actual world yet at the same time incapable of characterization except in reference to the latter as their incipience or the readiness to give rise to them.[52] Being "incipient with determination but not yet determinate"[53] the primordial unity and multiplicity of pattern and psychophysical energy within the substance of the Great Ultimate represent the kind of abstraction that is more in line with the fundamentally nondualistic and nonreductionistic intent of the substance-function distinction, unlike the metaphysical and metacosmic transcendence advocated, wittingly or unwittingly, by the prevalent Neo-Confucian qualified-dualistic constructions of the pattern-psychophysical relation. Even when abstracted from the dizzying array of the determinate thing-events that concretely exist, pattern in its original condition as the one Pattern, on the one hand, and psychophysical energy in its original condition of translucent unity and clear emptiness, on the other, are together not to be seen as constituting a sheer empty oneness. At the same time, neither are they to be construed as consisting in some kind of fully determinate manyness. The words "one" and "many" in this ontologically more basic state are figures of speech analogically taken from the determinations of one and many in the actual world and laboring in a dialectical relation to each other to convey the sense of the gestative ferment indicated by the notion of incipience or the readiness to give rise to something. With the dimension of limit-speech involved having thus been recognized, pattern and psychophysical energy in their original condition ought to be viewed as consisting in *the incipient or nascent unity of indeterminate and chaotic multiplicity* that quiescently lies at the irreducible beginnings[54] of the actual interrelated harmony of the world's determinate multiplicity. This incipient unity of indeterminate multiplicity, "after" activating itself (i.e., becoming functional in concrete reality), *pervades, orients, prompts,* and *becomes* that harmony through the incessant activity of creative harmonization that is the Great Ultimate as function.

Nongmun's characterization of both pattern and psychophysical energy in their original condition as the life-giving intention provides the key to understanding why the primordial unity of indeterminate and chaotic multiplicity characterizing the Great Ultimate as substance is an incipient or nascent unity. First of all, as can be observed in the following statement, Nongmun sees the primordial multiplicity inherent in the substance of the Great Ultimate as the sine qua non of its generative and life-giving power:

> The one Pattern is a wholly undifferentiated whole, yet all figures are luxuriantly present. Since the wholly undifferentiated whole is definitely the original substance, how can the luxurious presence [of all figures] not also be intrinsic to the original substance? If we were now to regard only the oneness of pattern to be the original condition and exclude manyness, then the so-called wholly undifferentiated whole would be vague and obscure, without anything present altogether. Accordingly, from the very moment it is to move to become active and to come to rest to become receptive, already it could not be in charge of anything to produce the receptive and active forces or the Five Phases and the myriad thing-events. Hence, if we are indeed to compel pattern [conceived as such] to fill the original substance, that would be possible only after the original substance is itself [conceived as being] merely completely empty, enormously vast, spotlessly pristine and clear, and thus without anything present altogether. I am afraid even Laozi's notion of vacuous nothingness does not go that far.[55]

Without the presence of primordial multiplicity, Nongmun argues, the Great Ultimate as the one Pattern becomes a sheer empty thing—far emptier than even the celebrated Daoist notion of the Way as Nothing that has been a constant object of criticism by the Neo-Confucians. If the substance of the Great Ultimate were a sheer empty One, he continues, it would then not have the wherewithal to generate the myriad thing-events of the world. In other words, the life-giving intention characterizing the operation of pattern in its original condition riding on psychophysical energy in its original condition would not be possible, if indeterminate and chaotic multiplicity were not an intrinsic part of the primordial unity of pattern and psychophysical energy.

It is to be admitted that Nongmun does not clearly articulate the how and why of the fecund plenitude of the substance of the Great Ultimate when it is conceived as consisting in both primordial oneness and primordial manyness, vis-à-vis the barren emptiness that would result if the same substance of the Great Ultimate were to be conceived as mere primordial oneness. Nonetheless, his definition of the life-giving intention as *empathy*, quoted below, offers a highly suggestive clue:

> Master Zhu had earlier asked a scholar, "If what fills the inside of one's belly is the heart-mind of empathy [惻隱之心], what fills the outside?" Do-am [Nongmun's teacher] interpreted his question to mean, "What fills both inside and outside of one's belly is altogether empathy." Do-am is correct on this. If we look at it [i.e., what fills both inside and outside] from the perspective of psychophysical energy, it is "vast, flood-like psychophysical energy"; if we look at it from the perspective of pattern, it is empathy. The two are in fact one. Empathy [惻隱] is what I have above called the life-giving intention.[56]

Nongmun's identification of the life-giving intention with empathy here no doubt reflects the long-standing Neo-Confucian tendency to cosmologize the core ethical notion of humanity (仁 *in*/*ren*), defined as empathy or sympathetic understanding, ever since Zhu Xi identified it with the universal and cosmic generative operation of pattern or the Great Ultimate as manifest in the fecund heart-mind of heaven earth. Nongmun goes further than Zhu Xi on this only insofar as he identifies humanity as empathy also with psychophysical energy in its original condition on the strength of his restoration of an intrinsic moral teleology to the "vast, flood-like psychophysical energy," contra Zhu Xi and Yulgok and following the original Mencian insight. However, Nongmun's assignment of a primordial, indeterminate, and chaotic multiplicity to the substance of the Great Ultimate, as the very condition of possibility for its creatively harmonizing, generative, and life-giving power, introduces an interesting and provocative twist to his continuation of the Cheng-Zhu identification of the life-giving intention with humanity as empathy. If the life-giving intention is to be identified with empathy, then Nongmun's argument, that the life-giving intention is predicated on the presence of the primordial multiplicity within the substance of the Great Ultimate, suggests that the life-giving intention as empathy may be seen as the function of a certain relational makeup of that primordial multiplicity—a relational makeup characterized by the existence of radical openness and mutual pull among the relata. But the question then becomes: Precisely how does a radically open and mutually attracting—that is, empathetic—relational makeup of indeterminate and chaotic multiplicity give rise to generativity or creativity? Going further, one may ask: Is it even possible to envisage the relational makeup of an *indeterminate* and *chaotic* multiplicity?

Since Nongmun does not himself raise or answer these questions, I will discuss them in the next, comparative chapter in dialogue with Whitehead and Deleuze. At this point, suffice it to say that Nongmun's distinct conception of the nonconcrete character of the Non-Ultimate or the Great Ultimate as substance, which is based on his thesis of the coextensive and equal actuality of pattern and psychophysical energy, enables him to advocate the equal primordiality of unity and multiplicity and thereby to resolve successfully the ontological problem of the penultimacy of multiplicity left unanswered—or answered only ambiguously—by Zhu Xi. The Non-Ultimate or the Great Ultimate as substance in Nongmun's conception does not refer merely to the one metaphysically abstract Pattern that is either deprived of difference and multiplicity, as in Zhu Xi's case, or forced to move on its own—that is, to become functional on the metaphysical and metacosmic plane—at the expense of systematic coherence in order to acquire difference and multiplicity, as in Toegye's case. According to Nongmun's innovative thesis, an indeterminate and chaotic kind of multiplicity is intrinsic even to the substance of the Great Ultimate, here conceived as the coextensive, equally actual, and inseparable yet mutually distinct union of pattern in its original condition with psychophysical energy in its original condition, even though he leaves unarticulated the precise relational makeup of that primordial multiplicity vaguely construed as empathetic.

Does Nongmun's thesis of the coextensive and equal actuality of pattern and psychophysical energy then successfully resolve the ethical issue regarding the universal efficacy of the heart-mind of the Way raised by Zhu Xi's qualified-dualistic construction of the pattern-psychophysical relation? To see whether it does so, one needs to examine his criticism of both *hohak* and *nakhak*. On the one hand, true to his way of discussing pattern always in its union with psychophysical energy, he agrees with the *hohak* claim that the concept of nature refers primarily to the so-called physical nature, namely, the individually unique natures of concretely existing thing-events determined and delimited by their specific physical endowments, and that human nature should therefore be seen as different from the natures of other thing-events. On the other hand, he sides with *nakhak* and takes *hohak* to task for not recognizing the universally efficacious presence of the original nature—i.e., pattern in its original condition or the one Pattern—precisely within those individual physical natures, thanks to the psychophysical energy of translucent unity and clear emptiness pervading the physical endowments determinative of those individual natures.[57] In fact, he even rejects the very distinction between the original nature and the physical nature on the ground that the individually unique natures of concretely differentiated thing-events universally retain their original impulse toward unity and harmony in the form of their shared life-giving intention.[58] In thus arguing for the universally efficacious presence of the original nature within the physical nature and going as far as to deny the very distinction between the two, Nongmun is in effect launching a critique of *nakhak* also, as the latter severely curtails the concrete efficacy of the original nature's unifying omnipresence, limiting it only to the case of the human heart-mind thought to be the only coalescence of psychophysical energy not to lose its original condition.

Nongmun and the proponents of *nakhak* at least agree on one point, that the human heart-mind in its unactivated state is just as purely good as the pattern embodied within it (i.e., the original human nature), with no distinction existing between the sages and ordinary people, owing to the heart-mind's constitution by the psychophysical energy of translucent unity and clear emptiness that fully resonates with original human nature's mandate of empathy and harmony. In fact, he insists on the original goodness of the human heart-mind to such an extent that he draws up the following corollaries to his main thesis: "The heart-mind and the nature are equally actual [心性同實 *simseong dongsil*]" and "The heart-mind and the nature completely correspond [to each other] [心性一致 *simseong ilchi*]."[59] Nonetheless, he has a much more expansive and dynamic view of psychophysical energy in its original condition than *nakhak*, in that he confers a universal, cosmic reach to its creatively harmonizing power beyond the confines of the human heart-mind in the form of the all-pervasive life-giving intention, although the human heart-mind's capacity for a fully empathetic and relational selfhood is the most complete manifestation of that power. He takes *nakhak*'s defense of the inherent moral subjectivity and agency of all human beings—the Mencian heritage—and establishes it within a wider ontological and cosmological scheme of things that is more systematically coherent than the dominant qualified-dualistic paradigm.

It is precisely on this point that Nongmun resolves the problem of the efficacy of the heart-mind of the Way. By virtue of the all-pervasive presence of psychophysical energy in its original condition carrying the universally harmonizing mandate of pattern in its original condition (i.e., of the original nature), the heart-mind of the Way can efficaciously realize itself in all heart-minds, be it the heart-mind of heaven and earth or the other creaturely heart-minds, through various expressions of the life-giving intention ranging from the vitality of plants and insects to the fully open, empathetic, and relational selfhood of the sage. The concrete manifestations of the efficacy of the heart-mind of the Way may vary. They will depend on whether the carriers of pattern's harmonizing mandate are whole or partial coalescences of psychophysical energy, as in the case of the difference between the human heart-mind and nonhuman heart-minds, or on how much of the "impurities" has been stirred up within human heart-minds all consisting of whole coalescences of psychophysical energy, as in the case of the difference between the sages and ordinary people.[60] All the same, the presence in all heart-minds of the creatively harmonizing power of pattern in its original condition, firmly in possession of effective dynamism to implement its telos, is never in doubt.

## The Apophatic Heart-Mind of the Way as Empathetic Space of Creative Freedom

At the end of chapter 3, I suggest a Whiteheadian reconstruction of Zhu Xi's notion of the Great Ultimate in which a conferral of primordial and ontologically ultimate multiplicity on the Great Ultimate enables its unending movement of generation to be conceived as truly spiral. The reconstructed Great Ultimate would always retain internal differences and contrasts—and therefore creative tensions—between the factual old and the hypothetical new, and thereby be able to ward off the threat of the totalizing metaphysics of one Heavenly Pattern. Such a genuinely spiral conception of the Great Ultimate's movement, I argue, would provide the requisite metaphysical context for a more liberating account of the process of self-cultivation in which the heart-mind of the sage is produced in a truly mutually reinforcing relationship between the heart-mind of the Way and the human heart-mind without a unilateral and unbalanced subjugation of "human desire" to the "Heavenly Pattern." At the same time, I claim also that such a revisionary work would be possible if pattern be deposed from its status as the only ontological ultimate and psychophysical energy be recast in such a manner that its differentiating dynamism productive of multiplicity be given ontological ultimacy by being reenvisioned as a creatively harmonizing dynamism capable of being the ground of order in the universe.

At the end of chapter 5, I also suggest that such a more interdependent and symmetrical construction of the pattern–psychophysical energy relation would be crucial to breaking through the impasse encountered by Toegye's—what may be called—"idealistic"[61] introduction of primordial multiplicity into the Great Ultimate. Toegye's ontologically symmetrical substance-function construction of the relationship between the one Pattern and many potential individual patterns within the triadic structure of the Great Ultimate's creatively harmonizing movement enables a conception of that movement as a spiral-dialectical one. In its active phase, the Great Ultimate issues from the Non-Ultimate's (i.e., the one Pattern's) undelimited pure potentiality for harmony into an infinite multiplicity of potentially harmonious or empathetic patterns, and, in its receptive phase, gathers the multiple patterns back into the Non-Ultimate and holds them together in an overarching plurisingular Harmony of harmonies full of fresh creative contrasts. At the same time, however, I argue that the Non-Ultimate's genuine receptivity to the multiple individual patterns is possible in the Toegyean paradigm only insofar as the Great Ultimate's creatively harmonizing movement is spoken "logically" in abstraction from psychophysical energy. In concrete reality, precisely because psychophysical energy is given no creatively harmonizing dynamic of its own except the indirect kind it acquires when it is "mounted" by many potential patterns, the independent harmonizing agency of the human and creaturely heart-minds apart from that of the heart-mind of the Way—epitomized by spontaneously emerging human feelings and desires—is devalued. The evaluative hierarchy thus created between the heart-mind of the Way and the multitude of human and creaturely heart-minds vastly narrows the range and scope of those individual patterns that can be considered as genuinely reflective of and contributory to the primordial and normative one Pattern, thereby courting a return of the totalizing metaphysics of one Heavenly Pattern.

I claim that Nongmun's innovative and systematically more coherent interpretation of the nondualism and nonreductionism of the Neo-Confucian dyadic scheme suggests a way forward, by helping us eliminate the deficiencies of the quasi-dualistic metaphysical visions of Zhu Xi and Toegye. Nongmun's thesis of the coextensive and equal actuality of pattern and psychophysical energy enables one to conceive the Great Ultimate entirely and always as a heart-mind, namely, as the most "spiritual" (*sin/shen*-like) embodiment of the pattern in psychophysical energy. In other words, one can imagine the Great Ultimate, both as substance and as function, to be the heart-mind of the Way, that is, the most wondrously creative embodiment of pattern in its original condition in the psychophysical energy of translucent unity and clear emptiness. The Great Ultimate as substance or the Non-Ultimate refers to the heart-mind of the Way as it is abstracted from the ongoing processes of creative harmonization and viewed as the incipient unity of indeterminate and chaotic multiplicity quiescently lying at the irreducible beginnings of the actual interrelated harmony of the determinately multiple heart-minds, both human and nonhuman. The Great Ultimate as function, by contrast, points to the heart-mind of the Way as the incessant activity of creative harmonization that pervades, orients, prompts, inspires, and ultimately becomes the concretely interrelated harmony of the myriad heart-minds.

This Neo-Confucian vision, inspired by Nongmun, is as panentheistic as the Toegyean version, because of the nondualistic, nonreductionistic, and interdependent manner in which the incipiently creative activity of the heart-mind of the Way and the actual interrelated harmonization of the myriad creaturely heart-minds are connected to each other, even as the former functions as the ontological ground and normatively governing telos of the latter. There are, however, three notable differences implying a conceptual breakthrough beyond the Toegyean impasse.

First, through the notion of psychophysical energy in its original condition, the Nongmunian panentheistic vision points to a way of conceiving the Great Ultimate as never "disembodied," even when abstracted from its creative harmonizing movement in the world of the myriad thing-events, while that intrinsic and perpetual "embodiment" in no way detracts from its transcendence of the world as the latter's ontological ground and normatively governing telos. Itself being a concretely unifying power transcending its own delimitation and determination into actual individual coalescences of psychophysical energy, the psychophysical energy of translucent unity and clear emptiness as the "physical" vessel of the one Pattern suggests what may be called *a panentheism of transcendent body* that abolishes the Toegyean vision's distinction between the "immanent trinity" of the One, the plurisingular Spirit, and the many Ways and the "economic trinity" of the One, the heart-mind of the Way, and human/creaturely heart-minds. This panentheism of transcendent body precludes the major failing of the Toegyean panentheism, namely, the serious dent made in the liberating potential of Toegye's symmetrical and interdependent construction of the Great Ultimate's substance-function relation by his asymmetrical and hierarchical construction of the pattern–psychophysical energy relation. The Nongmunian panentheism of transcendent body combines an asymmetrically interdependent dipolar construction of the Great Ultimate's substance-function relation with a symmetrical and interdependent dipolar construction of the pattern–psychophysical energy relation. Hence, pattern's embodiment in psychophysical energy in Nongmun's version does not transform the spiral dialectic between the One and many potential Ways in the "immanent trinity" into the empire of the One over many creaturely heart-minds in the "economic trinity." Similarly, the panentheism of transcendent body also challenges Hegel's trinitarian panentheism, which, despite its ontologically symmetrical conception of the relationship between the universal One (the "Father") and the particular Many (the "Son") within the abstract logical Idea (i.e., the "immanent trinity"), still opens an inviting door toward a dominion of one Master Spirit over finite spirits in the "economic Trinity," as Hegel regards all finite spirits as more or less plagued by the exigencies of their embodiment, namely, their varying degrees of closeness to the *an sich* spirituality of nature.

Second, by profiling the ontologically symmetrical relationship between the primordial unity and primordial multiplicity of the universe with far more conceptual clarity than is present in the Togyean version, the Nongmunian panentheism offers a fertile clue to the "mechanism"

(機 *gi/ji*) by which the primordial creativity of the universe comes to be. It is, of course, true that Toegye—along with Hegel—secures the equal primordiality and equal ontological ultimacy of unity and multiplicity. The Toegyean panentheism locks in the ontological ultimacy of multiplicity by assigning it to the function of the plurisingular Spirit (i.e., the Great Ultimate as function) within a symmetrically constructed substance-function relation on the abstract, metaphysical, and ontologically ultimate plane of pattern. It is also true that the Hegelian panentheism similarly secures the ontological ultimacy of multiplicity within the trinitarian-dialectical structure of the logical Idea conceived as abstract concrete unity and given the status of ontologically ultimate creativity. Neither of the two, however, offers an adequate insight into the *reason* for the abstract and nontemporal transition from the oneness of substance to the manyness of function or from the oneness of universality to the manyness of particularity. Put otherwise, neither Toegye nor Hegel provides a peek into the precise nature of the creative *restlessness* underlying the seemingly quiescent one Pattern or the universal One and prompting its nonconcrete transition to the dynamism of many potential patterns or the particular Many. Exactly how does the refusal to be content with the existing equilibrium or the constant "dialectical ferment,"[62] found in the creatively harmonizing dynamic of the Great Ultimate or the concretely uniting movement of the logical Idea, come to be?

The Nongmunian panentheism of transcendent body offers a provocative answer by changing the very terms of the question: The nonconcrete and nontemporal *transition* from abstract metaphysical oneness to abstract metaphysical manyness is not the issue, because the one Pattern or the universal One is in no need of issuing into many potential patterns or logically "positing" the particular Many. Within the paradigm of the Nongmunian panentheism, manyness is always already intrinsic to its oneness, albeit only of an indeterminate or incipiently determinate kind. In fact, it is actually the oneness of the one Pattern or the universal One that is to be explained in reference to the relational makeup of its indeterminate multiplicity. As we have seen, Nongmun opens a way toward construing the oneness of the substance of the Great Ultimate, which consists in the dipolar relation of pattern and psychophysical energy in their original condition, as the incipient unity of indeterminate multiplicity. Further, he points toward the possibility of conceiving the life-giving intention, interpreted as empathy, as the "bond" holding up that incipient unity. Following this lead, the panentheism of transcendent body imagines the quality prevailing in the relational makeup of the indeterminate many within the substance of the Great Ultimate not as mutual indifference but as mutual openness and attraction. It is precisely the empathetic relational makeup of the indeterminate and chaotic many that underlies the creative restlessness of the Great Ultimate as the heart-mind of the Way and leads to the always concrete and temporal transition from its substance to its function—that is, from the incipient unity of indeterminate multiplicity to the fulfilled or achieved unity of determinate multiplicity.

Third, by envisioning an indeterminate and chaotic kind of multiplicity to be intrinsic to the constitution of the substance of the Great Ultimate, the Nongmunian panentheism gestures toward an apophasis of the ontological ultimate within a basically rationalistic framework of construing the ontological ultimate. Moreover, precisely in so doing, it firmly grounds a liberating spiral-dialectical conception of its creativity initially suggested by Nongmun's symmetrical construction of the pattern–psychophysical energy relation. Given the conceptual difficulty of articulating concretely the relational makeup of *indeterminate* and *chaotic* multiplicity, the construal of the substance of the Great Ultimate as an empathetic unity of such multiplicity confers what may be called an apophatic, noncognitive depth to the ontological ultimate. At the same time, since the primordial empathetic unity implies a kind of internal interrelatedness productive of a creative urge toward order, albeit one that is minimally capable of being conceptualized, the primordial empathetic unity refuses to become the kind of apophatic ground and origin of the Great Ultimate that is wholly external to the Great Ultimate's principally knowable character as pattern—that is, something like the Daoist Non-Ultimate understood and criticized by the Neo-Confucians as empty nothingness.

Although not a totalizing void, however, precisely because it has an apophatic depth predicated on the indeterminate and chaotic nature of its multiplicity, the ontological ultimate does not allow itself to be construed overly kataphatically as either a single overarching Pattern pure and simple or a multitude of predetermined ideal patterns that is imposed on the way the multiplicity of the world is concretely harmonized. Such a moderately apophatic conception of the primordial creativity of the universe suggests a productive answer to the following question: Why is the substance of the Great Ultimate as the heart-mind of the Way capable of genuine and creative receptivity to the spontaneous achievements of the myriad thing-events returning to it in the receptive phase of the Great Ultimate's creatively harmonizing movement? As the incipient and nascent unity of indeterminate and chaotic multiplicity, the substance of Great Ultimate as the heart-mind of the Way offers an empathetic space of creative freedom for the myriad heart-minds of the universe. It offers a space in which the primordial empathetic interrelatedness of the chaotic many provides the condition of possibility and initial spur to the beginnings of the self-creative journeys of the myriad thing-events, each creating its own being-in-process fundamentally and initially as an empathetic unity of multiplicity. At the same time, being itself only indeterminate or incipiently determinate, the empathetic interrelatedness of the primordial many does not stand as a predetermined Order of orders presenting a competition to and demanding the submission of the achieved orders of the world returning to it. What it does, rather, is to propose ever anew radically novel possibilities of creative harmonization, which are not present antecedently in the returnees, on the strength of its own indeterminacy full of contingent possibilities of diverse determinate actualizations. In that sense, the substance of the Great Ultimate is a kind of "field of interrelated becoming" in which the myriad thing-events are nurtured and allowed to grow, to flourish on their own, and ultimately to offer their achieved orders in the moment of their waning as nourishment to novel others within the ever-renewing cycles of self-creation, rather than simply being dispersed into some kind of all-conquering totality or annihilating void. As such, the apophatic depth of the primordial and incipient creativity of the universe points to the kind of "virtual" creative order suggested by Deleuze's notion of *chaosmos*, that is, the creative harmony spontaneously emerging out of chaos and not preordained by any preexisting ideal order. This in turn resonates on multiple points with Whitehead's notion of the eternally concrescent togetherness of an infinite number of eternal objects in the primordial nature of God. This comparative discussion is the subject of the next chapter.

# 7 The Chaosmos and the Great Ultimate

## A NEO-CONFUCIAN TRINITY IN CONVERSATION WITH DELEUZE AND KELLER

In the preceding chapter, I offered an outline of what may be called a Neo-Confucian panentheism of transcendent body in which the empathetic interrelatedness of the primordial and chaotic many within the Non-Ultimate is offered as an explanation for the creative restlessness of the Great Ultimate as the heart-mind of the Way. At the same time, I left two questions unanswered or only preliminarily explored there: (1) By what "mechanism" (機 *gi/ji*) does the empathetic relational makeup of the indeterminate and chaotic multiplicity give rise to the creative urge toward order and harmony characterizing the Great Ultimate? (2) Further, and more fundamentally, what does it mean to say that the relational makeup of an *indeterminate* and *chaotic* multiplicity is characterized by empathy? Is it even possible to envisage or to characterize the interrelatedness of such multiplicity?

### The Empathetic Unity of the Great Ultimate and the "Unconscious" Primordial Nature of God in Whitehead

In an exploration of these questions, a comparison with Whitehead can be instructive, as the empathetic unity of indeterminate and chaotic multiplicity within the Non-Ultimate resonates on certain points with his notion of eternal objects within the primordial nature of God. We may recall that, for Whitehead, eternal objects as abstract, pure potentials do not exist in the primordial nature of God as a random, disjointed, and disjunctive multitude ("diversities in opposition") but as an all-encompassing set of disparate yet interrelated circles of mutually convergent conjunctive unities ("diversities in contrast"), thanks to God's infinite and complete conceptual valuation of all of them. As the general source of order and value harboring an intrinsic "appetite" for the beauty of harmonious multiplicity, God adjusts the togetherness of eternal objects so as to create infinitely multiple circles of mutually convergent pure potentials proposing an infinite number of possible concrescent harmonies, thereby providing metaphysical stability to *all* possible worlds conceptually realized—"envisaged"—in God's primordial nature. At the same time, being devoid of negative prehension, God's primordial nature does *not* adjust the larger togetherness of those infinitely multiple circles of mutually convergent eternal objects so as to propose a predetermined, overarching Order of some compossible orders that excludes some other incompossible orders. To put it another way, God does not choose the best among all possible worlds and thus does not preorder and predetermine the concrete paths of actual entities' interrelated becoming, despite the fact that such a predetermination of the best on God's part would only be a proposal and lure, not an imposition, thanks to God's always noncoercive dealings with the world.

A crucial point to note here regarding all these "acts" of God's primordial nature—"valuing," "adjusting," "conceptually realizing," and so on—is that they are not conscious acts in the full sense of the term. Since a full-fledged consciousness, according to Whitehead, involves *negation* in the form of the imaginative contrast between a given determinacy and a yet-to-be-realized alternative, God's primordial nature, with its conceptual realization of *all* possible orders without any negative prehension, is not really conscious. In other words, although named God's "mental" or "conceptual" pole, the primordial nature of God is not really mental or conceptual in the sense of involving conscious acts of cognition, evaluation, and judgment. This implies that the togetherness of eternal objects within God's primordial nature cannot be construed primarily in terms of logical coherence or conceptual unity, whether it is the ordered togetherness of compossible eternal objects forming the infinitely multiple circles of convergence or the larger, nonordered togetherness of those multiple circles of convergence. What kind of togetherness is it, then?

Given that Whitehead defines prehension, be it conceptual or physical, as *feeling*, God's conceptual prehension of all eternal objects is none other than God's conceptual *feeling* of them. To put it another way, by claiming that God as primordial is unconscious, Whitehead highlights the primarily *affective* quality of the togetherness present in God's primordial nature. Certainly what Whitehead means by *feeling* is not something purely subjective, referring only to the inner emotional state of the subject, but the subject's way of *experiencing* the object. Prior to any act of conceptual ordering on God's part, eternal objects are brought together within the "primordial mind" of God by God's certain way of feeling or experiencing them. A clue to God's way of feeling or experiencing them is offered by Whitehead's characterization of God as Love or Divine Eros consisting in an intrinsic appetition for harmony. Since God's primordial nature is unconscious, God's appetition for harmony is not—at least not yet—a desire for some kind of logical order or mathematical harmony, insofar as it is spoken in abstraction from the same appetition in God's consequent nature, which is conscious. Although Whitehead himself is not explicit on this, might it not be possible to say that, primordially, God's love of harmony takes the form of an unconscious or not-yet-conscious drive toward the kind of compossibility enabled by mutual openness and attraction, prior to and even apart from any kind of conceptual affinity?

If the answer to the above question is yes, then the seeming opposition between the ordered character of the infinitely multiple circles of convergent eternal objects and the nonordered character of the larger togetherness of those multiple circles of convergence begins to lose its dichotomizing force. The disparate or divergent interrelatedness of the multiple circles of convergence can still make sense as a kind of synthesis while not being outright a conjunctive unity formed of diversities in contrast like the circles of convergence themselves, if the former can be seen as sustained by the same affective, mutually attracting drive as the latter. If God's inherent "appetition"—the Divine Eros—for diversities in contrast gives rise to an infinite number of "efficient conjunctions," that is, circles of mutually convergent pure potentials productive of actual entities, it would be going against the grain of things to imagine the larger togetherness of those efficient conjunctions in turn to constitute nothing else than a "barren inefficient disjunction" of abstract potentialities suffering the futility of their mutual indifference. Although God's primordial nature may not order them into a single, conceptually all-encompassing Harmony of harmonies, insofar as they exist within God who is Love, it would be natural to think of their togetherness as somehow affected by their "divine milieu." Even if some circles of convergent pure potentials seem mutually incompatible and incompossible from a particular regional standpoint, be it that of the present cosmic epoch or of any actual entity, to conclude from that observation that they are, therefore, mutually indifferent or even opposed may only betray one's captivity to the totalizing dualistic logic of same and other. It is certainly possible from within the purview of Whitehead's thoroughly relational, organismic, and "panexperientialist"[1] paradigm to envisage their interrelatedness as characterized also by mutual openness and even mutual attraction, despite their radical difference and divergence.

By advancing the claim that the incipient unity of indeterminate and chaotic multiplicity within the substance of the Great Ultimate is an empathetic unity, the Neo-Confucian panentheism of transcendent body evinces the capacity for a sympathetic and affirmative reception of the above reading of Whitehead's God and eternal objects. First, the indeterminate and chaotic "all figures" within the Non-Ultimate may be likened to infinitely multiple circles of convergent abstract potentials, for the empathy seen to permeate the primordially indeterminate many strongly echoes the prelogical and preconceptual compossibility of the mutually open and mutually attracting eternal objects within God's primordial nature. Further, insofar as empathy is the name given to the life-giving intention of the Great Ultimate, suggesting a close relationship between empathetic interrelatedness and generative power, the *chaotic indeterminacy* of the "all figures" may be read to imply the *productive indeterminacy* of pure potentials brought together into circles of convergence by their affective affinity and harboring, like cosmic genetic codes, many divergent possibilities of determinate actualization. Once this twofold comparative analogy is established, a parallel may further be drawn between the incipient unity of the substance of the Great Ultimate as the one Pattern and the larger, nonordered togetherness of the infinitely multiple circles of convergence within God's primordial nature. Rather than being a unitary and conceptually all-encompassing Harmony of harmonies, the one Pattern may be envisaged as the boundless and infinite sum of peaceably interrelated yet disparate, divergent, and in some cases even incompossible circles of convergence sustained by the same relational force of empathy—mutual openness and attraction—as the individual circles of convergence themselves.

Nonetheless, notwithstanding all these rich and productive points of resonance between the substance of the Great Ultimate and the primordial nature of God, which has enabled a more concrete exposition of the empathetic and productive interrelatedness of the primordially indeterminate multiplicity within the substance of the Great Ultimate, substantial differences also exist between the two. The key point of divergence lies in Whitehead's purely ideal conception of eternal objects.

Because eternal objects as pure potentialities are merely ideal entities brought together in the "primordial mind" of God, they cannot "act" to feel, attract, and open themselves up and relate to one another; for only actual entities are subject-agents capable of self-objectification for and prehension of one another. This means that, if eternal objects are to be drawn into circles of convergence by being made affectively compossible, their mutual attraction must depend on the agency of a fully determinate actual entity that contains them all. In other words, their mutual attraction is strictly predicated on God's precognitive experiencing and envisioning of them in a corresponding affective mode.

By contrast, the primordial, chaotic, and indeterminate many within the substance of the Great Ultimate are not purely ideal entities brought together by a fully determinate thing-event's envisioning of them in a particular manner. We may recall that, for the panentheism of transcendent body, the Great Ultimate—both as substance and as function—is the one dynamic substance-in-process of all that is, not a particular thing-event or heart-mind. It is true, of course, that the Great Ultimate can in this case be called the heart-mind of the Way, but the latter never designates a particular heart-mind the way Whitehead's God is a determinate actual entity like all others. The primordial, chaotic, and indeterminate many are together not by being part of the "conceptual" or, more appropriately, "mental" experience of a particular heart-mind, but by actually making up the very being of the original condition of the dynamic substance-in-process, namely, the substance of the Great Ultimate or the Non-Ultimate. The critical point here is that, since the Great Ultimate is the one dynamic substance-in-process consisting in the dipolar relation of the one Pattern and the psychophysical energy of translucent unity and clear emptiness, the primordially indeterminate many themselves also consist of both pattern and psychophysical energy in their original condition. Given that pattern is what is "above form" and psychophysical energy what is "with form," the primordially indeterminate many can be seen to possess a kind of materiality and dynamism that warrants a conception of them as agents in a very preliminary and nascent sense of the term. In other words, their empathetic interrelatedness depends on their own "act" of relating to one another, not on a fully determinate thing-event or heart-mind thought to be capable of bringing them together purely "ideally" into productive circles of mutual compatibility. What this ultimately implies is that the Great Ultimate, which contains the incipient agents of becoming, is more like an all-encompassing field and matrix of interrelated becoming for the myriad things-events, closer to Whitehead's notion of creativity than to a fully determinate actual entity like Whitehead's God.

With a comparison of the Great Ultimate and creativity, we reach the level of ontologically ultimate categories. As we have seen in chapter 3, Whitehead's creativity is one of the three ultimate notions forming the Category of the Ultimate—creativity, one, and many—and the name for the ultimate metaphysical principle manifest in the cosmological fact of creative advance into novelty, namely, the all-pervasive cosmic process of creating unity out of multiplicity. Because creativity is a desubstantialized, abstract, and general notion of pure activity in need of further determination and characterization, the entities exemplifying creativity, both potential and actual (i.e., both eternal objects and actual occasions), may be viewed as self-creative and in that sense by themselves ontologically ultimate. Insofar as God is an actual entity, albeit a primordial, exemplary, and unique one encompassing all potential entities, God may also be construed as self-creative and therefore ontologically ultimate. This is tantamount to a claim that what is ontologically ultimate is none other than the empirically describable cosmos and that one cannot go "behind" the actual world, including the creativity which it characterizes and by which it is characterized, to find the reason for it. Such a claim is simply a restatement of Whitehead's "ontological principle" that refuses to ask the question, "Why is there something rather than nothing?"

Insofar as both the substance of the Great Ultimate and its function are made up of the dipolar relation of pattern and psychophysical energy, the Great Ultimate should be understood as "with form" through and through. In other words, the Great Ultimate as conceived by the panentheism of transcendent body shares to a certain extent the basic sensibility underlying Whitehead's ontological principle: The Great Ultimate cannot be viewed as a substantialized something standing "behind" the world of the myriad thing-events to be its raison d'être. Nonetheless, the Great Ultimate here has within itself an ontological depth that is not metaphysical or metacosmic in a dualistic sense. Despite the fact that both the substance of the Great Ultimate and its function consist of the same internally dipolar relation of what is "above form" and what is "with form," the Great Ultimate as substance represents the ontologically more basic state of the incipient unity of indeterminate multiplicity, whereas the Great Ultimate as function stands for the achieved harmony of determinate multiplicity constituting the actual world. Being "incipient with determination but not yet determinate,"[2] the primordial unity of indeterminate multiplicity within the substance of the Great Ultimate is ontologically creative in a way that can be characterized, barely but still meaningfully, as the very readiness to give rise to the cosmic process of the creative harmonization of determinate multiplicity.

Such a nondualistic and nonreductionistic account of the relationship between ontological creativity and cosmological creativity is another way of construing the fundamental paradigm of the panentheism of transcendent body, namely, the asymmetrically interdependent substance-function relation combined with the symmetrically interdependent pattern–psychophysical energy relation. Although similar to Whitehead's notion of creativity in its antisubstantialism, the conception of the Great Ultimate as the all-encompassing field and matrix of interrelated becoming is also different in the sense that it is capable of an account of ontological creativity. What is more, the account of the ontological creativity it offers is indeterminate and apophatic enough to preclude a totalizing metaphysics of one Heavenly Pattern while being determinate and kataphatic enough to resist a totalizing metaphysics of Nothingness. It suggests a fertile solution to the problem of the ontological arbitrariness and irrationality of metaphysical principles—such as the principle of creative advance toward novelty—within Whitehead's system by grounding their genesis in the primordial and only incipiently determinate "pattern" of empathetic interrelatedness within the ontologically more basic state of the Great Ultimate as substance.[3]

Now, at this point a question of substantial import needs to be asked: If the ontologically more basic state of the Great Ultimate as substance is a matrix of genesis filled with indeterminate or incipiently determinate agents of empathetically interrelated becoming, how are we to understand precisely their "acts" of feeling, attracting, and opening themselves up and relating to one another? In other words, if the incipient agents as bearers of ontological creativity are abstractions from the fully determinate subject-agents of the actual world yet can still be said to possess a kind of materiality and dynamism, how are we to comprehend their abstraction that is, apparently, not purely ideal? This question goes to the heart of the preliminary answer given in the previous chapter, that the incipient unity of chaotic and indeterminate multiplicity lies at the *irreducible beginnings* of the achieved harmony of determinate multiplicity in the actual world—an answer that is more of a metaphoric illustration than a theoretical explanation. Although we are here in the territory of limit-speeches with a very circumscribed prospect of articulating an answer fully, we have not yet reached the furthest limit of rational inquiry. I suggest that a comparison with Deleuze's provocative notion of "virtual" creative order suggested by his notion of *chaosmos*, that is, the creative harmony spontaneously emerging out of chaos, would be particularly helpful in pursuing the matter to that limit.

## The God of Anger and the God of Love: Difference and Relationality in Deleuze's Chaosmos

In his metaphysical treatise, *Difference and Repetition*, Gilles Deleuze (1925–1995), one of the most influential European philosophers in the second half of the twentieth century, proposes a cosmology that may be titled "a metaphysics of difference."[4] At the core of his metaphysics of difference stands what he calls "Idea"—a name designed as an intentional twist on the Platonic doctrine of Ideas. Deleuze's Ideas are not like the Platonic Ideas, which are unchanging universal essences independently and eternally subsisting behind changing particular phenomena and serving as the models or archetypes of the latter. Deleuze's Ideas are also dissimilar to Kant's Ideas of Reason as the regulative ideals of unity, which are postulated to enable both a transcendental condition of possibility for our experience of objects, on the one hand, and a rationalistic ethics, on the other. Deleuze's Ideas are aimed at providing an account of the conditions for the genesis of the objects themselves as they are given to us, not of the conditions for the possibility of our experience of them.[5] Further, Deleuze's Ideas do not explain the genesis of the objects in the way Hegel's logical Idea does, construing it as the creation of internally differentiated dialectical unities out of the contradiction and opposition between one and many, universal and particular. What Deleuze sees in the respective notions of Idea in Kant and Hegel is a continuation of the same Platonic scheme according to which difference is derived from identity in such a manner that speaking of the difference between *X* and *Y* assumes first the preexisting stable identities of *X* and *Y*. This Platonic prioritizing of identity over difference is exemplified in the hierarchical construction of the relationship between the Ideas as the eternal and self-identical models or archetypes, on the one hand, and the concrete, particular, and mutable things as copies or simulacra, that is, imperfect representations of the perfect Ideas, on the other.[6]

What Deleuze attempts with his concept of Idea is a reversal or overturning of Platonism[7]—a "Copernican revolution" in which identity comes to revolve around difference or, put otherwise, difference acquires "its own concept" rather than being subsumed under identity and turned into mere conceptual difference.[8] The nature of this Copernican revolution is encapsulated in the way Deleuze defines difference as "difference in itself,"[9] not as diversity or otherness predicated on preestablished identities.[10] By "difference in itself," Deleuze means that which differentiates itself from something that does not in turn differentiate itself from it:

> However, instead of something distinguished from something else, imagine something which distinguished itself—and yet that from which it distinguishes itself does not distinguish itself from it. Lightning, for example, distinguishes itself from the black sky but must also trail it behind, as though it were distinguishing itself from that which does not distinguish itself from it. It is as if the ground rose to the surface, without ceasing to be ground. There is cruelty, even monstrosity on both sides of this struggle against an elusive adversary, in which the distinguished opposes something which cannot distinguish itself from it but continues to espouse that which divorces it. Difference is this state in which determination takes the form of unilateral distinction.[11]

Difference in itself, in other words, means nondialectical, "affirmative" difference that differentiates itself unilaterally without its act of differentiating being dependent on that from which it differentiates itself—unlike the case of "negative" difference predicated on a preceding relation of opposition to another identity. Difference in itself is what Nietzsche calls "noble," namely, the powers capable of determining themselves positively and self-affirmatively, not in reaction to others and not following their lead in the attitude of *ressentiment*.[12]

Being, Deleuze argues, consists in difference in itself.[13] Everything, in that sense, should be understood as made up of forces that incessantly differentiate themselves from themselves—that is, again and again determine themselves unilaterally—as $X$ or $Y$, and then as $X_1$ or $Y_1$, and then yet again as $X_2$ or $Y_2$, ad infinitum. Further, this constant movement of self-differentiation goes all the way down: The smallest units of being consist in infinitesimally small changes, from $x$ to $x_1$ to $x_2$ and so on or from $y$ to $y_1$ to $y_2$ and so on, which in the language of mathematics are called "differentials" and denoted by the symbols $dx$, $dy$, and so on.[14] Being as Becoming, thus, is constituted by differential relations through and through. Everything is a series of infinitesimal differences that differentiate themselves from themselves—and thus create the series of differences that they are—without relying on a mediation with another by identity, analogy, opposition, or resemblance, that is, what Deleuze calls "the four shackles of mediation," all presupposing a prior conceptual unity.[15] The differential *dx* (or, for that matter, *dy*), therefore, stands for the nonreducible, ultimate character of reality as Change.

It is the differential *dx*, Deleuze argues, that stands for the Idea, which has a threefold character of being undetermined, determinable, and determined at the same time:

> The symbol *dx* appears as simultaneously undetermined, determinable and determination. Three principles which together form a sufficient reason correspond to these three aspects: a principle of determinability corresponds to the undetermined as such (*dx*, *dy*); a principle of reciprocal determination corresponds to the really determinable (*dy*/*dx*); a principle of complete determination corresponds to the effectively determined (values of *dy*/*dx*). In short, *dx* is the Idea.[16]

First of all, the respective magnitudes or values of differentials such as *dx*, *dy*, *dz*, and so on, which are all predicated on the self-differentiating and self-determining power of difference in itself, are completely undetermined. This is because Ideas consist of the *conditions* of the genesis of objects, not the objects given themselves, and, therefore, do not yet involve individuating or individuated states of *x*, *y*, *z*, and so on whose magnitudes of change or self-differentiation are measurable.[17] Second, as pure changes or differences, *dx*, *dy*, *dz*, and so on become determinable only when they are linked to one another and become functions of one another, as denoted by the symbol *dy*/*dx*.[18] An analogy would be the case of the convection process of water or air in which the rate of change in temperature is a function of the rate of change in density and vice versa. To use one of Deleuze's own examples, that of language, differentials are analogous to the phonemes "extracted from the continuous sonorous flux"[19] yet determinable only by their reciprocal relations, such as the English phonemes /b/, /p/, /d/, /t/, and so on, that are determinable only by their differences from one another. Of course, whereas these analogies assume measurable variables that are already individuating or individuated states (e.g., "intensities"[20] of temperature, density, pressure, and speed or "extensities" of qualities, forms, and parts, including phonemes), Deleuze's notion of differential relations within the Idea only establishes the relative determinability of the pre-*individual* terms or elements of the relations.

Last, the complete determination of the value of *dy*/*dx* is tantamount to the determination of *singularities* defined as thresholds or markers of phase transition in which the "becoming" of an event or object takes place.[21] To use the analogy of water again, water "becomes" water vapor, liquid water, or ice as its material flow undergoes qualitative changes of behavior at points where the instantaneous rates of change in temperature and density asymptotically approach zero to form the novel "events" of evaporation, precipitation, and freeze.[22] An important point to note here is that, again, we are speaking of pre-individuated states, whereas the analogies just used involve individuating states or individuals. Singularities are pre-individual. Nevertheless, singularities function as "attractors" distributed over the divergent fields of individuation (that is, fields within which events and objects come to be or become). The attractors give birth to and condition actual individual states as "trajectories" that approach the attractors always asymptotically—that is, always indefinitely close but never actually reaching them.[23] In other words, singularities are not themselves actual individual states but the stable points of value distributed over divergent fields of individuation and providing long-term tendencies by extending themselves into "infinite series of ideal events" capable of conditioning actually individuated trajectories.[24] The determination of the value of *dy*/*dx* is in that sense the determination of singular ideals to be actualized ever anew, differently and creatively, each time giving rise to multiple and divergent series of changing individual identities. To use an imperfect sports analogy—imperfect because it involves already individuated states—the Idea of football can be said to contain the differentials (the players, the ball, and the field), their reciprocal relations (the constantly changing ways in which the players, the ball, and the field interact), and singularities (the important thresholds or transition points, such as the players in possession of the ball entering the end zones or the ball crossing the goalposts under or above the crossbar). Changes in any or all of the three lead to divergent singularities productive of divergent lines or "trajectories" of football, such as rugby, American football, Australian football, soccer, which all asymptotically approach the Idea of football without completely corresponding to it.[25]

What is clear from the threefold character of the Idea is that, when Deleuze defines the Idea as *dx*, what he has in mind is a set of differential relations that form a transcendental *structure* or *system* providing the sufficient reason for the *genesis* of an object.[26] Because the differential *dx* has a determinate value only as linked to other differentials in relationships of reciprocal determination, the Idea is defined as a structure that consists of "the differential elements and relations along with the singular points which correspond to them" (210). The structure is transcendental in the sense that its differential elements "have neither sensible form nor conceptual signification, nor, therefore, any assignable function," and in that sense cannot even be considered as actually existent, being devoid of any concretely determinate identity (183). Similarly, the structure is transcendental to the extent that the differential elements' relations of reciprocal determination with one another are "non-localisable ideal connections" (183). Put otherwise, the reciprocal determination of the differential elements gives birth to merely ideal determinations of singular *values*, namely, generative or creative *ideals* to be actualized repetitively and serially (281).

Deleuze calls this transcendental structuring of the Idea "differen*t*iation" (207), and in so doing highlights its internal multiplicity (183). The internally differentiated multiplicity of the Idea does not, however, refer merely to the many or even to a combination of the many and the one, but rather to "an organisation belonging to the many as such, which has no need whatsoever of unity in order to form a system" (182). Within the Idea's structure or system, there is no point of view privileged over others, that is, "a centre which would unify the other centres" (209). When Deleuze says the complete reciprocal determination of the differential elements of an Idea produces a distribution of singularities, he is referring to none other than the decentered systematic character intrinsic to the internal multiplicity of the Idea, which makes that Idea a distinct type of "complex theme" (183) that is neither one nor many, neither universal nor particular, and neither general nor individual (176). Deleuze illustrates this pre-individual, singular character of the Idea's multiplicity by the analogy of white light. Unlike the general and generic idea of color obtained by a process of abstraction from the particular features of the individual colors (e.g., the removal from the red that which makes it red), white light, which is produced by having all the individual colors pass through a convex (convergent) lens, is a "complex of coexistence" (186) or "concrete universal" (176) that "*perplicates* in itself the genetic elements and relations of all the colours" (206; italics mine).

By the term "perplication," which is derived from the root word "pli" (fold), Deleuze points to the nature of the Idea as an "ontological fold"

(64) in which the genetic elements and relations of all the other Ideas coexist by "entering into" one another (187). Ideas are "varieties which include in themselves sub-varieties"; and the distinctions between Ideas are "inseparable from their types of varieties and from the manner in which each type enters into the others" (187). In other words, the distinctness of an Idea depends not on *what* kind of essential nature of its own it possesses but on *how* all the varieties of differential elements and relations are folded into one another within it to form its differentiated differential structure. It is in this sense that, while being neither one nor many, Ideas as concrete universals can be said to "contain all the varieties of differential relations and all the distributions of singular points coexisting in diverse orders 'perplicated' in one another" (206). Ideas are indeed distinguished from one another, but their mutual distinction is not static, as they are "objectively made and unmade according to the conditions which determine their fluent synthesis" (187). That is why "on each occasion, obscurities and zones of shadow correspond to their distinction" (187). Ideas as multiplicities are *obscure yet distinct* in contrast to the clear and distinct identity of essences.[27]

Deleuze uses the term "virtual"—or more infrequently, "embryonic" (Deleuze, *Difference and Repetition*, p. 209)—to refer to the internally differentiated and mutually perplicated differential structure of Ideas. What is virtual is not what is possible, for possibility is opposed to reality in the sense that it is only through "the limitation imposed by possibles upon each other" that the "realization" of the real takes place (212). Because abstract possibilities are infinite in number and variety, they are bound to include mutually incompatible possibilities or the incompossibles. This implies that the realization of possibilities can happen only in and through limitation, that is, a selection of some possibilities over other possibilities incompatible with them. Further, the real is supposed to resemble the possible (212), since the possible is conceived by taking the real and projecting its image into the realm of logical—if not temporal—priority taken as somehow "preexisting" the real. The virtual, by contrast, is not opposed to the real because it is already fully real (208), the reality of which being its structure (209–10). Rather than being "realized," therefore, the virtual is "actualized" (208). Deleuze calls the actualization of the virtual "differenciation" (207) in distinction from the differentiation—the structural character—of the virtual.

Deleuze casts the virtual-actual relation denoted by the concept of differenciation in terms of the relationship between a problem and its solutions: "Whereas differentiation determines the virtual content of the Idea as problem, differenciation expresses the actualisation of this virtual and the constitution of solutions (by local integrations)" (209; see also 207, 280). By calling the differentiated differential structure (i.e., the virtual content) of Ideas "perplication" with its connotations of perplexity, doubt, and hesitation, Deleuze intimates, perhaps unwittingly, the exhaustively problematic character of Ideas (187). The Idea as a problem to be solved, however, is not to be determined in essentialistic terms in the form of the question, "What is *X*?" Rather, the problem should take the form of the question, "How much, how, and in what cases?" which is tantamount to asking the manner in which all the varieties of differential elements and relations are folded through one another within the Idea to form its structure (188). Furthermore, Ideas as problems are not to be construed merely negatively as being identical to a domain of perplexity and doubt, for the problems also harbor a positive power of creation that manifests itself as a productive power of difference in the process of actualization or differenciation:

> The actualisation of the virtual . . . always takes place by difference, divergence or differenciation. Actualisation breaks with resemblance as a process no less than it does with identity as a principle. Actual terms never resemble the singularities they incarnate. In this sense, actualisation or differenciation is always a genuine creation. It does not result from any limitation of a pre-existing possibility. . . . For a potential or virtual object, *to be actualised is to create divergent lines which correspond to—without resembling—a virtual multiplicity*. The virtual possesses the reality of a task to be performed or a problem to be solved: it is the problem which orientates, conditions, and engenders solutions, but these do not resemble the conditions of the problem. (212; italics mine)

As indicated in this quotation, the problem-solution relation, which is captured by the notion of actualization or differenciation, does not consist in a production of copies from originals. Rather, differenciation, which "goes from structure to its incarnation, from the conditions of a problem to the cases of its solution" (183), is none other than a creation of "divergent lines" or heterogeneous series of differences that are merely oriented and conditioned by the virtual structure without resembling or copying it. When Deleuze construes the genesis of objects in terms of the "incarnation" of "the differential elements and their ideal connections" in "actual terms and diverse real [i.e., spatiotemporal] relations" (183), he is referring to the both transcendent and immanent character of the virtual problem (189), which "still objectively persists in the solutions to which it gives rise and from which it differs in kind" (280).

To use another one of Deleuze's own analogies, similar to that of "white light," the Idea of language can be likened to a "white language," which "contains in its virtuality all the phonemes and relations destined to be actualized in the diverse languages and in the remarkable parts of a same language" (206). When the differentiated differential structure of the Idea of language is actualized, the "fluent ideal distinctions" among the varieties of differential relations and their singularities are incarnate in the "specific and partitive distinctions" among distinct species of language each with its distinct, characteristic parts, without any of them being a copy of the Idea of language (206–7). This is what is meant by the claim that the actualization of the virtual structure of the Idea takes place by difference or the productive power of difference. Perhaps the analogy of "cosmic genetic codes" harboring many "divergent lines" of concrete actualization, which I have used as an illustration of Whitehead's eternal objects, could also be an appropriate metaphor here for the virtual structure of the Idea as the transcendental condition of the genesis of the objects given to our experience.

It is important at this juncture to note that the Idea's productive power of differenciation (actualization or individuation) is predicated on the way the power of difference and the power of communication are intertwined in the differentiated structure of the Idea. Deleuze appeals to the metaphors of anger and love to illustrate this core notion of his metaphysics of difference: "It is as though every Idea has two faces, which are like love and anger: love in the search for fragments, the progressive determination and linking of the ideal adjoint fields; anger in the condensation of singularities which, by dint of ideal events, defines the concentration of a 'revolutionary situation' and causes the Idea to explode into the actual" (191). To put it another way, the power of communication ("love"), which links heterogeneous differential elements and reciprocally determines them to produce singularities as complete determination of the creative value of their relations, is the sine qua non of the productive power of difference ("anger") that irrupts precisely from those singularities to produce divergent ideal series to be actualized.

Insofar as the process of actualization or differenciation is oriented and conditioned by the virtual structure of the Idea, one finds the "two faces" of the Idea incarnated or "objectively persisting" in that process.

Following Bergsan, Deleuze uses the word "intensive" to refer to the process of differenciation and in so doing captures the sense of the productive power of difference—"anger"—operating in it to produce gradients of extensities and qualities. When the "condensation of singularities" within the virtual Idea "causes the Idea to explode into the actual" (191), it is the power of difference that gives birth to divergent "intensive series" (281) as solutions to the "problematic" ideal series. At the same time, the distance between the divergent intensive series or "disparates," which form the fields of individuation within the intensive process, is bridged by "the establishing of communication between disparates" (246). It is precisely the productive power of communication operating in this act of bridging the heterogeneous intensive series that enables the integration of individuals. The act of individuation consists in "integrating the elements of the disparateness into a state of coupling which ensures its internal resonance" so that extensities (e.g., forms and qualities) could materialize as answers to the question "Who?" or "What is *X*?"[28]

Deleuze articulates the actualization or differenciation of the "two faces" of the Idea using the "trinity" of *complication*, *explication*, *implication*, expanding on the metaphor of enfolding and unfolding (*complicatio/explicatio*) that he absorbed from Nicholas of Cusa via Giordano Bruno:[29]

> The trinity complication-explication-implication accounts for the totality of the system—in other words, the chaos which contains all, the divergent series which lead out and back in, and the differenciator which relates them one to another. Each series explicates or develops itself, but *in* its difference from the other series which it implicates and which implicate it, which it envelops and which envelop it; *in* this chaos which complicates everything. The totality of the system, the unity of the divergent series as such, corresponds to the objectivity of a "problem." (Deleuze, *Difference and Repetition*, pp. 123–24)

Sharing the root word "pli" (fold) with the *perplication* of Ideas, the three terms, or poles, of the Deleuzean trinity point to the various ways actuality "folds" in response to the way virtual multiplicities "fold through" one another. First of all, *complication*, that is, "the chaos which contains all" or *enfolds* all that *fold together*, refers to "the womb in which finite determination never ceases to be born and to disappear" (43) and "the ultimate origin overturned into an absence of origin" (283). It designates the "formless *ungrounded* chaos" (69) that "retains and comprises all the actual intensive series which correspond to these ideal series, incarnating them and affirming their divergence" (281). In other words, complication should be understood as *chaotic actuality* whose "enfolded" materiality "corresponds" to the structured virtuality of Ideas and affirms the latter's incessantly diverging and decentering potential without resembling or "representing" that differentiated structure. Second, *explication* designates the divergent intensive series that *unfold* in and from the chaos in their mutual difference and, via the intensive process or the process of integration, come to form the actual extensities and qualities. It is here that "the totality of the solutions to the problem"—that is, differenciations and integrations—is traced out in the form of divergent individuated trajectories that together constitute the determinate actuality of the world (281). Finally, *implication* points to "the state of intensive series in so far as these *communicate* through their differences and *resonate* in forming fields of individuation" (281; italics mine). Despite their heterogeneity, when the divergent intensive series unfold in and from the enfolded chaotic actuality, they do so while *infolded* and enveloped in one another, thereby forming "fields" of resonance productive of individualized states.

Now, a crucial question needs to be asked: What is "the *differenciator* which relates them one to another"? (italics mine). What is this "force of some kind" (117) that enables heterogeneous series to communicate with one another and thereby to implicate and envelop one another? First of all, it must "relate different to different" by "connection in itself" (117), without any mediation by identity, resemblance, analogy, or opposition. Given that each of the heterogeneous series of differences in a system or world is constituted by the very differences between the terms *within* each series, the force of communication *between* those series is none other than that which "relates differences to other differences, constituting differences between differences within the system" (117). In other words, the "differenciator" is that which produces the second-degree differences that relate the first-degree differences to one another (117). That is why the "connection in itself"—or "difference in itself" (120)—is "a differenciation of difference" that "gathers the different outside of any possible representation" (117). Deleuze calls this differenciator "dark precursor":

> To begin with, what is this agent, this force? Thunderbolts explode between different intensities, but they are preceded by an invisible,

imperceptible *dark precursor*, which determines their path in advance but in reverse, as though intagliated. . . . There is no doubt that *there is* an identity belonging to the precursor, and a resemblance between the series which it causes to communicate. This "there is," however, remains perfectly indeterminate. . . . Given two heterogeneous series, two series of differences, the precursor plays the part of the differenciator of these differences. In this manner, by virtue of its own power, it puts them into immediate relation to one another: it is the in-itself of difference or the "differently different"—in other words, difference in the second degree, the self-different which relates different to different by itself. Because the path it follows is invisible and becomes visible only in reverse, to the extent that it is travelled over and covered by the phenomena it induces within the system, it has no place other than that from which it is "missing," no identity other than that which it lacks: it is precisely the object = *x*. . . . It perpetually *displaces* within itself and perpetually *disguises* itself in the series. (119–20)

The differenciator of differences which puts differences into immediate relation to one another is "dark"—invisible and imperceptible—because it is completely indeterminate. Being completely indeterminate, its absent presence can be known only by the "phenomena it induces" which, in the moment of their individuated emergence or mutually implicated explication, immediately "travel over and cover" the track left by their "precursor." That is why, "strictly speaking, difference should be inexplicable. . . . For difference, to be explicated is to be cancelled" (228). The differenciator as dark precursor, thus, is "the object = *x*" whose identity is precisely what it lacks in its perpetual concealment and displacement in the actualized or differenciated series of differences.

As can be seen, Deleuze's account of the virtual Idea and its actualization in the "trinity" of *complicatio—explicatio—implicatio* ends up verging on an *apophaticism* which, in its impossible effort to *think* difference, pushes the limits of human language to the point of producing near tautologies of the term "different," such as: "it is the in-itself of difference or the 'differently different' . . . the self-different which relates different to different by itself." His apophatic account posits the obscure yet distinct Ideas together with "the formless ungrounded chaos" and "the object = *x*" in order to identify, impossibly, the differential condition of the infolded unfolding of the actual world. The picture he presents is ultimately that of "the chaosmos from which the cosmos emerges" (199) or a "creative disorder" that is an "inspired chaos" (54). If there is a God in Deleuze's universe, it would be difference-in-itself, which combines the power of difference with the power of communication—"the God of anger" and "the God of love" (191)—to bring together heterogeneous actualities, that is, to create what may be called "the solidarity of those who have nothing in common."[30] This God would be the one who "at once affirms incompossibilities and passes through them"[31]—a schizophrenic yet loving God who does not even have to be one, for "given the variety among systems, this role is fulfilled by quite diverse determinations."[32]

## Empathy and "Connection-in-itself": The Affective Grounding of the Cosmos

The questions that led to the preceding exposition of Deleuze's ontology and cosmology can now be fully engaged. In what ways can Deleuze's provocative notion of the virtual Ideas and their actualization in the *chaosmos*, namely, the creative order spontaneously emerging out of chaos, be helpful in articulating the abstract yet not purely ideal creative agency of the indeterminate or incipiently determinate multitude—"all figures"—within the ontologically more basic state of the Great Ultimate as substance? Let me begin by highlighting a structural homology between the asymmetrically interdependent dipolar constitution of the Great Ultimate—that is, its substance and function—on the one hand, and the "unequal odd halves"[33]—one virtual, the other actual—that make up the Deleuzean chaosmos, on the other. First of all, insofar as the virtual is not merely possible but as real as the actual, the virtual structure of the Idea offers a provocative and innovative way to make sense of the incipient kind of materiality and dynamism possessed by the "all figures" within the Great Ultimate as substance. Because each of them consists in the symmetrically interdependent dipolar relation of pattern and psychophysical energy in their original condition, the indeterminate or incipiently determinate many within the Non-Ultimate can be conceived as realities, not merely ideal possibilities, although if taken by themselves they are still abstractions from the concretely determinate thing-events of the actual world. We may venture to take the incipiently determinate many within the Non-Ultimate as corresponding to the virtual Ideas with their differentiated structure, that is, the differential elements and their relations of reciprocal determination interspersed with singularities formative of ideal series. Further, the "luxuriant presence" of the incipiently determinate many with its connotation of mutual entanglement may be likened to the *perplication* of the obscure yet distinct Ideas as "complexes of coexistence" that are folded through one another.

Once this comparative analogy is established, what remains an obscure point within the Nongmunian panentheism of transcendent body can be further clarified, namely, the precise relationship between the "life-giving intention" permeating the "luxuriant" coexistence of the primordial many within the Non-Ultimate, on the one hand, and the empathetic relational makeup of that primordial multiplicity, on the other. The clarification comes by way of an analogy with the relationship between the "two faces" of the Idea, that is, the power of difference and the power of communication. As we have seen, without the power of communication, which brings heterogeneous differential elements together in relations of reciprocal determination to create singularities as the determinate value of their relations, there would be no *productive* power of difference that irrupts precisely from those singularities to produce divergent ideal series. Instead, there would remain only pure differences—mutually indifferent differential elements—whose magnitudes or values of change are completely undetermined because they are completely unrelated to one another. This intimate link between the power of communication and the productive power of difference, clearly visible in the differentiated virtual structure of the Ideas, is precisely what drives the process of differenciation or actualization of the Ideas, as seen in the trinity of *complicatio, explicatio, implicatio*. Without the "differenciator," which puts differences into immediate relation to one another, the intensive series unfolding divergently in and from the enfolded chaotic actuality would not at the same time be infolded and enveloped in one another to create the fields of resonance from which individualized states (qualities and extensities) emerge. Without the power of unmediated "connection in itself" to create the mutual implication, or "solidarity," of those that have nothing in common, the unfolding of divergent determinate actualities in and from the enfolded chaotic actuality would result in a stillbirth of the cosmos.

Now, if we take the indeterminate, or incipiently determinate, many within the Non-Ultimate to be like the Ideas' differentiated and perplicated multiplicities, the empathy permeating the former comes to mean no other than the power of communication between differences. The power of communication brings heterogeneous virtual differential elements together in relations of reciprocal determination to create the singularities of Ideas, on the one hand, and puts the divergent actual intensive series in immediate connection to one another to form the individuating fields of resonance, on the other. Likewise, being an affective power of mutual openness and attraction that does not rely on any kind of conceptual affinity, empathy can be said to put differences in unmediated relation to one another, relying solely on itself to traverse the distance created by the second-degree differences among the first-degree differences. The "life-giving intention" permeating the empathetic coexistence of the primordial many, then, can be understood to correspond to the power of difference as it is made fecund and productive, not barren and futile, by the power of communication. This comparative analogy clarifies the precise "mechanism" (機 *gi/ji*) by which the empathetic unity—the "humanity" (仁 *in/ren*)—of the indeterminate and chaotic multiplicity gives rise to the "origination" (元 *won/yuan*), namely, the creative urge toward order and harmony characterizing the Great Ultimate as the heart-mind of heaven and earth. The provocative aspect of this analogy is that the core Neo-Confucian metaphysical, cosmological, and ethicopolitical concept of humanity as empathy is deconstructed and reconstructed, so to speak, to take on the new signification of difference-in-itself that is at the same time connection-in-itself.

This Deleuzean rendition of the Nongmunian panentheism of transcendent body opens up an innovative way to conceptualize the relationship between the Great Ultimate as substance (or the Non-Ultimate) and the Great Ultimate as function. First, the relationship between the two is not to be conceived as one of resemblance between ideal, abstract possibility and real, concrete actuality, such as the relationship between the original one Pattern and many individual patterns understood to be its imperfect and inadequate copies. Rather, the relationship is to be envisioned as one between a problem and its solutions, between the transcendental and indeterminate—chaos-like—conditions of the genesis of the cosmos, on the one hand, and the divergent lines of determinate actualization that are drawn to one another into fields of unmediated, direct mutual resonance to give birth to the cosmos, on the other. This interpretation brings the much-needed elucidation to the time-honored Neo-Confucian metaphor of the moon's reflections in lakes and streams that is used to illustrate how the *entirety* of the Great Ultimate can be present in its myriad particularizations—namely, its *concrete universality*. The presence of the entirety of the Great Ultimate in its particularizations is difficult to conceptualize if its immanence in the world of myriad thing-events is understood in terms of the realization of a possibility via its delimitation, since such an understanding would "carve up" the whole Great Ultimate. By contrast, the concretely universal presence of the Great Ultimate can easily be construed as the "persistence" of a problem in its solutions, which it orients and conditions even as it differs from them, like the "presence" of a cosmic genetic code in its divergent individual articulations. This is all the more the case, since the empathetic unity of the incipiently determinate many within the Great Ultimate as substance is not to be envisaged as an overarching conceptual unity forming a predetermined archetype, but as an unmediated, direct, and nonhierarchical coexistence of the as-yet indeterminate many whose mutual attraction leads to repeated determinations of whole series of divergent patterns of coexistence, conceptual and otherwise. Hence, the transcendent immanence of the Great Ultimate in the world of myriad creatures may be put in the following way: (1) First, the unmediated empathetic coexistence of the indeterminate "all figures," which forms an incipient, "problematic" unity (what Neo-Confucians would call "equilibrium [中 *jung/zhong*]), underlies the creative restlessness of the Great Ultimate as substance; (2) In and through the Great Ultimate's transition to its function, the incipient unity *pervades, orients, prompts*, and *becomes* the myriad determinate patterns of coexistence (i.e., the achieved harmonies [和 *hwa/he*] of the myriad thing-events) as "resolutions" of that problematic unity.

Second, the Deleuzean interpretation of the Nongmunian panentheism of transcendent body enriches the notion of the spiral dialectic between the Great Ultimate as substance and the Great Ultimate as function. As argued in the previous chapter, due to the indeterminate or only incipiently determinate nature of the "all figures" bound to one another in empathy, the Non-Ultimate is given a moderately apophatic depth. It consists neither in a single overarching Pattern nor in a multitude of predetermined ideal patterns to be imposed on the way in which the myriad thing-events of the world are concretely harmonized. At the same time, its apophatic character does not go so far as to form a sheer indeterminate nothingness wholly alien to the Great Ultimate's principally knowable character as pattern. It is precisely this moderately apophatic depth which allows the substance of the Great Ultimate as the heart-mind of the Way to be capable of genuine and creative receptivity to the achieved orders of the myriad thing-events returning to it in the receptive phase of the Great Ultimate's movement. The Great Ultimate as substance or the Non-Ultimate offers a space of creative freedom in which the unmediated empathetic interrelatedness of the primordial, indeterminate many provides both the condition of possibility and initial spur to the beginnings of the myriad thing-events' self-creative journeys, even as it does not stand as a predetermined Order of orders that subsumes the achieved orders of the world returning to it. Could such a liberating spiral dialectic be further conceptually clarified by the notion of the "unequal odd halves" of the Deleuzean chaosmos, one virtual and the other actual?

I will venture to say yes, following Roland Faber's reading of the Deleuzean virtuality, which he likens to Whitehead's notion of real potentiality, as "the future openness and self-transcendence of the past with regard to the rising of new events."[34] As the virtual "half" or "image"[35] of one and the same chaosmos, the sphere of real potentiality in which the *perplicatio*—mutual folding through—of Ideas takes place does not constitute a separate realm; rather, it is found right in the midst of the *complicatio*, that is, the "womb" of enfolded chaotic actuality "in which finite determination never ceases to be born and to disappear."[36] Hence, the "problem" posed by the virtual Idea, which orients, conditions, and persists in the creation of divergent lines of actualities, is no other than "a variation of the old,"[37] that is, a renewal of the actual world in response to the "disappearance"—return—of finite determinations back into "the ultimate origin overturned into an absence of origin."[38] If we translate this into the terms of the Nongmunian panentheism of transcendent body, we can say that, on the strength of their indeterminate, "problematic" character, which demands divergent creative solutions, the incipiently determinate agents of creativity within the Non-Ultimate receive the achieved orders of the world and "codify," ever anew, novel patterns of creative harmonization. The novel codifications of the empathetic interrelatedness of the incipiently determinate multitude within the Non-Ultimate, then, are "let go" into the explosive freedom of spontaneous actualization in heterogeneous yet mutually related lines of myriad determinate thing-events.

Now, if we accept this Deleuzean rendition of the spiral dialectic of the Great Ultimate, would there be a place within the Nongmunian panentheism of transcendent body for the radically new, not merely a variation of the old? Given that there appears to be no space within the Deleuzean virtuality for what Faber identifies with Whitehead's notion of pure potentiality, namely, that which is "impossible because it does not in any way reside within the horizon of the possible before actually entering, wholly unexpectedly, into that horizon,"[39] the answer is seemingly no. There is no God who is the source and locus of *pure* potentiality in the Deleuzean philosophy of immanence. But we need to remember that, even as Nongmun conceives of the substance of the Great Ultimate as the coextensive, equally actual, and inseparable yet mutually distinct union of pattern in its original condition with psychophysical energy in its original condition, there exists a sense of ontological and normative priority placed on the former when he says, "The original substance of psychophysical energy is that which roots itself in pattern to emerge daily."[40] What he implies by this statement, as I indicated earlier, is not the kind of ontological causality between pattern and psychophysical energy affirmed by the dominant Cheng-Zhu school. Rather, what he conveys is the sense that the incessantly novel advent of the self-so or spontaneous creativity of the Great Ultimate as substance, which corresponds to psychophysical energy in its original condition of incipiently determinate multiplicity, follows and keeps to the rationally and normatively grounding operation of the same Great Ultimate as substance, which is called by the name of pattern in its original condition of incipiently determinate multiplicity. But since the self-codifications of the incipiently determinate multitude refer to the *conceptually unmediated* patternings of their *empathetic* interrelatedness, the fact that the self-so of the Great Ultimate as substance keeps to the rationally and normatively grounding operation of the same Great Ultimate as substance does not imply that some kind of predetermined conceptual and ideal foundation lies at the root of its self-so or spontaneous creativity. Rather, it means only that the dynamic ground of the world is ultimately tilted toward harmony and meaning—that is, it leans toward a cosmos rather than a barren and indifferent chaos, thanks to the affective power of mutual openness and attraction permeating it.

If the ontological and normative priority given to the rationally grounding operation of pattern in its original condition implies no more than that the spontaneous creativity of psychophysical energy in its original condition is fundamentally inclined toward a cosmos, then a path opens up toward a radicalization of the meaning of the word "spontaneous." It suggests that the novel self-codifications of the incipiently determinate multitude can be truly open and unfettered, insofar as they stand for an increase and intensification of the value of harmony. Provided that they orient and condition the creation of divergent lines of mutually implicated and resonant myriad thing-events, the novel patternings of their empathetic interrelatedness can be so utterly beyond what is to be expected of a given state of the world to fit the label "otherworldly." In other words, the Nongmunian panentheism of transcendent body allows a space for the possibility of envisaging pattern in its original condition as representing an opening toward radically new orders and harmonies. It is precisely in this sense that the asymmetrically interdependent dipolar construction of the Great Ultimate's substance-function relation confers a sense of ontological depth to the "virtual," or incipiently determinate, multitude making up the Non-Ultimate. The incipiently determinate "all figures" are agents of ontological creativity, that is, agents capable not only of merely rearranging the patterns of the old orders in response to their "homecoming" but also of connecting to one another in totally, radically unanticipated ways to produce wholly new patterns of actuality beyond the horizon of existing conceptual possibilities. If the core Neo-Confucian metaphysical, cosmological, and ethicopolitical concept of humanity as empathy points to the fundamentally affective grounding of the cosmos rather than a conceptual one, to the extent that it can be reconstructed to take on the signification of difference-in-itself that is at the same time connection-in-itself, then it is certainly possible to imagine the incipiently determinate multiplicity of the Non-Ultimate to be able to break through any horizon of predictable and anticipated conceptual possibilities. Although the vast majority of the variegated Confucian tradition has been in the thrall of the ancient and authoritative Heavenly patternings of humanity as empathy and their institutionalizations, which are prescribed in the classics of the sages mostly in paternalistic and hierarchical terms, the principal insight offered by that tradition has the wherewithal to transcend even the revered sages and provide valuable resources for a comparative-theological and comparative-philosophical reflection on the wild wind of the Spirit, which truly "blows where it will." The Neo-Confucian panentheism of transcendent body, which I have proposed and developed in dialogue with the Deleuzean philosophy of immanence, is one example of it.

## Change, Way, and Spirit: A Neo-Confucian Trinity in Conversation with the Chaosmos and Tehom

So far in this book, I have examined the Daoist and Confucian notion of psychophysical energy, tracing the various ways in which the nondualistic, equalizing, emancipatory, and holistic potentials of that notion have been shackled and domesticated by its being placed in the lower pole of the hierarchical binaries, whether the other, higher pole be the Way, Heaven, pattern, or the Great Ultimate. At the same time, my tracking of the "adventures" of the idea of psychophysical energy has shown, I hope, the resilience of the idea whose indomitable subversive potentials keep showing themselves creatively when put in dialogue with kindred yet disparate spirits in the theological and philosophical constellations of the modern or late-modern Western world. The Nongmunian panentheism of transcendent body, the rough contours of which I have sketched in this chapter and the previous one in dialogue with Whitehead and Deleuze, is the latest incarnation of that resilience.

At this point I would like to return to the original trinitarian *problematique* from which the odyssey was launched, and ask: Can the "adventures" of the nondualistic, holistic, and liberating idea of psychophysical energy, which I have followed, offer a way of constructing a pneumatocentric trinitarian theology that does justice to the originary biblical insight about God who is the liminal Spirit of creation, hovering back and forth between one and many, ideal and material, mind and body, and divine and creaturely? In answering this question, I would like first to take up the triadic formulation of the Great Ultimate offered by Yulgok (which was inspired by the well-known, earlier triadic formulation of the operations of Heaven put forward by Cheng Hao): "'The Great Ultimate' is also merely a forced name. Its substance is called Change (易 *yeok/yi*); its pattern is called the Way (道 *do/dao*); and its function is called Spirit (神 *sin/shen*)."[41] Yulgok, of course, interprets the Great Ultimate as metaphysical pattern (*li*), and therefore treats the triadic formulation merely as a different way of construing the essentially dyadic substance-function structure of pattern's operations. For him, Spirit as the Great Ultimate's function refers to the immanence of pattern or the Way in each individual thing-event that constitutes its normative measure ("that which it ought to be"), while Change as the Great Ultimate's substance designates pattern or the Way as the transcendent ontological ground of each thing-event ("that whereby it is").[42] In other words, Change as substance and Spirit as function refer to the dyadic modes of the Way's creative movement, one quiescent and receptive and the other dynamic and active. As Yulgok—contra Toegye—denies pattern's own dynamism, the dipolar movement back and forth between the substance of the Great Ultimate and its function, that is, between Change and Spirit, certainly involves psychophysical energy. Yet in his formulation psychophysical energy takes on a silent, subordinate role, serving as the vehicle and source of power for pattern's wondrous "spiritual" function of individuating itself and constituting the normative measures of the myriad thing-events.

What happens, then, if we apply his triadic formulation to the Great Ultimate as it is rendered by the Nongmunian panentheism of transcendent body with a Deleuzean inflection? The first thing one can notice is that, as the center of gravity, so to speak, shifts from the Great Ultimate as metaphysical pattern to the Great Ultimate as the metaphysical-physical dipolar union of pattern and psychophysical energy, a path toward a truly triadic formulation opens up—one that more closely reflects Cheng Hao's original formulation of the Neo-Confucian triad. Change and Spirit may be understood to refer, respectively, to the substance and the function of the dipolar union of pattern and psychophysical energy, which has yet a third mode, namely, that of "*pattern* (*li*)," understood primarily in the sense of "order" and called by the name of the Way. In terms of the Nongmunian-Deleuzean rendition of the Great Ultimate, Change as the substance of the Great Ultimate designates the "womb" of enfolded chaotic actuality within which is found the unmediated empathetic coexistence of the indeterminate "all figures" forming the incipient, virtual, and "problematic" unity—what may be called "equilibrium" (中 *jung*/*zhong*)—which ontologically undergirds the creative restlessness of that enfolded chaotic actuality. The Way as the pattern of the Great Ultimate, then, corresponds to the repeated unfolding of whole series of divergent patterns of actualities—the achieved harmonies of the myriad thing-events (和 *hwa*/*he*)—as "solutions" to the "problematic" unity of Change. Spirit as the function of the Great Ultimate, lastly, names humanity (仁 *in*/*ren*) as empathy, that is, the affective power of mutual openness and attraction, which brings together the divergent actual patterns of the Way and sustains their mutual infoldedness—their mutual implication and resonance—as they unfold in and from Change and fold back into it.

Is this triadic formulation pneumatocentric enough? At first sight, the answer appears to be no, given the asymmetrically interdependent construction of the Great Ultimate's substance-function relation within the Nongmunian-Deleuzean paradigm, which confers upon the substance of the Great Ultimate an ontological depth. Change is the locus of ontological creativity, that is, the emergence of the radically and irreducibly new, on account of the unmediated empathetic coexistence of the indeterminate "all figures" undergirding the creative restlessness of the chaotic matrix that it is. Nonetheless, we must not fail to note that, if Spirit is the power of empathetic communication that brings together the divergent actual patterns of the Way, we find the same affective power of mutual openness and attraction that puts in direct relation the virtual, incipiently determinate "all figures" within Change and gives birth to the productive power of difference, the "life-giving intention," permeating it. This means that Spirit also has an ontological depth or, alternatively, is the very reason for there being an ontological depth within Change. Without the power of unmediated "connection in itself" that is at the same time the productive power of difference-in-itself, the incipiently determinate many (the "all figures") would be incapable of being agents of ontological creativity—that is to say, incapable of connecting to one another in totally, radically unanticipated ways to produce wholly new patterns of actuality beyond the horizon of existing conceptual possibilities.

Seen in this way, the ontological depth of Spirit is precisely what sustains the perfect clarity, openness, and communicative resonance of pattern and psychophysical energy in their original condition despite their primordial and chaotic multiplicity within Change, making possible their all-pervasive and life-giving concrete universality as they unfold together in the Way. This means Spirit is at once that which enables Change to be what it is, namely, the enfolding of chaotically divergent actualities constantly being birthed from the mutual folding through of the virtual multiplicity, and also that which makes it possible for the Way to be what it is, namely, the mutually infolded unfolding of the myriad determinate patterns of coexistence emerging in and from Change. As the power of empathetic communication that is at the same time the power of difference made creative and productive, Spirit permeates Change, patterns it into the Way, and returns it to a new—even radically new—beginning, again and again in an unceasing *yin-yang* spiral movement. The trinitarian panentheism of transcendent body, as can be seen, is pneumatocentric through and through, for Spirit is subordinate not even to Change, let alone to the Way. True to the interdependent nature of the substance-function relation, Change as the substance of the Great Ultimate is a meaningless, indifferent, and inert chaos without Spirit, which is the Great Ultimate's function, just as Spirit "knows not where to abide"—is deprived of its context and become "disembodied"—without Change.

If we conceive of the Trinity in this way, substituting the Father with Change as the enfolded chaotic actuality harboring an unending irruption of transcendent novelty—even the radically new—from the virtuality of the Non-Ultimate within, then the Unoriginate Origin is no longer a determinate Creator who both logically and ontologically precedes the emergence of creation as cosmos. Rather, a determinate Creator is to be understood to emerge together with creation from Change in the very process of mutually infolded unfolding of the myriad determinate patterns of coexistence. The Creator is the name given to a specific pattern that is born from Change as a transcendent ideal or value and which is always already found incarnated in and luring the process of the unfolding of the cosmos in and from Change. In other words, the Creator is one of the many Ways that beckons us to follow. When this ideal or lure is projected back to the ultimate origin that is an absence of origin, Change is interpreted as a determinate Creator precisely in the shape of that ideal or lure. Hence, the theistic notion of a Creator, such as the Father with his various "personal" attributes, is derivative, not primordial. Even if he is to be perfectly imaged by his Son and conformed to by the lesser creaturely images through the agency of the Son and the Spirit, the Father cannot be thought of as the ultimate ontological archetype (for such a thing does not exist), just as the nontheistic notion of the one Heavenly Pattern cannot be conceived as the ultimate universal pattern of all thing-events predetermining the shape of reality as a particular kind of harmonious sociocosmic whole.

Perhaps Catherine Keller's account of *creatio ex profundis*, inflected by Deleuze and Whitehead among others, would help as an illustration here. Keller's "tehomic theology"[43] zooms in on the long-neglected and suppressed biblical metaphor of *tehom*, or the "deep," in the Genesis account of creation to launch a critique of the traditional creation theology of *creatio ex nihilo* and its underlying conception of God as a completely independent and self-sufficient Creator whose omnipotence enables "him" to fashion the world literally out of nothingness. In place of the Creator of the *creatio ex nihilo*, Keller installs what she calls a "tehomic trinity" (232):

> If the godhead, or rather the goodness, *"in" whom unfolds* the universe can be theologized as Tehom, the ocean of divinity, the divinity *who unfolds "in"* the all is called by such biblical names as Elohim, Sophia, Logos, Christ. The all in the divine, the divine in the all. . . . It does echo the Trinitarian intuition of complex relationality *immanent* to an impersonal Godhead and personalized in the *oikonomia* of the creation. Their relation to each other . . . can be resignified only through the icon of the oscillating Spirit. (219)

The first member of the tehomic trinity, Tehom, which she calls "the godhead," "the ocean of divinity, or "the goodness," is a "metonym of the divine womb" (227), which remains "neither God nor not-God but the depth of 'God'" (227). This depth of God is the "matrix of all relations" that is at the same time the "matrix of possibilities," for the relations, which are "*not differentiated but differential*" (161), are "the waves of our possibility" (227). As "the originary complexity" (164) not preceded by any absolute simplicity, Tehom is "the first place or *capacity* of genesis" (232) or "the real potentiality from which we emerge" (227). Keller uses the Deleuzean notion of *complicatio* to capture the differential-relational constitution of Tehom, its originary complexity: "This is a trinity of folds, *plis*, indicating a relationality of intertwining rather than cutting edges. *Complicatio*, 'folding together'. . . signifies 'the chaos which contains all.'"

Now a question can be asked: What does the "all" contained in the originary chaotic waters of Tehom refer to? It first of all refers, of course, to the universe in its incipience, for Tehom is none other than the divine womb "'*in*' *whom unfolds* the universe." But at the same time, in a Whiteheadian fashion, Keller construes Tehom also as the process of "indeterminate creativity" that gives birth to deity or divinity.[44] Tehom, she declares, is "the ocean of divinity," the divinity being the one "*who unfolds 'in'* the all" and called by the biblical names of Elohim, Sophia, Logos, Christ. If the divinity, *theos*, unfolds in the all, *pan*, which at the same time unfolds in the chaotic waters of Tehom, then both the divinity and the all can be said to unfold in and from Tehom in divergent yet thoroughly interrelated fashions. When Keller says "we" in this context, as in "waves of *our* possibility [italics mine]" or "the real potentiality from which *we* emerge [italics mine]," she is construing the divine plural Elohim, "gods," as "the all in the divine, the divine in the all." The pluris-ingular Elohim is the second member of the tehomic trinity, the "second capacity," which "could also be called the *explicatio*: that which 'unfolds' what otherwise remains 'folded together'" (232). Elohim designates the interrelated unfolding of the creator and the creation from Tehom—the process that is at once the "divination" of the deity and the actualization of the universe (232). In this process, "the divine and the world form the conditions of each other's becomings" to such an extent that "if divinity becomes incarnate in endless new forms, the metamorphoses of the creatures cast their effects back upon the divine" (227). For example, it is only when the divinity unfolds in humanity that the divinity acquires the determinations of a personal God: "Only, for instance, in the incarnation as the human does this deity get personal" (227). Through our creaturely creativity, Keller muses poetically, we humans "have *divined* the infinity with our painterly representations" (227). Put otherwise, we paint the surfaces of the "unhued" ocean of divinity (217).

If both the creator and the creation unfold from Tehom interdependently, then Tehom is the chaotic depth of both God and the world. Following Deleuze's construction of the virtual-actual relation as unequal—different—halves constituting a problem and its solutions, however, Keller underlines the fact that both God and the world, that is, Elohim, are not copies of Tehom, for the latter is "the *heterogeneous* depth of divinity and of world" (232; italics mine). Tehom as the divine womb and the ocean of divinity is not the origin "in" which familiar archetypes could be found; rather, it is the "place-holder of beginnings" (232)—the beginnings of divinity and world that take place ever anew, "not as absolutes but as irreducibles," thus ensuring the contingency and novelty of every beginning—*nova creatio ex profundis* (226). Tehom as the nonlocalizable depth of God, in that sense, is "the *difference* of God" (232), which "can be imagined to yield place to a difference called 'the creator' and a set of differences called 'the creation'" (220).

What about the third member, "the third capacity," of the tehomic trinity, then? It is "the icon of the oscillating Spirit," namely, Ruach, who, like the Deleuzean *implicatio*, relates difference to difference. Keller appeals here directly to Deleuze's notion of "differentiator as connector": "Rather than transcending or obliterating differences," Ruach lets differences be "intensified precisely by being brought into relation" (232). Ruach as "the relation of relations," or "the relationality itself," oscillates between Tehom and Elohim, between *complicatio and explicatio*, and creates, that is, allows the self-organizing process of the world to begin, again and again (232). Furthermore, it opens up, ever anew, "the 'third space' where Tehom could flow into language and Elohim, by a certain chiastic effect, might listen" (232). In other words, Ruach allows Elohim to obtain the names of Word, Wisdom, and Torah by bringing the divergent unfoldings of the Manyone into the height and depth of communication and mutual resonance, that is, by letting them "enter language" (232).

If we interpret the second member of the Nongmunian-Deleuzean trinity of the Great Ultimate, namely, the Way, through the "lens" of the interdependent becoming of God and creation advanced by Keller's notion of the tehomic trinity, then an anthropomorphically envisaged "personal" deity, be it the Abba of Jesus, the Lord on High (上帝 *sangje/shangdi*), or the Toegyean heart-mind of the Way (道心 *dosim/daoxin*), can be understood as the divine counterpart of and the transcendent lure for the human unfolding within the whole series of divergent patterns of actualities unfolding in and from Change. As Keller puts it, we humans paint the surfaces of the unhued ocean of divinity, that is, Change, following the specifically human patterns—*do* or *dao*—of unfolding actualities, be it "personhood," "self-consciousness," "subjectivity," "intellect," "will," "moral order," and so on within the vast mutually infolded unfolding of the myriad determinate patterns of coexistence constituting the cosmos. Spirit's role, then, particularly for humans, is to keep us humans and our deity in unmediated, empathetic relation to each other, enabling their mutual lure and mutually interrelated becoming—that is to say, both the incarnation or kenosis of the deity as the heart-mind of the Way and the divinization, or *theosis*, of human beings as human heart-minds. Lest we turn our icons into idols, Spirit, which is also our spirit, reminds us humans not to forget that we and our deity share the same moderately apophatical—that is, empathetically "codified"—ontological depth as the placeholder of always new, incipiently creative beginnings, and that we have "divined" the Way by *our* ways, by painting and patterning the surface of Change.

The Kellerian illustration of the trinity of the Great Ultimate, which I have just presented, may have the effect of highlighting a possible point of contention within the Nongmunian-Deleuzean paradigm of my trinitarian sketches. Although I point to the incipiently determinate multitude constituting the Non-Ultimate as providing an ontological depth that is not metaphysical or metacosmic in a dualistic sense, the construal of that ontological depth as "originary complexity," to quote Keller, may seem overdetermined and therefore too concrete and limiting to provide the kind of radical transcendence and novelty it claims to offer. Does not the ontological depth or creative ground of all, if it is truly transcendent and capable of introducing the genuinely new, have to be completely indeterminate, that is, radically apophatic? Robert C. Neville's own use of the notion of incipience to refer to the ontological depth of the Great Ultimate is a case in point. When he says that the ontologically more basic state of the Non-Ultimate is "incipient with determination but not yet determinate,"[45] and that it has no character whatsoever other than "the incipience of, or readiness to give rise to, the immanently defined state,"[46] he is pointing to the complete indetermination of the ontological ground or source of creation.

In fact, Neville's well-known defense of the doctrine of *creatio ex nihilo* is based on his insistence that a genuine ontological ground has to be completely indeterminate nothingness. From the metaphysical problem of the ontological contingency of the world, he deduces an abstract notion of the "creation" of a determinate world as such by the indeterminate source of creation and then uses that notion as a comparative category for the ideas about the ultimate religious object in different religious traditions.[47] According to Neville, the things of the world are characterized by their determinateness, and their determinateness implies their contingency. Because to be determinate is to be this particular thing and not that, determinateness as such means first of all relational contingency, which can also be called cosmological contingency, since relational features among concrete things are internal to the cosmos. At the same time, determinate things are not constituted by their cosmological relations alone, since to have an identity of its own—that is, to be determinate—a thing must also have essential features of its own without which there would be no thing of which relational determinations are relational determinations. The fact that things are thus necessarily *harmonies* of essential and relational (or conditional) features means, at the same time, that their existence is not entirely dependent on the cosmological, relational context, for there has to be something that makes the essential features of things come together so as to enable the relational context itself in the first place. This fact of *ontological contingency*, namely, that the very being of things is contingent on something other than their mutual relations, calls for a deeper context—what Neville calls "an ontological context of mutual relevance"[48]—which makes it possible for things to be together as harmonies of essential and relational features. In other words, the ontological contingency of things implies a deeper context that cannot be characterized by any cosmological features, be they essential or relational. Things *are*, because they are *created* from the utter indeterminacy (or nothingness) of the ontological context into the relational determinacy of their cosmic trajectories. Ontological causation, in that sense, should be understood in terms of creation out of nothingness.[49]

How does the creation ex nihilo take place concretely, then? Neville answers by giving an "archeological depth" to the notion of creation ex nihilo by means of three layers of interpretation. The three layers are (1) the comprehensive (ontological) layer in which the world is interpreted as a generically determinate creation from an indeterminate "source" that is further determined as a generic "creator" in that very act of creating; (2) the dimensional (cosmological) layer comparing tradition-specific interpretations of the generically determinate creation, particularly in regard to the different ways in which the dimensions or structural categories of the generically determinate creation are ordered, aligned, and mutually implicated by the religious world-interpretations, giving rise to different accounts of creation and creator; (3) the thematic layer comparing the world-interpretations of religious ideas, symbols, and narratives in regard to how, why, and with what justification they arose and developed in their historical contexts and with what transformative power they speak today.[50]

Crucial in this threefold interpretive scheme is the second, dimensional (cosmological), layer. The dimensions of the generically determinate creation are given in Neville's "primary cosmology," in which he calls the dimensions, following Plato, Limit, Unlimited, Mixture, and Cause of Mixture. They mean, respectively, order (forms), things-to-be-ordered (infinitely rich components with internal power), actuality (concrete things or harmonies), and normative measure (the paths things must follow or causal processes), or alternately, masculine, feminine, existential, and soteriological.[51] These dimensions or structural categories of the cosmos are not independent realities but four coordinated routes by which ontological causation occurs. In other words, they explain *how* the creation of determinate things as harmonies of essential and conditional features takes place. The particular category that gets emphasized by a religious tradition as the agency of creation determines the character of the creator in that tradition. To put it another way, the vague notion of creator is further specified as individual agent, transcendent principle, or pure consciousness, for example, depending on how each religious tradition focuses on particular features of the created cosmological order and envisions the act of creation that likely has given birth to a world having precisely those highlighted features as predominant elements.[52] For example, if a religious tradition emphasizes the formal or orderly dimension of the cosmos (i.e., the dimension of Limit, to use Neville's categories), then that tradition would interpret the act of creation accordingly as an act of fashioning the cosmos by keeping chaos at bay, and the creator as the Law-Giver or King, as in the Babylonian myth of Marduk creating the world by slaying the sea-monster (chaos-monster) Tiamat.

As is evident, Keller's *creatio ex profundis* and Neville's *creatio ex nihilo* agree with each other insofar as they both envision the interdependent emergence of both the creator and the creation from the ontologically creative ground via the creatures' interpretive acts, which project the perceived or experienced patterns of the unfolding of the cosmos back onto the ontological ground. The point of disagreement lies, rather, in the question of how far one can go in depicting, in a determinate fashion, the ultimate origin while still leaving its apophatic character as an absence of origin intact. If the ontological ground is made too determinate and circumscribed, a question inevitably arises regarding the provenance of those perceptual, linguistic, and conceptual limitations imposed on the ground, be it biology, culture, or history. It appears, however, that Neville's rendition of the source of creation as completely indeterminate implies the notion of a sheer act of creation, that is, the understanding of divine creative act as purely unconditioned, unbounded, spontaneous, and free activity. In this understanding I seem to hear a faint echo of the classical notion of the omnipotent creator God in the hyperbolized image of King and Law-Giver, although Neville has relegated such an image to being merely one among many tradition-specific interpretations of the ontologically creative ground.

In all fairness to Neville, his notion of ontological causation, especially when applied to the East Asian traditions of Daoism and Confucianism, resists such a facile characterization. For example, he locates the ontological causation of the Dao of the *Daodejing*, as it manifests itself in the world of Something, in the spontaneous emergence of novelty *right in the midst of* cosmic determinateness: "When and wherever a situation is underdetermined by antecedent conditions, the decisive determining is spontaneous relative to the past, and is the locus of ontological causation."[53] In other words, he construes the temporal manifestation of the ontologically creative ground in terms of an interplay between the existential achievement of structured and value-laden harmonies of cosmically internal forces, on the one hand, and the existential dislocation of those achieved harmonies in bursts of spontaneity that introduce the radically new, on the other.[54] Neville's "way of incipience" to refer to the ontological depth of the Great Ultimate is just another way of articulating the same understanding of ontological causation.

Seen in this way, both the Nevillian path of radical apophaticism and the Kellerian-Deleuzean path of moderate apophaticism allow a sense of the affirmative responsiveness of the ontological ground to the temporally and existentially achieved actualities of the past even as the ontological ground "acts" to give birth to something radically new. As such, either could provide ample resources to construct a spirally dialectical conception of the Great Ultimate's ontologically and cosmologically creative movement that is capable of resisting a totalizing metaphysics of one Heavenly Pattern or one empty Nothingness. But the Kellerian-Deleuzean path of moderate apophaticism taken by the Nongmunian panentheism of transcendent body, I believe, is capable of addressing better the question of why there is this creative restlessness of Origination (元 *won/yuan*)—that is, this creative ferment found within the deeper ontological context, which brings together the essential features of things so as to enable the cosmologically relational context itself within which the relational features of things are mutually determined. If the ontologically creative ground is the deeper ontological context of *mutual relevance*, what makes up this power of connection that relates mutually indifferent singular identities—namely, the essential features of things in abstraction from their relational features—with one another so that there would emerge harmonies of essential and relational features? The Kellerian-Deleuzean answer offered by the Nongmunian panentheism of transcendent body is that the power of connection consists in the mutually empathetic and nonconceptual "self-codification" of the incipiently determinate multitude, which brings them together into relations of direct, unmediated mutual relevance. Compared to the Nevillian answer, that the power of connection can only be a sheer creative act, the Nongmunian stance with a Kellerian-Deleuzean inflection is less susceptible, in my view, to a recolonization of the ontological depth by the classical notion of the unilateral exercise of creative power on the part of an omnipotent Creator. Furthermore, insofar as the empathetically "codified" ontological depth is the placeholder of always *irreducibly* new creative beginnings, to quote Keller, the Nongmunian panentheism of the transcendent body does not need the notion of *creatio ex nihilo* to secure the emergence of the radically new within the active-creative unfolding of the Great Ultimate from the receptivity of the Non-Ultimate.[55]

In the next, concluding chapter, I revisit the Donghak story of Ultimate Energy with which I began this examination of the adventures of the idea of psychophysical energy with a view to a pneumatocentric reconstruction of the Trinity. Just like Nongmun's idea of the equal actuality of pattern and psychophysical energy, the Donghak concept of Ultimate Energy represents one of the most prominent examples of the resistance of the notion of psychophysical energy to the attempts at its subordination to a higher metaphysical power or principle. But while Nongmun's idea stands for that resistance from within the ruling, hegemonic Neo-Confucian discourses, the Donghak concept embodies that same resistance from the perspective of the nonhegemonic discourses of the ruled, that is, from the perspective of the oppressed, exploited, and marginalized multitude of people. The Nongmunian panentheism of the transcendent body, which is a product of the conversation I have staged among Nongmun, Whitehead, Deleuze, and Keller, has still to undergo a further transformation in its encounter with the theology of Donghak.

# 8 The Democracy of Numinous Spirits

## THE PANENTHEISM OF "SUBALTERN" ULTIMATE ENERGY IN DONGHAK

In the late spring of 1860, after a year of spiritual wrestling involving an intense practice of prayer, Su-un, the founder of Donghak, heard the voice of Lord Heaven (originally the Korean 하늘님 [*haneullim*],[1] or the classical Chinese 天主 [*cheonju*]). According to the conversation recorded in the earliest Donghak scripture, *Dong-gyeong daejeon* (東經大全 The complete scriptures of Eastern Learning) and *Yongdam yusa* (龍潭諭詞 The instructional songs from the Dragon Pond),[2] Lord Heaven told Su-un not to fear but to receive his[3] teachings, and that he was the one whom people called by the name of Lord on High (上帝 *sangje*), namely, the traditional high god revered in both Confucian and Daoist traditions and also worshipped by a variety of popular religions in East Asia, including the Korean *mugyo*—"shamanistic"—tradition.[4] At the same time, Lord Heaven declared that she was in fact the real reference for and meaning of what people called "ghosts and spirits" (鬼神 *gwisin*).[5] The "ghost and spirits" was the comprehensive term for anthropomorphically envisaged deities, including the spirits of ancestors, natural features, and various locales, which were however rationalized in the Neo-Confucian philosophical tradition as representing the subtle, wondrous, and mysterious functioning of receptive and active psychophysical energies, not supernatural and metacosmic entities removed from the exigencies of the temporal and physical.[6]

### "Bearing Lord Heaven": Su-un's Revolutionary Subversion of the Confucian Way of Heaven

Having been educated as a Neo-Confucian scholar, Su-un subscribed to the philosophically sophisticated view of ghosts and spirits. Hence, given the self-identification with ghosts and spirits made by Lord Heaven, his developing understanding of Lord Heaven subsequent to that fateful encounter was intertwined with his understanding of the way psychophysical energy lay at the basis of the life of all creatures, from the movements of their bodies all the way to the wondrously "spiritual" functioning of their heart-minds.[7] Reinforcing this connection was the fact that Su-un's teacher, Choe Rim, was a scholar belonging to the *nakhak* school that affirmed the unsullied, creatively harmonizing presence of psychophysical energy in its original condition within the human heart-mind—that is, the affirmation that was taken up and expanded by Nongmun to apply to the entire universe.[8] At the same time, however, Su-un stood in the line of a Neo-Confucian school famous for the special reverence it accorded to Heaven understood as pattern (*li*). His father, Choe Ok (honorific name Geunam), was a widely renowned scholar in the school of Toegye. The dominant Cheng-Zhu Neo-Confucians in general called for the practice of "reverence" or "mindfulness" (敬 *gyeong/jing*) before the Heavenly Pattern, but the Toegyean school went furthest in cultivating a kind of religiosity before Heaven, assigning to it not only the highest transcendence, ontological priority, and ethical normativity but also creatively dynamic agency.[9]

Su-un himself underscores in both of the earliest Donghak scriptures the importance of revering the Heavenly mandate and following the Heavenly pattern.[10] In fact, one of the major points in his diagnosis of the ills of his time is that people are all busy looking after their own selfish interests—the sign that they have forgotten the teachings of the sages and no longer revere or follow Heaven.[11] But even though he sounds like a typical Neo-Confucian lamenting the deterioration of moral education and self-cultivation, Su-un introduces a novel interpretation of Heaven. Perhaps influenced by the ancient Korean indigenous worship of Heaven as the highest god and also by the monotheism of Western Learning (Catholic Christianity), he goes beyond even the strongly religious undercurrent of his own Neo-Confucian lineage to identify Heaven with Lord Heaven, a personal deity who speaks to human beings, reassuring them if they are fearful and imparting instructions on how to live the right Way. In other words, the new teaching of Eastern Learning, which Su-un proclaimed, pushed beyond the boundaries of its Neo-Confucian heritage to become a full-blown theistic Way, somewhat akin to the ancient classical Confucian worship of Heaven as Lord on High but now reinterpreted through the lens of a Neo-Confucian moral metaphysics with a heavy emphasis on psychophysical energy.[12]

Hence, Su-un's understanding of Lord Heaven occupies an interesting liminal space between transcendence and immanence. Even as he affirms Lord Heaven as the transcendent personal pole of divine-human relations, he identifies this deity as the primordial and ultimate form of psychophysical energy, which he calls *jigi* (至氣) or Ultimate Energy (literally, "ultimate psychophysical energy"). Here is the twenty-one-character devotional incantation that Su-un asks his disciples to recite:

> Ultimate Energy being all around me here and now, I pray for its great descent. I bear Lord Heaven; and [the Heavenly work of] creative becoming is being established in me. If I never forget [the Heavenly presence within], I will know all things.[13]

Given that Ultimate Energy is already present around them here and now, its "descent," which the disciples are to pray for, is no other than its descent on them, on their own bodies. In his commentary on this incantation, Su-un explains the "great descent" of Ultimate Energy on one's body as the harmonious becoming of one's psychophysical energy (氣化 *gihwa*).[14] What he means is that the recovery of the fundamental connection between one's own bodily psychophysical energy and Ultimate Energy, which takes place with the great descent, leads to one's deep understanding of and attunement to the others making up the world of myriad thing-events, as captured by the last part of the incantation, "I will know all things."

What, then, is this Ultimate Energy, which is another name for Lord Heaven, and the connection to which enables one to become intimately attuned to the entire universe? Here is the first part of Su-un's commentary on the twenty-one-character incantation:

> "Ultimate" [至 *ji*] means the utmost limit. "Psychophysical energy" [氣 *gi*] means what is empty and numinous [虛靈 *heoryeong*], all-pervasive, all-governing, and all-directing. Even as it appears to have form, it is difficult to discern its shape; it is as if one can hear it, although it is hard to see it. It could also be [called] one psychophysical energy of chaotic beginning [渾元之一氣 *honwon ji ilgi*]. . . . [Praying for] the "great descent" [大降 *daegang*] means desiring the harmonious becoming of one's psychophysical energy [氣化 *gihwa*)].[15]

According to Su-un's description, Ultimate Energy is "empty and numinous, all-pervasive, all-governing, and all-directing." Its "numinous" (or spiritual)[16] emptiness points to its transcendence, that is, the fact that it is the primordial and ultimate form of psychophysical energy. When Su-un says, "Even as it appears to have form, it is difficult to discern its shape; it is as if one can hear it, although it is hard to see it," he is articulating the truth that Ultimate Energy *is* psychophysical energy with physicality and materiality, yet beyond the concreteness of the myriad coalescences of psychophysical energy making up the universe. At the same time, despite its transcendence, he leaves no doubt that Ultimate Energy is truly immanent and intimately involved in the world of the myriad thing-events when he describes it as all-pervasive, all-governing, and all-directing. Perhaps the other name that Su-un gives Ultimate Energy, "one psychophysical energy of chaotic beginning" (渾元之一氣 *honwon ji ilgi*), provides the interpretive key to unlocking the seemingly paradoxical co-inherence of its transcendence and immanence.

As I have shown in chapter 1, the notion of one psychophysical energy (一氣 *ilgi/yiqi*)—or alternatively, Primordial Psychophysical Energy (元氣 *won-gi/yuanqi*)—is an ancient one in both Daoist and Confucian traditions, referring to psychophysical energy in its originally and primordially undifferentiated form before its differentiation into the complementary opposites of the receptive and active psychophysical energies. Within the shared triadic formulation of the relationship between the formless Way and the myriad thing-events with form, in which psychophysical energy occupies the mediating position, the one psychophysical energy is a concept subordinate to the Way as the metaphysical ultimate, be it the Daoist Way as the chaos-like (non-)origin of all thing-events or the Confucian Way as the Heavenly Pattern patterning all coalescences of psychophysical energy. Even though being without form like the Way, the one psychophysical energy is still physical and takes on physical forms to become the myriad vessels of the Way. As the firstborn of the Way, the one psychophysical energy is the source of all concrete coalescences of psychophysical energy, moving in perfect sync with the Way to generate its two modalities and ultimately the myriad thing-events of the world. Because of its complete attunement to the Way, the attainment of it is the primary goal of self-cultivation in both Daoist and Confucian traditions, that is, the practice of nurturing and conditioning one's bodily psychophysical energy in order to recover the primordial condition of the one psychophysical energy.

Su-un's interpretation of Ultimate Energy as the "one psychophysical energy of chaotic beginning" certainly shows his indebtedness to his intellectual and spiritual heritage, both the Seondo tradition (the Korean form of Daoism) and the Neo-Confucian tradition.[17] Nonetheless, what is missing in Su-un's version of the one psychophysical energy is its subordination to a higher, more ultimate metaphysical principle.[18] Rather than being the firstborn of the chaos-like Way, the one psychophysical energy of chaotic beginning is itself the chaotic beginning of all thing-events. In other words, Ultimate Energy is the originary chaos at the root of the world of the myriad creatures. The fact that this originary chaos is "numinous" (靈 *ryeong*)—implying efficaciousness, power, and potency[19]—and "empty" (虛 *heo*) means that the chaos can be seen to consist in a nonordered, *indeterminate* swirl of *potentialities* from which orders or harmonies bubble up, and can precisely in that sense be understood to transcend the determinate cosmos as such. This chaotic beginning or origin is, however, not to be conceived primarily in a cosmogonic sense, as that which stood before or at the temporal beginning of the universe. The words for the chaotic beginning or origin, *honwon* (渾元), also mean "chaotic primacy" or "chaotic supremacy," as befitting Ultimate Energy as the all-pervasive, all-governing, and all-directing ultimate power of the universe. As such, Ultimate Energy is not merely the primordially undifferentiated form of psychophysical energy but also what could be called the ultimate chaotic "ground" of all concrete coalescences of psychophysical energy. It is that which ultimately underlies the ten thousand thing-events *here* and *now*, giving birth to and sustaining them as orders or harmonies, and in that sense "governing" and "directing" them toward the fulfillment of their very nature as orders or harmonies. Given that Ultimate Energy is a dynamic, not static, reality, perhaps a better designation would be the ultimate chaotic "depth" of the myriad creatures—with the connotations of oceanic fluidity—rather than "ground." Whether "ground" or "depth," however, Ultimate Energy transcends the ground/surface or depth/surface binary, as it is itself psychophysical energy and is thus not merely the ideal or abstract Other of the concrete physical coalescences of psychophysical energy. It is not an external power governing and directing them from a metacosmic "outside."

According to the twenty-one-character incantation, the "great descent" of this ultimate chaotic ground or depth of all thing-events on human beings is related directly to their "bearing" of Lord Heaven (侍天主 *si-cheonju*).

The character for "bearing," *si* (侍), has the connotations of "embodying," "hosting," "serving," and "nurturing." In other words, "bearing" Lord Heaven implies "embodying," "hosting," "serving," and "nurturing" Lord Heaven.[20] Su-un's own commentary on *si* provides a clue to this intriguing notion. Here is the second part of his commentary on the twenty-one-character incantation:

> "Bearing" [侍 *si*] means that, having the numinous spirit within and the harmonious becoming of psychophysical energy without, people each know and do not leave. "Lord" [主 *ju*] refers to honoring and serving [Heaven] like one's own parents. "Creative becoming" [造化 *johwa*] means becoming without artificial action. "Being established" [定 *jeong*] indicates being united with the [Heavenly] virtue and centered on the [Heavenly] heart-mind. . . . "Know" [知] means to understand the [Heavenly] way and to receive the [Heavenly] wisdom. If you brighten, therefore, the [Heavenly] virtue and never forget it, always keeping it in your mind, you will become one with Ultimate Energy and attain the perfect sagehood.[21]

In the beginning sentence in which Su-un comments somewhat cryptically on *si*, the first thing that stands out is his reference to the "numinous spirit within" (內有神靈 *naeyu sinryeong*). What is this spirit? The first part of the twenty-one-character incantation, in which the great descent of Ultimate Energy is prayed for, is called "the incantation for the descent of the numinous spirit" (降靈呪文 *gangryeong jumun*).[22] Further, in a conversation recorded in the Donghak scriptures, other Confucian scholars come to him and ask whether it is true that the "Numinous Spirit of Heaven" (天靈 *cheollyeong*) has descended upon him.[23] From these references it becomes clear that Su-un identifies the descent of Ultimate Energy with the descent of the Numinous Spirit of Heaven. In other words, the Numinous of Spirit of Heaven is what human beings bear within themselves when they bear Lord Heaven.

Now, the possession of numinous spirituality, which is understood to manifest in the form of consciousness, feeling, intelligence, and will, has always been considered as the defining characteristic of human beings and the human heart-mind—though not belonging exclusively to them—within the Neo-Confucian tradition.[24] Since Su-un affirms this understanding of numinous spirituality,[25] it is not surprising that he construes the human bearing of the Numinous Spirit of Heaven in terms of the human bearing of Lord Heaven as a "personal" deity. What this all implies is that, when the recovery of the fundamental connection between the bodily psychophysical energy of human beings and Ultimate Energy takes place with the great descent, the all-pervasive governing and directing agency of that ultimate chaos-like power becomes "personal" or "suprapersonal," taking on what is similar to yet at the same time much more than the characteristic identity of a human person with consciousness, feeling, intelligence, and will.[26] I add "suprapersonal," because Su-un does not define or explain Heaven (*haneul* in Korean or *cheon* in classical Chinese), even as he explains "Lord" as a title of honor and respect akin to the one given to the parents, perhaps closer to the Korean original *nim* than the classical Chinese *ju* ("master"). Every time he refers to Heaven in his commentary on the incantation, he merely uses the possessive pronoun *gi* (其)—meaning "his," "her," or "its"—which I have translated as "Heavenly" and put in square brackets, as in "the [Heavenly] virtue," "the [Heavenly] heart-mind," and so on. In other words, there is what may be called an apophatic sensibility in Su-un's thoughts about Heaven, that is, an attitude of awe, reverence, and intellectual humility before a transcendent reality, however personal or even anthropomorphic a form in which Heaven is encountered.[27] Nevertheless, reflecting the nondualistic relation between Ultimate Energy and the concrete coalescences of psychophysical energy, Lord Heaven or the Numinous Spirit of Heaven as the transcendent personal pole of the divine-human relation *is* in some sense also the immanent personal pole, as captured well in one of the first utterances of Lord Heaven to Su-un: "My heart-mind is no other than your heart-mind."[28]

It is precisely this nondualistic relationship between Lord Heaven and human beings that the character for "bearing," *si* (侍) encapsulates with its connotations of "embodying," "hosting," "serving," and "nurturing." In a sense, the great descent of Ultimate Energy on human beings means the "birth" and "growth" of Lord Heaven both *within* human beings and *as* human beings. Alternatively put, the great descent implies the birth and growth of the Numinous Spirit of Heaven both within and as human spirits. This is tantamount to saying that the recovery of the connection between the bodily psychophysical energy of human beings and Ultimate Energy lies at the basis of the interrelated becoming of human beings and Lord Heaven, that is, the divinization of human beings and the humanization of Lord Heaven. The core Donghak theological notion of *si-cheonju*, "bearing Lord Heaven," expresses none other than this cardinal truth—namely, the mutually linked birth and growth of human beings becoming Heavenly numinous spirits, on the one hand, and the Numinous Spirit of Heaven becoming human spirits, on the other, both emerging from the same chaotic "depth" of Ultimate Energy.

The second thing that merits a careful reading in Su-un's commentary on the notion of "bearing" is his reference to the "harmonious becoming of psychophysical energy without" (外有氣化 *waeyu gihwa*). Bearing Lord Heaven, he avers, means having the harmonious becoming of one's psychophysical energy take place in relation to what is outside. To understand what he means, it is helpful to take a look at a similar expression found a few lines down in the same commentary on the twenty-one-character incantation. According to the text of the incantation itself, when human beings bear Lord Heaven, what they also experience is the establishment of "creative becoming" (造化 *johwa*) within them. Creative becoming, Su-un explains in his commentary, means "becoming without artificial action" (無爲而化 *muwi-i-hwa*).[29] In other words, the bearers of Lord Heaven become what they become "self-so" (自然 *jayeon*) or spontaneously, without artificial effort and exertion full of self on their part.[30] Given that the bearers of Lord Heaven are being divinized to become Heavenly numinous spirits with the possession of the heart-mind of Lord Heaven, their creative becoming as spontaneous self-becoming means their liberation from their captivity within the so-called self-interested heart-minds (各自爲心 *gakja wisim*), that is, the small and selfish concerns of their individual selves. When Su-un interprets the "establishment" (定 *jeong*) of creative becoming within human beings in terms of their being united with the Heavenly virtue and being centered on the Heavenly heart-mind, he is referring precisely to this decentered and decentering self-transformative process at the core of "becoming without artificial action." It implies their becoming part of the cosmic self, joining a much larger stream of life and achieving their divinity or Heavenly spirituality in and through the ultimate creative power of the universe.[31]

The fact that Su-un leaves Heaven undefined and unexplained, however, means that the Heavenly virtue and the Heavenly heart-mind—that is, the names for the larger cosmic self or the ultimate creative power of the universe—function as an empty placeholder for radical transcendence beyond human grasp. This implies that Su-un's apophaticism does not permit the creative becoming of human beings to be construed as a self-less act of submission to a transcendent reality determinately defined as a wholly external power. At the same time, precisely because Heaven cannot be defined as a wholly external power, it cannot be defined as a wholly internal power either. Radical transcendence, in other words, is the flipside of radical immanence—both are beyond human grasp. The larger, transcendent cosmic self, or the ultimate creative power of the universe, to which the bearers of Lord Heaven are to be joined and aligned, is located neither "inside" nor "outside" of them. Perhaps the best way to envisage this both radically transcendent and radically immanent reality is to imagine it as the ultimate "depth" shared by the self and the other. The only way to reach the depth "within" is to reach out at the same time to the depth "without"—the depth found at the core of the other's being as becoming—and vice versa. As the ultimate chaotic "depth" of all concrete coalescences of psychophysical energy, Ultimate Energy fits the bill. If the great descent of Ultimate Energy implies human beings' bearing Lord Heaven, which in turn implies their decentered creative becoming, then the great descent can be understood as the process in which the individual coalescences of psychophysical energy become intimately connected to one another and, precisely in so doing, come to be attuned to the very source and depth of their mutually intertwined self-creation, namely, Ultimate Energy. Su-un's identification of the great descent of Ultimate Energy with the harmonious becoming of psychophysical energy (氣化 *gihwa*), found in the earlier part of his commentary, only lends further credence to this reading.

Hence, Su-un's identification of *si-cheonju* with the "establishment of creative becoming" (造化定 *johwajeong*) is the key to understanding the connection between *si-cheonju* and the "harmonious becoming of psychophysical energy without" (外有氣化 *waeyu gihwa*). The "harmonious becoming of psychophysical energy without" turns out to be no other than the establishment of one's true being as a constant self-creative process that is thoroughly connected to the interrelated becoming of all thing-events in the universe and predicated on the ultimate creativity and life-giving power of the universe that is Ultimate Energy.[32] This intimate attunement of one's self-creativity to the larger cosmic creativity "outside" is the flip side of the birth and growth of divinity "inside" one's body, that is, one's bearing and nurturing the Numinous Spirit of Heaven "within." In other words, the divinization or spiritualization of the bearers of Lord Heaven, which is identical to their attainment of the heart-mind of Lord Heaven, means no other than the transformation of their mutually indifferent individual selves into the larger cosmic self via the recovery of their shared primordial connection to the all-pervasive

Ultimate Energy. This blurring of the boundaries between inside and outside, or the microcosmic and the macrocosmic, is what the nondualistic duality of the numinous spirit "within" and the harmonious becoming of psychophysical energy "without" captures in a nutshell. When Su-un says the bearers of Lord Heaven "know and do not leave," he is pointing first to their transformed, divine or spiritual self-understanding—namely, their embodied, experiential understanding of their fundamental relatedness to the larger cosmos and of their inextricable rootedness in the chaotic depth of all. Second, he is referring to their spiritual-communal practice of actually living out that understanding, with their bodies being always deeply attuned to one another and to the rest of the creaturely world and acting in perfect sync with the creative power of Ultimate Energy.

Su-un calls those who have thus attained divine or spiritual selfhood—the heart-mind of Lord Heaven—in both understanding and practice, in good Confucian fashion, "superior persons" (君子 *gunja*), or "sages" (聖人 *seongin*), or after the time-honored Daoist ideal now brought down to the earthly realm, "divine transcendents on earth" (地上神仙 *jisang sinseon*).[33] Nevertheless, even as he recognizes the continuing value of both the classic Confucian virtues of humanity, rightness, ritual propriety, and wisdom, on the one hand, and the traditional Daoist prescription of talismans, incantations, and elixirs of immortality, on the other, for achieving such transcendent selfhood,[34] he offers a new regimen of psychosomatic practices called "keeping the heart-mind and rectifying psychophysical energy" (守心正氣 *susim jeong-gi*).[35] The following saying of Su-un's from *Dong-gyeong daejeon* clarifies further what he means: "My Way consists in becoming without artificial action. If you keep the [Heavenly] heart-mind and rectify the [Heavenly] psychophysical energy, follow the [Heavenly] nature and receive the [Heavenly] teachings, your transformation will spring spontaneously from the midst of self-so."[36] Again Su-un uses the possessive pronoun 其 (*gi*), implying *haneul* or Heaven, to show that the heart-mind which we are to keep and the psychophysical energy which we are to rectify are Heaven's. If the homophonic alternative expression found elsewhere in the scripture, "cultivating the heart-mind and rectifying psychophysical energy" (修心正氣 *susim jeong-gi*), is also taken into consideration, "keeping the heart-mind" means taking good care of the heart-mind of Lord Heaven—or the Numinous Spirit of Heaven—within each of us, nurturing it and guarding it against diminishment and loss.[37] "Rectifying psychophysical energy," by contrast, refers to the effort to transform one's psychophysical energy into a state of complete attunement to the Heavenly psychophysical energy, i.e., Ultimate Energy. Given that one's psychophysical energy is not other to the Heavenly psychophysical energy, rectifying the former can also be understood as rectifying the latter or, even better put, the Heavenly psychophysical energy rectifying itself. Likewise, keeping the Heavenly heart-mind within us is in a sense the Heavenly heart-mind within us keeping itself, however strange this may sound to ears accustomed to the dualistic subject-object division. Such blurring of the boundaries between microcosm and macrocosm lies behind Su-un's ending remark in the above quote, that our transformation will spring spontaneously from the midst of self-so. Even as the practice of keeping the heart-mind and rectifying psychophysical energy certainly requires the self-creative effort of individual human selves, their effort is a part or moment of the creativity of the larger cosmic self and ultimate depth of all, which acts so without anything making it act so. That is why Su-un declares at the beginning of the quote that his Way consists in "becoming without artificial action."

Further, precisely because the practice of keeping the heart-mind and rectifying one's psychophysical energy means one's becoming completely attuned to Ultimate Energy as the ultimate depth of each and every one of the myriad thing-events, the practice at the same time implies one's becoming intimately connected to the heart of the others in relations of reciprocity and interdependent becoming. In other words, the practice of keeping the heart-mind and rectifying psychophysical energy aims for and results in the establishment of one's unity and communicative relationality with the ten thousand creatures of the world.[38] Su-un affirms this point, in a typically Confucian fashion, by speaking of the practice as leading to the establishment of the four cardinal virtues of humanity, rightness, ritual propriety, and wisdom, for which becoming truly human in relations of empathetic reciprocity is the key. What is more, using the traditional language of Neo-Confucian self-cultivation, Su-un construes the practice of keeping the heart-mind and rectifying psychophysical energy more concretely in terms of the practice of sincerity (誠 *seong*) and reverence (敬 *gyeong*).[39]

One crucial difference, however, lies between the traditional Neo-Confucian teaching on self-cultivation and his new teaching. The Neo-Confucian self-cultivation, especially the way it is theorized and practiced by the hegemonic Cheng-Zhu school, has always emphasized learning the classics of the sages, because it has interpreted both the four cardinal virtues and the practice of sincerity and reverence primarily in reference to the authoritative—and predominantly hierarchical—patternings of human relations prescribed in those classics. It is precisely the practice of sincerity and reverence within the context of the classically prescribed patterns of human relations—the so-called Heavenly Pattern—which is demanded of the vast majority of people who have been born with turbid and impure kinds of psychophysical energy, if they are to have even a modicum of a chance to rectify their bodily constitution, to overcome their human desire, and to become genuinely human. The major implication of this has been that only those who have the means and leisure for many years and decades of study—that is, the land-holding or government-employed ruling class of literati—can properly engage in self-cultivation in the true sense of the term. Moreover, the cardinal virtues thus achieved by means of self-cultivation largely legitimate and reinforce the hierarchical patternings of human relations, although the principle of empathetic reciprocity built into them has tended to prevent the worst forms of domination and tyranny.

By contrast, the Donghak self-cultivative practice of keeping the heart-mind and rectifying psychophysical energy constitutes the "easy Way."[40] Even as Su-un does not deny the continuing value of the study of the Confucian classics in attaining the cardinal virtues, he sees it as having been superseded by his version of the practice of sincerity and reverence that has a third component added to it, namely, trust (信 *sin*).[41] By trust, he means the trust in Lord Heaven and her teachings encapsulated in the twenty-one-character incantation, just as by sincerity and reverence he means the sincerity and reverence toward Lord Heaven.[42] What is noteworthy here is that, in his version, trust has priority over sincerity and reverence because it is what undergirds the other two and makes them possible. The attitude of sincerity and reverence toward Lord Heaven starts from the trust in the teachings embodied in the incantation and summarized in the claim that human beings are bearers of Lord Heaven.[43] Moreover, because the teaching includes the idea that human beings and, in fact, all myriad thing-events bear Lord Heaven, the trust in that teaching naturally translates into an attitude of sincerity and reverence toward all.[44] If the attitude of sincerity and reverence toward the Numinous Spirit of Heaven within corresponds to the microcosmic practice of keeping the heart-mind, then the attitude of sincerity and reverence toward the ten thousand Heavenly numinous spirits without corresponds to the macrocosmic practice of rectifying psychophysical energy.[45] Since the only thing required to develop and nurture sincerity and reverence is one's trust in the embodied presence of Lord Heaven within and without, as taught by the incantation, the self-cultivative practice of keeping the heart-mind and rectifying psychophysical energy does not presuppose decades of classical studies practically possible only for those born into wealth and privilege.[46]

The pivotal role of trust in the Donghak self-cultivation is the reason for Su-un's characterizing of his Way as "becoming without artificial action." By trusting the presence of Lord Heaven within and without, one lets one's self-creative process carried by the waves of the ultimate creative depth of the universe without any blockage caused by self-interested and self-assertive action. The emphasis on trust is also why Su-un gives his teaching of Eastern Learning another name, "the Learning of the Heart-Mind" (心學 *simhak*).[47] The attainment of the ideal selfhood of the sage, or the divine transcendent, which is the attainment of the heart-mind of Lord Heaven, comes directly through the paradoxical trust in the indwelling of the heart-mind of Lord Heaven that is always already there in all of us and through the accompanying attitude of sincerity and reverence that is directed outward expansively to all creation. What underlies this whole paradigm of self-cultivation, centered on the attitude of the heart-mind, is the notion of the all-pervasive, chaotic creative depth of Ultimate Energy absently present in each of the myriad coalescences of psychophysical energy and enabling their fundamental and intimate connection with one another.

The revolutionary and socially explosive implications of Su-un's teaching of *si-cheonju* become clear here. By declaring that everyone is a bearer of Lord Heaven and that everyone can become the sage, or the divine transcendent, simply by trusting in Lord Heaven and the teachings contained in the mere twenty-one-character incantation, Su-un cuts the age-old tie between the Confucian ideal of the virtuous human being fit to lead and rule, on the one hand, and the hierarchical stratification of society based—in practice if not in principle—on birth and bloodline, on the other.[48] Although there may indeed be the difference of noble and base between people with varying psychophysical constitutions, the difference is based solely on whether or not they practice the "easy Way" of Eastern Learning. "Superior persons" (君子 *gunja*) and "inferior persons" (小人 *so-in*) are what they respectively are because the former have rectified their psychophysical energy in complete attunement to Ultimate

Energy and centered their heart-minds on the Heavenly heart-mind, thereby uniting their self-creativity with the ultimate creativity of the cosmos, while the latter have not.[49] The universally accessible character of the self-cultivative regimen of keeping the heart-mind and rectifying psychophysical energy, which is carried out in and through the practice of trust, sincerity, and reverence, delegitimizes from the outset any hierarchical patterning of human relations and social structures based on the intrinsically superior virtues of some over the rest. Su-un expresses this egalitarian ideal at the core of his teaching with the phrase "returning together to form one body" (同歸一體 *dong-gwi-il-che*).[50] The "opening of a new heaven and earth" (開闢 *gaebyeok*),[51] which is Su-un's way of putting in words the dawn of a new age, would be characterized by the advent of a free, egalitarian society of Heavenly numinous spirits who recognize their deep and primordial mutual connection in Ultimate Energy and reverence one another as bearers of Lord Heaven. The bearers of Lord Heaven form "one body" in solidarity precisely because their overcoming of their selfish interests, through the self-cultivative practice of keeping the heart-mind and rectifying psychophysical energy, is not beholden to and dictated by the hierarchical patternings of empathetic reciprocity prescribed in the classics.

Su-un's successor, Haewol, deepens and expands the egalitarian and democratic thrust of Su-un's Way when he teaches the followers of Eastern Learning to "nourish Lord Heaven" (養天主 *yang-cheonju*) in oneself and in one another, and to "treat every human being as Heaven" (事人如天 *sa-in yeo cheon*) because "humanity is Heaven" (人是天 *in si cheon*).[52] Much more explicitly than Su-un, Haewol condemns the social hierarchy between the elite literati class of *yangban* and the commoners, on the one hand, and the domestic hierarchy between the children of the official wife and the offspring of the concubines, on the other. Among the followers of Eastern Learning, he admonishes, there should be no fixed social pyramid because everyone is an offspring of Lord Heaven and is to be shown as much reverence as another.[53] Even though due order or even a chain of command may be a necessity in any group of people, the differences in power and prestige need to be always kept fluid, since those in higher positions are not intrinsically better than those in lower positions. Even those traditionally placed in the lowest strata, mainly women and children, can be one's elders and teachers, as they are no less bearers of Lord Heaven than the others.[54]

Furthermore, Haewol brings to the fore the ecological implications of his predecessor's teachings by enlarging the notion of *si-cheonju* explicitly to include nonhuman creatures, as seen in the numerous passages from *Haewol sinsa beopseol* (The sermons of Haewol the divine teacher) quoted in the prologue of this book.[55] From the premise that "among the myriad creatures, there is none that does not bear the Lord of Heaven" (萬物莫非侍天主 *manmul makbi si-cheonju*), Haewol derives his notion of "reverence for things" (敬物 *gyeongmul*).[56] This notion is a natural outgrowth of his understanding that all the myriad thing-events of the world emerge and live by "bearing the psychophysical energy of the Numinous Spirit of Heaven" (侍天靈氣 *si-cheollyeong gi*)[57] that is "Heaven's psychophysical energy of chaotic beginning" (天混元之氣 *cheon honwon ji gi*)[58]—namely, Ultimate Energy. For Haewol, not only no human being is to be treated as a nonperson just because he or she happened to be born a peasant, a slave, or a woman, but also an animal, a bird, or even a single blade of grass is to be honored and respected as an embodiment of the ultimate creative power of the universe.

Haewol brings his notion of reverence for things into the comprehensive principle of "three reverences" (三敬 *samgyeong*)[59]—reverence for Heaven, reverence for humanity, and reverence for things—in order to present the vision of a new world in which Su-un's egalitarian and solidary ideal of "returning together to form one body" (同歸一體 *dong-gwi ilche*) is realized to its maximum extent. Haewol's famous phrase, "feeding Lord Heaven by means of Lord Heaven" (以天食天 *i-cheon sikcheon*), is the consummate expression of the Donghak ideal of the myriad coalescences of psychophysical energy, all of which are Heavenly numinous spirits born of the chaotic depth of Ultimate Energy, forming one body in profound communion, mutual dependence, and respectful solidarity. It is for a reason that Haewol interprets the "harmonious becoming of psychophysical energy without" as pointing to the process of mutual help, mutual nurture, and mutually implicated becoming captured by the phrase, "feeding Lord Heaven by means of Lord Heaven."[60] Haewol's last instruction—"Set up the offerings to face yourselves" (向我設位 *hyang-a seolwi*)[61]—merely pushes the logic of the phrase, "feeding Lord Heaven by means of Lord Heaven," to its religiously and sociopolitically revolutionary conclusions. In consecrating the food and drink offerings to themselves, that is, by returning the fruit of their own labor to themselves, the unholy, ignoble, subjugated, and colonized multitude would be resisting the forces that tried to sever the vital link of psychophysical energy connecting all. In the revolutionary resistance of 1894, the Donghak teachings provided the moment of kairos for an irruption of the suppressed life-force of the subjugated multitude against the forces that tried to sever the free circulation of psychophysical energy between heaven and earth, the holy and the unholy, the human and the nonhuman, the noble and the base, male and female, the ruler and the ruled, the colonizer and the colonized. The "opening of the later heaven" (後天開闢 *hu-cheon gaebyeok*)[62]—which is Haewol's own formulation of Su-un's "opening of a new heaven and earth" (開闢 *gaebyeok*)—is the vision of a new world in which there would be the "harmonious becoming of psychophysical energy" in the entire cosmos without the artificial obstruction and excessive concentration of that cosmic energy in the hands of just a few or even one.

## "Ugeumchi Phenomenon": The Countercurrents of Ultimate Energy in History

Having explored the Donghak teaching of *si-cheonju* in the entire web of its meanings, we are in a better position to understand the full implications of Su-un's criticism of Western Learning (Christianity), that its adherents lack "the spirit of the harmonious becoming of psychophysical energy" (氣化之神 *gihwa ji sin*) in them. What is notable about the phrase, *gihwa ji sin*, is that it combines "the numinous spirit" (神靈 *sinryeong*)—in the abbreviated form of "spirit" (神 *sin*)—and "the harmonious becoming of psychophysical energy" (氣化 *gihwa*). In other words, Su-un faults Western Learning for its ignorance of the teaching and practice of having the numinous spirit within and the harmonious becoming of psychophysical energy without—namely, the teaching and practice of *si-cheonju*. Western Learning, he claims, does not teach and practice the divinization or spiritualization of the bearers of Lord Heaven by means of their attainment of the heart-mind of Lord Heaven. This is tantamount to saying that Western Learning has no understanding of human or creaturely fulfillment in terms of the transformation of self-seeking, mutually indifferent individual selves into the larger cosmic self via the recovery of their shared primordial connection to the ultimate creativity and life-giving power of the universe that is Ultimate Energy.

Hence, Su-un castigates Western Learning for envisioning Lord Heaven as a completely transcendent being separate from human and nonhuman creatures and dwelling in a heavenly palace. He is particularly critical of the corollary of such a view of divinity, that is, the selfish pursuit of individual salvation from this world imagined to consist in the postmortem entrance into the supposed heavenly dwelling place of Lord Heaven.[63] From the perspective of Eastern Learning, the problem at the core of Western Learning is that its understanding of divinity is purely ideal and metaphysical, without the critical mediating notion of psychophysical energy that would provide the vital and intimate connection between divinity and humanity, between human beings, and between human and nonhuman creatures.[64] Because it lacks such an organic and relational understanding of what may be called "theanthropocosmic"[65] reality, Western Learning excels in the production of violent instruments of domination, as proven by the seemingly invincible industrial and military might of the Western imperial powers, even as it propagates its message of "selfish" salvation offered by God as a perfectly transcendent patriarch and monarch, the Father and King of the universe.[66] Although Su-un's understanding of Christianity may be narrow and inadequate, pretty much limited to the teachings of the missionary Catholic Christianity underground in Korea in his times, he has a keen insight into the cancer at the core of the then dominant forms of imperial Christianity that were legitimating and buttressing the imperialistic aggressions of the Western industrial civilization against both human and nonhuman creatures of this planet.

Western Learning's destructive role is merely one prominent symptom of the ignorance of the truth of *si-cheonju* that has resulted in the all-pervasive reality of domination and subjugation characterizing the old era leading up to the present, namely, what Haewol calls "the former heaven" (先天 *seoncheon*).[67] Although they have had their part in instructing and guiding people, the ancient and established teachings of Confucianism, Buddhism, Christianity, and so on all belong to the old age and have proven themselves to fall short of the true Way of *si-cheonju*.[68] For Su-un, Donghak signals the advent of the new age, for its followers have in their bodies *gihwa ji sin*, the spirit of the harmonious becoming of psychophysical energy. They bear the Numinous Spirit of Heaven (Lord Heaven) within and, being deeply attuned to one another and the rest of the creaturely world, act in perfect sync with the creative power of Ultimate Energy. They are heralds and inaugurators of the "later Heaven" in which the myriad thing-events creatively come to be in harmony and solidarity without the artificial obstruction of the free movement of their psychophysical energy among one another—the very obstruction represented by the hierarchical dualisms of heaven and earth, the holy and the unholy, the human and the nonhuman, the noble and the base, male and female, the ruler and the ruled, and the colonizer and the colonized.

It is instructive at this point to hear a story told by one of the most creative contemporary interpreters of the Donghak movement and thought, the Korean poet and playwright Kim Ji-ha, in regard to the revolutionary resistance of 1894.[69] One day, while watching the rapid currents of polluted water flow down like a waterfall between the cement stepping-stones across the stream in front of his house after a heavy rainfall, he was amazed to see small fish swimming upstream and jumping from below to cross over the stepping-stones, striving against the torrential downflow in order to reach their birthplace. Faced with the mystery of the power of the small, feeble fish to ride such strong down currents upward, he pondered various possible explanations, such as an evolutionary adaptation to the environmental conditions most suitable for reproduction, or a mysterious creativity of the Creator. Finally, he came to the understanding that the fish's seemingly impossible power emerged when the "spiritual psychophysical energy" (神氣 *sin-gi*) of the fish was united with the same energy of the water. According to him, if the active (*yang*) movement of the psychophysical energy of the water consists in the water's downward flow, the receptive (*eum*) movement of the same psychophysical energy consists in the water's *upward* flow. In other words, the psychophysical energy of the water flow moves in both directions, downward and upward, at the same time. The fish have the power to move upstream against the down currents because, with their psychophysical energy united with the receptive movement of the water's psychophysical energy, the fish ride the invisible countercurrents of the water flow moving upward.

The psychophysical energy of both the fish and the water flow, Kim Ji-ha avers, is "spiritual" (神 *sin*) psychophysical energy, and is therefore capable of "awakening" (覺 *gak*) itself to numinous self-consciousness, especially in human beings. Human beings, in other words, are capable of riding the countercurrents of spiritual psychophysical energy in history with self-awareness and in freedom.[70] Relating this insight to the historical arena of the revolutionary resistance of 1894, Kim claims that what happened in that year, culminating in the climactic battle at the mountain pass of Ugeumchi, was not merely a class struggle, a rebellion to throw off the yoke of a rigid social caste system, or an explosion of the accumulated *han* of the *minjung*, that is, the "multitude of people" oppressed, exploited, and marginalized.[71] In Kim's own words, what happened, rather, was the following:

> With what kind of power did the hundreds of thousands of the minjung, who were nearly bare-handed even though they had things like matchlock muskets and bamboo spears, try to climb over the pass through the devilish onslaught of the machine gun fires of the Imperial Japanese Army and the Korean government troops? What was the source of the power that enabled them to advance toward their liberation, forming a mountain of corpses and a sea of blood, experiencing failure after failure, and climbing over dead body after dead body? . . . In short, the answer lies in the great awakening of the collective spiritual psychophysical energy of the minjung through the teachings of Donghak. The minjung became aware of and put into practice the numinous spirit of the harmonious becoming of psychophysical energy, i.e., the endlessly and expansively evolving, [self-]organizing, self-sanctifying, and self-spiritualizing Ultimate Energy. The entire event was a great cosmic movement in which the minjung's collective spiritual psychophysical energy, which had become self-conscious, struggled to unite itself with the primordial spiritual psychophysical energy of history, with its receptive-active movement, even in the midst of the demonic currents of history that cascaded down upon them. I will call this the "Ugeumchi phenomenon."[72]

What Kim Ji-ha calls the "Ugeumchi phenomenon" was the movement of the spiritual psychophysical energy of the oppressed, exploited, marginalized, and yet now collectively awakened, multitude of people to break through the seemingly insurmountable historical power structures of hierarchical dualism that blocked the harmonious becoming of psychophysical energy in the cosmos. Like the polluted waters flowing downstream in Kim's account, the power structures stand for the immoderately self-assertive forces of *yang* historically prevailing over the suppressed countervailing forces of *eum* (*yin*). They stand for the "enlightening" and "civilizing" enterprises consisting in concentrated wealth, dominating power, controlling and manipulative knowledge (technology), and ideals for individual moral perfection and harmonious social order insofar as they are predicated on a hierarchy of artificially created values in the service of the hegemonic group over the others. The heaven, the holy, the human, the noble, the male, the ruler, and the colonizer—these constitute the dominating forces of *yang* in the "former heaven" where their relational counterpart, namely, the earth, the unholy, the nonhuman, the base, the female, the ruled, and the colonized, are not let to be so of themselves, but instead "othered" and treated as external objects of suppression, control, and exploitation.

What the collectively awakened multitude of oppressed and exploited people tried to do at the pass of Ugeumchi was to bear the suppressed forces of *eum* and to enable the countercurrents of psychophysical energy in history to flow creatively "backward" to its origin in Ultimate Energy against the unrelenting global imperial march of modern "progress." By releasing the stifled life-energy of the earth, the unholy, the nonhuman, the base, the female, the ruled, and the colonized, the awakened minjung attempted to rectify the colossal and monstrous historical imbalance between the receptive and the active, between *eum* and *yang*, created by the human civilizations of the former heaven. For the multitude of downtrodden people climbing up the Uguemchi pass, the former heaven was embodied by the premodern agricultural "East" of the patriarchal and elitist Korean Confucian local power and the modern capitalist-industrial "West" of the equally patriarchal and elitist Japanese Empire. Their attempt, however, was not simply their own doing. As bearers of Lord Heaven in possession of the spirit of the harmonious becoming of psychophysical energy (or spiritual psychophysical energy), their bodies were already in sync with the creative power and movement of Ultimate Energy. What happened at Ugeumchi was in fact the Ultimate Energy "striving" to right its own creatively harmonizing movement, which had gone accumulatively out of balance over many thousands of years, in and through the explosive discharge of the suppressed life-force of the subaltern multitude, that is, the subjugated and abjected *eum* of history. The revolutionary resistance of 1894 was in that sense a case of "becoming without artificial action" (無爲而化 *muwi i hwa*), a consummate sociohistorical and cosmic example of the Daoist *wuwei* (無爲), or nonassertive action, in which the bearers of Lord Heaven became what they became "self-so" (自然 *jayeon*) or spontaneously, without artificial effort and self-ful exertion on their part.

Nevertheless, the revolutionary resistance of the sociohistorical and cosmic forces of the subjugated *eum* in 1894 seems to have failed in the face of the entrenched forces of the monstrously self-assertive *yang*. Does this mean the ultimate creative power of the universe, Ultimate Energy, failed to right itself, to restore balance to its own historical movement?

Here we must ask the meaning of one of Lord Heaven's sayings to Su-un in their very first encounter, that Lord Heaven has been "striving without results" (勞而無功 *no i mugong*) for fifty thousand years until finally finding success in Su-un.[73] Although the record of the encounter is couched in terms reflective of Su-un's affirmation of the significance of his own mission, the important point is the way the powerlessness of Lord Heaven without human and creaturely participation is underscored. Lord Heaven cannot be effectively creative in the world without the creativity of the myriad creatures.[74] Even to a greater extent, the creative power of Lord Heaven in history is meaningless when unrelated to the self-creativity of humans, particularly the life-energy of the oppressed, exploited, and marginalized multitude, who, when awakened, can work to stop the pendulum of history from swinging too far in the direction of collective and institutional self-assertion and domination of the other, that is to say, the "self-interested heart-minds" (各自爲心 *gakja wisim*) in the civilizational sense of the term. Su-un's apophatic refusal to define the term "Heaven" alludes to the nonsubstantial, nondualistic character of Lord Heaven—the fact that she is not a substantial entity separate from her bearers. This nondualistic apophaticism provides an empty, fluid, relative, historical, and relationally defined space of transcendent value and honor for the bearers of Lord Heaven to grow into and to occupy, thereby achieving the title of "lord" and "master"[75] and becoming the rightful subject-agents of creative and solidary historical praxis.[76]

Hence, to ask whether Ultimate Energy did or did not fail to right itself in 1894 is to ask the wrong question, to make a category mistake of a sort. Ultimate Energy is never itself a concrete subject-agent. It is always the chaotic matrix out of which the concrete subject-agency of creative historical praxis arises; and at the transcendent ideal pole of the subject-agency stands Lord Heaven or the Numinous Spirit of Heaven, while at its immanent pole stand the bearers of Lord Heaven who possess the spirit of the harmonious becoming of psychophysical energy. The concrete subject-agents, particularly humans among them, can fail properly to bear and to nurture the cosmic heart-mind of Lord Heaven within themselves despite its beckoning and, with each "self-interested heart-mind" curving back on itself in a gesture of dominating self-assertion, create ruptures in the web of the harmoniously intertwined becoming of their individual psychophysical energies. The immoderately and unilaterally self-assertive forces of *yang* prevailing in the former heaven, that is, the collective and institutional subjugation and domination of "the others," have been products of human subject-agents' unbalanced and nonrelational exercise of their self-creative power. By contrast, the countervailing forces of *eum*, which have surfaced in various forms ranging from peasant revolts to "day-to-day forms of resistance," including insubordination, withdrawal, migration, and subversive cultural practices,[77] represent the discharge of the suppressed self-creative life-force of the othered multitude. Sometimes the countervailing forces of *eum* acquire more *yang* in the sense of taking on more self-consciously ideal and even programmatic characters, subversively inhabiting the hegemonic discourses and positing alternative institutional visions, and precisely in so doing come closer to achieving a harmony of receptive and active, as in the cases of *revolutionary* resistance and even outright institutional revolution. The Donghak Peasant Revolution of 1894, with its highly literate yet subversive inhabitation of the ruling Neo-Confucian ideology and institutions by a significant part of its leadership, was one such case.[78] When such revolutionary resistances or institutional revolutions succeed, Ultimate Energy can be said to have righted itself, to have achieved an alignment of the currents and countercurrents of psychophysical energy in history with its own creatively harmonizing movement represented by the time-honored binary symbol of the Great Ultimate.

## Ultimate Energy, Lord Heaven, and Spirit: The Donghak Trinity and the Democracy of Numinous Spirits

At the end of the last chapter, I stated that Nongmun's notion of the equal actuality of pattern and psychophysical energy represented the resistance of the idea of psychophysical energy against its suppression from within the ruling, hegemonic Neo-Confucian discourses, whereas the Donghak concept of Ultimate Energy embodies that same resistance from the perspective of the nonhegemonic discourses of the ruled, that is, the oppressed, exploited, and marginalized multitude of people. Hence, the Nongmunian panentheism of the transcendent body, which is a product of the conversation I have staged among Nongmun, Whitehead, Deleuze, and Keller, needs to face the theology of Eastern Learning if my project of tracing the adventures of the idea of psychophysical energy is to accomplish its stated goal of arriving at a comparative theology of Spirit that is at once also a decolonizing Asian theology of Spirit. Given the trinitarian structure of the Nongmunian panentheism of the transcendent body, such an encounter certainly calls for a trinitarian reflection. At the same time, the prominent place given to the historical role of the minjung in Donghak thought, especially as it is interpreted by Kim Ji-ha, demands a serious engagement of the question of the resistant and revolutionary subject-agency of the oppressed, exploited, and marginalized multitude.

First, a trinitarian reflection: As discussed at the end of the last chapter, in the Nongmunian panentheistic scheme with a Deleuzian-Kellerian inflection, the ultimate creative power of the universe, the Great Ultimate, is the triad of Change (易 *yeok*), Way (道 *do*), and Spirit (神 *sin*), each of which consists in a dipolar union of pattern and psychophysical energy. Change as the substance of the Great Ultimate designates the "womb" of enfolded chaotic actuality that is creatively restless. What ontologically undergirds the creative restlessness of that chaotic actuality is the chaotic virtuality of the Non-Ultimate that consists in the unmediated empathetic coexistence of indeterminate multiplicity (the so-called "all figures") forming an incipient, "problematic" unity—what may be called "equilibrium" (中 *jung/zhong*). The Way as the pattern of the Great Ultimate corresponds to the repeated unfolding of divergent patterns of actualities—the achieved harmonies of the myriad thing-events (和 *hwa/he*)—as "solutions" to the "problematic" unity of Change. Spirit as the function of the Great Ultimate, lastly, names humanity (仁 *yin/ren*) as empathy, that is, the affective power of mutual openness and attraction, which brings together and puts in direct relation the incipiently determinate "all figures" within Change, on the one hand, and the divergent actual patterns of the Way, on the other. Spirit overcomes the explosive tension between differences forced into unmediated coexistence and gives birth to the "life-giving intention" permeating Change and patterning the Way. That is why Spirit is precisely what sustains the perfect clarity, openness, and communicative resonance of pattern and psychophysical energy in their original condition despite their chaotic multiplicity within Change, making possible their all-pervasive and life-giving concrete universality as they unfold together in the Way.

A distinctive feature of this panentheistic trinitarian scheme is that it interprets the second member of the trinity, the Way, through the "lens" of the interdependent becoming of God and creation. It envisions the divinity, *theos*, as emerging together with the cosmos from Change in the very process of mutually infolded unfolding of the myriad determinate patterns of coexistence. The divinity is the name given to the specific pattern that is born from Change as a transcendent ideal, or value, of creation and which is always already found incarnated in and luring the process of the unfolding of the cosmos from Change. When this ideal or lure is projected back to the ultimate (non-)origin, the "surface" of Change is "painted"—to use Keller's terms—precisely in the shape of that ideal, that deity. The anthropomorphically envisaged personal deities are in that sense *both* the transcendent ideals and lures for the specifically human patterns of unfolding actualities—"personhood," "self-consciousness," "subjectivity," "intellect," "will," etc.—*and* the products of human interpretations of Change in accordance with those specifically human patterns of unfolding actualities. Spirit's role, particularly for humans, is to keep us humans and our deity in unmediated, empathetic relation to each other, enabling their mutual lure and mutually interrelated becoming, i.e., both the incarnation or kenosis of the deity as the heart-mind of the Way and the divinization or theosis of human beings as human heart-minds. In this way, Spirit, which is also human spirit, keeps both the deity and humans rooted in and attuned to the empathetically codified ontological depth of Change as the placeholder of always new, incipiently creative beginnings.

Does this triadic and trinitarian panentheistic scheme resonate with the theology of Donghak? Some studies of Donghak theology have highlighted the duality—not trinity—of Ultimate Energy and Lord Heaven, seeing Lord Heaven as an anthropomorphic personalization of Ultimate Energy that is experienced in human consciousness as a responsive being, on the one hand, and Ultimate Energy as Lord Heaven's primordial, all-pervasive universal mode of being, on the other.[79] I agree on the presence of such a duality, but I also see the potential for a triadic or trinitarian framework of interpretation. The triad would consist of Ultimate Energy (至氣 *jigi*), Lord Heaven (天主 *cheonju*), and the Spirit of the harmonious becoming of psychophysical energy (氣化之神 *gihwa ji sin*). Although this triad has much in common with the Nongmunian triad, there are major differences. The differences have most of all to do with the fact that the Donghak "trinity" is based on what may be called a monism of psychophysical energy,[80] whereas the Nongmunian "trinity" still retains the qualified-dualistic framework of the Cheng-Zhu Neo-Confucianism, presenting a picture of the Great Ultimate as a dipolar union of pattern and psychophysical energy, while subverting that framework from within and thereby rendering itself open to a dialogue with Whitehead, Deleuze, and Keller. Hence, there is a great potential for mutual enrichment that would lead to a better constructive vision.

To begin with, Ultimate Energy as the one psychophysical energy of chaotic beginning would correspond to the ultimate chaotic depth and source of all that becomes, and can be seen to consist in a nonordered, indeterminate swirl of potentialities from which orders or harmonies bubble up, befitting its characterization as "numinous" (靈 *ryeong*)—implying efficaciousness, power, and potency—and "empty" (虛 *heo*). To this interpretation of the ultimate creative power of the universe, the Nongmunian-Deleuzian-Kellerian rendition of Change as the "womb" of enfolded chaotic actuality can bring in the needed conceptual precision. Particularly beneficial is the distinction made in the latter scheme between virtuality and actuality, because the notion of chaotic virtuality as the creative "lure" of enfolded chaotic actuality adds further ontological depth and helps explain the reason for the creative restlessness—the "bubbling up" of novel orders and harmonies—characterizing Ultimate Energy. Because the virtual-actual relation is one of unequal—different—halves constituting a "problem" and its "solutions," if the distinction between virtuality and actuality is introduced into the notion of the nonordered, indeterminate swirl of potentialities constituting Ultimate Energy, it ensures that whatever patterns or harmonies emerge from the one psychophysical energy of chaotic beginning are not imperfect and subordinate copies of some perfect model or archetype. It guarantees that Ultimate Energy remains the *heterogeneous* depth of all that becomes, and that the unfolding of divergent patterns of actualities—the myriad thing-events—would be genuinely spontaneous, free, and new, beholden to no predetermined ideal Pattern.

At the same time, the monism of psychophysical energy represented by the Donghak notion of Ultimate Energy may stand as a criticism of the Nongmunian trinity for opening up what could be a slippery slope toward conferring a sense of ultimacy to pattern (理 *li*) and thereby repeating, all over again, the historical subordination of psychophysical energy to a higher metaphysical principle. The Nongmunian panentheism of transcendent body conceives the chaotic virtuality in Change as a dipolar union of pattern and psychophysical energy in their original condition of indeterminate multiplicity. But owing to the historical baggage carried by the notion of pattern with its close association with the Heavenly Pattern as the imperial and colonizing archetype whose concrete shape is prescribed in the authoritative tradition of the Confucian classics, the conception of the chaotic virtuality in Change as the dipolar union of pattern and psychophysical energy is constantly dogged by one nagging question: Can it ever fully and successfully be cast as ontological "problem" rather than as ontological model? Of course, the saving grace for the Nongmunian appropriation of the Deleuzian notion of virtuality in the previous chapter is that it envisions pattern in its original condition as the placeholder for an opening toward the radically new from within the physicality and materiality of psychophysical energy in its original condition, not a separate and independent metaphysical principle with logical, ontological, and normative priority over the latter. Nevertheless, if the possibility of the radically new can be secured without having recourse to a notion with as much ambiguous historical impact as pattern, then that would be a trajectory of thought worth entertaining.

Within the Donghak "trinity" that I am putting forward, the notion of Lord Heaven initially appears to provide an alternative way of allowing a space for the radically new. Lord Heaven represents the transcendent ideal or lure for the becoming of the myriad thing-events, which emerges together with the myriad thing-events themselves from Ultimate Energy in the same way that divinity and world, the heart-mind of the Way and the creaturely heart-minds, emerge interdependently from Change within the Nongmunian paradigm. Hence, the fact that Heaven is left undefined and unexplained apophatically intimates the possibility that the transcendent ideal or lure does not consist in mere realignments of the patterns of the old orders but also in totally, radically unanticipated patterns of becoming for the myriad thing-events beyond the horizon of conceptual possibilities. But since Lord Heaven is only a "creature" of Ultimate Energy, even with its apophatic character the concept of Lord Heaven can only symbolize the possibility of the radically new, not explain how the radically new is possible in the first place. Since the Donghak notion of Ultimate Energy as the ultimate creative depth of all does not by itself provide an explanation, we seem to have come upon a roadblock.

Here the Nongmunian-Deleuzian-Kellerian notion of Spirit as the power of empathetic communication and relation may offer a possible path forward. Within the panentheism of transcendent body, Spirit names empathy, namely, the affective power of mutual openness and attraction that brings together and puts in unmediated relation the incipiently determinate multiplicity within Change, making possible both the enfolding of chaotic actuality and the folding through of chaotic virtuality underlying the former's creative restlessness. Further, Spirit is the power of empathetic connection, which keeps the divergent patterns of the Way infolded in one another as they unfold in and from Change, enabling their mutual lure and mutually interrelated becoming, including humans and their divinity. As such, the concept of Spirit within the Nongmunian panentheistic framework affirms the fundamentally affective grounding of the cosmos rather than a conceptual one, since the birth of orders, patterns, and harmonies is ultimately predicated on the direct and mutually empathetic coexistence of the incipiently determinate multitude within Change. If, however, the emergence of the cosmos depends on the direct, empathetic "self-codification" and "self-problematization" of the incipiently determinate many without any preexistent primordial pattern guiding them, then it is certainly possible for the primordial multitude to be agents of ontological creativity—that is, capable of connecting to one another in such a manner as to give birth to wholly new patterns of actuality beyond the horizon of existing and predictable conceptual possibilities.

This pneumatological explanation of ontological creativity, or the creation of radical novelty, shows that it is possible to argue that the Nongmunian panentheism does not really need to retain, as it does, the loaded notion of pattern in its original condition in the "virtual" ontological depth of Change, however narrowed its semantic range may be. From the Nongmunian perspective, the point of retaining the notion of pattern in its original condition is to signify that the utterly free spontaneity of the "all figures" within Change is intrinsically and ultimately inclined toward a cosmos, not a sheer, barren chaos, and that therefore the radically new consists in radically new *orders* and *harmonies*. The structural/normative ground of the world and the dynamic ground of the world still need to be distinguished from each other and structured in a symmetrically dipolar relation within Change, if a *creative*, not annihilating, ontological depth is to be assigned to it. But from the perspective of the Donghak monism of psychophysical energy, the retention of the Cheng-Zhu qualified-dualistic paradigm on the part of the Nongmunian panentheism hints at a continuing veiled distrust of psychophysical energy, despite the repeated affirmation of the concretely universal presence of psychophysical energy in its original condition with its own affectively unifying and harmonizing power. There may be no need for such a conceptual fail-safe as the notion of pattern in its original condition, if the spontaneous dynamism of psychophysical energy in its original condition can be fully trusted to be creative, not pointless and futile. In other words, the structural/normative ground of the world, which is distinguished from the dynamic ground of the world and stands in a dipolar relation to the latter, is not only superfluous but can also be a threat to the fully integral conception of psychophysical energy in its original condition.

Given that Nongmun's thesis of the equal actuality of pattern and psychophysical energy itself represents a potentially subversive rewriting of the hegemonic Neo-Confucian discourse, the choice between the Nongmunian qualified dualism and the Donghak monism may not be one between a continuing subordination of psychophysical energy and its full liberation. Nonetheless, the argument from history, pointing to the baggage attached to the notion of pattern, cannot be taken lightly, especially if a continued employment of that notion leads to a not totally unfounded suspicion that a concealed devaluation of psychophysical energy may be operative. Further, if we take the Donghak advice and jettison the notion of pattern in its original condition of indeterminate multiplicity as superfluous in the end, even to the Nongmunian trinity itself, the result may not be that we end up with a barren chaos. Ultimate Energy as the one psychophysical energy of chaotic beginning pure and simple may still be regarded as the site of new creative beginnings, thanks to Spirit's power as connection-in-itself. The power of mutual openness and attraction permeating the incipiently determinate many is precisely what keeps their dynamism creative of harmonies and orders, even radically and irreducibly novel ones. Spirit frees the transcendent ideal and lure of Lord Heaven to be determined by the spontaneous self-codification and self-problematization of the primordial many, not by some eternally preexistent original Heavenly Pattern whose concrete shape is conveniently prescribed in the ancient and venerable works of the sages. Spirit's fundamentally nonconceptual, affective grounding of the cosmos enables Ultimate Energy to remain the *heterogeneous* depth of all that becomes, despite the fact that it consists of the same psychophysical energy as the myriad coalescences of psychophysical energy unfolding from it.

Another significant comparative point to note is that the Nongmunian Spirit's power to keep the divergent patterns of the Way infolded in one another as they unfold in and from Change, enabling their mutual lure and mutually interrelated becoming, helps explain the operation of *gihwa ji sin*, that is, the Spirit of the harmonious becoming of psychophysical energy, within the Donghak triad. As previously made clear, the notion of *gihwa ji sin* encapsulates the truth of *si-cheonju*, the bearing of Lord Heaven, for it combines having the numinous spirit within and the harmonious becoming of psychophysical energy without. It refers to the divinization or spiritualization of the bearers of Lord Heaven by means of their attainment of the heart-mind of Lord Heaven, which is the same as the transformation of their self-seeking, mutually indifferent individual selves into the larger cosmic self via the recovery of their primordial connection to the creatively transforming power of Ultimate Energy. What the introduction of the Nongmunian idea of Spirit does is that it conceptually clarifies the ontological ground of the creaturely freedom at the core of this Donghak pneumatological notion of *gihwa ji sin*.

As argued, Spirit's power as connection-in-itself provides the basis for the determination of the transcendent ideal and lure of Lord Heaven by the spontaneous self-codification and self-problematization of the primordial many in Ultimate Energy, not by some eternally preexistent original Heavenly Pattern dictating and imposing itself upon Ultimate Energy. But given that Ultimate Energy is the shared ultimate creative depth of the bearers of Lord Heaven, the incipiently determinate many at the heart of Ultimate Energy also point to the creative chaos within each and every one of the bearers of Lord Heaven. In other words, neither the heart-mind of Lord Heaven, which the bearers are to attain, nor the creative depth of Ultimate Energy, to which the bearers are to connect themselves, represents a "higher power" external to them and demanding their submission. This means that the concrete shape or pattern of Lord Heaven or—to say the same thing—the larger sociohistorical and cosmic self, which the bearers of Lord Heaven are to bear, to nurture, to grow into, and to form in empathy and solidarity, is determined by the spontaneous self-creativity of the bearers in tune with their own yet heterogeneous creative depth. If so, then the "one body," to which they are to "return together" in empathy and solidarity, cannot be a homogeneous body. Because it is a joint product of the spontaneous self-creativity of each and every one of the bearers of Lord Heaven, the "one body" is bound to be fraught with differences—it is bound to be a genuine *multitude*.[81] Nonetheless, the Spirit of the harmonious becoming of psychophysical energy is the power of empathy that brings differences into unmediated relation, opening up a space for their mutual lure and mutually interrelated becoming. Since this Spirit is the spirit of the bearers themselves, the Donghak trinity proposed here offers a radical vision of the creative freedom of the bearers of Lord Heaven, that is, a radical democracy of Heavenly numinous spirits without any Heavenly Overlord and Master, which defies the logic of the One—the logic of empire—with the mutual empathy of the resistant multitude.

The vision of a democracy of numinous spirits briefly glimpsed here brings to the table the second issue raised at the beginning of this section, namely, the place of the resistant and revolutionary subject-agency of the oppressed, exploited, and marginalized multitude within the meeting of the Nongmunian-Deleuzian-Kellerian panentheism of transcendent body with the theology of Donghak. As discussed in the previous chapter, the panentheism of transcendent body shows how the movement between the active phase of the Great Ultimate as function and the receptive phase of the Great Ultimate as substance (or the Non-Ultimate) can be genuinely spiral, thereby ensuring the self-creative freedom of the myriad thing-events on both microcosmic and macrocosmic levels. On the strength of their indeterminate, "problematic" character, which demands divergent creative "solutions," the empathetically enfolded multitude within the Great Ultimate in its receptive phase offers a heterogeneous space of creative freedom for the achieved orders of the world returning to it. In this space of creative freedom, the primordial multitude of potentialities "codify," ever anew, novel—even radically novel—patterns of creative harmonization that are not present antecedently in the past harmonies. The novel codifications of the empathetic interrelatedness of the incipiently determinate multitude, then, provide in the active phase of the Great Ultimate both the heterogeneous condition of possibility for and the initial spur to the spontaneous unfolding of the myriad thing-events that are "let go" into different yet mutually infolded lines of self-creation.

Nevertheless, as Kim Ji-ha has pointed out, the history of the former heaven—the last fifty thousand years—has been one of colossal and monstrous imbalance between the receptive and the active, between *eum* and *yang*, created by the excessively self-assertive forces of *yang* embodied in human civilizations and their institutional power structures of hierarchical dualism that have blocked the harmonious becoming of psychophysical energy in the cosmos. The return of the achievements of human civilizations and their proud rulers to their chaotically multiple and heterogeneous (non-)origin in Ultimate Energy has been hampered again and again, stopping the pendulum of history from swinging back and leading to the permanent "othering" of the bearers of *eum* awaiting them at their chaotic (non-)origin—that is, the earth, the unholy, the nonhuman, the ignoble, the female, the ruled, and the colonized.

Instead, the rulers of human civilizations have installed the ossified Heavenly Pattern at their imagined origin, which allegedly authorizes their exclusive reign, in order to keep at bay the din of the "othered" multitude, the clamor of the heterogeneous and chaotic (non-)origin, which is returning to them and to which they are returning, despite their obstinate denial. The authoritative tradition of the classics of the sages has suppressed and preempted the power of the excluded multitude to "re-problematize" and to "re-codify" the grand historical enterprises of the masters, which is the same thing as suppressing their power to "re-problematize" and "re-codify" the use of their very life-energy hitherto in docile servitude to those enterprises.

If Ultimate Energy is to restore the balance of its historical movement so that its historical folding and unfolding could be in sync with its primordial movement represented by the symbol of the Great Ultimate, it is imperative that the multitude, who occupy a spectrum along the lowest end of the historically subjugated and abjected *eum*, exercise their creative freedom. They are to be free to "problematize" and to "codify" their mutual empathetic connections so that a space of possibility may be created for the emergence of Lord Heaven for them to bear as the transcendent ideal and lure for new, liberating, and life-giving forms of human civilizational praxis—what Su-un calls "later Heaven." What signal the beginning of the countervailing movement of the *eum* for the restoration of Ultimate Energy's historical balance are the "day-to-day forms of resistance"—such as protests, insubordination, withdrawal, migration, subversive cultural practices, and even riots and popular revolts—which exemplify the rebounding of the suppressed self-creative life-force of the othered multitude.[82] Such forms of resistance represent the increase of entropy, of disorder, within the "progressive" currents of psychophysical energy in history and precisely in that sense embody the countercurrents of psychophysical energy that carry the orderly achievements of human civilizations "backward" to its chaotic (non-) origin, to the unruly multitude. Indeed, present among the multitude are those whom Gayatri Chakravorty Spivak has named "subaltern"—those "structurally and systematically written out or excluded from any hegemonic ideology, official history, developed economic structure, or political system of representation"[83]—whose resistance can take the form, if at all, only of a sheer, inarticulate discharge of suppressed life-force. But insofar as the resistant role of the multitude is to bear, grow, and historically manifest in concrete forms of collective living the transcendent ideal and lure of Lord Heaven, as the Donghak teaching insists, the countervailing forces of *eum* are to take on more features of *yang* and not retain the purely deconstructive role of the externalized, "subaltern" *eum* confined to "the sheer heterogeneity of decolonized space."[84] In other words, the movement of Ultimate Energy to rectify its historical imbalance of receptive and active, *eum* and *yang*, involves forms of resistance of the multitude that have more self-consciously ideal and even programmatic characters, subversively inhabiting the hegemonic discourses and positing alternative institutional visions, as was the case in the revolutionary resistance of 1894 with its subversive rewriting of the ruling Neo-Confucian ideology. Su-un, the founder of Donghak, was himself a paradigmatic example of such forms of resistance.

In fact, in reflecting on the role of the resistant and revolutionary subject-agency of the multitude within the historically self-rectifying movements of Ultimate Energy, the value of the Donghak teachings is that they show how the multitude's resistance can inhabit the hegemonic discourses and become more "active," "positive," and "constructive" while remaining nontotalitarian; that is, they can remain egalitarian and democratic with chances of domination and exclusion minimized. Even as it puts forward, as the goal of self-cultivation, the traditional moral and political ideal of the sage-ruler in firm possession of the fully empathetic heart-mind of the Way and the four Heavenly cardinal virtues of empathetic reciprocity, the Donghak teaching of keeping the heart-mind and rectifying psychophysical energy cuts out the pivotal mediation of the classical literate tradition of learning that has made the attainment of the ideal the privilege of an elite class. Instead, the multitude are called on simply to trust in and reverence the embodied presence of Lord Heaven both within and without, as taught by the twenty-one-character incantation. To put it another way, the teaching is for the multitude to give birth to the heart-mind of Lord Heaven and to grow into its likeness by letting their self-creative process be attuned to the chaotic yet creative waves of Ultimate Energy that is in each and every one of them and, precisely in so doing, to come to form an egalitarian and democratic form of collective life characterized by creative freedom in empathy and solidarity. Hence, rather than signaling a purely critical, deconstructive posture, the apophatic nondefinition of Heaven points to the fluid, relative, historical, and relationally defined shape of the transcendent ideal and creative lure that the collectively awakened multitude give birth to and grow into in order to become the subject-agents of creative and solidary historical praxis. The experiment in democratic self-government, which the collectively awakened bearers of Lord Heaven briefly carried out in the part of Korea under their control in 1894, was one of the historical crests of such "active" and "constructive" resistances by the subjugated and excluded multitude whose depth of creative life-energy and freedom could no longer be contained.

# Epilogue

## THE SPIRIT-QI OF THE MULTITUDE UNDER THE CROSS OF EMPIRE

The journey I have taken in this book has all along been in search of what Whitehead calls "a democracy of fellow creatures" in response to Su-un's critique of the "spirit-less" theology of missionary Christianity. It is an attempt to decolonize Christian theology from its colonization by the logic of empire, namely, the logic of the One, so that its suppressed capacity for *chaophilia* could be released. It is an endeavor to come up with a pneumatocentric conception of God that resists and subverts the hierarchical binaries of one and many, ideal and material, mind and body, spirit and nature, abstract and concrete, and universal and particular, which have plagued the Christian theological tradition in the West—or the North Atlantic world—and now globally, thanks to the missionary expansion. For this work I have enlisted the help of the East Asian cosmo-ontological notion of psychophysical energy, following its "adventures" in the Daoist and Confucian traditions and observing how its suppressed nondualistic, equalizing, emancipatory, and holistic potentials keep showing themselves resiliently, and thus enabling a richly productive dialogue with various analogues in the theological and philosophical constellations of the modern or late-modern Western world. At the end of the journey, I have arrived at what I hope is a fertile pneumatocentric and panentheistic conception of the Trinity underpinning a liberating pneumatology of the divine-creaturely multitude, that is, the vision of what may be called "a democracy of numinous spirits." Before I conclude, however, I would like to provide a brief sketch of a possible constructive development of the theology of Spirit-Gi (or Spirit-Qi) in response to the present postcolonial-neocolonial global context.

At the beginning of the twenty-first century, we are witnessing the global dominance of a newest form of immoderately self-assertive *yang* with its own subtle power structures of hierarchical dualism. Called "Empire" by the political philosophers Michael Hardt and Antonio Negri, this latest incarnation of human civilizational excess is different from the empires of the recent past in the sense that it is not a product of the expansion of the territory, power, and influence of a nation-state via military, political, economic, and cultural domination. Empire, according to Hardt and Negri, is a "network power"[1] or a "new global form of sovereignty," which includes as its "nodes"—its primary elements—the dominant nation-states along with supranational institutions such as major transnational corporations.[2] Although it has no unified center and is thus unlike previous forms of imperialism, it does have internal divisions and hierarchies, as some elements in Empire's network, such as the dominant nation-states and transnational corporations, have enormous power over the other elements. But despite its internal divisions and hierarchies, all the elements and powers in Empire's network cooperate to create and maintain the current global order.[3]

Even as Empire aspires to a total domination of the globe, however, there are forces of resistance growing within it, for the globalization of Empire's transnational network of power implies at the same time a creation of new circuits of transnational cooperation and collaboration. Hardt and Negri call the networked forces of resistance to Empire "multitude." Unlike the unitary notion of *people* assuming a single identity, or the *masses* implying an indifferent, indistinct conglomerate in which differences are submerged and drowned, or the *working class* denoting exclusively waged workers, the *multitude* is an open and expansive network in which all differences—cultures, races, ethnicities, genders, sexual orientations, forms of labor, ways of living, views of the world, and desires—can express freely and equally, communicate with one another, and act in common.[4] What enables the multitude so to network, communicate, and collaborate is the fact that they are producers of the "common," which they share to begin with (xiv). By the "common," Hardt and Negri first of all refer to the biophysical, economic, and cultural conditions of their communication and collaboration: "We share bodies with two eyes, ten fingers, ten toes; we share life on this earth; we share capitalist regimes of production and exploitation; we share common dreams of a better future" (128). But at the same time, the common refers to the *immaterial production* of the multitude, namely, their production of ideas, knowledge, forms of communication, and affective relationships. In other words, the immaterial production of the multitude both presupposes and produces the common: "Our common knowledge is the foundation of all new production of knowledge; linguistic community is the basis of all linguistic innovation; our existing affective relationships ground all production of affects; and our common social image bank makes possible the creation of new images" (148).

The common, in fact, is not only both the condition and the product of the immaterial production but also the middle or mediating link, as the processes of the immaterial production are themselves communicative and collaborative. A notable feature of the current form of economic and social production is the emergence of what might be called post-Fordist forms of production: service work, caring labor, intellectual and cognitive labor, and affective labor, carried out by food servers, salespersons, health workers, teachers, computer engineers, and so on. These workers, usually without long-term contracts, form flexible, mobile, and unstable labor units designed to respond rapidly to changing market conditions, but at the same time always involving affective communication and collaboration (107–8, 113). These forms of immaterial production constitute the fastest growing sector in the dominant nation-states within Empire's network. Although not yet quantitatively dominant, they have become hegemonic in qualitative terms in the sense that the other forms of production such as industry and agriculture are adopting their characteristics, as seen for instance in the trend to informationalize and network (109, 114–15).

The crucial claim made by Hardt and Negri here is that, being affectively communicative and collaborative, the immaterial production is *biopolitical*. Expressed otherwise, even as it puts to work the ideas, emotions, and bodily affects of the workers from which the workers themselves are alienated (109–11), by virtue of its inherently communicative and collaborative nature, the immaterial production is conducive to the production of a network-based democratic political subjectivity that is involved in network struggles against Empire's network of power (82–91, 211–19).[5] By network struggles, Hardt and Negri mean the kind of resistance taking the form of a distributed-network in which "each local struggle functions as a node that communicates with all the other nodes without any hub or center of intelligence" (217). Network struggles involve a kind of "swarm intelligence" based fundamentally on communication—for which the Internet, with its various nodes remaining different yet mutually connected, and with its external boundaries open, is a good model (xv, 91). Unlike the bourgeoisie who needed a unifying absolute authority—the modern nation-state—to become a political subject, the multitude is capable of forming a political society autonomously and thereby becoming a political subject precisely because of the multitude's networked intelligence based on affectively communicative and collaborative relationships of production (xvii–xviii). That is why the multitude is a *biopolitical* concept, at once economic and political (103–5), forming a political body without hierarchy: "Rather than a political body with one that commands and others that obey, the multitude is *living flesh* that rules itself" (100). Furthermore, those who are excluded from waged labor—the poor, the migrant, the unemployed, and the homeless—are not excluded from the multitude, as can be seen from the inclusion of the migrant poor in various forms of service work and the increasingly central role they play in agriculture (129). More generally, social production as biopolitical—"immaterial"—production, such as "the production of knowledge, information, linguistic forms, networks of communication, and collaborative social relationships," tends to involve all of society (129–30). Hence, the external boundaries of the multitude are porous, allowing the inclusion of industrial workers, agricultural workers, the poor, and migrants as active subjects of biopolitical production and biopolitical self-rule (137–38). The other name of the multitude, *legion*, captures well the defining character of the multitude as "an internally different, multiple social subject whose constitution and action is based not on identity or unity (or much less, indifference) but on what it has in common" (100).

Even as Hardt and Negri present a penetrating analysis of the regnant global order, Empire, their account of the multitude as a democratic political subject leaves something to be desired. The trio of theologians of Empire, Néstor Miguez, Joerg Rieger, and Jung Mo Sung, have advanced what in my view is a necessary supplement and corrective to the account of Hardt and Negri on how democracy can and does emerge in the midst of the current global imperial order. According to them, the Empire analyzed by Hardt and Negri is the empire of globalized late financial capitalism, in which "the true network that contains the Empire is the international financial network, to which the people and their expectations, cultures and nations must submit."[6] Whereas Empire is a "particular configuration of power" that consists of economic, military, political, and civil institutions and organizations either under or beyond the umbrella of government structures (5), it is the financial-capitalist "economic core" that pulls everything together (10). Because of this, the laws of the market come to constitute the only legitimate way of organizing human life and, precisely in so doing, come to determine even the very significance and meaning of human life within Empire (13). In other words, the various elements and powers that configure Empire's network are fed by a "spirit"—"an *ethos*, a way of thinking and doing, a *Weltanschauung*, and even a certain theology"—that emerges from and sustains the laws of the market as the only legitimate organizing principle of Empire (1). The spirit of Empire in that sense comprises the "conditions of subjectivity and of cultural self-conception" that are both a result and a condition of the totalitarian nature of late financial capitalism's dominance of the globe (2).

What then precisely constitutes the spirit of Empire so as to give rise to the kind of subjectivity and cultural self-conception regnant within it? Given that the laws of the market place the competitive maximization of profit at the heart of Empire's system of valorization, the spirit of Empire is characterized by an ethos of total competition among human beings that elevates egoism from being a mortal sin to being a salvific virtue (13–14). According to the conception of human life as dictated by the spirit of Empire, "The connection to the other is denied: the other is always a competitor, never a neighbor. The other is a threat to my freedom, never an opportunity for working together" (14). The regnant form of subjectivity within Empire, both individual and collective, is therefore imbued with a spirit of domination, which, unable to let the other be the other, will not tolerate the existence of alternative ways of imagining and organizing human life. The subjectivity of "imperial subjects"—the small minority of elites controlling the market—is driven by the idea of unity, that is, "of making Empire and humanity coincide" (4), with the goal of defining "what it is that the totality of humanity wants, or needs, what is good for all, and finally, what cannot be avoided" (6). Concretely speaking, the dominant subjectivity of Empire works to create the cultural self-conception in which "the desires established by the market are the only valid ones, the only possible ones, the only path that leads us to that fullness enjoyed by imperial subjects" who are seen as truly human subjects (17–18). Hence, the unity that Empire imposes on the totality of humanity is "the dispersed unity of individualized humanity" grounded in the illusory commonality of desires and aspirations created by the market (15). This imperial "unity," based on an extreme form of individualism, "is essentially anti-democratic because it destroys the concept of *demos*" as a political subject and installs in place of civil society and politics the "invisible hand" of the market as the regulatory mechanism that guides and directs the actions of mutually isolated and indifferent individuals (15).

Democracy as a government of the demos, according Míguez, Rieger, and Sung, is "anti-imperial" insofar as "the people, as *demos*, will always be an ambiguous and disarticulated conjunction, bearing struggles and oppositions, conflictive and diverse, with their hegemonies and disputes, with their ambiguities and tragedies" (190). Since the demos as a political subject includes all of the social forces that seek political representation, democracy necessarily assumes a certain degree of ambiguity, a certain incapacity to resolve differences, tensions, and conflicts finally and conclusively (19). The creative freedom let loose by the ambiguity of democracy is therefore diametrically opposed to the imperial spirit with its totalitarian fantasy of uniting the world with one overarching and hegemonic "imperial consensus" that excludes or co-opts any struggle for representation, which is the essence of politics (19). Although there are many nation-states forming the global network of Empire that are formally democratic in the sense that they have representational forms of government, the spirit of Empire empties the democratic formality of its demos by neutralizing the political representation and social insertion of desires, interests, and forces other than those dictated by the market. The spirit of Empire achieves this by the power of its hegemonic symbolic structures and discourses, which internalize the imperial consensus—the vision of truly human life as one of total competition in the market—within the dominated, thereby inducing the latter's participation in the totalizing ideological space of the imperial subjects (19).

Despite its aspiration for a full realization of the "logic of the One" propelled by the desire for domination, however, Empire harbors an "untouched remainder" (173) who are excluded from the benefits and resources to sustain human life within it in a dignified manner, such as the economic activity within the market, political participation, the enjoyment of individual and collective rights, and cultural identity and creativity (174). Míguez, Rieger, and Sung call this remainder, the excluded, *laos*, signaling a broader group of people than the demos (xi). In fact, the excluded remainder actually constitutes the majority of humanity, though there are differences within the group in regard to the extent and severity of exclusion affecting them (174). The *laos*, as the unrecognized and disavowed limit of Empire, exercises force that is both exterior to the system but at the same time subversively "hidden" within it, waiting for the right moment to irrupt to disrupt the system, which the three theologians of Empire call the "laocratic moment": "When this force (*kratos*) appears with such magnitude that the system cannot disavow it and is upset by it, we can say that we are in a 'laocratic moment'" (176). Like the unexpected presence of the beggars at the banquet in Jesus' parable (Luke 14:15–25), in the laocratic moment the excluded are included as a question, critique, and challenge to the ruling system (176).

Nevertheless, even as Empire fears the prophetic voice, the "laocratic cry" representing "the reality of the fundamental dissatisfaction of the majorities" (21), democracy cannot be established merely by "the negativity of the excluded" (190). Barring the extreme form of an "uncontrollable chaos" (176), which the laocratic can take, its primary mode of question and protest simultaneously encompasses a vision of the possibility of change and of alternative ways of organizing human life (190–91). When this vision becomes discursive, that is, when it becomes an ideological configuration, the laocratic appropriates "previously existing elements, whether in the hegemonic forces or in the resistances that have already been generated in the system, as well as popular memories and other laocratic moments," including the utopian (178). In other words, the laocratic inserts itself into the space of political representation in the form of "the popular" or "populism" (178), which "assumes the interests and representations of the most neglected sectors of society, even, sometimes, against certain potential majorities influenced by hegemonic currents" (179). Of course, this insertion of the laocratic into the space of political representation is necessarily an ambiguous phenomenon, "since any popular construction is certainly also a bearer of elements of the hegemony in the midst of which it formed" (178). Precisely by representing the laocratic in the political space, populisms "formalize" it and open up space for a new exclusion, for the creation of a new "other" (182). But despite this ambiguity, if democracy is to be reestablished, it is imperative that the *laos* enter the political space by way of the popular and become a demos, thereby "bringing validity to the *res publica* not just as a formality but with substance" (21). It is precisely at this point that the trio of theologians differ from Hardt and Negri, who claim that the multitude itself is the political agent of democracy. By contrast, the trio argue that democracy comes into being only when the *laos* becomes a demos (21–22).

The entrance of the *laos* into the democratic political space does not mean its absorption by a demos, as the laocratic is "the necessary exteriority that antagonizes the democratic 'from below'" (183–84) and revitalizes it by reestablishing the delicate balances of power that make democracy possible (184). The laocratic, in that sense, constitutes the "dialectic of the immanent and the transcendent" (176) of any established power structures of hierarchical dualism that attempt permanently to "other" the excluded remainder, be it Empire or democracies. In theological terms, it is "the irruption of the messianic *kairos*" (184) from within, which at the same time "includes a 'given,' an illumination that comes to it from outside, the transcendent that establishes meaning" (191). Hence, the real transcendence that dismantles the claim of the spirit of Empire is not to be located in the democratic but in the laocratic: "the crisis, the chaotic, the uncontained." In the words of Miguez, Rieger, and Sung, "God exists, but is not at the foundation of the democratic task; rather he [*sic*] is in its permanent question 'from below,' from the location of the laocratic, from the excluded that transcends it, from the messianic irruption that is not based on power but calls it into question" (188). The spirit of the "Kingdom of God," which opposes itself to the spirit of Empire and subverts it from within, could in that sense be named the spirit of "laocracy" (173).

Having examined the globally reigning structures of hierarchical dualism and the resistances to them with the help of Hardt and Negri and the trio of theologians, I would like at this point to ask the following questions: Could we say that the spirit of Empire, with its market-driven totalizing ethos of total competition among human beings, embodies the "progressive" currents of immoderately self-assertive *yang* advancing a peculiar totalizing metaphysics of one Heavenly Pattern—that is to say, a metaphysics that patterns human civilizations into a single overarching but dispersed unity of individualized human beings each in the grip of the "self-interested heart-mind" (各自爲心 *gakja wisim*)? Could we say that the spirit of laocracy, which resists and subverts the spirit of Empire with the messianic irruption of the chaotic and uncontained, refers to the historical countercurrents of the suppressed forces of *eum*/*yin* that carry Empire's network of power "backward" to its chaotic (non-)origin in Ultimate Energy, to the creative depth of the unruly multitude? Would it be reasonable to assert that the transformation of the *laos* into a demos can be accomplished by the self-cultivative practice of keeping the heart-mind and rectifying psychophysical energy? In other words, does it make sense to contend that the laocratic vision of the possibility of change becomes discursive formations capable of political representation, when the excluded multitude come to bear the transcendent ideal and lure of Lord Heaven that subversively inhabits and challenges the hegemonic political discourses? Is there an insight to be gained by declaring that the laocratic ambiguity of democracy, kept fully alive by the unresolved differences within, points to the internally heterogeneous one body of Heavenly numinous spirits that is always perched on the edge of the chaos within each and every one, thus ensuring creative freedom?

The historical and comparative adventures of the idea of psychophysical energy, which I have respectively followed and myself attempted in this book, can find in this final, albeit brief, comparative exercise a sociohistorically concrete theological meaning for today. The democracy of numinous spirits, that is, the democracy of the bearers of Lord Heaven, which I propose as another way of naming the growing opposition to the global imperial order of late financial capitalism, represents a sociohistorically concrete comparative-theological articulation today of the resistant power of the idea of psychophysical energy to the continual attempt at its subordination to a higher metaphysical principle. The idea of the democracy of numinous spirits arises from the trinitarian theological paradigm of Ultimate Energy, Lord Heaven, and the Spirit of the harmonious becoming of psychophysical energy. As an alternative to the Empire's totalizing unification of mutually indifferent human beings, it posits a particular sociohistorical—both material and discursive—configuration of the transcendent ideal and lure of Lord Heaven, namely, the internally heterogeneous social body of numinous spirits held together in mutual empathy by the Spirit. What keeps differences alive and not excluded within this particular form of democracy—that is, what prevents it from achieving an imperial consensus and thereby losing its defining characteristic as a democracy—is Ultimate Energy as the restless, heterogeneous creative depth within each and every bearer of Lord Heaven, all of whom constitute the democratic social body. Insofar as the heterogeneous depth of Ultimate Energy is made constantly and newly creative by the Spirit's power to bring differences into direct empathetic connection, the concrete discursive and material configuration of Lord Heaven is always fluid, relative, and open-ended, thereby making the boundaries of the democratic social body porous to any excluded remainder. Hence, the Spirit of this democracy is opposed to the spirit of Empire, which can bring about only a dispersed unity of mutually indifferent differences by means of hegemonic discursive formations that reinforce structures of hierarchical dualism.

At the present moment in history, the Spirit of the democracy of numinous spirits is the Spirit of the displaced, wandering, oppressed, and exploited multitude that constitute the planetary outcasts of the globalizing world, to use Spivak's notion of planetarity as both the excluded remainder of the globality of transnational capitalism and that which hosts, nourishes, and sustains the latter.[7] Insofar as the resistance to the empire of globalized late financial capitalism can become effective only when the multitude, the *laos*, become a political subject, a demos, it is pivotal that the multitude are "awakened" through the self-cultivative practice of keeping the heart-mind and rectifying psychophysical energy and reborn as the emancipatory and solidary divine-human subject-agents of history. That is what the multitude did in 1894 and in numerous other historically "kairotic" moments, including the "occupy Wall Street" movement of today whose future is yet uncertain. The awakening of the multitude takes place when the forms of their resistance go beyond mere random reboundings of their suppressed life-energy—as in the "day-to-day forms of resistance" mentioned earlier—to take on the form of a discursive coalition of political subject-agencies driven and lured by Lord Heaven which they bear in their bodies. The awakening of the multitude, in that sense, represents a "quickening" of the countervailing movement of Ultimate Energy in the direction of a new restoration of the civilizational balance of receptive and active, *eum/yin* and *yang*. It does not mean a return to the chaotic origin imagined to be present in some sociohistorically concrete form, that is, a return to a kind of anarchic self-rule of the unruly multitude frolicking in the divine "ocean" of Ultimate Energy itself.

I will end with one final reflection: Moon Dong-hwan, the last living doyen of the first generation of Korean minjung theologians, has spoken of the "awakening" (覺 *gak*) and resolute "cutting" (斷 *dan*) of the minjung, developing a seminal insight of Kim Ji-ha.[8] According to Moon, it is only through the accumulation of the sociohistorical experience of suffering, injustice, and oppression that the exploited multitude come to see evil for what it is—that is, they come to experience the "awakening." It is only through their awakening to the hard and brutal truth, that they are the excluded 99 percent of the imperial system, that they can finally "cut off" their addiction to the hegemonic but false dream of climbing up the ladder of the global market to be part of the top 1 percent of humanity, namely, the imperial subjects. The "awakening" and the "cutting" constitute God's way of educating God's people, Moon adds, as shown in the history of the covenant people of God recounted in the Bible. Appealing to the Donghak ideal of self-cultivation, he has called for "the education through the harmonious becoming of psychophysical energy" as that which would bring about the awakening of the multitude. It is the kind of sociohistorically concrete experiential learning in which the multitude look in the face of the reality of their constant exploitation and exclusion and come to affirm their deep, fundamental relatedness to the divine, the cosmos, and one another, despite Empire's constant mapping of them onto the hierarchical grid of competitive living, the constant rat race to prove themselves to be the masters of the global market.

If the awakening of the multitude can come about only through the accumulation of the sociohistorical experience of suffering, injustice, oppression, exploitation, and marginalization, then the trinity of Ultimate Energy, Lord Heaven, and the Spirit of the harmonious becoming of psychophysical energy cannot help being cruciform. The transcendent ideal and lure of Lord Heaven, to which the multitude are awakened, bears the trace, the stigmata, of their historical suffering. The Spirit, who has throughout history tried to configure the communal and social body of the multitude into the shape of Lord Heaven, carries the scars of the repeated defeat of empathetic solidarity before the structures of domination sustained by the power of the self-interested heart-minds. Even at this very moment, Ultimate Energy suffers from its banishment to the outer fringes of Empire, where it cries out through the chaotic depth of the restless multitude for the recognition of the truth that it is no other than the exploited and abjected body of Empire itself, what Spivak calls the "planetarity" that sustains the globalized world. The countercurrents of psychophysical energy in history, the countervailing forces of *eum/yin*, then point to the resurrection of the crucified trinity of Ultimate Energy, Lord Heaven, and the Spirit of harmonious becoming of psychophysical energy—the resurrection that is no other than the resurrection of the crucified multitude. Hence, when its movement is conceived as the kind of liberating and creative spiral dialectic that I have been trying to envision and to articulate in this book, the Great Ultimate as the symbol of psychophysical energy can even serve as the symbol of the "return" of the very body of Empire to reconfigure and to reconstitute itself into the "later heaven," also called by the name of the Kindom of God, however much it stands under the shadow of the cross in the present historical moment.

# NOTES

## *Prologue: A Meeting of Two Stories*

An earlier version of this section was published in *TheoSpirit*, the biennial newsletter of Drew University Theological School, as "Consecrate the Offerings to Yourselves," *TheoSpirit* 9, no. 2 (2011): 14–16.

1. Choe Si-hyeong (Haewol), *Haewol sinsa beopseol* [The sermons of Haewol the divine teacher], in *Cheondogyo gyeongjeon* [Cheondogyo scriptures], ed. Chondogyo jung-ang chongbu (Seoul: Cheondogyo jung-ang chongbu chulpanbu, 1988), 19:2. For citations from *Haewol sinsa beopseol*, I will give the chapter number followed by the verse number(s).
2. Shin Yong-ha, *Donghak nongmin hyeongmyeong-ui sahoesa* [Social history of the Donghak peasant revolutionary movement] (Seoul: Jisik saneopsa, 2005), pp. 130–229.
3. Thomas H. Reilly, *The Taiping Heavenly Kingdom: Rebellion and the Blasphemy of Empire* (Seattle: University of Washington Press, 2004); Jonathan D. Spence, *God's Chinese Son: The Taiping Heavenly Kingdom of Hong Xiuquan* (New York: W. W. Norton, 1996).
4. Min Gyeong-bae, *Hanguk gidok gyohoesa: Hanguk minjok gyohoe hyeongseong gwajeongsa* [History of the Korean Christian church: A history of the process of the formation of the Korean national church] (Seoul: Yonsei daehak chulpanbu, 2007), pp. 66–120.
5. For a biographical account of Su-un's life, see Pyo Yeong-sam, *Donghak 1: Su-unui sarmgwa sang-gak* [The life and thought of Su-un] (Seoul: Tongnamu, 2004).
6. When the Korean and Chinese pronunciations of a classical Chinese character differ from each other, I will present them both with a slash in between. When the pronunciations of the classical Chinese characters are given in the context of discussing particular texts or figures, either Korean or Chinese, I will give the corresponding pronunciation. For romanization, I use the Revised Romanization system for Korean and the pinyin system for Chinese.
7. Choe Je-u (Su-un), *Dong-gyeong daejeon* [The complete scriptures of Eastern Learning], in *Cheondogyo gyeongjeon*, "Jumun [Incantations]," p. 89. For citations from *Dong-gyeong daejeon*, I will give the book title followed by the verse number(s) preceded by the abbreviation v. or vv. When verse numbers are not available, I will give page numbers.

8. Dong-gyeong Daejeon, "Nonhangmun (Writings to discuss learning)," v. 6.
9. Ibid., v. 4.
10. Ibid., vv. 4, 9. See also "Podeongmun (Writings to propagate virtue)," vv. 5, 8; Choe, *Yongdam yusa* (The instructional songs from the Dragon Pond), in *Cheondogyo gyeongjeon*, "Gwonhakga (Songs to encourage learning)," v. 8.
11. For the biographical account of Haeweol, see Pyo Yeong-sam, *Donghak 2: Haweorui gonan yeokjeong* (Haewol's life-course of hardship and suffering) (Seoul: Tongnamu, 2005).
12. *Haewol sinsa beopseol*, 7:4.
13. Ibid., 8:12.
14. Ibid., 10:5.
15. Ibid., 2:11.
16. Ibid., 8:9.
17. In fact, Su-un did not appear to have an understanding of the existence or activity of the Holy Spirit in "Western Learning." Kim Yong-hae, "Geurisdogyowa cheondogyoui singwan bigyo [A comparison of the view of God in Christianity and the religion of the heavenly way]," in *Han-gugui sasang-ga sibin: Su-un Choe Je-u* [Ten Korean thinkers: Su-un Choe Je-u], ed. Oh Mun-hwan (Seoul: Yemun seowon, 2005), p. 234.
18. See Ex 31:3; Prov 8:1–36.
19. Gen 15:1; 1 Sam 3:21; 1 Kgs 18:1, 31; 19:9–11; Ps 33:4, 6; Jer 1:4–5. The close connection between *ruach* and *dabar* is seen in Gen 1, when one takes into consideration the fact that, when God "spoke" the divine word in creation, God breathed out ("spirated").
20. For a good summary of the various meanings of "spirit" found in the Bible, see G. T. Montague, "The Fire in the Word: The Holy Spirit in Scripture," in *Advents of the Spirit: An Introduction to the Current Study of Pneumatology*, ed. B. E. Hinze and D. L. Dabney (Milwaukee: Marquette University Press, 2001), pp. 35–44. See also the extensive analysis of the biblical meanings of "spirit" in P. C. Hodgson, *Winds of the Spirit: A Constructive Christian Theology* (Louisville, Ky.: Westminster John Knox Press, 1994), pp. 276–82. Another helpful biblical analysis is found in Mark I. Wallace, *Finding God in the Singing River: Christianity, Spirit, Nature* (Minneapolis: Fortress Press, 2005), pp. 36–39.
21. Here I am using the Revised Standard Version.
22. For a trenchant analysis of Aquinas's classical trinitarian theology, see Anselm K. Min, *Paths to the Triune God: An Encounter between Aquinas and Recent Theologies* (Notre Dame, Ind.: University of Notre Dame Press, 2005), pp. 168–238.
23. Laurel C. Schneider, *Beyond Monotheism: A Theology of Multiplicity* (London: Routledge, 2009), p. 1.
24. J. N. D. Kelly, *Early Christian Doctrines*, rev. ed. (San Francisco: Harper and Row, 1978), pp. 275–76. The question of the "double procession" of the Spirit from the Father and the Spirit—the famous *filioque* question—is an ecumenically sensitive issue that I do not need to go into at this point, except to note that I am taking the Western position in my exposition.
25. The divine nature that the Father communicates to the Son and the Spirit is identical "numerically," not "specifically" as in creatures. Also, the distinctions among the divine persons are relational or "relative" oppositions not founded on quantity, action, or passion (that is, power difference). Anselm K. Min, "God as the Mystery of Sharing and Shared Love: Thomas Aquinas on the Trinity," in *The Cambridge Companion to the Trinity*, ed. Peter C. Phan (New York: Cambridge University Press, 2011), pp. 91–95.

26. See Jürgen Moltmann, *The Trinity and the Kingdom of God: The Doctrine of God* (San Francisco: Harper and Row; London: SCM Press, 1981); John D. Zizioulas, *Being as Communion: Studies in Personhood and the Church* (Crestwood, N.Y.: St. Vladimir's Seminary Press, 1985); Leonardo Boff, *Trinity and Society*, trans. Paul Burns (Maryknoll, N.Y.: Orbis, 1988).
27. Dale T. Irwin, "The Trinity and Socio-political Ethics," in *The Cambridge Companion to the Trinity*, p. 403.
28. Based on Heb 1:3 (New Revised Standard Version): "He is the reflection of God's glory and the exact imprint of God's very being."
29. Min, "God as the Mystery," p. 92.
30. Killian McDonnell is careful to note that the subordination of the Spirit, which is found in the classical theologians whom we now recognize as orthodox—including Gregory of Naziansus who presided over the Council of Constantinople in 381 that affirmed the divinity of the Holy Spirt—is cast in economic, salvation-historical categories rather than essentialist or ontological ones, making their subordinationism more prominent in their treatment of the "economic" Trinity than the "immanent" Trinity. Killian McDonnell, *The Other Hand of God: The Holy Spirit as the Universal Touch and Goal* (Collegeville, Minn.: Liturgical Press, 2003), pp. 121–47.
31. See Schneider, *Beyond Monotheism*, pp. 67–73 for this monarchical transformation of the classical doctrine of the Trinity within the context of the Christian Roman Empire.
32. Joerg Rieger notes, however, that because of what he calls "christological surplus" (p. 9), Christ could never be entirely contained by the figures of the imperial Christ, as shown in the subversive interpretations and representations that continued to resist the imperial co-optation of Jesus. Joerg Rieger, *Christ and Empire: From Paul to Postcolonial Times* (Minneapolis: Fortress Press, 2007), pp. 69–117.
33. The coequality of Christ with God presupposed the hierarchical elevation of his divinity at the expense of his humanity. Hence, as Christ's coequality with God was applied to human imperial rulers, it made the latter quasi-divine, especially in the Byzantine East. Ibid., 82–88.
34. Some examples are Hodgson, *Winds of the Spirit*; Elizabeth A. Johnson, *She Who Is: The Mystery of God in Feminist Theological Discourse* (New York: Crossroad, 2002), Catherine Keller, *Face of the Deep: A Theology of Becoming* (London: Routledge, 2003); Philip Clayton, *Adventures of the Spirit: God, World, Divine Action* (Minneapolis: Fortress Press, 2008); Mark. I. Wallace, *Fragments of the Spirit: Nature, Violence, and the Renewal of Creation* (New York: Continuum, 1996); Sharon V. Betcher, *Spirit and the Politics of Disablement* (Minneapolis: Fortress Press, 2007); Mayra Rivera, *The Touch of Transcendence: A Postcolonial Theology of God* (Louisville, Ky.: Westminster John Knox Press, 2007); Shelly Rambo, *Spirit and Trauma: A Theology of Remaining* (Louisville, Ky.: Westminster John Knox Press, 2010).

## *Introduction: A Decolonizing Asian Theology of Spirit as a Comparative Theology of Spirit-Qi*

This chapter is an expanded and revised version of my paper, "Being Hospitable to the Subaltern Others of Religious Others: Comparative Theology as a Decolonizing

Theological Practice in Asia," published by the Program Area on Faith, Mission and Unity (Christian Conference of Asia) in *CTC Bulletin* 28, no. 2 (2012).

1. "Ecumenical" in the wider sense of "interacting with and sharing resources with communities other than one's own across a variety of boundaries." Sebastian C. H. Kim, ed., *Christian Theology in Asia* (New York: Cambridge University Press, 2008), p. xii.
2. Of the various terms used in missiology to capture the dynamic between the gospel and the "field" of mission, such as "indigenization," "accommodation," "acculturation," "adaptation," "incarnation," "inculturation," "contextualization," and so on, three have been the subject of prolonged debates: "indigenization," "inculturation," and "contextualization" (Stephen B. Bevans, *Models of Contextual Theology* [Maryknoll, N.Y.: Orbis Books, 2002], pp. 26–27; Ruy O. Costa, "Introduction: Inculturation, Indigenization, and Contextualization," in *One Faith, Many Cultures: Inculturation, Indigenization, and Contextualization*, ed. Ruy O. Costa [Maryknoll, N.Y.: Orbis Books; Cambridge, Mass.: Boston Theological Institute, 1988], pp. ix–xvii; Robert J. Schreiter, *Constructing Local Theologies* [Maryknoll, N.Y.: Orbis Books, 1985], 5–6). Because of its connection with colonialism and imperialism (e.g., the British Empire's policy of replacing British personnel in colonial government with local "indigenous" leadership), the word "indigenization" has come to be questioned (Schreiter, *Constructing Local Theologies*, p. 5). It is true that the European conquerors, settlers, missionaries, and capitalist entrepreneurs saw "the indigenous" in opposition to what they thought was their advanced and universal civilization. Nonetheless, the nineteenth-century missiologists Henry Venn, Rufus Anderson, and John L. Nevius advanced the mission method of establishing "indigenous" churches with the principle of three "selfs" (self-supporting, self-governing, self-propagating) that emphasized local "indigenous" leadership. Later known as the "Nevius method," this mission strategy assumed a symmetrical relation of the missionaries to the indigenous cultures (i.e., each culture was to be approached in its own terms) and rejected the mechanical replication model of mission. The Nevius method was, however, largely rejected in the age of imperialism and racism, most notably by the missionaries in China where Nevius had developed his method through much field experience, except in Korea where it was enthusiastically accepted with much positive result (Wilbert R. Shenk, "The Missionary Encounter with Culture since the Seventeenth Century," in *Appropriate Christianity*, ed. Charles H. Kraft [Pasadena, Calif.: William Carey Library, 2005], pp. 38–45). In the light of this more positive assessment of the category of indigeneity in regard to the power dynamic involved, I am going to use the terms "indigenization" and "inculturation" more or less synonymously, preferring "inculturation" as a broader category. Peter C. Phan also understands the category of inculturation to encompass indigenization (Peter C. Phan, *In Our Own Tongues: Perspectives from Asia on Mission and Inculturation* [Maryknoll, N.Y.: Orbis Books, 2003], pp. 4–9). For the twin tasks of cultural indigenization/inculturation and social liberation, see David M. Thompson, "Introduction: Mapping Asian Christianity in the Context of World Christianity," in *Christian Theology in Asia*, ed. Sebastian C. H. Kim (New York: Cambridge University Press, 2008), pp. 11–14. For the presence of similar tasks in Africa, see Emmanuel Martey, *African Theology: Inculturation and Liberation* (Maryknoll, N.Y.: Orbis Books, 1993).
3. Here I follow Schreiter's preference for the phrase "local theology" over "contextual theology" (Schreiter, *Constructing Local Theologies*, p. 6).

4. Some examples are Kosuke Koyama, *Water Buffalo Theology* (Maryknoll, N.Y.: Orbis Books, 1974); C. S. Song, *Third-Eye Theology: Theology in Formation in Asian Settings* (Maryknoll, N.Y.: Orbis Books, 1979); K. P. Aleaz, *Christian Thought through Advaita Vedanta* (Delhi: ISPCK, 1996); M. Thomas Thangaraj, *The Crucified Guru: An Experiment in Cross-Cultural Christology* (Nashville: Abingdon Press, 1994); Yoon Sung-bum, *Gidokgyowa hanguk sasang* [Christianity and Korean thought] (Seoul: Daehan gidokgyo seohoe, 1964); Ryu Dong-sik, *Hanguk sinhagui gwangmaek* [The mineral vein of Korean theology] (Seoul: Dasan Geulbang, 2003); Jung Young Lee, *The Trinity in Asian Perspective* (Nashville: Abingdon Press, 1996).
5. Song, *Third-Eye Theology*, pp. 11–13.
6. Schreiter, *Constructing Local Theologies*, pp. 6–12. In the view of Kim Kyoung-jae, one of the most prominent *tochakhwa* (indigenizing) theologians of Korea, the sowing model—championed by the fundamentalist Western missionaries—is more like Schreiter's translation model, as it regards the soil as a barren and desolate wilderness full of weeds and thistles (i.e., traditional religions) that needed to be pulled out. Kyoung Jae Kim, *Christianity and the Encounter of Asian Religions: Method of Correlation, Fusion of Horizons, and Paradigm Shifts in the Korean Grafting Process* (Zoetermeer: Uitgeverij Boekencentrum, 1994), p. 121.
7. The seed, when sprouted, *uses* the nutrients in the soil to grow. In another one of Kim Kyoung-jae's model, that is, the "yeast" model, this sense of unilaterality is stronger, as yeast penetrates the dough and transforms it, akin to H. Richard Niebuhr's model of "Christ the Transformer of Culture." Kyoung-jae Kim, *Christianity and the Encounter of Asian Religions*, p. 131.
8. Ibid., pp. 135–41. Here Kim is relying on the ideas of Ryu Dong-sik, one of the pioneers of Korean *tochakhwa* theology.
9. Robert J. Schreiter, *The New Catholicity: Theology between the Global and the Local* (Maryknoll, N.Y.: Orbis Books, 1997), pp. 43–44. Peter Phan goes a step further to introduce the notion of "inter-multicultural" theology within the context of a multicultural society like the United States. Peter C. Phan, *Christianity with an Asian Face: Asian American Theology in the Making* (Maryknoll, N.Y.: Orbis Books, 2003), p. 10.
10. Schreither, *New Catholicity*, pp. 65–68; Kim, *Christianity and the Encounter of Asian Religions*, pp. 140–41. Another model discussed by Kim, the "converging" model pioneered by the minjung theologian Suh Nam-dong, also resonates with the bilateral nature of Schreiter's intercultural model, as its ruling metaphor depicts two streams (the gospel and the local culture) coming together to form a larger river. Nonetheless, Kim regards it as not as satisfactory as the grafting model, because it sees no qualitative difference between the two tributaries and in so doing fails to appreciate fully the ultimacy of the cross and resurrection events of Jesus Christ for Christians. Kim, *Christianity and the Encounter of Asian Religions*, pp. 132–35.
11. For the indigenization-contextualization debate, see Shoki Coe, "Contextualizing Theology," in *Third World Theologies: Mission Trend No. 3*, ed. Gerald H. Anderson and T. F. Stansky (New York: Paulist Press; Grand Rapids: Eerdmans, 2002), pp. 19–24. The concept of contextualization was introduced in 1972 by the World Council of Churches in response to the need of mission to address social issues, especially the struggles for justice and human rights in the Third World. *Ministry in Context*, published by the WCC Theological Education Fund (of which Coe was the director), states: "Indigenization

tends to be used in the sense of responding to the Gospel in terms of a traditional culture. Contextualization, while not ignoring this, takes into account the process of secularism, technology and the struggle for human justice, which characterizes the historical moment of nations in the Third World [*Ministry in Context*, 20]" (quoted in Costa, "Introduction: Inculturation, Indigenization, and Contextualization," xii). Whether or not the indigenization model was already doing much of what the new contextualizing model claimed to do, as Simon Kwan argues, the need for a genuine local theology to tackle the issue of social liberation was certainly highlighted by the debate. Simon Shui-Man Kwan, "From Indigenization to Contextualization: A Change in Discursive Practice Rather Than a Shift in Paradigm," *Studies in World Christianity* 11, no. 2 (2005): 236–50.

12. Thompson, "Introduction: Mapping Asian Christianity," pp. 11–12.
13. See the seminal essays in *Minjung Theology: People as the Subjects of History*, ed. the Commission on Theological Concerns of the Christian Conference of Asia (Maryknoll, N.Y.: Orbis Books, 1983).
14. David Kwang-sun Suh, *The Korean Minjung in Christ* (Hong Kong: Christian Conference of Asia, 1991).
15. See the essays, formative of the movement, in *A Reader in Dalit Theology*, ed. Arvind P. Nirmal (Madras: Gurukul Theological Seminary, 1990). See also Sathianathan Clarke, *Dalits and Christianity: Subaltern Religion and Liberation Theology in India* (Oxford: Oxford University Press, 2000).
16. Ruy O. Costa defines the concept of contextualization succinctly vis-à-vis indigenization and inculturation: "In summary: discussions on inculturation focus on the symbolic exchange between the faith being preached and the receiving culture. Debates over indigenization include this cultic agenda but go a step further with the inclusion of conscious power struggles between foreign missionaries and national leaders. Reflections on contextualization represent a third level of interpretation of the faith, in which, to the cultic aspects and the intrachurch power struggles is added a process of conscientization about power struggles in the world, in which the church participates either actively or passively" (Costa, "Introduction: Inculturation, Indigenization, and Contextualization," pp. ix–xvii). The indigenization-contextualization debate of the 1970s and 1980s has highlighted the category of contextualization as a category capable of embracing both cultural indigenization/inculturation and social liberation. Schreiter, *Constructing Local Theologies*, pp. 12–16.
17. Stephen D. Moore and Fernando F. Segovia, eds., *Postcolonial Biblical Criticism: Interdisciplinary Intersections* (London: T & T Clark, 2005); Catherine Keller, Michael Nausner, and Mayra Rivera, eds., *Postcolonial Theologies: Divinity and Empire* (St. Louis: Chalice Press, 2004).
18. Homi K. Bhabha, *Location of Culture* (London: Routledge, 1994), pp. 11, 36.
19. Spivak understands postcoloniality as a heritage of imperialism that the postcolonial critic must inhabit intimately yet deconstructively: "Postcoloniality—the heritage of imperialism in the rest of the globe—is a deconstructive case. As follows: Those of us from formerly colonized countries are able to communicate with each other and with the metropolis, to exchange and to establish sociality and transnationality, because we have had access to the culture of imperialism. Shall we then assign to that culture, in the words of the ethical philosopher Bernard Williams, a measure of 'moral luck'? I think there can be no question that the answer is 'no.' This impossible 'no' to a structure which one

critiques, yet inhabits intimately, is the deconstructive philosophical position, and the everyday here and now of 'postcoloniality' is a case of it. Further, the political claims that are most urgent in decolonized space are tacitly recognized as coded within the legacy of imperialism: nationhood, constitutionality, citizenship, democracy, socialism, even culturalism. Within the historical frame of exploration, colonization, and decolonization, what is being *effectively* reclaimed is a series of regulative political concepts, the supposedly authoritative narrative of whose production was written elsewhere, in the social formations of Western Europe. They are thus being reclaimed, indeed claimed as concept metaphors for which no *historically* adequate referent may be advanced from postcolonial space." Gayatri Chakravorty Spivak, *Outside in the Teaching Machine* (New York: Routledge, 1993), pp. 280–81.

20. According to Spivak, the access to citizenship (i.e., to civil society) granted one when one becomes a voter represents one of the notable examples of the symbolic circuit of mobilizing subalternity into hegemony: "When a line of communication is established between a member of subaltern groups and the circuits of citizenship or institutionality, the subaltern has been inserted into the long road to hegemony." This, Spivak argues, is absolutely to be desired, against the illusion of "preserving subalternity championed by romantic purists or primitivists. The political activist encourages the effacement of the subalternity of the subaltern out of 'moral love.'" Gayatri Chakravorty Spivak, *A Critique of Postcolonial Reason: Toward a History of the Vanishing Present* (Cambridge, Mass.: Harvard University Press, 1999), p. 310. Spivak's usage of the term "responsibility"—like her dialogic understanding of "speaking"—signifies not only the act of response that completes the transaction of speaker and listener, but also the ethical stance of making discursive room for the Other to exist. What she means by "ethical singularity" or "secret encounter" is no other than this call to a relationship with the Other in nonessential terms. Gayatri Chakravorty Spivak, "Translator's Preface and Afterword to Mahasweta Devi, *Imaginary Maps*," in *The Spivak Reader*, ed. Donna Landry and Gerald Maclean (New York: Routledge, 1996), pp. 269–70.

21. For the notion of strategic essentialism, see Gayatri Chakravorty Spivak, "Subaltern Studies: Deconstructing Historiography," in *The Spivak Reader*, pp. 214–21. She calls this strategic appropriation of essentializing metaphysical structures or metanarratives also by the name of "deconstructive embrace" (*Critique of Postcolonial Reason*, 427). Serene Jones has drawn attention to the fact that the poststructuralist theoretical assumptions about the always oppressive nature of binarisms do not necessarily hold up under the pressures of concrete political struggles, and that in order to strengthen the bond of solidarity for a coalition of diverse social and cultural identities, what is called for is some kind of grand narrative that clearly defines the powers to be resisted and dismantled. Serene Jones, "Cultural Labor and Theological Critique," in *Converging on Culture: Theologians in Dialogue with Cultural Analysis and Criticism*, ed. Delwin Brown, Sheila Greeve Davaney, and Kathryn Tanner (Oxford: Oxford University Press, 2001), pp. 166–68.

22. R. S. Sugirtharajah, *The Bible and the Third World: Precolonial, Colonial, and Postcolonial Encounters* (Cambridge: Cambridge University Press, 2001), pp. 175–243.

23. Pui-lan Kwok, *Postcolonial Imagination and Feminist Theology* (Louisville, Ky.: Westminster John Knox Press, 2005); Marcella Althaus-Reid, *Indecent Theology: Theological Perversions in Sex, Gender, and Politics* (London: Routledge, 2000).

24. Namsoon Kang, "Who/What Is Asian?: A Postcolonial Theological Reading of Orientalism and Neo-Orientalism," in *Postcolonial Theologies*, ed. Keller, Nausner, and Rivera, pp. 100–117.
25. Taken from Roland Robertson, "Glocalization: Time-Space and Homogeneity-Heterogeneity," in *Global Modernities*, ed. Mike Featherstone, Scott Lash, and Roland Robertson (London: Sage, 1995). See also Namsoon Kang , "Reconstructing *Asian* Feminist Theology: Toward a *Glocal* Feminist Theology in an Era of Neo-Empire(s)," in *Christian Theology in Asia*, ed. Kim, p. 222.
26. Joerg Rieger, "Liberating God-Talk: Postcolonialism and the Challenge of the Margins," in *Postcolonial Theologies*, ed. Keller, Nausner, and Rivera, pp. 219–20.
27. See Namsoon Kang's distinction between the Empire as the globally hegemonic metanarrative of the West and the empires as locally hegemonic—mostly religious ("kyriarchal")—narratives. "Reconstructing *Asian* Feminist Theology," p. 220. Richard McBride has shown that the customary distinction between elite, hegemonic, religion and popular, "subaltern," religion is problematic, as seen in the case of the elite-led Maitreya cult of Silla Kingdom in Korea. Richard McBride, *Domesticating the Dharma: Buddhist Cults and the Hwaŏm Synthesis in Silla Korea* (Honolulu: University of Hawai'i Press, 2008).
28. For an example of comparative theologies that claim to remain faithful to the symbolic framework of the Christian tradition while adopting the cultural-hermeneutical framework of another religious tradition (e.g., an attempt to reformulate the symbol of God with the categories of Buddhist ontology), see Joseph S. O'Leary, *Religious Pluralism and Christian Truth* (Edinburgh: Edinburgh University Press, 1996). It is, however, questionable whether a clear-cut distinction between religion or faith, on the one hand, and cultural framework of interpretation, on the other, can indeed be made. Claude Geffré argues that the encounter between Christianity and a non-Western culture is always an encounter between two cultures ("Double Belonging and the Originality of Christianity as a Religion," in *Many Mansions? Multiple Religious Belonging and Christian Identity*, ed. Catherine Cornille [Maryknoll, N.Y.: Orbis Books, 2002], pp. 93–105); Geffré quotes Panikkar's question, "Must one be spiritually a Semite and intellectually a Greek to be a Christian?" to argue that Christianity *is* Semite and Greek. Inculturation, he claims, does not mean Christianity ceasing to be Western in order to be African or Asian, for there is no original, pure Christianity beyond all the doctrinal and theological developments of the intervening centuries. Inculturation is, therefore, more a conversation between Asian and African theologies and European theology, in which the cultural and historical baggage of the Christian faith of the past centuries is relativized. By the same token, it is a myth to think of inculturation as an encounter between Christianity and a pagan culture while ignoring the religious traditions that have shaped the latter's value systems and symbolic resources. Such an attitude, he claims, reflects the modern Western prejudice priding itself on the autonomy of a secular culture and forgets that the modern Western culture is a post-Christian culture, much of whose symbolic resources derive from Christianity. In the light of this, he calls for a more positive understanding of syncretism.
29. I am using the word "community" somewhat loosely for the larger human community or the international community—that is, without implying the communitarian notion of community formed around a definite notion of common good. The common economic,

political, and cultural space, be it local or transnational, refers in that sense to a much more tangible, physical, reality of togetherness, namely, a common *geopolitical* space. In addition to the formerly colonizing Western nation-states, instances of religiously and ethnically plural nations born in the aftermath of political decolonization are numerous — India, Indonesia, Malaysia, Sudan, South Africa, Northern Ireland, to name just a few—of which some have been secular (such as India and Indonesia) and some have not (such as Sudan). On the transnational level, there is a kind of global culture and institution emerging from the gradually forming consensus in the international community on what constitutes the minimum conditions of human well-being, such as the global culture of human rights undergirded by the International Criminal Court or the mandate for environmental stewardship stipulated by various global accords and treaties, all of which are goaded on and further challenged by a global coalitional politics of various nongovernmental organizations and social movements against the neocolonial, labor-exploitive, and environmentally destructive forces of global capitalism. For the emergence of the global culture of human rights and the challenges made against it in the name of religious and cultural identity, see Michael Singer, "Relativism, Culture, Religion, and Identity," in *Religious Fundamentalisms and the Human Rights of Women*, ed. Courtney W. Howland (New York: Palgrave, 2001), pp. 45–54, and Radhika Coomaraswamy, "Different but Free: Cultural Relativism and Women's Rights as Human Rights," in the same book, pp. 79–90.

30. Alan Race first introduced the typology two decades ago in *Christians and Religious Pluralism: Patterns in the Christian Theology of Religions* (Maryknoll, N.Y.: Orbis Books, 1982), p. 7. "Exclusivism" designates the theological position that salvation requires an explicit faith in Jesus Christ and that other religions are therefore of little or no value. "Inclusivism," by contrast, refers to the position that other religions do have salvific significance, but only by virtue of the hidden and unrecognized redemptive work of Christ in them, requiring their fulfillment in Christianity. "Pluralism" is the view that non-Christian religions are legitimate ways of salvation apart from the way of Jesus Christ, the latter being merely one of many equally valid ways. Examples of exclusivism are Justin Martyr's view of Greco-Roman pagan religions and Cyprian's dictum *extra ecclesia nulla salus* (although originally directed against Christian heretics and schismatics rather than other religions). Inclusivist views can be seen in Justin Martyr's view of pagan philosophers as implicit Christians (*Apology* 1.46, which argues that, just as Abraham had an implicit knowledge of the Word of God—the eternal Logos Spermatikos—a pagan such as Plato also had some inkling of the Word through his philosophic wisdom), Origen's universalist view of salvation, and Aquinas's notion of "baptism of desire." In the modern era exclusivism has tended to be the view of evangelical Protestant Christians while inclusivism that of Roman Catholics and mainline Protestants. Thus, while exclusivism and inclusivism have been long-standing dominant theological options in the history of Christianity, with their foremost recent exponents being Karl Barth and Karl Rahner, respectively, pluralism is a relatively new theological model proposed and worked out from the 1970s on by theologians such as John Hick, Paul Knitter, W. C. Smith, and Raimundo Panikkar. See James L. Fredericks, *Faith among Faiths: Christian Theology and Non-Christian Religions* (New York: Paulist Press, 1999), 23. Paul Knitter has introduced a new classificatory scheme consisting of replacement model, fulfillment model,

mutuality model, and acceptance model (to include postliberal theology, the "many salvations" approach of S. Mark Heim, and comparative theology). Paul F. Knitter, *Introducing Theologies of Religions* (Maryknoll, N.Y.: Orbis Books, 2002).

31. The literature of comparative theology is sizable, but for a programmatic overview of comparative theology as a theological movement and method, see Francis X. Clooney, *Comparative Theology: Deep Learning across Religious Borders* (Chichester, UK: Wiley-Blackwell, 2010).
32. James L. Fredericks, "A Universal Religious Experience? Comparative Theology as an Alternative to a Theology of Religions," *Horizons* 22, no. 1 (1995): 83. See also Francis X. Clooney, *Theology after Vedanta: An Experiment in Comparative Theology* (Albany: State University of New York Press, 1993), p. 3.
33. James L. Fredericks, *Faith among Faiths: Christian Theology and Non-Christian Religions* (New York: Paulist Press, 1999), pp. 139–61. He reads the story of Krishna and the Milkmaids from the Hindu tradition, which tells of Krishna's love that cannot be exclusively possessed by one person, in comparison with the New Testament parable of the Prodigal Son. Another comparative exercise in the book is his reading of the Pauline understanding of death and resurrection in the light his reading of the Zen master Dogen, who preaches the notion of the nonduality of life and death. Another leading comparative theologian, Francis X. Clooney, also advocates using the texts of other religious traditions as the context in which the texts of the Christian tradition are to be read: a "dialectical activity of reading and rereading the Bible and other Christian texts in the new context of non-Christian texts." Francis X. Clooney, "Reading the World in Christ," in *Christian Uniqueness Reconsidered: The Myth of a Pluralistic Theology of Religions*, ed. Gavin D'Costa (Maryknoll, N.Y.: Orbis Books, 1990), p. 64.
34. George A. Lindbeck, *The Nature of Doctrine: Religion and Theology in a Postliberal Age* (Philadelphia: Westminster Press, 1984), pp. 112–13, 135, n. 1. The "postliberal" designation is based on the view that pluralism is a continuation of nineteenth-century liberal Protestant theology's apology to the Enlightenment, which construed religious doctrines, symbols, rituals, and practices as historical and cultural expressions of a common, universal religious experience that was in itself ineffable yet paradoxically known to underlie all religions. See also Fredericks, "Universal Religious Experience?" pp. 67–72.
35. Asymmetrical cultural relations are implicit in Lindbeck's notion of "a universe of discourse embracing others without itself being embraced." See George A. Lindbeck, "The Gospel's Uniqueness: Election and Untranslatability," in *The Church in a Postliberal Age*, ed. James J. Buckley (Grand Rapids, Mich.: William B. Eerdmans, 2003), p. 232.
36. Lindbeck, *Nature of Doctrine*, pp. 30–45; J. A. DiNoia, "Pluralist Theology of Religions: Pluralistic or Non-Pluralistic?" in *Christian Uniqueness Reconsidered*, ed. D'Costa, pp. 122–28; Paul J. Griffiths, "The Uniqueness of Christian Doctrine Defended," in *Christian Uniqueness Reconsidered*, ed. D'Costa, pp. 157–73, and *Problems of Religious Diversity* (Oxford: Blackwell, 2001).
37. See Fredericks, "Universal Religious Experience?" p. 82, for his critique of postliberal theology: "Christians end up being able to talk to no one but themselves."
38. Clooney, *Theology after Vedanta*, p. 158: "The comparative reader sees not only how the *Summa Theologiae* presumes and entails a complete Christian worldview but also how that worldview reaches no farther than its margins, what it has been able to say in its vocabulary, rules of language, and accumulated set of reference."

39. Clooney, *Theology after Vedanta*, p. 158.
40. Ibid., pp. 7, 159.
41. Francis X. Clooney, *Hindu God, Christian God: How Reason Helps Break Down the Boundaries between Religions* (Oxford: Oxford University Press, 2001), pp. 27–28.
42. Clooney, *Theology after Vedanta*, pp. 5–6. Comparative theology involves the issue of truth, he argues, because it is a theological enterprise and not an exercise in comparative religion, which simply catalogues the views of different religious traditions on salvation and so on or merely attempts to understand and to interpret what certain texts mean to certain communities. Here he appeals to David Tracy's notion of the religious classic.
43. Fredericks, *Faith among Faiths*, p. 163.
44. Ibid., pp. 171–77.
45. Clifford Geertz, *The Interpretation of Cultures: Selected Essays* (New York: Basic Books, 1973), pp. 87–125; Lindbeck, *Nature of Doctrine*, p. 20.
46. Talal Asad, *Genealogies of Religion: Discipline and Reasons of Power in Christianity and Islam* (Baltimore: Johns Hopkins University Press, 1993), pp. 30–54.
47. Kathryn Tanner, *Theory of Culture: A New Agenda for Theology* (Minneapolis: Fortress Press, 1997), pp. 38–58.
48. Russell T. McCutcheon, *Manufacturing Religion: The Discourse on Sui Generis Religion and the Politics of Nostalgia* (Oxford: Oxford University Press, 1997); Timothy Fitzgerald, *The Ideology of Religious Studies* (Oxford: Oxford University Press, 2000); Tomoko Mazusawa, *The Invention of World Religions: Or, How European Universalism Was Preserved in the Language of Pluralism* (Chicago: University of Chicago Press, 2005); Richard King, *Orientalism and Religion: Postcolonial Theory, India, and "The Mystic East"* (London: Routledge, 1999).
49. This is convincingly demonstrated by the widely acclaimed work of Tomoko Masuzawa. In it she shows how the universalizing and supersessionistic agenda of Anglo-European liberal Protestant Christianity of nineteenth-century comparative theology, encapsulated in the concept of world religion (especially the possession of a written sacred scripture), has been carried over and preserved today by the "scientific" comparative studies of religion, especially in their pluralistic and egalitarian emphasis on the rich diversity of "great" world religions founded upon a unity of religious experience. Masuzawa, *Invention of World Religions*, pp. 72–104, 259–328.
50. See Fitzgerald, *Ideology of Religious Studies*, p. 222; King, *Orientalism and Religion*, pp. 59–60; Asad, *Genealogies of Religion*, pp. 53–54, 198–99.
51. I borrow Min's helpful definition of religion as "concrete totalities": "a system of symbols that comprises beliefs, rituals, and practices that embody the collective self-understanding of its adherents within a 'plausibility structure' (Peter Berger), i.e., those objective socio-historical conditions that render such self-understanding plausible." Anselm Kyongsuk Min, "Dialectical Pluralism and Solidarity of Others: Towards a New Paradigm," *Journal of the American Academy of Religion* 65, no. 3 (1997): 590.
52. Mary McClintock Fulkerson, "'We Don't See Color Here': A Case Study in Ecclesial-Cultural Invention," in *Converging on Culture: Theologians in Dialogue with Cultural Analysis and Criticism*, ed. Delwin Brown, Sheila Greeve Davaney, and Kathryn Tanner (Oxford: Oxford University Press, 2001), pp. 140–57.
53. Hugh Nicholson, "Comparative Theology after Liberalism," *Modern Theology* 23, no. 2 (2007): 238.

54. Spivak, *Critique of Postcolonial Reason*, p. 167.
55. Nicholson, "Comparative Theology," pp. 238–39.
56. Ibid., pp. 239–40, 244–45. In essence Nicholson construes the practice of comparative theology as involving two steps: first, a political restoration of symmetry à la comparative study of religion; second, the practice of comparative theology proper via metaphorical redescription.
57. Ibid., pp. 236–37, 242–43.
58. Ibid., pp. 230–33, 243–44.
59. King, *Orientalism and Religion*, p. 215.
60. John J. Thatamanil, "Comparative Theology after 'Religion,'" in *Planetary Loves: Spivak, Postcoloniality, and Theology*, ed. Stephen D. Moore and Mayra Rivera (New York: Fordham University Press, 2011), pp. 241–45.
61. Echoing this thought is King, *Orientalism and Religion*, p. 215.
62. Thatamanil, "Comparative Theology," pp. 253–57.
63. See note 41.
64. John J. Thatamanil, "God as Ground, Contingency, and Relation: Trinitarian Polydoxy and Religious Diversity," in *Polydoxy: Theology of Multiplicity and Relation*, ed. Catherine Keller and Laurel C. Schneider (London: Routledge, 2010), pp. 238–57.
65. David Chidester, "Anchoring Religion in the World: A Southern African History of Comparative Religion," *Religion* 26, no. 2 (1996): 155.
66. Ibid.
67. Edward W. Said, *Orientalism* (New York: Vintage Books, 1978). For the Orientalist debate initiated by Said, see King, *Orientalism and Religion*, pp. 82–85.
68. For example, when Hindu communities in India and the diaspora today advocate an idealized and monolithic representation of Hinduism devoid of internal complexity and diversity, put an undue emphasis on the sacred texts and their translation for missionary purposes, and construct the Other—usually Islam—to explain the past and present ills of Hinduism, one needs to question whether all these constitute a postcolonial nativist reaction to the history of humiliation and nonrecognition rather than an uninterrupted extension and expression of whatever they claim to be their traditional and "pure" identity (Sharada Sugirtharajah, *Imagining Hinduism: A Postcolonial Perspective* [London: Routledge, 2003], pp. 133–43). The Islamists' angry rejection of the "Western" and "Christian" discourses of women's rights and pluralistic democracy in the name of the past golden age of a pure form of Islam could be understood in a similar vein, as a nativist oppositional politics which merely tries to turn the essentializing binary scheme of hierarchical evaluation around on Europe and America and in the course of doing so squelch the heterogeneous discourses welling up within itself. For instance, Mahnaz Afkhami points out the similarity between the Western Orientalists' reports of traditional Islamic societies and contemporary Islamists' descriptions of the supposedly homogeneous and harmonious Muslim societies before Western corruption that are used to bolster their claims of legitimacy. Mahnaz Afkhami, "Gender Apartheid and the Discourse of Relativity of Rights in Muslim Societies," in *Religious Fundamentalisms*, ed. Howland, p. 70.
69. Originally coined by Patricia Hill Collins, quoted in Michelle Voss Roberts, "Gendering Comparative Theology," in *The New Comparative Theology: Interreligious Insights from the Next Generation*, ed. Francis X. Clooney (London: T & T Clark, 2010), p. 115.

70. Kwok Pui-lan advocates the helpful notion of "multifaith hermeneutics," which pays attention to both the "high" intellectual and hermeneutical tradition formed around the ancient scriptures and classical texts of a non-Christian tradition and its "popular" culture consisting of stories, fables, and legends. Kwok Pui-lan, *Discovering the Bible in the Non-Biblical World* (Maryknoll, N.Y.: Orbis Books, 1995), pp. 66–68.
71. For the multiculturalism debate around the curriculum of public education, see Paul Berman, ed., *Debating P.C.: The Controversy over Political Correctness on College Campuses* (New York: Laurel, published by Dell, 1992). See also Ward Churchill, "White Studies: The Intellectual Imperialism of U.S. Higher Education," in *Theorizing Multiculturalism: A Guide to the Current Debate*, ed. Cynthia Willet (Malden, Mass.: Blackwell, 1998), pp. 334–56.
72. Nancy Fraser, "Recognition without Ethics?" in *Recognition and Difference*, ed. Scott Lash and Mike Featherstone (London: Sage, 2002), p. 24. Anselm Min draws our attention to the fact that the ideal condition of dialogical reason is dependent on and either fostered or obstructed by material and sociohistorical conditions, such as inequalities in political and economic power ("Dialectical Pluralism," pp. 598–99). I agree in the sense that the ideal condition of dialogue presupposes free agency, and as the inclusion of economic rights in addition to civil and political rights in the human rights discourse shows, free agency is either nurtured or hampered by the amount of material and cultural resources to which one has access, such as the level of income and education. Especially in situations where there is a gross inequality of power among religious communities and within each of them, mutual recognition of free participatory agency would have to involve recognition of the need for some degree of intercommunal and intracommunal redistribution of resources, on the one hand, and institutional measures against the tyranny of majority. on the other. Nancy Fraser makes a similar observation about the *objective conditions* of participatory parity (Fraser, "Recognition without Ethics?" in p. 29).
73 Kwok, *Postcolonial Imagination*, pp. 204–5.
74. See Fanon's essay "The Negro and Recognition" in Frantz Fanon, *Black Skin, White Masks*, trans. Charles Lam Markmann (New York: Grove Press, 1967), pp. 210–22. I have been helped in my reading of Fanon by Alfred J. López, although in my view he does not clearly show that what is at stake for Fanon is recognition of identity and worth. Alfred J. López, *Posts and Pasts: A Theory of Postcolonialism* (Albany: State University of New York Press, 2001), pp. 121–42.
75. I agree with Axel Honneth that in order for there to be a sense of social solidarity, social esteem conferred by recognition of worth (of one another's abilities, skills, and ways of life) is necessary. Axel Honneth, "Recognition or Redistribution? Changing Perspectives on the Moral Order of Society," in *Recognition and Difference*, pp. 49–50.
76. Charles Taylor, "The Politics of Recognition," in *Multiculturalism: Examining the Politics of Recognition*, ed. and introduced by Amy Gutmann (Princeton, N.J.: Princeton University Press, 1994), pp. 63–73.
77. Kwok, *Postcolonial Imagination*, p. 204.
78. Thatamanil, "Comparative Theology," p. 251.
79. Nicholson, "Comparative Theology," p. 239. Nicholson is summarizing David Tracy's well-known formulation of the transformative power of classics and the worldviews they express. See David Tracy, *The Analogical Imagination: Christian Theology and the Culture of Pluralism* (New York: Crossroad, 1981), pp. 112–15.

80. Tracy Sayuki-Tiemeier, "Comparative Theology as a Theology of Liberation," in *The New Comparative Theology*, ed. Clooney, pp. 129–49. Clooney has made a similar effort in *Divine Mother, Blessed Mother: Hindu Goddesses and the Virgin Mary* (Oxford: Oxford University Press, 2005), although, as he himself acknowledges, the texts on female divinity that he examines are all male-authored (p. 233).
81. Spivak, *Critique of Postcolonial Reason*, p. 384.
82. Ibid.
83. Ibid., p. 427.
84. Ibid., pp. 382–83.
85. Arvind Mandair finds in the largely negative attitude of postcolonial theorists and critics toward religions a continuation of modern Western *secular* universalism. His contention is that postcolonial theorists, including Spivak, see non-Western cultural traditions as "religions" beholden to authoritative bodies of tradition that are believed to be ahistorical and unchanging (what Spivak calls "transcendental figurations"), and thereby at odds with true historicity, that is, transcendental self-consciousness and the accompanying sense of *secular* historical agency ("freedom") touted by Western modernity. As a consequence, the West, now even more secular and "modern," continues to be regarded by postcolonial critics as the sole locus of genuine (critical) thinking and theorizing (Arvind Mandair, "The Repetition of Past Imperialism: Hegel, Historical Difference, and the Theorizing of Indic Religions," *History of Religions* 44, no. 4 [2005]: 278–99). This criticism is shared by Robert Young, who chastises his postcolonialist colleagues for being blind to prophetic and messianic religious movements—such as Mahdi movements in East Africa and South Asia—that assert traditional indigenous cultures in the name of a utopic decolonized future, providing althernative value systems: "Postcolonial theory, despite its espousal of subaltern resistance, scarcely values subaltern resistance that does not operate according to its own secular terms" (Robert J. C. Young, *Postcolonialism: An Historical Introduction* [Oxford: Blackwell, 2001], p. 338). It is indeed a brilliant stroke on Mandair's part to recognize, in postcolonial theory's mostly or exclusively *secular* attempt to conceptualize speech-agency on behalf of subaltern groups against the religious nationalism of neocolonial elites, precisely the same kind of modern colonial heritage that infects the latter. It is certainly true that, as a result of the colonial legacy, non-Western religions have been infected by and inscribed within the Western metanarrative; for they exhibit tendencies to see themselves as "religions," especially "world religions" possessing authoritative bodies of tradition encapsulated in written scriptures and pointing to the ahistorical and unchanging "religious" or "sacred" domain—i.e., the very sign of their capacity for universalization (i.e., for becoming "world religions"). That is why Spivak, even as she makes somewhat half-hearted positive assessment of the "ethno-philosophical" ideas of Tao, Zen, or Sunyvada, and the like (*Critique of Postcolonial Reason*, p. 429), ultimately takes the side of "animist liberation theologies" (or "original practical ecological philosophies") of the Fourth World against the "transcendental figurations" of world religions (*Critique of Postcolonial Reason*, pp. 382–83). Nonetheless, I agree with Richard King's counter to Spivak that, even as there can be no return to a pure nativism—a search for some kind of pure "lost origin"—beyond the epistemic violence of colonialism, we should not concede defeat to colonialism and Western modernity: "Spivak is right in her refusal to endorse a nativist or atavistic nostalgia for lost origins. Colonialism may have inextricably transformed

non-Western forms of knowledge. I refuse to believe, however, that it has wholeheartedly eradicated them. Moving forward, then, must also involve looking back with renewed vigour at the legacy of precolonial forms of indigenous knowledge. To fail to do so is to concede defeat to colonialism and to accept as unproblematic Western-derived notions of 'modernity,' thereby cutting ourselves off from our disparate pasts. . . . Accepting that the modern world is rooted in a variety of historical tributaries and that these traditions remain alive *within* and *in spite of* modernity is a first step in the displacement of this central post-Enlightenment dichotomy [of tradition and modernity]" (King, *Orientalism and Religion*, pp. 213–14). Hence, I wholeheartedly agree with Mandair's call for both philosophy of religion and history of religion to recognize the contemporaneity and contemporary theoretical relevance of non-Western "religious" traditions. We are no longer to treat non-Western traditions as "religious" with the accompanying theoretical devaluation based on the spurious and imperial opposition between the secular/modern (self-critical, historically self-aware, and therefore theoretical) West and the "traditional" East (Mandair, "Repetition of Past Imperialism," pp. 298–99).

86. Gayatri Chakravorty Spivak, *Death of a Discipline* (New York: Columbia University Press, 2003), pp. 71–72.
87. Schreiter, *New Catholicity*, pp. 29–30.
88. Ibid., p. 30.
89. Ibid., pp. 79–80.
90. Ibid., p. 80.
91. Ibid., p. 70.
92. Ibid., p. 71.
93. Raimon Panikkar, *The Intrareligious Dialogue* (New York: Paulist Press, 1978), p. 16.
94. Here I am following the insistence of Ahn Byung-mu, one of the pioneers of minjung theology, that Christian theology in East Asia needs to reflect on the nondualistic notion of psychophysical energy as corresponding to the notion of Spirit in Christianity. Byung-mu Ahn, *Minjung sinhak yiyagi* [Story of minjung theology], rev. ed. (Seoul: Hanguk sinhak yeon-guso, 2005), pp. 216–17.
95. The character 神 (*sin/shen*) is often translated as "spirit," as seen in my translation of the phrase 氣化之神 (*gihwa ji sin*) into "the spirit of the harmonious becoming of psychophysical energy." The culturally codified meanings of 神, however, are already included in the wider range of meanings possessed by 氣 (*gi/qi*), which leads to the frequently found genitive construction "*sin* of *gi* (*shen* of *qi*)" in pretty much the same manner as the theological phrase "Spirit of God." Hence, taking 神 as the dynamic equivalent of "spirit" does not suggest any alternative possibility of encoding the word "spirit" that has not already been offered by 氣.

## *1. The Psychophysical Energy of the Way in Daoist Thought*

1. "Material force" has been a conventional translation. Daniel K. Gardner has translated the term into "psychophysical stuff" (Chu Hsi, *Learning to Be a Sage: Selections from the Conversations of Master Chu, Arranged Topically*, trans. with a commentary by Daniel K. Gardner [Berkeley: University of California Press, 1990], p. 49, n. 52). I will slightly modify his translation into "psychophysical energy," although a more precise translation would be "psycho-bio-physical energy."

2. Maebayashi Kiyokazu, Sato Koetsu, and Kobayashi Hiroshi, *Giui bigyo munhwa* [A comparative-cultural analysis of gi], trans. Park Mun-hyeon and Sekine Hideyuki (Seoul: Doseo chulpan hanul., 2006), pp. 16–21. See also Zhang Liwen, *Giui cheorak* [A philosophy of gi], trans. Kim Gyo-bin (Seoul: Yemun seowon, 2004), pp. 63–75.
3. The classical period in East Asia (1000 B.C.E.–500 C.E.) refers to the period ranging from the Chinese Zhou Dynasty (1046–256 B.C.E.), whose later years of long decline overlapped with the Spring and Autumn Period (770–403 B.C.E.) and the Warring States Period (403–221 B.C.E.), to the early imperial era covering the founding and consolidation of imperial China by the Qin Dynasty (221–206 B.C.E.) and the Han Dynasty (206 B.C.E.–220 C.E.) and the following interregnum of nomadic invasions and disunion (220–c. 500 C.E.).
4. See Yuasa Yasuo, *Momgwa uju* [The universe and the body], trans. Yi Jeong-bae and Yi Han-yeong (Seoul: Jisik saneopsa, 2004), pp. 72–109, 325; , *Giui cheorak*, pp. 37–44.
5. For the historical origin of the symbol, see Julia Ching, *Religious Thought of Chu Hsi* (Oxford: Oxford University Press, 2000), pp. 32–37.
6. The complementary and mutually interpenetrating relationship between the receptive and active psychophysical energies is clearly theorized in the ancient text of Chinese medicine, *Huangdi neijing* [Yellow Emperor's inner classic] Zhang, *Giui cheorak*, p. 116. For one of the classic explanations of the fractal structure of the receptive-active relation, see the sixteenth-century Korean Neo-Confucian Yi Hwang's Cheonmyeong do seol [Explanation of the Diagram of Heavenly Mandate]," in *Toegye Jeonseo* [Complete works of Toegye], ed. Toegyehak chongseo pyeon-gan wiwonhoe (the Committee for Publication of the Study of Toegye Series) (Seoul: Toegyehak yeon-guwon, 1989–), XIII, sokjip [extended collection], 8.15b–16a, p. 93: "Pattern is pattern in such a way that its substance is originally vacuous, and being vacuous, without internal contrasts or opposites. Because it is without inner contrasts or opposites, when pattern is immanent in people and thing-events, it is one, truly without anything added to or taken away from it. When it comes to psychophysical energy, from its very beginning there appears the figure of the opposition of the receptive (*eum*) and the active (*yang*). The opposites function as the root of each other, so that the receptive inevitably has in its midst the active, while the active also inevitably has the receptive at its core. Further, it is impossible for the active within the receptive also not to have in its very middle the receptive, while it is also impossible for the receptive within the active not to have the active at its very center. In the myriad transformations of the receptive and active, each is never without its opposite. In general, therefore, when thing-events are endowed with pattern and psychophysical energy, there is no gap between them insofar as their respective natures are concerned, but their psychophysical constitutions cannot be without the distinctions of balanced and unbalanced."
7. The constantly changing balance of the active and receptive forces is articulated further by the Theory of Five Phases (五行 o-*haeng/wuxing*), which names symbols for the five representative combinations of the active and receptive forces: water (greater *eum/yin*), metal (lesser *eum/yin*), earth (neutral), wood (lesser *yang*), and fire (greater *yang*). See Fung Yu-lan, *A History of Chinese Philosophy*, trans. Derk Bodde, vol. 2, *The Period of Classical Learning from the Second Century* B.C. *to the Twentieth Century* A.D. (Princeton, N.J.: Princeton University Press, 1953), pp. 11–22.

8. I will translate 物 (*mul/wu*) as "thing-event," given the processual nature of any given "thing" as a dynamic and constantly changing coalescence of psychophysical energy in its binary modes.
9. The notion of psychophysical energy as the field and medium of interaction among all thing-events was based on the so-called correlative thinking articulated first by Dong Zhongshu 董仲舒 (179–104 B.C.E.). Correlative thinking assumes the idea of the universe as a moral cosmos (an orderly and harmonious moral pattern), which, together with its microcosm, i.e., the human political order, constituted a set of mutually resonant systems. See Nathan Sivin, "State, Cosmos, and Body in the Last Three Centuries B.C.," *Harvard Journal of Asiatic Studies* 55, no. 1 (1995): 6–22. See also Yuasa, *Momgwa uju,* pp. 84–85.
10. The sixty-four hexagrams (卦 *gua*) of the Classic of Change (*Yijing*) symbolize such markers of time. Yuasa, *Momgwa uju*, pp. 92–93. There is no sense of space and time as empty vacuum within which entities are located (pp. 94–95).
11. Such a notion is already seen in as ancient a document as the Classic of Change (*Juyeok* [Classic of Change from Zhou Dynasty], trans. Choe Won-sik [Seoul: Hyewon chulpansa, 2000], p. 253; Geum Jang-tae, *Gwisin-gwa jaesa* [Spirits and the ritual of ancestor veneration] [Seoul, JNC, 2009], p. 44). See also J. A. Adler, "Varieties of Spiritual Experience: *Shen* in Neo-Confucian Discourse," in *Confucian Spirituality*, ed. Tu Weiming and M. E. Tucker (New York: Crossroad, 2004), 2:120–43.
12. Haneunim (하느님), the Korean sky god, and Amaterasu-ōmikami (天照大神), the Japanese sun goddess, can be seen as variants of the common East Asian worship of Heaven (天), who was originally a sky god. Angus C. Graham, *Disputers of the Tao: Philosophical Argument in Ancient China* (La Salle, Ill.: Open Court, 1989), p. 1.
13. Geum, *Gwisin-gwa jaesa,* pp. 42–53. The ritual practices in preclassical China revolved around the worship of ancestors who were conceived as forming a hierarchy of spiritual powers in which the most distant ancestors were akin to powerful nature spirits (the spirit of earth, mountains, rivers, etc.), at the apex of which sat Lord on High or Heaven, exercising power over both the natural and human worlds. The point of sacrifices made to the ancestors was to persuade them to work on behalf of the living to obtain support from the more powerful nonancestral powers, and it was seen as supremely important especially for the rulers to have access to the highest power and to be a vehicle of its potency to order their realms in peace and harmony. See Sarah Allan, *The Way of Water and Sprouts of Virtue* (Albany: State University of New York Press, 1997), pp. 18–21; Jordan Paper, *The Spirits Are Drunk: Comparative Approaches to Chinese Religion* (Albany: State University of New York Press, 1995), pp. 268–69; Michael Puett, *To Become a God: Cosmology, Sacrifice, and Self-Divinization in Early China* (Cambridge, Mass.: Harvard University Asia Center for the Harvard-Yenching Institute, 2002), p. 26.
14. Geum, *Gwisin-gwa jaesa,* pp. 19–27.
15. Mary Evelyn Tucker, "The Philosophy of Ch'i as an Ecological Cosmology," in *Confucianism and Ecology,* ed. Mary Evelyn Tucker and John Berthrong (Cambridge, Mass.: Harvard University Center for the Study of World Religions, 1998), pp. 187–207.
16. *Juyeok*, p. 270.
17. *Juyeok*, p. 252.

18. The word 氣 (*gi/qi*) or 陰陽 (*eum/yin yang*) is mentioned rather sparsely in the Appended Remarks and virtually never in the Classic of Change itself. But the quoted phrase actually defines 道 (*do/dao*) in terms of the movement of the receptive and active psychophysical energies: "But in actuality we may not really know what *yin* and *yang* are or how these two words are used in the Yi text. In asserting that 'the alternation of one *yin* and one *yang* is to be called the *dao*,' we must notice the use of the term '*zhi-wei*' (之謂 'is to be called') as distinct from the term '*wei-zhi*' (謂之 'is called'). The former indicates a real definition which consists in an insight into the nature of things which leads to the definition of a thing in light of that insight, whereas the latter indicates a conventional definition which consists in identifying a use of descriptive language by convention." Chung-ying Cheng, "The *Yi-jing* and the *Yin-Yang* Way of Thinking," in *History of Chinese Philosophy*, ed. Bo Mou (New York: Routledge, 2009), p. 72.
19. *Juyeok*, pp. 253, 268. The two modes are the two horizontal lines, one broken and the other unbroken, called 爻 (*yao*), symbolizing the receptive and the active. The four images consist of four different combinations of the lines, namely, 大陰 (greater *yin*), 小陰 (lesser *yin*), 小陽 (lesser *yang*), and 大陽 (greater *yang*). The eight trigrams consist of eight different combinations of the lines, each combination being made up of three stacked lines, and form the basis of the entire set of sixty-four hexagrams.
20. The word "laozi" literally means "old master" or "old child." *Daodejing* means "the Classic of Way and Virtue (or Power)." The *Laozi* was compiled sometime between the early or mid-fourth and mid-third centuries B.C.E. as an anthology of units of verse-like sayings both earlier and then current, and edited into a "full-scale philosophical poem" (Graham, *Disputers of the Tao*, p. 214) attributed to a fictitious and mythological figure named Laozi. The text has served throughout Chinese history both as a scripture to be meditated on and ritually recited by the practitioners of the organized Daoist religion, on the one hand, and as a classic to be studied and commented on by the educated strata of Chinese society in general, on the other. See Graham, *Disputers of the Tao*, pp. 214–34; Michael LaFargue, trans., *The Tao of the Tao Te Ching: A Translation and Commentary* (Albany: State University of New York Press, 1992), pp. 196–98; Max Kaltenmark, *Lao Tzu and Taoism*, trans. Roger Greaves (Stanford: Stanford University Press, 1969), pp. 13–15; D. C. Lau, trans., *Tao Te Ching: A Bilingual Edition* (Hong Kong: Chinese University of Hong Kong, 2001), pp. 133–41.
21. I use the text of the received (Wang Bi) recension of the *Laozi* as found in the 2001 bilingual edition prepared by D. C. Lau. I use Lau's translation throughout, but when it does not in my view fully do justice to the meaning of the text, I amend it myself or use alternative translations, particularly Philip Ivanhoe's *The Daodejing of Laozi* (New York: Seven Bridges Press, 2002).
22. I have modified Lau's translation of 强爲之名 (*qiang wei zhi ming*), which is "I give it the makeshift name of 'the great.'"
23. I have modified Lau's translation of 逝 (*shi*), which is "receding."
24. The alternative translations of 微 (*wei*), 希 (*xi*), 夷 (*yi*) in chapter 14 as "invisible," "inaudible," and "imperceptible" are Richard Lynn's. Richard J. Lynn, trans., *The Classic of the Way and Virtue: A New Translation of the Tao-te ching of Laozi as interpreted by Wang Bi* (New York: Columbia University Press, 1999), 72. I have modified Lau's translation of 無狀之狀, 無物之象 (*wuzhuang zhi zhuang, wuwu zhi xiang*) in the same chapter, because

his use of "substance" for *wu* ("thing" or "entity") introduces the Western metaphysical connotations associated with the term.

25. Found in chapters 22 and 28, respectively.
26. The word "dao" has two meanings, that of "way," or "path," and that of "speech"—thus the pun.
27. Various nonmetaphysical interpretations have been given to the notion of the Way as it is presented in the classical Daoism of the *Laozi* and the *Zhuangzi*. It has been identified with nature (Wing-tsit Chan, Chen Guying, H. G. Creel, Joseph Needham), resulting in the characterization of the *Laozi* as "organic naturalism," "naturalistic pantheism" (Needham), "simplistic naturalism" (Chen), "nature mysticism" (B. Morris), etc. Wing-tsit Chan, trans., *The Way of Lao Tzu (Tao-te ching)* (Indianapolis: Bobbs-Merrill, 1963), p. 9; Joseph Needham, *Science and Civilization in China*, vol. 2, *History of Scientific Thought* (Cambridge: Cambridge University Press, 1956), pp. 37–38; Chen Guying, *Lao Tzu: Text Notes and Commentary*, trans. Rhett Young and Roger T. Ames (Taibei: Chinese Materials Center, 1981), pp. 8–34; Herrlee G. Creel, *What Is Taoism? And Other Studies in Chinese Cultural History* (Chicago: University of Chicago Press, 1970), pp. 41–42; Brian Morris, "Taoism, Confucianism, and the Chinese Self," *International Journal of Moral and Social Studies* 8, no. 3 (1993): 274–89. Hans-Georg Moeller, *The Philosophy of the Daodejing* (New York: Columbia University Press, 2006). Michael LaFargue interprets the Way as a perspectival, radically pluralist, nonreferential, and "existentially foundational" (*Tao of the Tao Te Ching*, p. 208) ethico-religious ideal of organic harmony. See Michael LaFargue, *Tao and Method: A Reasoned Approach to the Tao Te Ching* (Albany: State University of New York Press, 1994), pp. 269–93. Somewhat similarly, Roger Ames and David Hall present the Way as a radically perspectival, decentered, and aesthetically ordered "acosmotic cosmology" that is nonmetaphysical and nonreferential (Roger T. Ames, "The Local and Focal in Realizing a Daoist World," in *Daoism and Ecology: Ways within a Cosmic Landscape*, ed. N. J. Girardot, James Miller, and Liu Xiaogan [Cambridge, Mass.: Center for the Study of World Religions, Harvard Divinity School, 2001], p. 273; see also David L. Hall, "From Reference to Deference: Daoism and the Natural World," in *Daoism and Ecology*, pp. 246–61). The nonmetaphysical and nonreferential interpretation of the Way given by Ames and Hall construes the relationship of the things of the world and the Way as an interdependent, symmetrical relationship between "focus" and "field" (Roger T. Ames and David L. Hall, trans., *Daodejing "Making This Life Significant": A Philosophical Translation* [New York: Ballantine Books, 2003], pp. 11–21). Chad Hansen has attempted to strip the term *dao* of metaphysical and religious significance chiefly by means of linguistic analysis (translating *dao* into socioconventionally generated "prescriptive discourse" [207] that guides behavior) (Chad Hansen, *A Daoist Theory of Chinese Thought: A Philosophical Interpretation* [New York: Oxford University Press], 1992). In view of all these antimetaphysical interpretations, I would like note that, since Max Weber's pioneering comparative study of China and the West on the basis of the notion of an evolutionary development of rationality (Max Weber, *The Religion of China: Confucianism and Taoism*, trans. and ed. Hans H. Gerth [Glencoe, Ill.: Free Press, 1951]), the scholarship on early Chinese thought and religion has largely fallen into two camps. Those who follow the cultural-essentialist model (M. Granet, J. Needham, A. C. Graham, R. Ames, D. Hall) see in early China the cultural type or pole opposite of the West,

dominated by intuitive, organic, and correlative thinking vis-à-vis rational, mechanical, and analytic thinking, and therefore lacking a genuine sense of transcendence (in the sense of a deeper ontological context unconditioned by the world that depends on it), even when they understand both types of thinking as universal modes of thought that are present in different measures of strength in different cultures (Graham, Ames, Hall). (See Marcel Granet, *La pensée chinoise: La vie publique et la vie privée* [Paris: Editions Albin Michel, 1948]; Needham, *Science and Civilization in China*; Graham, *Disputers of the Tao*; Roger T. Ames and David L. Hall, *Thinking from the Han: Self, Truth, and Transcendence in Chinese and Western Culture* [Albany: State University of New York Press, 1998].) By contrast, those who adhere to the evolutionary model of Weber (Fung Yu-lan, B. Schwartz) locate early Chinese culture in a universal developmental path of cultures from mythos to logos, religion to philosophy, and immanence to transcendence, although they differ in their assessment of how early a sense of transcendence has emerged in China and what kind. (See Fung Yu-lan, *History of Chinese Philosophy*; Benjamin Schwartz, *The World of Thought in Ancient China* [Cambridge, Mass.: Belknap Press of Harvard University Press, 1985].) The strength of studies by Nathan Sivin, John Henderson, and Michael Puett, which avoid both cultural-essentialist and evolutionary models, is their thoroughly historical approach, tracing the rise and decline of Chinese correlative cosmology to show that what is usually regarded as a typically Chinese (or non-Chinese) mode of thought has its own historical vicissitudes within Chinese history. (See Sivin, "State, Cosmos, and Body"; John B. Henderson, *The Development and Decline of Chinese Cosmology* [New York: Columbia University Press, 1984], and Puett, *To Become a God*.) Their studies indicate that the real question is whether a sense of transcendence already existed in early China as *a particular historical development within* the Chinese culture. The scholarship on early Chinese religion demonstrates that a sense of transcendence did exist in early China, with far-reaching implications for the way we understand religious and philosophical concepts, such as the Dao, that originated in that context. My interpretation of the Dao as a normative religious-metaphysical order relies on the studies of early Chinese religion produced by Roth, Slingerland, Puett, Sivin, and others to reject the largely cultural-essentialist denial on the part of Ames and Hall of the notion of transcendence (in the sense of a deeper ontological context unconditioned by that which depends on it) to early China. For other religio-metaphysical readings of the Dao, see, among others, Mou Zhongjian, "Laozi's Discourse on the Way and Its Significance Today," *Contemporary Chinese Thought* 30, no. 1 (1998): 75–79; Chung-ying Cheng, "Chinese Metaphysics as Non-metaphysics: Confucian and Taoist Insights into the Nature of Reality," in *Understanding the Chinese Mind: The Philosophical Roots*, ed. Robert E. Allinson (Hong Kong: Oxford University Press, 1989), pp. 192–203; Robert C. Neville, "Daoist Relativism, Ethical Choice, and Normative Measure," *Journal of Chinese Philosophy* 29, no. 1 (2002): 6–8; Thomas Michael, *The Pristine Dao: Metaphysics in Early Daoist Discourse* (Albany: State University of New York Press, 2005).

28. I changed Lau's translation of 先 (*xian*) as "forefather" to "ancestor."
29. I use the present tense "is" instead of "was" as used by Lau in order to avoid the misunderstanding that the nameless was merely temporally prior and ancestral to heaven and earth rather than being their enduring condition of possibility.
30. "The myriad creatures in the world are born from something (有 *you*), and something from Nothing" (40.89). Norman Girardot has disclosed the creation-mythological

theme of *hundun* (混沌 chaos) operating underneath the structure of thought in the *Laozi* and articulated with mythic symbols such as "mother," "ancestor," "water," or "dark" (*xuan*) or more abstract terms such as "nothing" (*wu*) or "empty" (*xu*) (Norman J. Girardot, *Myth and Meaning in Early Taoism: The Theme of Chaos [hun-tun]* [Berkeley: University of California Press, 1983], pp. 1–52). Attempts have been made to give voice to the ontologically indeterminate yet creative nature of *wu*—in opposition to the Western metaphysical notion of nothingness as negative negativity (i.e., negativity that is opposed to being)—in terms of a void that harbors all potentialities (Kaltenmark, *Lao Tzu and Taoism*, p. 34) or a "divine Matrix" that is active or creative potentiality (Joseph A. Bracken, *The Divine Matrix: Creativity as Link between East and West* [Maryknoll, N.Y.: Orbis Books; Herefordshire, UK: Gracewing, 1995], pp. 133–35). A. T. Nuyen calls the Dao as *wu* "positive negativity" or nonbeing that is paradoxically being or reality, something similar to Heidegger's *Seyn*, which conceals in revealing and leaves only its trace in nature and human language. A. T. Nuyen, "Naming the Unnameable: The Being of the Tao," *Journal of Chinese Philosophy* 22, no. 4 (1995): 487–97.

31. I translated *fan* as "overflows" instead of Lau's "is broad" to highlight the Way's waterlike quality (life-giving and all-reaching).
32. Other passages that affirm the constancy and strength of the way's life-giving power are: "From the present back to antiquity, its name never deserted it" (21.49a); "The spirit of the valley never dies" (6.17); "The way is empty, yet use will not drain it. (4.11).
33. According to Tateno Masami, the ontological significance of *de* is that it is the phenomenal expression of the way in the realm of actual being, as the *de* of perfected self, of exquisite paintings and performances, etc. (Tateno Masami, "A Philosophical Analysis of the Laozi from an Ontological Perspective," in *Religious and Philosophical Aspects of the Laozi*, ed. Mark Csikszentmihalyi and Philip J. Ivanhoe [Albany: State University of New York Press, 1999], p. 182). See also Mou Zhongjian, "Laozi's Discourse," p. 82; Philip J. Ivanhoe, "The Concept of *de* ('Virtue') in the Laozi," in *Religious and Philosophical Aspects of the Laozi*, pp. 239–57; Allan, *Way of Water and Sprouts of Virtue*, pp. 105–6. As Waley's influential translation has pointed out, *de* originally had a premoral sense as "latent power" or "virtue inherent in something" (Arthur Waley, *The Way and Its Power: A Study of the Tao Tê Ching and Its Place in Chinese Thought* [London: George Allen and Unwin; New York: Macmillan, 1934], p. 32). *De* points to the potential or inner power of a given thing, which, like a fluid from the stream, was generated ultimately from *di* or *tian* and then transmitted hereditarily (associated with semen and female sexual fluids) in the form of *jing* (quintessence or innate vital energy) (Allan, *Way of Water and Sprouts of Virtue*, p. 105). With Confucius, the notion took on an ethical and moral connotation as cultivated virtue (Allan, *Way of Water and Sprouts of Virtue*, p. 106) that radiated moral charisma, "a kind of psychological power to attract and retain the support of others" (Ivanhoe, "The Concept of *de*," p. 240). In the *Laozi* the notion is used in both senses, as the *de* of human sages models itself after that of nature (Ivanhoe, "Concept of *de*," pp. 242–45).
34. For 物壯則老 (*wu zhuang ze lao*) I have used Philip Ivanhoe's translation rather than Lau's emendation of the text to *wu zhuang zei lao* ("a creature in its prime doing harm to the old"). As Lau himself admits (*Tao Te Ching*, p. 175), his emendation can no longer be supported after the discovery of the earlier Mawangdui text, which has 物壯而老 (*wu zhuang er lao*) (and 物壯即老 *wu zhuang ji lao* in ch. 55). Although Lau translates the

Mawangdui texts as "a creature old in its prime" for both chapters 30 and 55, in my view the temporally sequential sense of *er* is reinforced by its juxtaposition with *ji*, which lends support to my decision to use Ivanhoe's translation (*Daodejing*, p. 16).

35. *Arche* means origin or principle; *archos* and *archon* mean leader, first, chief, etc. *An-arche, an-archon, an-archos,* etc. mean, therefore, without rule, principle, or origin. David L. Hall has highlighted this "un-principled" and "an-archic" character of the Way as chaos in *The Uncertain Phoenix: Adventures toward a Post-Cultural Sensibility* (New York: Fordham University Press, 1982), p. 53.
36. R. C. Neville locates the ontological causation of the Dao, as it manifests itself in the world of Something, in the spontaneous emergence of novelty: "When and wherever a situation is underdetermined by antecedent conditions, the decisive determining is spontaneous relative to the past, and is the locus of ontological causation" (Neville, "Daoist Relativism," p. 9). In his reading of the "dialectical metaphysics" of classical Daoism, he distinguishes eternal ontological creativity (the eternal unnameable Dao) from its temporal manifestation (the nameable Mother Dao) and construes the latter in terms of an interplay between the existential achievement of structured and value-laden harmonies of internal forces (*you*) and the existential dislocation of those achieved harmonies in bursts of spontaneity (*ziran*) (pp. 9–11). It is the latter pole of the interplay, he argues, that enables human intervention that moves with rather than against the forces of creation (*wuwei*) (p. 13). Isabelle Robinet points out that many of the traditional Chinese commentators also saw the world as constantly re-creating itself by drawing on the omnipresent Dao, its source, and read the notion of *ziran* accordingly as self-creation. Isabelle Robinet, "The Diverse Interpretations of the Laozi, " in *Religious and Philosophical Aspects of the Laozi*, ed. Mark Csikszentmihalyi and Philip J. Ivanhoe (Albany: State University of New York Press, 1999), p. 144.
37. Since 自然 (*ziran*) in its common classical usage is a modifier (adjective) indicating a mode or manner of being, not a noun (as is clear in 17.46), I amended Lau's translation "that which is naturally so." An alternative translation would be "being of itself what it is." Chan translates it as "Nature" in accordance with his reading of the *Laozi* as a naturalistic philosophy (Chan, *Way of Lao Tzu,* p. 9). As a philosophical concept, though, *ziran* has been used in Chinese history as a noun to mean spontaneity or "naturalness," but not "nature or "natural world," which is a modern Chinese use of *ziran* invented under Western influence. In classical Chinese, nature in the modern Western sense corresponded to *tian* (heaven) or *tiandi* (heaven and earth) or *wanwu* (the myriad creatures or ten thousand things). Still, *ziran* can be translated as "nature" insofar as the latter word refers to the essential quality or fundamental character of something that is developed without external prompting and interruption. Liu Xiaogan, "Naturalness (Tzu-jan), the Core Value in Taoism: Its Ancient Meaning and Its Significance Today," in *Lao-tzu and the Tao-te-ching*, ed. Livia Kohn and Michael LaFargue, (Albany: State University of New York Press, 1998), pp. 212–13.
38. See the text in Rudolf G. Wagner, *A Chinese Reading of the Daodejing: Wang Bi's Commentary on the Laozi with Critical Text and Translation* (Albany: State University of New York Press, 2003), pp. 271–72 (translation mine): "It [great completion] achieves completion in deference to things, and does not become a single image; therefore, it 'seems incomplete.' Great fullness, being plentiful, gives in deference to things and does not show favoritism; therefore, it 'seems empty.' It [great straightness] straightens in

deference to things, and not on the basis of a single standard; therefore it 'seems bent.' Great skill completes vessels in accordance with their spontaneous nature, and does not produce extraordinary features; therefore it 'seems awkward.' Great eloquence speaks in deference to things and does not contrive anything; therefore it 'seems tongue-tied.'"

39. Jung H. Lee has highlighted the importance of the virtue of *ying* in early Daoist ethics (Jung H. Lee, "Finely Aware and Richly Responsible: The Daoist Imperative," *Journal of the American Academy of Religion* 68, no. 3 [2000]: 511–36). David Hall's use of the term "deference" also underscores the meaning of *ying* as "yielding to the perspective of the things" and letting them be themselves. Hall, "From Reference to Deference," p. 248.

40. This is Rudolf Wagner's translation of *bu zi sheng* (Wagner, *Chinese Reading of the Daodejing*, 141). Ivanhoe's translation is "do not live for themselves" (*Daodejing of Laozi*, p. 7), whereas Waley has "do not foster their own lives" (*Way and Its Power*, p. 150), both of which in my view are better translations than Lau's "do not give themselves life" (*Tao Te Ching*, p. 11 ).

41. See Schwartz, "The Thought of the Tao-te-ching," in *Lao-tzu and the Tao-te-ching*, ed. Livia Kohn and Michael LaFargue (Albany: State University of New York Press, 1998), pp. 200–2. In regard to what aspects of human life is "being so of itself" or not, Graham Parkes puts it best when he says: "It seems natural, for example, for humans to seek shelter in caves, and further—on the model of animals that build nests, hives, or dens—to construct houses to live in. But we might want to say of a life that is lived in hermetically sealed, air-conditioned apartments, cars, and office buildings, such that one rarely comes into contact with a molecule of unprocessed air, water, or earth, that it is a somewhat unnatural existence. The issue would then be to distinguish those forms or features of civilization that detract from naturalness, to the point where human flourishing is impaired, from those that are comparable with such flourishing." (Graham Parkes, "The Place of the Human in Nature: Paradigms of Ecological Thinking, East and West," in *Is There a Human Nature?* ed. Leroy S. Rowner [Notre Dame, Ind.: University of Notre Dame Press, 1997], pp. 152–53). According to Sarah Allan, in the early Confucian texts such as the *Analects* and the *Mencius*, the *dao* is more narrowly modeled on a channel or course of stream, i.e., a conduit guiding people in their actions or a condition in which everything follows its natural course, both in the natural and human worlds, and is therefore always with a modifier. Since without channels water flows in every direction, creating a flood, the image of flood control and irrigation is central to their understanding of civilization as 文 (*wen*) or identifiable patterns of proper behavior. Because channeled water, not water as such, is important, it is possible to say that either there is *dao* in the world (*tian xia you dao*) or there is not, depending on whether there is a ruler with Heaven's mandate (*tian ming*). In the *Laozi*, by contrast, the *dao* is the Dao, i.e., a principle constantly manifested both in the movements of heaven and earth and in human beings (Allan, *Way of Water and Sprouts of Virtue*, pp. 66–74). Because the Dao is always present (*zai*) in the world, like water as such, it implies a loss of civilizational and moral imperatives (p. 138). What Allan confirms by highlighting the root metaphor of the notion of the Dao is that, for the *Laozi*, civilizational and moral imperatives that are considered *ziran* follow the qualities of (nonchanneled) water as such, namely, the "female" qualities of being quiet, still, weak, submissive, and resting in the lower position, that are identified with the virtue of nondiscriminating and self-effacing simplicity.

42. The question of why this deviation from the Dao happens in the case of human beings, when they cannot separate themselves from the Dao that is everywhere, is neither really answered by the *Laozi* nor by its Chinese commentators historically (Robinet, "Diverse Interpretations," p. 147). For Schwartz and Ames, it is "mysterious" and "unexplained" (Schwartz, "Thought of the Tao-te-ching," p. 200; Roger T. Ames, *Art of Rulership: A Study of Ancient Chinese Political Thought* [Albany: State University of New York Press, 1994], p. 35). See also Graham, *Disputers of the Tao*, p. 172.
43. I use the translation by Schwartz ("Thought of the Tao-te-ching," p. 200) instead of Lau's "great hypocrisy" (*Tao Te Ching*, p. 27).
44. The *Laozi* has two different uses of the term *shengren*—one to designate the proto-Confucian culture heroes who were the initiators of the "great artifice" (as in 19.43) and the other to refer to the true sage-rulers who can reverse the pathology of civilization thus begun, and whose authority is "as 'natural' as the presence of the dominant male in the group life of many higher mammals" (Schwartz, Thought of the Tao-te-ching," p. 203). According to Graham, a constant assumption in early Chinese political thought was that government was by nature authoritarian and that the only alternative to absolutism was a severe reduction or even abolition of government, which was an ideal set in antiquity practically implying a minimalization of interference from above in the affairs of individuals, families, clans, and villages in accordance with local traditions and customs. In other words, antiauthoritarianism in early China was antipolitical, inclining not to democracy but to anarchism. Insofar as the necessity of government was acknowledged, therefore, no one conceived any limits to power except moral limits—which meant that good government was thought to depend on the moral goodness of those who governed (Graham, *Disputers of the Tao*, p. 299). The Confucian appeal to Zhou feudalism in opposition to the bureaucratic absolutism of the Legalist School (*fajia*) was in that sense a "hierarchical anarchism" that envisioned social order as the harmonizing of human beings' spontaneously emerging moral inclinations, such as the attitude of deference found in patriarchal families; the Daoist emphasis on unlearning socioconventionally inculcated desires and patterns of behavior by means of the charismatic influence of the sages' perfectly clear awareness was a "paternalistic anarchism" (pp. 302–3).
45. Hall, "From Reference to Deference," p. 257. For Hall, the term denotes an action carried out in deference to the recognized excellence or *de* of particular things, seeing beneath the accreted layers of artifice that masks their naturalness. For Allan, *wuwei* is what water does, which moves spontaneously downward following the contours of the landscape (*Way of Water and Sprouts of Virtue*, p. 79). Although the term *wuwei* emerged relatively late in pre-imperial China, occurring first (and only once) in the Analects (Creel, *What Is Taoism?* pp. 57–59; Allan, *Way of Water and Sprouts of Virtue*, p. 79), according to Slingerland it represented, one of the central themes of the early Chinese religion, namely, the spiritual ideal of being in a state of "fitting" (*yi*) with the normative order of the cosmos (Heaven or the Way), which is found as early as in the Classic of Odes (*shijing*) and the Classic of History (*shujing*). For Confucians and Daoists of the Warring States period, it denoted an ability to move through the world and human society in a manner completely spontaneous and yet still fully in harmony with the Way as the normative order of the natural and human worlds. As an ideal of perfectly skilled action, not

nonaction, it referred to "a state of personal harmony in which actions flow freely and instantly from one's spontaneous inclinations—without the need for extended deliberation or inner struggle—and yet nonetheless perfectly accord with the dictates of the situation at hand, display an almost supernatural efficacy, and (in the Confucian context at least) harmonize with the demands of conventional morality" (Edward Slingerland, "Effortless Action: The Chinese Spiritual Ideal of Wu-Wei," *Journal of the American Academy of Religion* 68, no. 2 [2000]: 300). *Wuwei* was connected to the ideal of ordering the world through the power of one's virtue (*de*), found in the two Classics (the Classic of Odes and the Classic of History) as the martial and social virtues of the aristocratic lord, and for the early Confucians in the ideal of the Confucian gentleman (*junzi*) which Confucius embodied and exemplified with the spontaneity and naturalness of his ritual mastery. Whereas the disagreement between the early Confucians Mencius and Xunzi was whether *wuwei* embodied the full realization of responses natural to humans or a virtue hard-won from the initially recalcitrant human nature after years of training and submission to cultural forms, the early Daoists put emphasis on the end state of *wuwei* to criticize what they perceived as the Confucian obsession with the means of achieving that state, such as an overelaborated and consciously sought set of (conventionally moral) goals and practices, which purportedly turned the end result into a forced behavior, a hypocrisy (Slingerland, "Effortless Action," pp. 295–306). Hansen's anachronistic reading, which treats *wuwei* as some kind of linguistically and pragmatically oriented anticonventionalism, ignores this religious context (Hansen, *Daoist Theory of Chinese Thought*, pp. 213–14). Because the spontaneity evinced in *wuwei* does not represent subjectivity in the sense of individual autonomy as in the modern West but the highest degree of objectivity associated with the will of Heaven or the way of the Way, the effortless actions of the sages "are not so much their actions as they are the *Dao* acting through them" (Ivanhoe, "Concept of *de*," p. 249). In that sense, *wuwei* could be translated as "nondual action," i.e., the kind of action without a sense of agent/self apart from the action itself. David R. Loy, "Loving the World as Our Own Body: The Non-Dualist Ethics of Taoism, Buddhism, and Deep Ecology," in *Asian and Jungian View of Ethics*, ed. Carl B. Becker (Westport, Conn.: Greenwood Press, 1999), pp. 89–91.

46. Following David Hall, "no-knowledge" and "no desire" could be translated as "unprincipled knowing" and "objectless desire" in the sense that what they reject is both artificially principled knowledge of things and the supposedly lasting objects of desire provided by such knowledge. Hall, "From Reference to Deference," pp. 253–55, 258–61.

47. For the *Laozi*, to know the myriad things just the way they are is to know them within the context of the Way's constant flow, i.e., the constant an-archic movement between Nothing and Something: "To know harmony is called the constant; to know the constant is called 'discernment (*ming*)'" (55.126). Because discernment as nonsubjective knowledge of things gives the most accurate picture of the world, it "penetrates the four quarters" (10.24), and as a result, "Without stirring abroad one can know the whole world; without looking out of the window, one can see the way of heaven" (47.106). The opposite of *wuzhi* is *qian shi* ("foreknowledge")—"Foreknowledge is the flowery embellishment of the way and the beginning of folly" (38.84)—which refers to the principled knowing of one who has already made up one's mind before entering the situation, i.e., one who "knows" beforehand what is proper and right. The perfectly clear perception of the

myriad things that is *wuzhi* is an end product of the mystical inner cultivation exercises, as Graham puts it: "The Taoist relaxes the body, calms the mind, loosens the grip of categories made habitual by naming, frees the current of thought for more fluid differentiations and assimilations, and instead of pondering choices lets his problems solve themselves as inclination spontaneously finds its own direction, which is the Way" (*Disputers of the Tao*, p. 235).

48. I have translated *xin* as "heart-mind."
49. For *tianxia* I have used "the world" in place of Lau's "the empire."
50. Again, for *tianxia* I have used "the world."
51. According to Graham, the *Laozi's* preference for the female terms of the binaries is strategically deconstructive; it is designed to counter the already existing massive accumulation of the male pole in human civilization. It does not mean one should be fixated on the female as an enduring and independent absolute. *Disputers of the Tao*, pp. 228–30.
52. "If the sage who is free from desire ever desires anything, it is that he "desires not to desire [*yuwuyu*] . . . in order to help the myriad creatures to be so of themselves [*ziran*]" (translation modified from "to be natural") (64.156).
53. *Shang xian* was one of the central tenets of the Confucian and Mohist doctrines of government (Lau, *Tao Te Ching*, p. xxix).
54. I have modified Lau's translation ("It happened to us naturally") in order to avoid the use of the word "natural" for *ziran*.
55. I have modified Lau's translation, which merely phonetically reproduces 陰 and 陽 as *yin* and *yang*.
56. I have modified Lau's translation of 沖氣以為和, which is "are the blending of the generative forces of the two."
57. According to the ground-breaking studies produced by Harold Roth and others, early Daoism consisted of a shared tradition of "mystical" self-cultivation practices called "inner cultivation" (內業 *neiye*), which were practiced and passed on by different master-disciple lineages and were accompanied by metaphysical and cosmological speculations explaining the nature of the self-transformative mystical experiences attained by those practices. Inner cultivation may have originated from the trance-inducing practices of shamans. "Inner cultivation" is referred to in the *Zhuangzi* as the practice of "sitting and forgetting (*zuowang*)" (Harold D. Roth, "The Laozi in the Context of Early Daoist Mystical Praxis," in *Religious and Philosophical Aspects of the Laozi*, ed. Mark Csikszentmihalyi and Philip J. Ivanhoe [Albany: State University of New York Press, 1999], p. 69). The earliest extant statement of this practice, the Inward Training (內業), speaks of "cleaning out the lodging place of the numinous (*shen*)," strongly suggesting a shamanic purification ceremony that prepares one for the descent of some divinity (Harold D. Roth, *Original Tao: Inward Training (Nei-yeh) and the Foundations of Taoist Mysticism* [New York: Columbia University Press, 1999], pp. 189–90, and "Laozi," pp. 61–62, 68–69). According to Graham's reading of the Inward Training, the descent of *shen* was understood in terms of *qi* (wind/air/breath), the life-energy that circulates as the air, permeates everything, and vitalizes the body. At its purest and most vital, *qi* is *jing*, the "quintessential," which is perfectly luminous as the heavenly bodies, circulates in the atmosphere as *kuishen* ("the ghostly and daimonic"), centered within each being as its essence, and descends into—or congeals within—human beings as the physiological substrate of their *shen* ("daimon"), rendering them *shenming* ("daimonic and clear

seeing"), i.e., enabling them to perceive all things with perfect clarity. In order to achieve the descent of *shen*, which is called the obtainment of *de* ("virtue" or "power"), the practitioners must use *xin* (the heart as the organ of both thought and emotion, or, to quote Kirkland, "the ruling agency in the individual's biospiritual nexus" [76]) to guide and concentrate *qi* as it courses through their body—a practice that involves moderation in diet, adjustment of posture, controlled breathing, and stilling of passions and senses. Graham, *Disputers of the Tao*, pp. 100–102; Russell Kirkland, "Varieties of Taoism in Ancient China: A Preliminary Comparison of Themes in the *Nei Yeh* and Other Taoist Classics," *Taoist Resources* 7, no. 2 (1997): 74–77.

58. *Nanhua zhenjing* (bk. 4, ch. 22, *Zhibeiyou*), in *Zhonghua daozang*, ed. Zhang Jiyu, vol. 13 (Beijing: Huaxia chubanshe, 2004), p. 46.
59. *Nanhua zhenjing* (bk. 3, ch. 17, *qiushui*), in *Zhonghua daozang*, p. 33.
60. *Nanhua zhenjing* (bk. 3, ch. 18, *zhile*), in *Zhonghua daozang*, p. 37. Here I am using Paul Kjellberg's translation, which seems to capture the sense of the passage perfectly (Philip J. Ivanhoe and Bryan W. Van Norden, eds., *Readings in Classical Chinese Philosophy*, 2nd ed. [Indianapolis: Hackett, 2001], p. 247). For the *Zhaungzi*'s notion of the Way as a primal chaos, see the story of the emperor of the center, 混沌 (*hundun*) in chapter 7. *Nanhua zhenjing* (bk. 2, ch. 7, *yingdiwang*), in *Zhonghua daozang*, p. 17.
61. For the notion of the "fasting of the heart-mind (心齋)," *Nanhua zhenjing* (bk. 1, ch. 4 *renjianshi*), in *Zhonghua daozang*, p. 8. See also *Nanhua zhenjing* (bk. 2, ch. 7, *yingdiwang*), in *Zhonghua daozang*, p. 17. For the notion of "sitting and forgetting [坐忘]" and "great communication [大通]," *Nanhua zhenjing* (bk. 2, ch. 6, *dazongshi*), in *Zhonghua daozang*, p. 16. The "great communication" means to nourish one's psychophysical energy until one connects to "that by which all things were created [物之所造]," i.e., the Way. See *Nanhua zhenjing* (bk. 4, ch. 19, *dasheng*), in *Zhonghua daozang*, p. 38.
62. Zhang, *Gi ui cheorak*, pp. 94–95.
63. For *Huainanzi*, see Zhang, *Gi ui cheorak*, pp. 124, 132. For *Liezi*, see Maebayashi, Sato, and Kobayashi, *Giui bigyo munhwa*, p. 28.
64. Being the oldest complete commentary on the *Laozi*, the *Heshang Gong* commentary was produced in the second century C.E. by an anonymous author and is considered part of *the* so-called Huang-Lao tradition that flourished during the Han dynasty era (Alan K. L. Chan, *Two Visions of the Way: A Study of the Wang Pi and the Ho-shang Kung Commentaries on the Lao-Tzu* [Albany: State University of New York Press, 1990], p. 118). See also Yi Seok-myeong, trans., *Noja dodeokgyeong hasang-gong jang-gu* [The Heshang Gong commentary to Laozi's Daodejing] (Seoul: Somyeong chulpansa, 2005), pp. 11–12. For the Heshang Gong commentary's development of the triadic structure of the Way, psychophysical energy, and the myriad thing-events, see pp. 14–15.
65. Yi, *Noja dodeokgyeong*, p. 92 (ch. 10); p. 269 (ch. 42). The commentary even identifies the Primordial Psychophysical Energy with the Way itself, though only once in ch. 2 (p. 58).
66. Yi, *Noja dodeokgyeong*, pp. 266–68 (ch. 42).
67. In the words of Alan Chan, the One as One Psychophysical Energy represents the *ideal order* in contrast to the *ideal chaos* of the Way (*Two Visions of the Way*, p. 132).
68. Yi, *Noja dodeokgyeong*, p. 117 (ch. 14); p. 51 (ch. 1). For the notion of Great Peace, p. 139 (ch. 18), p. 228 (ch. 35), p. 322 (ch. 55). For the translator's excellent introduction to the notion, pp. 19–22.

69. Iain Thomson, "Ontotheology? Understanding Heidegger's *Destruktion* of Metaphysics," in *International Journal of Philosophical Studies* 8, no. 3 (2009): 297–327.
70. Hall, *Uncertain Phoenix*, p. 59.
71. Catherine Keller, *Face of the Deep: A Theology of Becoming* (London: Routledge, 2003), pp. 103–23.
72. Hall, *Uncertain Phoenix*, pp. 53–60, 77–85.
73. Guo Xiang, the most famous editor and commentator of *Zhuangzi*, whose commentaries accompanied the traditional editions of the text, is one such case. Brook Ziporyn, *The Penumbra Unbound: The Neo-Taoist Philosophy of Guo Xiang* (Albany: State University of New York Press, 2003).
74. "The democracy of creation" is taken from Catherine Keller's *God and Power: Counter-Apocalyptic Journeys* (Minneapolis: Fortress Press, 2005), p. 135. It is a slightly modified version of Whitehead's original coinage: "We find ourselves in a buzzing world, amid a democracy of fellow creatures." Alfred North Whitehead, *Process and Reality: Corrected Edition*, ed. David Ray Griffin and Donald W. Sherburne (New York: Free Press, 1978), p. 50.
75. Hall, *Uncertain Phoenix*, p. 216.
76. Ibid., p. 279.
77. Hall's own formulation (coined in homage to Zhuangzi's perspectivalism) is "the non-coherent sum of all orders." Hall, "From Reference to Deference," p. 247.
78. Used to mean "culture" or "civilization," *wen* originally meant decorations carved into wood. Sandra A. Wawrytko, "The Problem of the Problem of Evil: A Taoist Response," in *The Problem of Evil: An Intercultural Exploration*, ed. Sandra A. Wawrytko (Amsterdam: Rodopi, 2000), p. 24.
79. Michael Puett, *The Ambivalence of Creation: Debates concerning Innovation and Artifice in Early China* (Stanford: Stanford University Press, 2001), pp. 40–50.
80. As in the text of the *Laozi*, chapter 18: "When the great way falls into disuse, there are benevolence and rectitude; when cleverness emerges, there is great hypocrisy; when the six relations are at variance, there are filial children; when the state is benighted, there are loyal ministers" (18.42). Here the *Laozi* attacks the Confucian emphasis on rites/propriety (*li*), which refers to "correct behavior and fulfillment of obligations within existing hierarchies" (Livia Kohn, "Chinese Religion," in *The Human Condition*, ed. Robert C. Neville [Albany: State University of New York Press, 2001], p. 26). See also chapter 38: "The rites are the wearing thin of loyalty and good faith and the beginning of disorder" (38.84). Also, "Exterminate sageliness, discard wisdom, and the people will benefit a hundredfold; exterminate benevolence, discard rectitude, and the people will again be filial; exterminate ingenuity, discard profit, and there will be no more thieves and bandits. These three, being false adornments (*wei wen*), are not enough. And the people must have something to which they can attach themselves; exhibit the unadorned and embrace the uncarved block. Have little thought of self and as few desires as possible" (19.43–43a).
81. Against the early Chinese religious tradition of exhorting the human world to pattern itself after Heaven as the ultimate deity (sky god) turned spiritual principle and power of the universe, the *Laozi* substitutes the Way for Heaven as such a principle and power, now much more "apophaticized," and turns Heaven into a subordinate principle: "Man models himself on earth, Earth on heaven, Heaven on the Way, And the Way on that which is naturally so" (25). See Schwartz, "Thought of the Tao-te-ching, pp. 190–92;

Allan, *Way of Water and Sprouts of Virtue*, pp. 22, 66–75; Roth, *Original Tao*, p. 181. In chapter 5, with an almost shocking rhetorical use of hyperbole, the *Laozi* distances itself from preachers of morality: "Heaven and earth are not humane, and treat the myriad creatures as straw dogs; the sage is not humane, and treats the people as straw dogs" (5.14). (Instead of Lau's "ruthless," which implies a disposition diametrically opposed to benevolence, I have used "not humane" for *buren*.) The point here is not that heaven and earth or human beings who are one with the Way are ruthless and callous—which would merely be the moral binary opposite of being humane and thus part of the same evaluative hierarchy—but that the Way is impartial because it is accommodating of all, and therefore does not favor one or another according to some preset criteria of evaluation such as benevolence, to the extent that it appears almost indifferent (see also 16.38). Although the Way as the generous Mother may sound similar to the plenitude of Divine Goodness praised and glorified by apophatic or negative theology, the Way is not benign or humane.

82. Girardot, *Myth and Meaning*, p. 2.
83. Ibid., p. 42
84. Ibid., pp. 40–41.
85. Ames, *Art of Rulership*, p. 46.
86. The most famous of which were the Celestial Masters, the earliest Daoist sect that presented an independent political and religious social structure, and the Yellow Turban Rebellion, the first of many Daoist-inspired rebellions, both at the end of the Han dynasty. See Terry F. Kleeman, *Great Perfection: Religion and Ethnicity in a Chinese Millennial Kingdom* (Honolulu: University of Hawai'i Press, 1998); Barbara Hendrischke, *The Scripture on Great Peace: The Taiping jing and the Beginnings of Daoism* (Berkeley: University of California Press, 2006); Stephen Bokenkamp, *Early Daoist Scriptures* (Berkeley: University of California Press, 1997).
87. Isabelle Robinet, *Taoism: Growth of a Religion*, trans. Phyllis Brooks (Stanford: Stanford University Press, 1997), pp. 184–211.
88. This is similar to Laurel Schneider's critique of the totalizing Buddhist metaphysics of emptiness, which evacuates the One (singularity) into emptiness on the basis of the claim that each object is in an excess of totality and therefore empty of its own being. Laurel C. Schneider, *Beyond Monotheism: A Theology of Multiplicity* (London: Routledge, 2009), pp. 143–44.
89. Ch. 10 and 22.
90. Ch. 42.

## 2. *The Psychophysical Energy of the Great Ultimate: A Neo-Confucian Adventure of the Idea in Zhu Xi*

This chapter is a revised and expanded version of the first half of an essay published earlier as "'Empty and Tranquil, and Without Any Sign, and Yet All Things Are Already Luxuriantly Present': A Comparative-Theological Reflection on the Manifold Spirit," in *Polydoxy: Theology of Multiplicity and Relation*, ed. Catherine Keller and Laurel C. Schneider (London: Routledge, 2010), pp. 126–50.

1. For early Daoism's striking departure from the centrality of Heaven and the more limited usage of the word "dao" in other early Chinese religio-philosophical traditions, Benjamin

Schwartz, "The Thought of the Tao-te-ching," in *Lao-tzu and the Tao-te-ching*, ed. Livia Kohn and Michael LaFargue (Albany: State University of New York Press, 1998), pp. 190–92; Sarah Allan, *The Way of Water and Sprouts of Virtue* (Albany: State University of New York Press, 1997), pp. 22, 66–75; Harold D. Roth, *Original Tao: Inward Training (Nei-yeh) and the Foundations of Taoist Mysticism* (New York: Columbia University Press, 1999), p. 181.

2. Angus C. Graham, *Disputers of the Tao: Philosophical Argument in Ancient China* (La Salle, Ill.: Open Court, 1989), p. 3.
3. Ibid., pp. 9–21, 33–50, 111–32, 235–66. See also Roger T. Ames, *Art of Rulership: A Study of Ancient Chinese Political Thought* (Albany: State University of New York Press, 1994), pp. 28–35; Michael Puett, *The Ambivalence of Creation: Debates concerning Innovation and Artifice in Early China* (Stanford: Stanford University Press, 2001), pp. 40–78.
4. Edward Slingerland, "Effortless Action: The Chinese Spiritual Ideal of Wu-Wei." *Journal of the American Academy of Religion*. 68, no. 2 (2000): 311–12. See also his *Effortless Action: Wu-wei as Conceptual Metaphor and Spiritual Ideal in Early China* (Oxford: Oxford University Press, 2003).
5. This innovation was shared by the itinerant shi (士) class, originally the retainers ("knights") of hereditary ministers (公卿大夫) of small states but now itinerant office seekers, but Kongzi was probably the earliest. For the notion of shi idealists, see Michael LaFargue, *The Tao of the Tao Te Ching: A Translation and Commentary* (Albany: State University of New York Press, 1992), pp. 192–94, and *Tao and Method: A Reasoned Approach to the Tao Te Ching* (Albany: State University of New York Press, 1994), pp. 292–93. Yet despite their anticonventional stance, the shi idealist fully accepted the contemporary sociopolitical structure and their officially assigned place in it, their goal being to "rule from the middle" as advisers to the rulers. For the different ways the shi idealist such as Kongzi, Mozi, Mengzi, Xunzi, and others conceived the way of Heaven, see Graham, *Disputers of the Tao*, pp. 9–21, 33–50, 111–32, 235–66. See also Ames, *Art of Rulership*, pp. 28–35, and Puett, *The Ambivalence of Creation*, 40–78. For the different ways in which the shi such as Kongzi, Mozi, Mengzi, Xunzi, and others understood self-cultivation as the way of obtaining virtue, see Michael Puett, *To Become a God: Cosmology, Sacrifice, and Self-Divinization in Early China* (Cambridge, Mass.: Harvard University Asia Center for the Harvard-Yenching Institute, 2002), pp. 26, 98–104, 122–40, 318–19. On the whole Kongzi did not necessarily assume the ability of those divine or spiritual beings to accept the performance of the rituals and to take pleasure in the offerings. The rituals were seen as efficacious in creating social and cosmic harmony primarily on the basis of the right spirit and attitude of the people performing the rituals. Kongzi's attitude was an "agnostic," "rationalistic," and "practical" attitude toward beings transcendent but not really "supernatural." See Zhu Xi, *Non-eo jipju* [Collected commentaries on Analects], trans. with commentary by Seong Baek-hyo , rev. and exp. ed. (Seoul: Jeontong munhwa yeon-guhoe, 2006), p. 90 (3.12); p. 117 (6.20); p. 205 (7.20); p. 303 (11.11).
6. The notion of "superior man" embraced, in principle, both men and women, as the Confucian tradition always left open a limited access to learning (and virtue thereby acquired) by women. Nonetheless, because of the formal confinement of women to the realm of *nei* (內)—the realm of domestic skills and household management and their exclusion from the realm of *wai* (外), the realm of literary learning and public service,

women could realize the ideal of "superior man" in a only very limited fashion. See Li-Hsiang Lisa Rosenlee, *Confucianism and Women: A Philosophical Interpretation* (Albany: State University of New York Press, 2006), pp. 69–94.

7. *Ren* (仁) is also translated as "humaneness," or "benevolence."
8. See Zhu Xi, *Non-eo jipju*, p. 118 (4.15), where *ren* (仁) is construed in terms of integrity (忠 *zhong*) and sympathetic understanding (恕 *shu*).
9. Tu Wei-ming defines the Neo-Confucian notion of transcendence as such. See "A Confucian Perspective on Learning to Be Human," in *Confucian Thought: Selfhood as Creative Transformation* (Albany: State University of New York Press, 1985), pp. 51–65.
10. See Zhu Xi, *Maengja jipju* [Collected commentaries on Mencius], trans. with commentary by Seong Baek-hyo (Seoul: Jeontong munhwa yeon-guhoe, 1991), p. 88 (2A2). Hereafter *Maengja jipju*. I am partially borrowing Graham's translation of the phrase as "the flood-like *ch'i*." See *Disputers of the Tao*, p. 127.
11. Ibid., p. 322 (6A6) See also p. 327 (6A8); pp. 103–4 (2A6); p. 226 (4A27); p. 326 (6A7).
12. Ibid., p. 373 (7A1).
13. Ibid., p. 322 (6A6); pp. 103–4 (2A6) The distinction between the Four Sprouts and the Seven Feelings, which have their respective roots in *Mencius* 2A6 and the *Liji* [The book of rites], ch. 9. See, for instance, one of the most famous references to the distinction found in Zhu Xi, *Zhuzi yulei* [Conversations of Master Zhu, arranged topically], ed. Li Jingde and Wang Xingxian (Beijing: Zhonghua shuju, 1986), 4:1297 (hereafter *Yulei*—for citations from *Yulei*, I give the volume number followed by the page number).
14. *Maengja jipju*, p. 88 (2A2).
15. Ibid., pp. 88–89 (2A2).
16. Ibid., p. 338 (6A15). The heart-mind is the faculty of reflecting on and judging the relative importance of our various appetites and moral inclinations. Without it, "the senses simply yield to the attraction of what excites them and withdraw attention from everything else. We notice again that general assumption of his tradition, that moral thinking starts when the senses are already responding to stimulation from outside, and that its function is to choose between reactions in the light of the fullest knowledge" (Graham, *Disputers of the Tao*, pp. 131–32). See also *Mengzi: With Selections from Traditional Commentaries*, trans. Bryan W. Van Norden (Indianapolis: Hackett, 2008), p. xxxiv.
17. Zhang Liwen, *Giui cheorak* [A philosophy of gi], trans. Kim Gyo-bin (Seoul: Yemun seowon, 2004), pp. 131–36; Maebayashi Kiyokazu, Sato Koetsu, and Kobayashi Hiroshi, *Giui bigyo munhwa* [A comparative-cultural analysis of Ggi], trans. Park Mun-hyeon and Sekine Hideyuki (Seoul: Doseo chulpan hanul, 2006), .p. 76.
18. I follow A. C. Graham in translating *li* as "pattern." "The Ch'eng-Chu Theory of Human Nature," in *Studies in Chinese Philosophy and Philosophical Literature* (Singapore: Institute of East Asian Philosophies, 1986), p. 421. A. S. Cua, "Reason and Principle in Chinese Philosophy: An Interpretation of *Li*," in *A Companion to World Philosophies*, ed. E. Deutsch and R. Bontekoe (Malden: Blackwell, 1999), pp. 201–13.
19. See his reply to Huang Daofu's letter ("Da Huang Daofu") in Zhu Xi, *Zhuzi wenji* [Collected literary works of Master Zhu], ed. Chen Junmin (Taibei: Defu wenjiao jijinhui, 2000), 6:2798 (hereafter *Wenji*—for citations from *Wenji*, I give the volume number followed by the page number).

20. The concept of pattern (*li*) vis-à-vis psychophysical energy (*qi*) was initially derived by Cheng Yi from the Huayan Buddhist notion of the mutual nonexclusion of pattern (*li*) and fact (事 *shi*). Tomoeda Ryutaro, "Yi T'oegye and Chu Hsi: Differences in Their Theories of Principle and Material Force," in *The Rise of Neo-Confucianism in Korea*, ed. Wm. Theodore de Bary and JaHyun Kim Haboush (New York: Columbia University Press, 1985), pp. 246–47. Zhu Xi combines the moralistic and rationalistic interpretation of pattern (i.e., as regularities or coherences in natural processes and in human behavior) by Cheng Yi and the question about the source of the generation and production of all things (the Supreme Ultimate for Zhou Dunyi, the Supreme Void for Zhang Zai, and the Change for Cheng Hao) (A. C. Graham, *Two Chinese Philosophers: The Metaphysics of the Brothers Ch'eng*, 2nd ed. [La Salle, Ill.: Open Court, 1992], 108). The word "structuring" or "patterning" is the translation of pattern given by Don Baker in his *Korean Spirituality* (Honolulu: University of Hawai'i Press, 2008), pp. 48–49. My designation of pattern as dynamic *ontological* creativity is based on the tendency observed in both Cheng Yi and Zhu Xi to view psychophysical energy—the very "stuff" of the universe—itself as constantly being produced and reproduced by pattern, although they refrain from speaking of pattern as the active "agent" of production and opt to refer to psychophysical energy's spontaneous self-production in accordance with pattern. See Cheng Hao, and Cheng Yi, *Er Cheng ji* [Collected works of the Cheng Brothers], ed. Wang Xiaoyu (Beijing: Zhonghua shuju, 1981), 1:149: "The Way produces all thing-events spontaneously. Those that have been produced in the spring and matured in the summer—they are all offspring of the Way. In regard to those produced in the next season, we cannot say that the psychophysical energy that has already been used for production (in this season) will be used again. The Way gives birth spontaneously without ceasing." See also *Er Cheng ji*, 1:163: "In general, when thing-events disintegrate, their psychophysical energy is accordingly exhausted. There is no pattern by which it returns to its source. What is between heaven and earth can be likened to an immense furnace. Even living thing-events melt and cease to exist. How can then the psychophysical energy that has already dispersed be present again? How can the creative processes of the universe use the psychophysical energy that has already dissipated? As a matter of course, the creative transformation of psychophysical energy consists of psychophysical energy that is vital." Zhu Xi follows Cheng Yi's view in saying the following: "Psychophysical energy that has already dispersed has already changed and no longer exists; but that which roots itself in pattern to emerge daily is truly vast, flood-like and infinite." "Da Liao Zihui [Reply to Liao Zihui]," in *Wenji*, 5:2021. See also *Yulei*, 1:48.
21. Zhu Xi follows Cheng Hao in focusing on the creative nature of Change, as declared in the Classic of Change, chapter 5: "Producing—or giving birth—again and again is Change (生生之謂易)," and links it with pattern via the symbol of the Great Ultimate. Julia Ching, *Religious Thought of Chu Hsi* (Oxford: Oxford University Press, 2000), pp. 247–48; Graham, *Two Chinese Philosophers*, p. 108.
22. Chung-ying Cheng, "Reality and Divinity in Chinese Philosophy," in *A Companion to World Philosophies*, ed. Eliot Deutsch and Ron Bontekoe (Malden, Mass.: Blackwell, 1999), pp. 185–93. See also Ching, *Religious Thought of Chu Hsi*, pp. 32–37.
23. Or in Julia Ching's translation, "the Infinite" or "the Limitless" (*Religious Thought of Chu Hsi*, p. 35).

24. See Fung Yu-lan, *A History of Chinese Philosophy*, trans. Derk Bodde. 2 vols. Princeton, N.J.: Princeton University Press, 1952–1953), pp. 438–42. While acknowledging the Daoist and Buddhist influence on Zhou's *Diagram* (*Religious Thought of Zhu Xi*, pp. 18–20), Julia Ching sees in it a truly innovative attempt by Zhou to articulate a cosmological vision with the help of Yin-yang and Five Phases theories. Still, she recognizes the heavy influence of Daoist philosophy on him as seen in his emphasis on *wu* (nothingness) and *jing* (stillness or tranquility) (p. 37). Relying on the work of Imai Usaburo, she even accepts the alternative, seven-word version of the controversial first phrase—自無極而爲太極 ("from the Non-Ultimate to become the Great Ultimate")—as the more original, authentic version coined by Zhou (p. 22).
25. Such a hierarchical interpretation of the relationship between the two Ultimates was prefigured by Kong Yingda's following subcommentary on Wang Bi's commentary on the Appended Remarks of the Classic of Change: "The Great Ultimate refers to the chaotically mixed and unified state of Primordial Psychophysical Energy before the division of heaven and earth. It is precisely [what is called] the Great Beginning or the Great One. Hence, the *Laozi* says, 'The Way gives birth to One.' This [the One] is no other than the Great Ultimate." As evident, Kong interprets the Great Ultimate as the cosmological symbol of the one psychophysical energy subordinate to the Way as the metaphysical ultimate (*Zhouyi zhengyi* [Correct meaning of the Classic of Change of the Zhou Dynasty], vol. 1 of *Shisanjing zhushu* [Commentaries and subcommentaries to the thirteen classics], ed. Ma Xinmin and Li Xueqin [Beijing: Beijing daxue chubanshe, 2000], p. 340). Unlike Kong's subcommentary, however, Wang Bi's commentary identifies the Great Ultimate with the Way itself rather than with psychophysical energy: "In general, being necessarily has its origin in nonbeing. Hence, the Great Ultimate gives birth to the two Modes. The Great Ultimate is the designation for that which has no designation. Because we cannot name it, we take the ultimate limit to which being can be extended and treat it as corresponding to the Great Ultimate." While Zhou Dunyi's hierarchical structuring of the relationship between the Non-Ultimate and the Great Ultimate mirrors Kong Yingda's between the Way and the Great Ultimate, Zhu Xi, who has read Wang's commentaries with great care, incorporates into his own reading of the passage Wang's elevation of the Great Ultimate to the status of the Way, and ends up identifying the Great Ultimate with the metaphysical ultimate, that is, pattern: "Change is the transformation of *yin* and *yang*; the Great Ultimate is its pattern." Zhu Xi, *Zhouyi benyi*, in *Zhuzi quanshu* [Complete works of Master Zhu], ed. Zhu Jieren et al. (Shanghai: Shanghai guji chubanshe; Hefei: Anhui jiaoyu chubanshe, 2010), 1:133. See Richard Lynn's introduction to *The Classic of Changes: A New Translation of the I Ching as Interpreted by Wang Bi*, trans. Richard John Lynn (New York: Columbia University Press, 1994), p. 7.
26. Ching, *Religious Thought of Zhu Xi*, pp. 43, 48.
27. See Zhu Xi, *Taiji tushou jie* [Commentary on the Explanation of the Diagram of the Great Ultimate], in *Zhou Dunyi ji* [Collected works of Zhou Dunyi], ed. Chen Keming (Beijing: Zhonghua shuju, 1990), 3 (hereafter *Tushou jie*), where Zhu Xi says, "The doings of High Heaven [i.e., the Great Ultimate] is without any sound or smell, yet it is in fact the pivot of creative transformation and the root of the differentiation of all things. That is why Master Zhou says, 'the Non-Ultimate and the Great Ultimate.' It is not the case that there is the Non-Ultimate outside of the Great Ultimate." The Non-Ultimate,

he adds, is "the very condition in which [the patterns of] *yin* and *yang* and the Five Phases are dissolved into one another with no gap left between them" (*Tushou jie*, p. 5).

28. Zhu Xi, *Yulei*, 1:1, 2. For Zhu Xi's "kataphatic" construal of the metaphysical ultimate vis-à-vis Buddhism, see *Yulei*, 6:2365, 2376. The Neo-Confucian rejection of Daoist and Buddhist "nihilism" comes from their concern that too transcendent an interpretation of the ultimate might lead to escapism, that is, a metaphysical flight from the world. See Ching, *Religious Thought of Chu Hsi*, pp. 48–51.
29. Zhu Xi, *Yulei*, 6:2374. He makes it clear that he is using the Great Ultimate as a metaphysical and ontological symbol, not a cosmological symbol: "The Great Ultimate is the Way above physical form; *yin* and *yang* are vessels with physical form" (*Tushou jie*, p. 3).
30. Zhu Xi, *Yulei*, 1:3, 101. See *Tushou jie*, p. 7.
31. The Neo-Confucian notion of the mutual interdependence of substance and function is encapsulated in the following dictum of Cheng Yi, an important predecessor of Zhu Xi: "Substance and function are of a single origin; there is no gap between what is manifest and what is hidden" (*Yizhuan xu* [Preface to the commentaries on the Classic of Change], in *Er Cheng ji*, 3:689). Zhu Xi interprets this dictum as follows: "The meaning of 'substance and function are of a single origin' is that, although substance has no trace, function is already in its midst; the saying, 'There is no gap between what is manifest and what is hidden,' refers to the fact that what is hidden is present in the midst of what is manifest. Before heaven and earth come into being, the ten thousand things are already furnished—that is the meaning of substance having function within itself. Once heaven and earth are established, the patterns [of the ten thousand things] also continue to be—that is the meaning of what is manifest having in its midst what is hidden" (*Yulei*, 5:1654). See also Zhu Xi, *Yulei*, 1:101, where he says, "When speaking of *yang*, *yang* is substance, and *yin* is function; when speaking of *yin*, *yin* is substance, and *yang* is function."
32. See Zhu Xi, *Yulei*, 1:3 where he says pattern is "without feeling, intention, deliberation, and productive activity" in contrast to psychophysical energy, which can "coalesce, congeal, and produce" concrete thing-processes. Pattern is certainly in the midst of psychophysical energy's creative movement, he says, but without activity of its own. Zhu Xi is careful to interpret Zhou Dunyi's statement, "The Great Ultimate moves and produces *yang*; it comes to rest, and produces *yin*," in such a way as to ensure that the Great Ultimate's "movement" and "rest" are understood as referring to the *patterns* of movement and rest, not movement and rest themselves, which he assigns to psychophysical energy (*Yulei*, 1:1, 6:2373). See also Ching, *Religious Thought of Chu Hsi*, pp. 29–30.
33. Precisely for this reason, Tu Wei-ming rejects the interpretation of *li* as creativity in favor of its interpretation as the "ground of being" underlying the creative process, although he does not refer to the substance-function relation: "In short, Chu Hsi envisioned principle [*li*]to be singular, unitary, above-form, permanent, and omnipresent. It is *being* rather than activity, *reason* rather than practice, and the *ground* underlying cosmic transformation rather than the actual creative impulse that engenders heaven, earth, and the myriad things. Principle in itself is neither dynamic nor tranquil, for it transcends categories of this kind. Indeed, principle is ineffable and beyond ordinary human experience." Tu Wei-ming, "T'oegye's Creative Interpretation of Chu Hsi's Philosophy of Principle," *Korea Journal* 22, no. 2 (1982): 12.

34. Robert Neville argues that the ontological creativity of pattern should be envisaged not so much in terms of ontological "causation" as in terms of ontological creation of value: "The special focus of Confucian ontogenesis, however, is less the grounding of physical existence than the grounding of the real value that existence bears and of the very definition of the human as the value-seeker." Robert C. Neville, *Boston Confucianism: Portable Tradition in the Late-Modern World* (Albany: State University of New York Press, 2000), p. 75.
35. In his effort to relate Zhu Xi's thought to the tradition of American naturalism, particularly to that of Justus Buchler, John H. Berthrong argues that pattern's priority over psychophysical energy is epistemological, not ontological. Pattern is prior to psychophysical energy in the order of our knowing the myriad thing-events, because "we learn about new objects and events by recognizing something different, some novel pattern that attracts our attention—namely, *li* 理 as a coherent, ordered principle or pattern that makes the thing or event stand out from the rest of the ten thousand things and events. . . . It is this recognition of principle that happens first, that is all" (*Expanding Process: Exploring Philosophical and Theological Transformations in China and the West* [Albany: State University of New York Press, 2008], p. 97). Further, as Zhu Xi firmly believed in the concrete, factual togetherness of pattern and psychophysical energy, he "has a theory of ontological parity, not of ontological priority" (ibid). Although Berthrong points to a fresh way of interpreting one of the most ambiguous points in Zhu Xi's thought, the force of the statements such as the following—well-known—one seems to resist his naturalistic approach: "The so-called pattern and psychophysical energy are definitely two different things. But when looked at from the standpoint of concrete thing-events, the two are merged with each other and cannot be separated into their respective locations. This, however, does not hinder the two from each being one thing. When looked at from the standpoint of pattern, before things existed, their pattern had already existed" ("Da Liu Shuwen [Reply to Liu Shuwen]," in *Wenji*, 5:2095). Further, the ontological priority of pattern is quite clearly presented in this statement quoted earlier: "Psychophysical energy that has already dispersed has already changed and no longer exists; but *that which roots itself in pattern* to emerge daily is truly vast, flood-like and infinite" ("Da Liao Zihui [Reply to Liao Zihui]," in *Wenji*, 5:2021; italics mine).
36. Zhu Xi, *Yulei*, 1:1; 6:2371, 2374.
37. "The Great Ultimate is not a separate entity. It is present in *yin* and *yang* as *yin* and *yang*, in the Five Phases as the Five Phases, in the ten thousand thing-events as the ten thousand thing-events. It is [nonetheless] only one Pattern. Because of its ultimate reach, it is named the Great Ultimate" (Zhu Xi, *Yulei*, 6:2371). See also 6:2372: "Question: 'How was it before anything existed?' Answer: 'There existed a shared Pattern of all under heaven, not the patterns of individual thing-events.'"
38. Zhu Xi, *Yulei*, 1:61; 4:1177.
39. According to Zhu Xi, "The Great Ultimate is simply the supremely excellent and perfect normative pattern. . . . What Master Zhou called the Great Ultimate is the exemplary virtue of all that is good and most excellent in heaven and earth, in people and thing-events" (*Yulei*, 6:2371). Fung Yu-lan compares the Great Ultimate with Plato's Idea of the Good and Aristotle's God in his *History of Chinese Philosophy*, 2:537.
40. Zhu Xi, *Yulei* 6:2409.

41. Cheng Hao and Cheng Yi, *Er Cheng ji*, 1:153. I am using Wing-tsit Chan's translation of this saying with one modification, substituting "all figures" for "all things." Wing-tsit Chan, *A Source Book in Chinese Philosophy* (Princeton, N.J.: Princeton University Press, 1963), p. 555.
42. Cheng Yi, "Da Yang Shi lun xi ming shu [Reply to Yang Shih's letter on the Western inscription]," in *Er Cheng ji*, 2:609.
43. See Zhu Xi, *Yulei*, 6:2437, where he says the phrase "empty and tranquil, and without any sign" is none other than an explanation of "the Non-Ultimate and the Great Ultimate."
44. Zhu Xi, "Da Lü Ziyao [Reply to Lü Ziyao]," in *Wenji*, 5:2186.
45. See also Zhu Xi, *Tushou jie*, p. 9: "In regard to his [Cheng Yi's] saying, "substance and function constitute one source,' from the standpoint of the ultimate hiddenness of pattern, the saying refers to the Great Ultimate being 'empty, silent, and without any sign,' while all thing-events, shimmering, are already present in it. In regard to his saying, "there is no gap between what is manifest and what is hidden,' from the standpoint of the ultimate manifestness of things, the saying refers to pattern being everywhere, in every entity or state of affair. When speaking of pattern, substance comes before pattern, but the function of pattern is already present in its substance. That is why the two constitute one source; when speaking of states of affairs, what is manifest comes before what is hidden, but in every state of affair the pattern of its substance can be seen. That is why there is no gap between the two."
46. See Zhu Xi, *Yulei*, 4:1286: "Heaven and earth are merely one psychophysical energy, but it spontaneously divides itself into *yin* and *yang*. Consequently, the two forces of *yin* and *yang* interact, and in so doing give rise to the myriad thing-events. Nothing, therefore, is without its opposite. Heaven is the opposite of earth; life is the opposite of death; speech and silence, movement and rest—these are likewise opposites, each according to its kind." For a detailed account of the birth of the myriad thing-events of the world from the creative transformation of psychophysical energy, see *Tushou jie*, p. 5. For the various analogies used by Zhu Xi to explain this process, see *Yulei*, 1:58, 73.
47. The phrase "moral metaphysics" was coined by Mou Zhongsan to point to the fact that in Zhu Xi's Neo-Confucianism pattern functions as the metaphysical basis of authentic human existence. Tu Wei-ming, "T'oegye's Creative Interpretation," p. 10.
48. For Zhu Xi's identification of human nature with pattern, see *Yulei*, 1:67. See also his commentary on *The Doctrine of the Mean*, 1.1—the alleged origin of that identification—in Zhu Xi, *Daehak Jungyong jang-gu* [Collected commentaries on the Great Learning and the Doctrine of the Mean], rev. ed., trans. with commentary by Seong Baek-hyo (Seoul: Jeontong munhwa yeon-guhoe, 2006), p. 82. For Zhu Xi's identification of humanity (*ren*) with human nature, which can be traced back to Mencius, 2A6, see his commentary on the passage in *Maengja jipju*, p. 104.
49. Zhu Xi, *Yulei*, 1:40, 85, 95. Zhu Xi acknowledges that nonhuman creatures also have heart-minds and consciousness, albeit without a capacity to deliberate upon feelings (*Yulei*, 4:1431). Due to the partial and obstructed type of psychophysical energy with which they are endowed, they simply respond to their environment spontaneously without exhibiting the "spiritual" qualities of the human heart-mind. Their spontaneous psychosomatic responses, however, are in most cases conducive to harmony on account of the harmonizing pattern present in them as their respective natures, although the

kinds of harmony they manifest are incomplete compared to harmonies possible in human relations (*Yulei*, 1:59).

50. See the succinct description of the Neo-Confucian moral psychology by Michael Kalton in the introduction to *The Four-Seven Debate: An Annotated Translation of the Most Famous Controversy in Korean Neo-Confucian Thought*, trans. Michael C. Kalton et al. (Albany: State University of New York Press, 1994), pp. xxii–xxv. For the relationship among the heart-mind, the human nature and feelings, see Zhu Xi, *Yulei*, 1:89, 92, 94–95. For the role of intentional deliberation (意 *yi*), see *Yulei*, 1:96. For Zhu Xi, desires are intensifications of feelings; and people have evil desires when their feelings become excessive and unbalanced to the point of being uncontrollable (*Yulei*, 1:93–94).
51. Originating in the obscure phrase in the *Shujing* (the Classic of History), "The heart-mind of the Way (*Daoxin*)" became a widely used term among the Neo-Confucians to designate the human heart-mind fully enacting the human nature within, including Zhu Xi who wrote a commentary on the above phrase in the introduction to his *Collected Commentaries on the Doctrine of the Mean*. See Zhu Xi, *Daehak Jungyong jang-gu*, pp. 73–74.
52. Zhu Xi, *Yulei*, 1:113: "Humanity [*ren*] implies the life-giving intention."
53. For Zhu Xi's identification of humanity with the "fecund heart-mind of heaven and earth," see Zhu Xi, *Yulei*, 1:111, 7:2633. See also his "Renshuo" [A treatise on humanity], in *Wenji*, 7:3391–92. Zhu Xi argues that the heart-mind of heaven and earth, which can be said to be a "lord and master," is in fact none other than pattern, and that this heart-mind is creative and conscious ("numinous"), though not really with deliberation and purpose. He seems to entertain a theistic language while at the same time qualifying it in a nontheistic direction. See *Yulei*, 1:4, where he says, "One cannot say that the heart-mind of heaven and earth is without numinous consciousness (靈 *ling*). Its numinous consciousness, however, cannot be compared to the way humans reflect and deliberate. Yichuan [Cheng Yi] said, 'Heaven and earth has no heart-mind yet accomplishes transformations; the sage has a heart-mind yet does not act' . . . The heart-mind [of heaven and earth] is a lord and master in terms of its basic intent. Nonetheless, the so-called 'lord and master' is simply pattern." Ultimately, Zhu Xi's notion of the heart-mind of heaven and earth seems to be the name for the one Pattern when its embodiment is taken universally and generally "across the world" and given certain vague qualities of consciousness and intention that are directly related to its creative "urge" and proportionally analogous to the one Pattern's more individual instances of embodiments in human and creaturely minds with varying degrees of intensity of consciousness. See Jonathan R. Herman, "Human Heart, Heavenly Heart: Mystical Dimensions of Chu Hsi's Neo-Confucianism," *Journal of the American Academy of Religion* 69, no. 1 (2001): 103–28. See also Ching, *Religious Thought of Chu Hsi*, p. 252.
54. As David L. Hall's process interpretation suggests, *yin* may be construed as the data of the past actualized world (the objective immortality of actual occasions) whereas *yang* could be interpreted as an activity of integrating the data of the past into a novel event. See David L. Hall, *The Uncertain Phoenix: Adventures toward a Post-Cultural Sensibility* (New York: Fordham University Press, 1982), pp. 221–22. Robert Neville shares this process interpretation of the Great Ultimate's movement: "A more primordial meaning is that yin has to do with the conditions of matrix, a situation out of which things can arise

and to which they can return for replenishment. Yang on the other hand has to do with expression, with moving out from home base, with extension beyond the situation in which everything is mutually reinforcing, particularly with making something new that goes beyond the resources of yin. Change is thus a series of adventuring moves which must return to their source, or resource, for a renewal of their own power. . . . Change, or we may say creativity, involves a pulsation away from the given source and a contraction back to it. . . . Creativity is not an act making something out of nothing, as in the Western Hebrew-Platonic tradition, but the very being of process weaving novelties out of matrices filled with incipiencies and then reconstituting itself as at one with its sources." Robert C. Neville, *Behind the Masks of God: An Essay Toward Comparative Theology* (Albany: State University of New York Press, 1991), p. 54.

55. Julia Ching reads Zhu Xi's account of the Great Ultimate's creatively harmonizing movement cyclically (*Religious Thought of Chu Hsi*, p. 248). But there is nothing that prevents a spiral reading, given that Zhu Xi never spoke of it as some kind of "eternal return of the Same."

56. Zhu Xi, "Da Huang Shangbo [Response to Huang Shangbo]," in *Wenji*, 5:2075 (quoted also in *Yulei*, 1:57): "If we discuss it from the perspective of the single origin of the myriad thing-events, pattern unites, while psychophysical energy differentiates." See also *Yulei*, 1:59: "What makes them similar is their pattern; what makes them different is their psychophysical energy."

57. Zhu Xi says, "When looked at from the perspective of the myriad thing-events' different [physical] bodies, their psychophysical energies appear to be similar to each other while their [respective] patterns are definitely not alike." "Da Huang Shangbo [Response to Huang Shangbo]," in *Wenji*, 5:2075.

58. Ching, *Religious Thought of Chu Hsi*, pp. 98–101. Zhu Xi, *Yulei*, 1:69: "Human nature is always good, yet there are some who are good from the time of their births, and there are those who are evil from the time of their births. This is due to the differences in their physical endowment. . . . The goal of learning is to transform the physical endowment, although such transformation is very difficult."

59. In his *Conversations*, Zhu Xi makes the following statement: "The Great Ultimate is that which gathers [總 *zong*] the patterns of heaven and earth, and of all things" (*Yulei*, 6:2375). Lao Siguang distinguishes between two meanings of *zong* (總), i.e., as "subsume" (總攝 *zong she*) and "comprise" (總和 *zong he*), and argues that Zhu Xi uses the term more in the latter sense, i.e., as pointing to the sum of all the individual patterns, while criticizing him for being unclear and confusing on this matter. Siguang Lao, *Jung-guk cheorhaksa* [History of Chinese philosophy], trans. Jeong In-jae (Seoul: Tamgudang, 1987), pp. 329–30. See also *Yulei*, 6:2365, where Zhu Xi says, "The so-called Great Ultimate refers merely to the patterns of the Two Forces [*yin* and *yang*] and the Five Phases. It is not the case that there is a separate entity which constitutes the Great Ultimate."

60. Zhu Xi, *Tushou jie*, pp. 3–4.

61. See Zhu Xi, *Tushou jie*, p. 4, where he says, "The subtlety of the Non-Ultimate is never absent from each individual entity. . . . When it comes to the very condition of the Great Ultimate being what it is, which can first be spoken of as being without sound or smell, that is the way the substance of the nature of thing-events is. . . . But in the production of the Five Phases, what thing-events are endowed with differs according to their respective

psychophysical constitution; and that is the so-called 'each has its one nature.' 'Each has its own nature' means that the entirety of the indeterminate Great Ultimate never fails to be present within each thing-event." See also Zhu Xi's comment in *Yulei*, 6:2409: "Fundamentally there is only one Great Ultimate, yet the ten thousand thing-events are each endowed with it. Furthermore, they each have one Great Ultimate in its entirety." The meaning of "one Great Ultimate in its entirety" is a bit clearer in *Taiji tushou jie*, p. 5: "In general, to speak comprehensively, the myriad thing-events altogether embody one Great Ultimate; to speak analytically, each thing-event individually has one Great Ultimate." See also *Yulei*, 6:2409: "The saying, 'Many and one are each right; small and large are [each] determined,' refers to the fact that many are one, and one is many. All thing-events together embody one Great Ultimate; but each single thing-event individually has one Great Ultimate." Fung Yu-lan compares this notion of the Great Ultimate with the Huayan Buddhist concept of the Jewel Net of Indra or the *tathagata-garba* (storehouse of the absolute), while recognizing the difference between the notions in that, whereas the Buddhist concept envisions that within each concrete thing-event all other concrete thing-events are physically present, Zhu Xi's Neo-Confucian notion sees within each concrete thing-event only the *patterns* of all other concrete thing-events (Fung, *History of Chinese Philosophy*, 2:541–42). What this implies is that when each individual thing-event partakes of the Great Ultimate beause its pattern participates in the one Pattern, all the other individual patterns of all the other thing-events of the world are co-present within each at the same time.

62. Here an analogy could be drawn with Whitehead's concept of the eternal objects in the primordial nature of God minus God's agency, that is, without God's act of enabling their "ingression" into the process of concrescence so that they could become the initial subjective aim of actual occasions. See Alfred North Whitehead, *Process and Reality: Corrected Edition*, ed. David Ray Griffin and Donald W. Sherburne (New York: Free Press, 1978), pp. 342–51.
63. See n. 58.
64. See n. 13.
65. Zhu Xi, "Da He Shujing [Reply to He Shujing]," in *Wenji*, 4:1746. As Stephen Angle points out, for the Cheng-Zhu Neo-Confucians, Heavenly Pattern (天理 *tianli*)—which Angle translates as "universal coherence"—is objectively settled (定 *ding*) and unchanging (常 *chang*), having been discovered by the early sages who had deep insights into human nature. Those who have thoroughly acquired the Confucian virtues instituted by the sages, such as a ruler's humaneness and a subject's reverence, to the point of manifesting them in action with spontaneous ease, are therefore one with the Heavenly Pattern, although that does not mean the virtuous ones merely follow a settled rule universally applicable to various relational situations and contexts. Stephen C. Angle, *Sagehood: The Contemporary Significance of Neo-Confucian Philosophy* (New York: Oxford University Press, 2009), pp. 35–36.
66. See the criticism of Dai Zhen, a Qing Dynasty Neo-Confucian, directed against the Song and Ming Neo-Confucians for claiming the authority of the Heavenly Pattern to justify their own parochial interests and desires: "Of those who regard pattern as something obtained from Heaven and endowed in the heart-mind, there is none who does not replace it with their personal opinions." Dai Zhen, *Mengzi ziyi shu zheng* [An evidential

commentary on the meanings of terms in Mencius], in *Dai Zhen quanshu* [Complete works of Dai Zhen], ed. Zhang Dainian (Hebei: Huangshan shushe, 1995), 6:155.

## 3. *Creativity and a Democracy of Fellow Creatures: The Challenge of Whitehead's Radical Ontological Pluralism*

The phrase "a democracy of fellow creatures" is from Alfred North Whitehead, *Process and Reality: An Essay in Cosmology,* corrected edition, ed. David Ray Griffin and Donald W. Sherburne (New York: Free Press, 1978), p. 50.

1. Alfred North Whitehead, *Process and Reality: An Essay in Cosmology,* corrected edition, ed. David Ray Griffin and Donald W. Sherburne (New York: Free Press, 1978), pp. 342–43. References to this book in this discussion are given by page number within parentheses in the text.
2. See also ibid., p. 19: "The ontological principle can be summarized as: no actual entity, then no reason."
3. Ibid., p. 21: "'Creativity' is the principle of novelty." See also ibid., p. 28: " 'Becoming' is a creative advance into novelty."
4. Ibid., p. 35: "There is becoming of continuity, but no continuity of becoming. The actual occasions are the creatures which become, and they constitute a continuously extensive world. In other words, extensiveness becomes, but 'becoming' is not itself extensive. Thus, the ultimate metaphysical truth is atomism. The creatures are atomic." See also page 69: "The conclusion is that in every act of becoming there is the becoming of something with temporal extension; but that the act itself is not extensive, in the sense that it is divisible into earlier and later acts of becoming which correspond to the extensive divisibility of what has become. . . . The creature is extensive, but . . .its act of becoming is not extensive." Judith Jones has coined the phrase "relational atomism" for this. Judith A. Jones, *Intensity: An Essay in Whiteheadian Ontology* (Nashville: Vanderbilt University Press, 1998), p. 4.
5. See also page 24 of Whitehead, *Process and Reality,*: "A nexus is a set of actual entities in the unity of the relatedness constituted by their prehensions of each other, or—what is the same thing conversely expressed—constituted by their objectifications in each other." See also Alfred North Whitehead, *Adventures of Ideas* (New York: Free Press, 1967), p. 197: "Any set of actual occasions are united by the mutual immanence of occasions, each in the other. To the extent that they are united they mutually constrain each other. Evidently this mutual immanence and constraint of a pair of occasions is not in general a symmetric relation. For, apart from contemporaries, one occasion will be in the future of the other. Thus the earlier will be immanent in the later according to the mode of efficient causality, and the later in the earlier according to the mode of anticipation, as explained above. Any set of occasions, conceived as thus combined into a unity, will be termed a nexus." Nonetheless, the mutual immanence of actual occasions and their causal relations, which underlie the formation of nexuses take place diachronically, not synchronically. According to Whitehead, insofar as each actual occasion's self-creation is a free act, contemporary occasions are causally independent of one another (*Process and Reality*, p. 61). See *Adventures of Ideas*, p. 198: "The causal independence of contemporary occasions is the ground for the freedom within the Universe." See also page 195: "It is the definition of contemporary events that they happen in causal independence of each

other. . . . The mutual independence of contemporary occasions lies strictly within the sphere of their teleological self-creation. The occasions originate from a common past and their objective immortality operates within a common future. Thus indirectly, *via* the immanence of the past and the immanence of the future, the occasions are connected. But the immediate activity of self-creation is separate and private, so far as contemporaries are concerned."

6. See also Whitehead, *Adventures of Ideas*, p. 236: "Then each event, viewed in its separate individuality, is a passage between two ideal termini, namely, its components in their ideal disjunctive diversity passing into these same components in their concrete togetherness. There are two current doctrines as to this process. One is that of the external Creator, eliciting this final togetherness out of nothing. The other doctrine is that it is a metaphysical principle belonging to the nature of things, that there is nothing in the Universe other than instances of this passage and components of these instances. Let this latter doctrine be adopted. Then the word Creativity expresses the notion that each event is a process issuing in novelty. Also if guarded in the phrases Immanent Creativity, or Self-Creativity, it avoids the implication of a transcendent Creator." Roland Faber reads the self-creative nature of actual entities' concrescence as the creation of "self-value": "The concept of 'creation' has been altered, referring now not to causation, but to the relational creating of self-value, that is, self-creativity within the process of a concrescence." Roland Faber, *God as the Poet of the World*, trans. Douglas W. Stott (Louisville, Ky.: Westminster John Knox Press, 2008), pp. 143–44.
7. The actual world is "a community of entities which are settled, actual, and already become." Whitehead, *Process and Reality*, p. 65.
8. Ibid., p. 40: "Hence 'feeling' is the term used for the basic generic operation of passing from the objectivity of the data to the subjectivity of the actual entity in question." See also page 41: "An actual entity has a perfectly definite bond with each item in the universe. This determinate bond is its prehension of that item. A negative prehension is the definite exclusion of that item from positive contribution to the subject's own real internal constitution. . . . A positive prehension is the definite inclusion of that item into positive contribution to the subject's own real internal constitution. This positive inclusion is called its 'feeling' of that item."
9. Ibid., p. 29: "Actual entities 'perpetually perish' subjectively, but are immortal objectively. Actuality in perishing acquires objectivity, while it loses subjective immediacy. It loses the final causation which is its internal principle of unrest and it acquires efficient causation whereby it is a ground of obligation characterizing the creativity."
10. They are eternal "objects" in the sense that they are eternally objectified or given as object to be conceptually prehended by actual entities; they are never by themselves subjects.
11. Ibid., p. 60: "The 'organic doctrine' demands a 'real essence' in the sense of a complete analysis of the relations, and inter-relations of the actual entities which are formative of the actual entity in question, and an 'abstract essence' in which the specified actual entities are replaced by the notions of unspecified entities in such a combination; this is the notion of an unspecified actual entity. Thus the real essence involves real objectifications of specified actual entities; the abstract essence is a complex eternal object." Also p. 24: "A proposition is the unity of certain actual entities in their potentiality for forming a nexus, with its potential relatedness partially defined by certain eternal objects which have the unity of one complex eternal object."

12. Catherine Keller, *Face of the Deep: A Theology of Becoming* (London: Routledge, 2003), p. 198.
13. Whitehead, *Process and Reality*, p. 23: "The term 'ingression' refers to the particular mode in which the potentiality of an eternal object is realized in a particular actual entity, contributing to the definiteness of that actual entity."
14. Ibid., p. 32: "'Relevance' must express some real fact of togetherness among forms. The ontological principle can be expressed as: All real togetherness is togetherness in the formal constitution of an actuality. So if there be a relevance of what in the temporal world is unrealized [eternal objects], the relevance must express a fact of togetherness in the formal constitution of a non-temporal actuality. But by the principle of relativity there can only be one non-derivative actuality, unbounded by its prehensions of an actual world. Such a primordial superject of creativity achieves, in its unity of satisfaction, the complete conceptual valuation of all eternal objects. This is the ultimate, basic adjustment of the togetherness of eternal objects on which creative order depends. It is the conceptual adjustment of all appetites in the form of aversion and adversions. It constitutes the meaning of relevance. Its status as an actual efficient fact is recognized by terming it the 'primordial nature of God.'"
15. Ibid., p. 348: "God and the World are the contrasted opposites in terms of which Creativity achieves its supreme task of transforming disjointed multiplicity, with its diversities in opposition, into concrescent unity, with its diversities in contrast. In each actuality there are two concrescent poles of realization—'enjoyment' and 'appetition,' that is, the 'physical' and the 'conceptual.' For God the conceptual is prior to the physical, for the World the physical poles are prior to the conceptual poles."
16. Ibid., p. 244: "What is inexorable in God, is a valuation as an aim towards 'order'; and 'order' means 'society permissive of actualities with patterned intensity of feeling arising from adjusted contrasts.'"
17. I borrow this phrase from Tim Clark. Tim Clark, "A Whiteheadian Chaosmos? Process Philosophy from a Deleuzean Perspective," in *Process and Difference: Between Cosmological and Poststructuralist Postmodernists*, ed. Catherine Keller and Anne Daniel (Albany: State University of New York Press, 2002), p. 199.
18. The passage from *Process and Reality* deserves to be quoted in full: "This final entity is the divine element in the world, by which the barren inefficient disjunction of abstract potentialities obtains primordially the efficient conjunction of ideal realization. This ideal realization of potentialities in a primordial actual entity constitutes the metaphysical stability whereby the actual process exemplifies general principles of metaphysics, and attains the ends proper to specific types of emergent order. By reason of the actuality of this primordial valuation of pure potentials, each eternal object has a definite effective relevance to each concrescent process. Apart from such orderings, there would be a complete disjunction of eternal objects unrealized in the temporal world" (Whitehead, *Process and Reality*, pp. 39–40). Tim Clark rightly rejects Gilles Deleuze's "chaosmological" reading of Whitehead's notion of God's primordial nature, particularly regarding the effectively relevant "togetherness" of eternal objects within the primordial nature. In the light of the presence of an element of "decision" or limitation in God's primordial valuation of all possible worlds (i.e., the fact that not all of the incompossible worlds are positively affirmed by God), Clark correctly differentiates Whitehead's sense of God's "orderings" of worlds from Deleuze's "chaosmological" explanation of the emergence of

orders. Deleuze explains the emergence of orders in reference to a chaotic matrix of order in which the different (disjunctive others) are held together and kept in communication "polytheistically" via a multitude of "dark precursors" or "differenciators"—i.e., the "difference-in-itself that relates different to different." Clark, "Whiteheadian Chaosmos?" pp. 192–205. Catherine Keller appears to hold the middle ground, identifying Whitehead's notion of creativity with chaos, i.e., "a boiling ocean of incessant relatedness" whose "crash and clash of difference [is] not yet organized into contrast," while retaining God as the principle of cosmos. Catherine Keller, "Process and Chaosmos: The Whiteheadian Fold in the Discourse of Difference," in *Process and Difference: Between Cosmological and Poststructuralist Postmodernists,* ed. Catherine Keller and Anne Daniell (Albany: State University of New York Press, 2002), p. 65.

19. The constitution of God's preliminary subjectivity in and through God's evaluation of eternal objects is strongly hinted at on page 32 of *Process and Reality*: "Such a primordial superject of creativity achieves, *in its unity of satisfaction*, the complete conceptual valuation of all eternal objects" (italics mine).

20. Quoting Whitehead's statement that "in every respect God and the world move conversely to each other in respect to their process" (*Process and Reality*, p. 349), Marjorie Suchocki argues that God's satisfaction in the proper sense of the term takes place in the primordial nature of God, unlike all the other actual occasions for which satisfaction comes at the end of their concrescence: "God 'originates' in a decision which is a primordial valuation of all possibilities; Whitehead calls this an envisagement which contains within it an appetition for realization in actuality. Thus the satisfaction of God lies in this conceptual atemporality; it is primordial, underlying and pervading the reality of God. This being the case, the concrescence of God cannot move *toward* satisfaction; it can only move *from* satisfaction. Nor can it move toward an increasing simplification of data and subjective aim; it must move instead toward an ever increasing complexity in continual and dynamic realization of that satisfaction" (Marjorie Hewitt Suchocki, *The End of Evil: Process Eschatology in Historical Context* [Albany: State University of New York Press, 1988], p. 139). I believe, however, that this interpretation loses sight of the fact that the primordial nature of God functions almost as an object to the consequent nature of God, although God's fully achieved subjectivity does have as its precondition the primordial nature. I am indebted to Catherine Keller for this important point. In my reading, the primordial nature of God achieves a kind of unity and "satisfaction" that is preliminary; and this preliminary achievement of divine subjectivity is logically, not temporally, prior to the consequent nature of God.

21. See also Thomas E. Hosinski, *Stubborn Fact and Creative Advance: An Introduction to the Metaphysics of Alfred North Whitehead* (Lanham, Md.: Rowman and Littlefield, 1993), pp. 85–88.

22. Whitehead, *Process and Reality*, p. 108: "Thus an originality in the temporal world is conditioned, though not determined, by an initial subjective aim supplied by the ground of all order and of all originality."

23. This pairing of "subject" and "superject" is meant to highlight the emergent character of the subject: The subject is one that throws or projects itself beyond (*super*) itself.

24. Sometimes Whitehead refers to the eternal objects in the primordial nature of God as "lures of feeling" (*Process and Reality,* pp. 87–88), whereas at other times he designates

God as the lure: "He [God] is the lure for feeling . . .the initial 'object of desire' establishing the initial phase of each subjective aim" (p. 344).

25. Ibid., p. 347: "The primordial permanence of God, whereby the creative advance ever re-establishes itself endowed with initial subjective aim derived from the relevance of God to the evolving world."
26. Ibid., p. 350: "Every actuality in the temporal world has its reception into God's nature. The corresponding element in God's nature is not temporal actuality, but is the transmutation of that temporal actuality into a living ever-present fact. An enduring personality in the temporal world is a route of occasions in which the successors with some peculiar completeness sum up their predecessors. The correlate fact in God's nature is an even more complete unity of life in a chain of elements for which succession does not mean loss of immediate unison."
27. Although temporally achieved, this actual, physical unity of God's being as becoming—i.e., God's consequent nature—is not temporal in the sense of itself experiencing passage of time and thus "perishing." As a single actual entity, God is a quantum of becoming; but this divine quantum of becoming encompasses all of time. In other words, God's concrescence extends over all of time. This is the meaning of the "everlasting" nature of God's satisfaction (Hosinski, *Stubborn Fact and Creative Advance,* p. 194). See Whitehead, *Process and Reality*, pp. 31–32: "By reason of its character as a creature, *always in concrescence and never in the past*, it receives a reaction from the world; this reaction is its consequent nature. It is here termed 'God'" (italics mine).
28. That is, energy equals mass times the velocity of light squared.
29. In other words, God's consequent nature is temporal, finite, and incomplete, because the physical world is. God's capacity for physical prehension is in fact unlimited and infinite. Hosinski, *Stubborn Fact and Creative Advance*, p. 194.
30. Whitehead, *Process and Reality*, p. 347: "In this way God is completed by the individual, fluent satisfactions of finite fact, and the temporal occasions are completed by their everlasting union with their transformed selves, purged into conformation with the eternal order which is the final absolute 'wisdom.'"
31. Despite Whitehead's principle of the causal independence of contemporary occasions, the nonperishing, everlasting satisfaction of God's consequent nature can be prehended by novel actual occasions because, strictly speaking, God is nontemporal and cannot therefore be conceived as temporal in the same sense as other actual entities. See Hosinski, *Stubborn Fact and Creative Advance,* p. 221.
32. See Faber, *God as the Poet of the World*, p. 188.
33. Whitehead, *Process and Reality*, p. 24: "A proposition is the unity of certain actual entities in their potentiality for forming a nexus, with its potential relatedness partially defined by certain eternal objects which have the unity of one complex eternal object. The actual entities involved are termed the 'logical subjects,' the complex eternal object is the 'predicate.'" See also p. 25: "It is an essential doctrine in the philosophy of organism that the primary function of a proposition is to be relevant as a lure for feeling. . . . The 'subjective aim,' which controls the becoming of a subject, is that subject feeling a proposition with the subjective form of purpose to realize it in that process of self-creation."
34. John Cobb and Lewis Ford extend Whitehead's notion of the superjective nature of God, so that the ingression of eternal objects from the primordial nature of God into the

concrescent actual entities comes to be identified with (or replaced by) the actual entities' prehension of the propositions produced and realized in the consequent nature of God (John B. Cobb Jr., *A Christian Natural Theology: Based on the Thought of Alfred North Whitehead* [Philadelphia: Westminster Press, 1965], pp. 155–56; Lewis Ford, "Divine Persuasion and the Triumph of Good," in *Process Philosophy and Christian Thought*, ed. Delwin Brown, Ralph E. James Jr., and Gene Reeves [Indianapolis: Bobbs-Merrill, 1971], pp. 291–93). John Cobb has, however, revised his earlier proposal in the second edition to distinguish the actual occasions' feeling of the initial aim—the feeling of eternal objects in God's primordial nature—and the formation of their final subjective aim in and through their feeling of the propositions in God's consequent nature. The former, Cobb avers, involves the latter but is not replaced by it (John B. Cobb Jr., *A Christian Natural Theology: Based on the Thought of Alfred North Whitehead*, 2nd ed. [Louisville, Ky.: Westminster John Knox Press, 2007], pp. 131–32).

35. See F. Bradford Wallack, *The Epochal Nature of Process in Whitehead's Metaphysics* (Albany: State University of New York Press, 1980), p. 302.
36. Whitehead, *Process and Reality*, p. 80.
37. See n. 5.
38. Julia Ching, *Religious Thought of Chu Hsi* (Oxford: Oxford Univ.University Press, 2000), p. 256.
39. Whitehead, *Process and Reality*, p. 344.

### *4. The Great Ultimate as Primordial Manyone: The Promise and Peril of Toegye's Neo-Confucian "Heterodoxy"*

This chapter is a heavily revised and expanded version of the second half of an essay published earlier as "'Empty and Tranquil, and without Any Sign, and Yet All Things Are Already Luxuriantly Present': A Comparative-Theological Reflection on the Manifold Spirit," in *Polydoxy: Theology of Multiplicity and Relation*, edited by Catherine Keller and Laurel C. Schneider (London: Routledge, 2010), pp. 126–50.

1. The Neo-Confucian analogue to the Christian notion of salvation would be the ideal of self-cultivation aimed at being truly human. Robert C. Neville, *Behind the Masks of God: An Essay toward Comparative Theology* (Albany: State University of New York Press, 1991), pp. 115–26.
2. Toegye's dynamic conception of pattern tries not to deviate too much from Zhu Xi's own conception of pattern's "movement and rest," i.e., the notion that pattern provides, logically and causally speaking, the *pattern* of movement and rest, i.e., the ontological condition of possibility for psychophysical energy's movement and rest, as can be seen from the following statements: "Master Zhu once said, 'Pattern has movement and rest; therefore, psychophysical energy has movement and rest. If pattern did not have movement and rest, on what grounds would psychophysical energy have movement and rest?' In general, once pattern moves, psychophysical energy follows it and arises; once psychophysical energy moves, pattern follows it and manifests itself. When Lianxi [Zhou Dunyi] says, 'The Great Ultimate moves and gives birth to *yang*,' he is referring to the movement of pattern and the consequent emergence of psychophysical energy." See Yi Hwang, "Dap Jeong Ja-jung byeolji [Reply to Jeong Ja-jung, addendum]," in *Toegye Jeonseo* [Complete works of Toegye], ed. Toegyehak chongseo pyeon-gan wiwonhoe

(Seoul: Toegyehak yeon-guwon, 1989–), VII, 25.35a, p. 33 (hereafter *Jeonseo*—for citations from *Jeonseo*, I give the volume number in roman numerals, the book number and the page number in the traditional format, and then the page number in the modern pagination). The quotation within the quotation is from "Reply to Zheng Zishang," in Zhu Xi, *Zhuzi wenji* [Collected literary works of Master Zhu], ed. Chen Junmin (Taibei: Defu wenjiao jijinhui, 2000), 6:2721 (hereafter *Wenji*—for citations from *Wenji*, I give the volume number followed by the page number)].

As is clear from the way he carefully delineates psychophysical energy's coming into being as a process of self-arising in accordance with pattern, not as a process of production by pattern (even going against the plain sense of Zhou Dunyi's statement which he quotes), Toegye does not appear to see the "activity" of pattern in the same way as the activity of psychophysical energy, i.e., as an exercise of some kind of efficient causality. Whereas Yun Sasoon sees implicit contradictions in the way Toegye introduces activity to pattern while attempting to distinguish pattern's activity clearly from psychophysical energy's activity (Yun Sasoon, *Critical Issues in Neo-Confucian Thought: The Philosophy of Yi T'oegye*, trans. Michael C. Kalton [Seoul: Korea University Press, 1990], pp. 70–83), Michael Kalton sees a gradual evolution of Toegye's thought over the course of his life away from his earlier, more strictly orthodox view of pattern's "activity" toward a more truly dynamic and productive conception of it, based on his conception of the substance-function relation and its application to the operation of pattern. See Michael C. Kalton, trans. and ed., *To Become a Sage: The Ten Diagrams on Sage Learning*, by Yi T'oegye (New York: Columbia University Press, 1988), p. 48.

3. Yi Hwang, "Sim mu cheyong byeon [Regarding the theory that the heart-mind is without substance and function]," in *Jeonseo*, X, 41.17a–b, pp. 8–9.
4. See Bae Jong-ho, *Han-guk yuhaksa* [A history of Confucian learning in Korea] (Seoul: Yonsei daehakgyo chulpanbu, 1973), pp. 94–95.
5. Although acknowledging the existence of the two levels of the substance-function distinction in Toegye's thought, Yun Sasoon argues that Toegye fails to make clear just how the substance-function distinction works on the level of pattern in the same way he conceives of it on the level of concrete thing-events, i.e., in terms of potentiality and its actualization. In other words, Toegye does not explain how the Great Ultimate as substance in its totally void condition of pure possibility come to actualize itself as the patterns of all thing-events and to include them existentially within itself, given that Toegye understands the phrase "empty and tranquil, and without any sign" to express how "all figures," which are "luxuriantly present," belong—paradoxically—to the level that transcends concrete form (see Yun, *Critical Issues in Neo-Confucian Thought*, pp. 65–68). Given his careful analysis and assessment of Toegye's metaphysics as having some fundamentally contradictory points, Yun's claim, that "his thesis of substance and function as applied to pattern is not theoretically solid" (p. 68), appears to be not without grounds. Nonetheless, despite the absence in Toegye's text of a clear articulation of the substance-function relation on the level of pattern, one could read his formulation of the relationship between the emptiness/formlessness of the substance of the Great Ultimate (i.e., the Non-Ultimate) and the presence of the individuated patterns within the function of the Great Ultimate not as contradictory but dialectical, especially given his introduction of movement to the Great Ultimate as pattern. For a dialectical reading of

the relation between the Non-Ultimate and the Great Ultimate, see Jeon Duha, "Toegye-ui cheoragui haeksim [The heart of T'oegye's philosophy]," in *Toegye Hakbo* 19 (December 1978): 144–45, although Jeon reads the Non-Ultimate–Great Ultimate relation more in terms of the pattern–psychophysical energy relation than in terms of the substance-function relation.

6. Yi Hwang, "Dap Yi Gong-ho munmok [Reply to Yi Gong-ho's topical questions]," in *Jeonseo*, IX, 39.28a–b, pp. 94–95.
7. Huang Mianzhai switches the original location of the verb 生 (*sheng*)—meaning "give birth to" or "produce"—from *before* the object, "active and receptive [forces]," to after it, thereby changing the transitive sense of the verb into an intransitive one ("arise"). See Yun, *Critical Issues in Neo-Confucian Thought*, p. 70.
8. Kalton, *To Become a Sage*, p. 48.
9. "Cheonmyeong do seol [Explanation of the Diagram of Heavenly Mandate]," See in *Jeonseo*, XIII, sokjip [extended collection] 8.15b–16a, p. 93.
10. Yi Hwang, "Eonhaeng nok [Record of sayings and acts]," in *Jeonseo*, XVII, 1.11b–12a, p. 10.
11. Yi Hwang, "Dap Gi Myeong-eon [Reply to Gi Myeong-eon]," in *Jeonseo*, V, 16.32a, p. 63. See also his "Seonghak sipdo [The ten diagrams on sage learning]" in *Jeonseo*, III, 7.24b–25a, pp. 46–47. Toegye adds that, although there can be no Four Sprouts outside of the Seven Feelings, there is a difference in their respective meanings according to their respective origination ("Dap Gi Myeong-eon," in *Jeonseo*, V, 16.34a, p. 64). Toegye appeals to one of the most famous references to the distinction between the Four Sprouts and the Seven Feelings, found in Zhu Xi, *Yulei*, 4:92, as an authoritative support for his own position. See Yi Hwang, "Dap Gi Myeong-eon [Reply to Gi Myeongeon]," in *Jeonseo*, V, 16.23b–24a, p. 59.
12. "In general, pattern and psychophysical energy combine and produce the human body. The two, therefore, mutually have an issuing function, and their issuing adhere to each other. Because it is a mutual issuance, one can see that each has its predominant role; because they adhere to each other, one can see that they are included in each other's issuing. Since they are included in each other's issuing, one can certainly speak of them as mixed; since they each have their predominant role, it is not impossible to speak of them separately" ("Dap Gi Myeong-eon," in *Jeonseo*, V, 16.30b, p. 62).
13. See Yi Hwang, "Seonghak sipdo [The ten diagrams on sage learning]," in *Jeonseo*, III, 7.28b, p. 48. See also Yi Hwang, "Dap Yi Suk-heon," in *Jeonseo*, V, 14.35b, p. 24: "What is born of the materiality of psychophysical energy is called the human heart-mind; what originates from the mandate of human nature is called the heart-mind of the Way." See also "Dap Yi Gweng-jung [Reply to Yi Gweng-jung]," in *Jeonseo*, IX, 36.2b, p. 21: "The human heart-mind refers to the Seven Feelings; the heart-mind of the Way refers to the Four Sprouts." My argument is that the common usage does not carry the specific connotation of Toegye's use of it, i.e., a transhuman agency not totally dependent on psychophysical energy for its dynamism.
14. Yi Hwang, "Seonghak sipdo," in *Jeonseo*, III, 7.31b, p. 50. See also "Dap Yi Gweng-jung," in *Jeonseo*, XIII, sokjip 6.6a, p. 56. He makes it clear, however, that he applies the name "Lord on High" to pattern in a metaphorical sense, as a poetic way of describing pattern's wondrous creativity that gives an appearance of someone in command ("Dap Yi Dal Yi Cheon-gi [Reply to Yi Dal and Yi Cheon-gi]," in *Jeonseo*, IV, 13.17a, p. 100). In this sense,

he follows Zhu Xi (*Yulei*, 1:5, 63), yet his conferral of active agency to pattern puts the metaphor in a significantly more panentheistic light. On the religious dimension of Toegye's philosophy of mindfulness, see Park Sung-bae, *Toegye Sasang-ui jong-gyojeok seong-gyeok* [The religious aspects of Toegye's thought], in *Toegyehak yeon-gu nonchong* [Collected essays on Toegye studies], ed. Song Hwi-chil and Shin Gwi-hyeon (Daegu: Gyeongbuk daehakgyo Toegye yeon-guso, 1997), 9:247–58. See also Choe Yeong-jin, *Toe Yurui yigiron-gwa segye yinsik* [The theories of yi-gi relations by Toegye and Yulgok and their worldviews], in *Toegyehak yeon-gu nonchong* [Collected essays on Toegye studies], ed. Yi Wan-je and Yun Cheon-geun (Daegu: Gyeongbuk daehakgyo Toegye yeon-guso, 1997), 2:515–27.

15. Yi Hwang, "Dap Yi Suk-heon byeolji [Reply to Yi Suk-heon, addendum]," in *Jeonseo*, V, 14.18b–19a, pp. 15–16. "Mindfulness" is Michael Kalton's translation of the term. An alternative is Daniel K. Gardner's translation of it as "inner mental attentiveness" (Chu Hsi, *Learning to Be a Sage: Selections from the Conversations of Master Chu, Arranged Topically*, trans. Daniel K. Gardner [Berkeley: University of California Press, 1990], p. 89). The standard Neo-Confucian regimen of self-cultivation in the school of Zhu Xi prescribes the "investigation of things and thorough probing of patterns" (*gyeongmul gungli/gewu qiongli*) and the practice of mindfulness as the necessary preparation for it. Toegye differs from the standard regimen in that he regards mindfulness not merely as the preparation but the very thing that enables the comprehension of pattern. The practice of mindfulness consists first in returning one's heart-mind to its original state of tranquillity before feelings and intentions have issued, and thereby attaining an unobstructed and undistorted access to the human nature or the pattern within. The second step is to follow closely the issuance of feelings and intentions, reflect on them, and correct them when they are unbalanced. See Yi Hwang, "Dap Gim Don-seo [Reply to Gim Don-seo]," in *Jeonseo*, VII, 28.17a–b, p. 85; "Cheonmyeong doseol," in *Jeonseo*, XIII, sokjip 20a–b, p. 95; and "Seonghak sipdo," III, 7.24b–25a, pp. 46–47.
16. See Yi Hwang, "Dap Gi Myeong-eon byeolji [Reply to Gi Myeong-eon, addendum]," in *Jeonseo*, V, 18.31a–b, p. 111.
17. Although he is somewhat ambiguous on the presence of all individual patterns in each concrete thing, Toegye is clear on the reality of such presence in the human heart-mind. See "Dap Gi Myeongeon byeolji," in *Jeonseo*, V, 18.12b–13a, pp. 101–2: "Pattern and psychophysical energy combine to form the heart-mind; and the heart-mind naturally has the wondrous qualities of emptiness, numinosity, and consciousness. What is at rest, harboring all patterns, is the [human] nature; and that which contains and bears the [human] nature is the heart-mind. What moves and responds to all circumstances is feeling; and that which applies feelings far and wide is the heart mind. It is said, therefore, 'The heart-mind commands the nature and feelings.'" See also "Sim mu cheyong byeon," in *Jeonseo*, X, 41.18b, p. 9: "As a universal presence, what is 'empty and silent, and without any sign' is the substance of the Non-Ultimate and the Great Ultimate; and all things are already present in it. As a presence in the human heart-mind, it is the utmost emptiness and stillness of substance; and all functions are completely furnished in it. As a presence in concrete things, it is the active manifestation and operation of function, and it is present everywhere, at all times and in all places."
18. I borrow the term "preworldly Trinity" from Hodgson, *Winds of the Spirit*, p. 151.

19. The Ultimate of Nonbeing is merely the indeterminate, abstract aspect of the Great Ultimate, and thus different from the trends within Western negative theology that see God beyond God or the One as more ultimate than the Trinity.
20. This is in contrast to the classical conception in which the dynamism to move things is given to the Father while to the Spirit is assigned only the role of the mediator of the Father's dynamism. See, for instance, John Calvin's *Institutes of Christian Religion*, trans. Henry Beveridge (Grand Rapids, Mich.: W. B. Eerdmans, 1989), p. 126: "To the Father is attributed the beginning of action, the fountain and source of all things; to the Son, wisdom, counsel, and arrangement in action, while the energy and efficacy of action is assigned to the Spirit."
21. I have been inspired in this formulation by Yi I (honorific name Yulgok), who gives a triadic interpretation of the Great Ultimate as follows: "The 'Great Ultimate' is merely a forced name. Its substance is change (易 *yeok*); its pattern is the way (道 *do*); and its function is spirit (神 *sin*)." This triadic formulation is originally by Cheng Hao (one of the Cheng brothers), but unlike him, Yulgok applies the formulation to the Great Ultimate. See "Yeok su chaek [A treatise on calculating change (or divination)], in Yi I, *Gugyeok Yulgok Jeonseo* [Complete translated works of Yulgok], ed. Han-guk jeongsin munhwa yeon-guwon jaryo josasil (Gyeonggi-do Seongnam-si: Han-guk jeongsin munhwa yeon-guwon, 1984–88), IV, 14.48a–b, p. 15. My formulation here, however, changes the order of the triad, putting spirit in the middle.
22. Zhu Xi, "Da He Shujing [Reply to He Shujing]," in *Wenji*, 4:1746. See also Yi Hwang, "Dap Yi Pyeong-suk," in *Jeonseo*, IX, 37.28b, p. 54.
23. *G. W. F. Hegel: Theologian of the Spirit*, ed. Peter C. Hodgson (Minneapolis: Fortress Press, 1997).

## 5. *From the Divine Idea to the Concrete Unity of the Spirit: Hegel's Shapes of Freedom and the Domination of Nature*

1. G. W. F. Hegel, *The Encyclopedia Logic*, trans. T. F. Garaets, W. A. Suchting, and H. S. Harris (Indianapolis: Hackett, 1991), pp. xxvi–xxvii. Harris and the co-translators use "overgrasp" to translate *übergreifen*, which is a literal translation with perhaps a stronger connotation of subjectivism than Hegel intended.
2. G. W. F. Hegel, *Encyclopedia of Philosophical Sciences*, §20R (hereafter *Enc.*). See also G. W. F. Hegel, *Lectures on the Philosophy of Religion*, ed. Peter C. Hodgson, trans. R. Brown, P. Hodgson, and J. Stewart, with the assistance of J. P. Fitzer and H. S. Harris, vol. 1, *Introduction and the Concept of Religion* (Berkeley: University of California Press, 1984), pp. 204–5 (hereafter cited as *LPR*, 1). Although there is at present no single English translation of the entire *Enzyklopädie der philosophischen Wissenschaften*, parts of it have been translated separately. In order to simplify citation, therefore, I will be using the section numbers (with the symbol § standing for the sections themselves, R for Remarks [*Anmerkungen*], and A for Additions [*Zusätze*] following the section numbers) in the German original and common to all of the translations. For direct quotations, I will be using the following translations: *The Encyclopedia Logic*, trans. T. F. Garaets, W. A. Suchting, and H. S. Harris (Indianapolis: Hackett, 1991); *Hegel's Philosophy of Nature*, ed. and trans. M. J. Petry, 3 vols. (London: Allen and Unwin; New York: Humanities Press, 1970);

*Philosophy of Subjective Spirit*, ed. and trans. M. J. Petry. 3 vols. (Dordrecht: D. Reidel, 1979); (for the sections on objective spirit) *Hegel's Philosophy of Mind*, trans. William Wallace and A. V. Miller (Oxford: Clarendon Press, 1971); (for the sections on absolute spirit) *G. W. F. Hegel: Theologian of the Spirit*, ed. Peter C. Hodgson (Minneapolis: Fortress Press, 1997). For the German original, see *Werke*, ed. Eva Moldenhauer and Karl Markus Michel, 20 vols. (Frankfurt am Main: Suhrkampf, 1969–71).

3. *LPR*, 1:347. For Hegel theology is therefore philosophy and, ultimately, philosophy of religion (*Enc.*, §36A; *LPR*, 1:84, 116–17, 366–68). Hegel's description of philosophy in the 1821 manuscript is in this sense worth quoting: "God is the beginning of all things and the end of all things. . . . God is the one and only object of philosophy. [Its concern is] to occupy itself with God, to apprehend everything in him, to lead everything back to him, as well as to derive everything particular from God and to justify everything only insofar as it stems from God, is sustained through its relationship with him, lives by his radiance and has [within itself] the mind of God. Thus philosophy *is* theology, and [one's] occupation with philosophy—or rather *in* philosophy—is of itself the service of God" (*LPR*, 1:84).
4. Charles Taylor, *Hegel* (Cambridge: Cambridge University Press, 1975), pp. 29–50.
5. *Enc.*, §§2, 6, 23, 23R, 24, 24R. Harris and the other translators use "thinking-over" to translate this term (*Enc.* §2), but they have "meditative thinking" as an alternative translation, which also nicely captures the nonsubjectivistic meaning of the term (§7). *Nachdenken*, when genuinely philosophical, becomes "speculative thinking" (*spekulative Denken*, §9). In this mode of thinking, thoughts are "objective thoughts" (*objektive Gedanken*), though Hegel has reservations about using the term "objective" on account of its common usage to designate nature in opposition to spirit (§24).
6. Hegel's *Phenomenology of Spirit*, which he wrote as an introduction to his system, makes clear that the revelatory religion (Christianity) and its grasp of the truth of God as infinite subjectivity—i.e., as infinite power and freedom to endure and overcome the anguish of otherness and difference—is what makes possible the final transition of human consciousness to absolute knowing or the philosophical point of view (G. W. F. Hegel, *Phenomenology of Spirit*, trans. A. V. Miller [Oxford: Oxford University Press, 1977], hereafter cited as *PhS*). This shows that both the logical idea of his *Encyclopedia Logic* and the trinitarian divine idea of his philosophy of religion lectures are a philosophical elaboration of his fundamentally religious insight into the "deep structure" of reality—the insight that serves as the key to the intelligibility of his whole system. See also the preface to the second edition of *Encyclopedia of Philosophical Sciences*, in *Encyclopedia Logic*, pp. 11–12.
7. For example, the juxtaposition of the trinitarian "persons" or divine "attributes" in the one being of God, the unity of divine and human "nature" in the "God-man," or the salvation in and through Christ happening "back then," "now," and in the future parousia. For Hegel's discussion of representation, see *LPR*, 1:238–40, 247–50, 333–34, 396–406. See also *Enc.*, §565. For Hegel even the word "God" is a representation (*LPR*, 1:222–23, 230).
8. See the preface to the second edition of *Encyclopedia of Philosophical Sciences*, in *Encyclopedia Logic*, pp. 6–17; *Enc.*, §§1, 5; *LPR*, 1:397, 406.
9. G. W. F. Hegel, *Lectures on the Philosophy of Religion*, ed. Peter C. Hodgson, trans. R. Brown, P. Hodgson, and J. Stewart, with the assistance of J. P. Fitzer and H. S. Harris, vol. 3, *The Consummate Religion* (Berkeley: University of California Press, 1985), p. 91 (hereafter cited as *LPR*, 3).

10. According Hegel's logic, the category of particularity (*Partikularität* or *Besonderheit*) stands for differentiation, separation, and mutual externality opposite the category of universality represented by the logical Idea, whereas the category of singularity (*Einzelheit*) or individuality (*Individualität*), to which human beings as finite spirits are assigned, denotes integration and internally differentiated—concrete— unity. Hegel's philosophy of nature defines nature as "the [logical] Idea in the form of otherness" (*Enc.*, §247), i.e., as particularity, externality, and difference that constitute the opposite of the concrete unity of the divine Idea. This is tantamount to saying that nature's logical definition is a sheer chaos of nothingness (*Enc.*, §248). Human beings as individual finite spirits are therefore not characterized essentially by naturalness, but their individuality can become involuted into itself, making them external to one another and impeding their achievement of universal, infinite, and absolute unity (see *Hegel's Science of Logic*, trans. A. V. Miller [Atlantic Highlands, N.J.: Humanities Press, 1969], pp. 605–22 [hereafter cited as *SL*]). In his philosophy of religion lectures, he defines humanity existing "*according* to nature [*nach der Natur*]" as "the willing of separation, the setting of one's singularity against others" (*LPR*, 3:102, 298; italics mine). In other words, humanity existing as natural humanity means existing as singular subjects that have always already willed and chosen involuted subjectivity and self-seeking in opposition to the universal: "The human being is human as a subject, and as a natural subject it is *this* single individual; the will involved is this singular will, and it is fulfilled with the content of its singularity. This means that natural humanity is selfish" (*LPR*, 3:299). Evil lies, therefore, not in singularity or individuality as such but in singularization or privatization (*Vereinzelung*). I am indebted to Peter Hodgson for this point. Hodgson detects here the Pauline theology of divided will (*kata sarka* and *kata pneuma*) found in Romans 7 (*LPR*, 3:92n90). See also Peter C. Hodgson, "Alienation and Reconciliation in Hegelian and Post-Hegelian Perspective," *Modern Theology* 2, no. 1 (1985): 49–50.
11. *LPR*, 3:317–18; see also 116, 217. Hegel's exposition of Jesus' teaching of the kingdom of God is much more pronounced and detailed in his lecture manuscripts of 1821.
12. *LPR*, 3:123, 116.
13. *LPR*, 3:109.
14. *LPR*, 3:118, 218.
15. *LPR*, 3:317–21.
16. *LPR*, 3:318, 217; see also pp. 117–20. The biblical passages which Hegel interprets are: the Sermon on the Mount (Mt 5.3–8), the Mosaic dispensation of the law (Mt 5.20ff.), "Consider lilies of the field" (Mt 6.31), "Who is my mother, and who are my brothers?" (Mt 19.21), "I have come not to bring peace, but a sword" (Mt 10.34–37).
17. *LPR*, 3:116, 216; see also p. 319.
18. *LPR*, 3:123. Unlike in the lecture manuscripts of 1821, where Hegel discusses the life of Jesus as in conformity with his teaching, he skips it in the 1824 and 1827 lectures and focuses on his death and resurrection.
19. This understanding of Jesus' death as a martyr is highlighted in both the 1821 manuscripts and the 1827 lectures: Jesus "does not shun the hazards and the death that he must expect because of what he has begun among his people" (and seals his faith by his death, a fate shared by many others) (*LPR*, 3:122); the suffering and death of Christ is "a natural death, brought about by injustice, hatred, and violence" (*LPR*, 3:322); Jesus "became, humanly speaking, a martyr to the truth in a way that coheres closely with his earlier

role, because the establishment of the kingdom of God stands in stark contradiction to the worldly authority [*vorhandenen Staate*], which is grounded upon another mode, a different determinate form, of religion" (*LPR*, 3:320–21).

20. *LPR*, 3:310–11, 212–13.
21. *LPR*, 3:216. See also pp. 121–22.
22. *LPR*, 3:110.
23. *LPR*, 3:219, 125, 327–28.
24. *LPR*, 3:124–25. See also pp. 214, 315.
25. *LPR*, 3:468.
26. *LPR*, 3:125.
27. *LPR*, 3:325.
28. *LPR*, 3:128–29. This point, that death as both the extreme limit of finitude and the sublation of everything pertaining to natural existence is tantamount to the death of the natural will, is most explicit in the 1821 manuscript, although the 1824 and 1827 lectures also imply it. *LPR*, 3:220, 326.
29. He continues, "If this symbol of dishonor is made into a badge [of honor] and is raised up as a banner whose positive content is at the same time the kingdom of God, then the inner disposition [of the citizens] is at root withdrawn from the life of the state and from civil affairs. The substantial foundation of public life is removed, and this whole structure no longer has any actuality." *LPR*, 3:129–30. See also the 1831 lectures in *LPR*, 3:323n199.
30. *LPR*, 3:125. See also pp. 219–20.
31. "Thus what this life of Christ brings to representation for us . . . [is] this process of the nature of spirit—God in human shape. In its development, this [process is] the going forth of the divine idea into the uttermost cleavage, even to the opposite pole of the anguish of death, which is itself the absolute reversal, the highest love, containing the negation of the negative within itself [and being in this way] the absolute reconciliation, the sublation of the prior antithesis between humanity and God" (*LPR*, 3:132).
32. *LPR*, 3:370. See also the 1831 lectures, p. 323, n. 199.
33. *LPR*, 3:132. See also p. 220.
34. *LPR*, 3:133, 221–22, 322–25.
35. *LPR*, 3:311–12, 215.
36. *LPR*, 3:215. See also pp. 310, 312, 315–16.
37. *LPR*, 3:327. See also pp. 220, 370.
38. *LPR*, 3:77–78, 189, 275–76. Hegel regards the traditional doctrinal language in which the Trinity is expressed in terms of the relationship of three divine persons—Father, Son, and Spirit—as a "childlike relationship, a childlike form" (3:194). In his own formulation, the Trinity designates "the God who differentiates himself but remains identical with himself in the process" (3:192). This logical reformulation of the intradivine relations symbolized by the language of persons enables him to construe God as the logical "deep structure" that is "the *ultimate* condition of possibility for the *totality* of experience and for religious experience in particular," as Hodgson aptly puts it. G. W. F. Hegel, *Lectures on the Philosophy of Religion*, ed. Peter C. Hodgson, trans. R. Brown, P. Hodgson, and J. Stewart, with the assistance of H. S. Harris, one-volume edition, *The Lectures of 1827* (Berkeley: University of California Press, 1988), pp. 28.
39. *LPR*, 3:279.

40. Hegel's important definition of love as internally differentiated—concrete—unity is as follows: "Love is a distinguishing of two, who nevertheless are absolutely not distinguished for each other. The consciousness or feeling of the identity of the two—to be outside of myself and in the other—this is love. I have my self-consciousness not in myself but in the other. I am satisfied and have peace with myself only in this other—and I *am* only because I have peace with myself. . . . This other, because it likewise exists outside itself, has its self-consciousness only in me, and both the other and I are only this consciousness of being-outside-ourselves and of our identity; we are only this intuition, feeling, and knowledge of our unity" (*LPR*, 3:276). See also *LPR*, 3:78.
41. *LPR*, 3:286. See also pp. 192–94.
42. *LPR*, 3:78, 284–85.
43. *LPR*, 3:276. For Hegel's crucial claim that the Spirit, not the Father, is the most proper name for God, see pp. 195, 219, 284 n. 93, 364. See also *Enc.*, §567. Hegel and the classical Christian view agree that the Father is the unoriginate source or ground of the Godhead and that the Persons are essentially relational. But whereas the classical doctrine of Trinity places the relations between the Persons outside the divine essence, generating a tension between the monotheism of divine nature and tritheism of Persons, Hegel identifies the Father with the Godhead as such and regards the Persons or subsistent relations as internal to the Godhead of the Father, in essence seeing the immanent Trinity as contained within the Father. An implication of this is that, insofar as an originating, pluralizing, and reintegrating principle is posited within the one Godhead of the Father to which ontological priority is given as the unoriginate ground of the divine nature in its unity, God in the most proper sense of the term comes to designate not the Father but the Spirit as the concrete unity in love of the trinitarian Persons within the Father. See Anselm K. Min, "The Trinity and the Incarnation: Hegel and Classical Approaches," *Journal of Religion* 66, no. 2 (1986): 183–85.
44. *LPR*, 3:292.
45. *LPR*, 3:292. See also pp. 189, 195, 78.
46. *LPR*, 3:292. See also p. 86; *Enc.*, §247A. According to Emilio Brito ("La Création chez Hegel et Schelling," *Revue Thomiste* 87, no. 2 [1987]: 260–79), Hegel construes God's creation of the world as a necessary consequence of God's rational freedom and will in order to counter the view of freedom prevalent in the Lutheran *theologia crucis*, namely, nominalism's formalistic view of freedom as arbitrary and contentless power of free choice. But neither does Hegel straightforwardly accept the emanationism of monistic Neoplatonism by which he was partially influenced, owing to his conception of God as absolute negativity, which he inherited from German mysticism. The combination of his conception of God as absolute negativity and his view of creation as a necessary act results, Brito claims, in an impoverishment of the Christian concept of God, because the creative act of God is seen to be motivated solely by the divine need to realize itself as Spirit, i.e., "by the poverty of God's love of godself, and not by the plenitude of love which God shares" (p. 264). For Brito, Hegel's view of the Trinity is both "subordinationism in reverse" (p. 267), in which the Father is "subordinated" to the more concrete moments of the Son and above all of the Spirit (pp. 267–68), and "crypto-modalism" in which the first two Persons are presented as deficient "modes" of the Spirit (pp. 268–69). With all due respect to Brito, however, it must be pointed out that Hegel clearly distinguishes between

the primal division within God, which gives birth to the Son, and the second division, the creation of the world: "The absolute act of the first judgment or division [is] *implicitly* the same as the second. . . . In fact they should be distinguished and held apart" (*LPR*, 3:87). Hegel in fact rejects the conflation of the two as "a false interpretation" leading to pantheism. Hodgson sees Hegel's view as that of panentheism, i.e., the position that the world is in and dependent on God but not identical with God, which does have an affinity with Neoplatonism and German mysticism on account of its assumption of an implicit and teleological—eschatological—identity between the world and God (*LPR*, 3:17). On Brito's contention that Hegel's notion of God is impoverished because of its teleology of divine self-becoming, the following passage from Hegel about absolute spirit throws much doubt: "Absolute truth cannot be a result; it is what is purely and simply first, unique. It is what takes up simply everything into itself—the *absolute plenitude* in which everything is but a moment" (*LPR*, 1:322). Hegel's reference to God as "the absolute womb" and "the infinite fountainhead" (*LPR*, 1:374) speaks against Brito's characterization of God's creativity as a product of God's poverty and neediness.

47. *LPR*, 3:275.
48. *LPR*, 1:374.
49. A narrative reading of the Hegelian construal of the trinitarian divine life is the central theme of Cyril O'Regan's *Heterodox Hegel* (Albany: State University of New York Press, 1994).
50. *LPR*, 3:89, 293.
51. Hegel's philosophy of nature logically defines nature as "the [logical] Idea in the form of otherness" (*Enc.*, §247), i.e., as particularity, externality, and difference that constitute the opposite of the concrete unity of the divine idea. This is tantamount to saying that nature's logical definition is a sheer chaos of nothingness (*Enc.*, §248). But insofar as this nothingness is posited by the divine idea, one could say that, for Hegel, God creates out of God's own being, God being the only source of the being of all beings. Min, "Trinity and Incarnation," p. 175.
52. This point is most clearly made in *LPR*, 1:222–32. Hegel contends that it is the (consummate) religious standpoint, which—especially when elevated to philosophical cognition—recognizes the trinitarian logical idea as the truth of God, that enables us to view nature in this way, alive and "spiritual" in a mode of prefigurement. Philosophically speaking, the consummate religious standpoint is the speculative point of view, which enables one to go beyond Kant's notion of productive imagination or figurative synthesis in the First Critique and intuitive intellect in the Third Critique, and to recognize not only a regulative but a constitutive function in the inner, materially objective purposiveness manifest in nature, seeing it as a disclosure of the Idea (Daniel O. Dahlstrom, "Hegel's Appropriation of Kant's Account of Teleology in Nature," in *Hegel and the Philosophy of Nature*, ed. Stephen Houlgate [Albany: State University of New York Press, 1998], pp. 167–75; Sally S. Sedgwick, "Hegel's Treatment of Transcendental Apperception in Kant," *Owl of Minerva* 23, no. 2 [1992]: 153–63). The divine idea, thus speculatively revealed, upholds the logical "deep structure" that functions as the universal form of the entire range of the worldly sphere and yields a bewilderingly and inexhaustibly rich variety of finite configurations and forms: "God's internal self-development has thus the same logical necessity as the development of the universe, and the latter is implicitly

divine only to the extent that, at each of its stages, it is the development of this form" (*LPR*, 1:231; see also *LPR*, 3:88–90). Hegel's philosophy of nature (*Enc.*, §§245–376) shows how the divine logical idea increasingly makes itself manifest as the concretely uniting power of being as it moves from the lowest, simplest level of nature (space and time) to its highest and most complex level (life). Hegel sums this up nicely at the end of *Encyclopedia*: "It may also be recalled in this connection that although philosophy certainly has to do with *unity* in general it is not, however, with abstract unity, mere identity, and the empty absolute, but with *concrete* unity, and that in its whole course it has to do with nothing else. Thus every stage in its advance is a *distinct determination* of this concrete *unity*, and the deepest and last of the determinations of unity is that of absolute spirit. . . . The distinctiveness of all natural, inorganic, and living things, and the entire difference between them, rests solely on the *diverse determinacy of this unity*" (*Enc.*, §573R). See also §38A: "We can therefore say that there is no 'matter'; for whenever it exists it is always something determinate and concrete."

53. *LPR*, 3:90, 195. See also pp. 192–93: "Everything concrete, everything living contains contradiction within itself. . . . But the contradiction is also resolved in the idea, and the resolution is spiritual unity." It needs to be pointed out that, for Hegel the divine idea's "progress" in nature toward (animal) life is not an evolutionary process in time but a notional or categorial hierarchization. See Martin Drees, "Evolution and Emanation of Spirit in Hegel's Philosophy of Nature," *Bulletin of the Hegel Society of Great Britain* 26 (1992): 53–59.
54. *LPR*, 3:90. For Hegel the subjectivity of an animal organism is only a prefiguration of the self-conscious subjectivity of human beings, and the mutual interaction between living individuals of nature only a prefiguration of the intersubjective relation of self-conscious persons. See Karl-Heinz Ilting, "Hegels Philosophie des Organischen," in *Hegel und Naturwissenschaften*, ed. Michael John Petry (Stuttgart-Bad Cannstatt: Frommann-Holzboog, 1987), pp. 367–68.
55. Nature as "slumbering spirit" was a metaphor often used by the Romantic poets and philosophers, but Hegel more directly appropriated it from Schelling. Daniel Berthold-Bond, "Can There Be a 'Humanistic' Ecology? A Debate between Hegel and Heidegger on the Meaning of Ecological Thinking," *Social Theory and Practice* 20, no. 3 (1994): 156.
56. *LPR*, 3:91. In the *Encyclopedia*, Hegel has a clear and succinct summary of the trinitarian history up to this point of furthest extreme: "In the moment of *particularity* [Besonderheit], of judgment or primal division [Urteil], this concrete eternal being is what is *presupposed*, and its movement [is] the coming to be of *appearance*, the falling apart of the eternal moment of mediation, of the only Son, into an independent opposition: on the one hand is heaven and earth, elemental and concrete nature, and on the other hand, standing in *relationship* to it, is spirit, which therefore is *finite*. Finite spirit, as the extreme of inherent negativity, makes itself independent and becomes evil; it is that extreme by its relation to a nature that stands over against it and by its own resulting naturalness. Yet, amid that naturalness, it is, when it thinks, directed toward the eternal, but for this reason stands in external relationship to it" (*Enc.*, §568).
57. *LPR*, 3:91. According Hodgson (*LPR*, 3:11–12), Hegel's conception of the "turning point" of the divine history changed over time. In his 1821 manuscript Hegel structures his philosophical redescription of the Christian religion in two triads, one within the other.

The outer triad is the analytic framework applied to each of the determinate or finite (historical) religions, namely the triad of abstract concept (of God), concrete representation (i.e., the theoretical relationship to God via symbols, images, and other thought-categories), and cultus (the practical, participating relationship to God). The inner triad, in contrast, presents the concrete representation of God found in the Christian religion as the consummate religion, which consists of the idea of God in and for itself (the immanent Trinity), the idea in diremption or differentiation (the creation and preservation of the natural world), and the appearance of the idea in finite spirit (the history of estrangement and reconciliation/redemption). Hegel's construction of the inner triad discloses a tension in Hegel's thought, because the inner triad's concrete representation of God of the Christian religion is not structured in a trinitarian manner but in accordance with the philosophical triad of the logical idea, nature, and (finite) spirit in the *Encyclopedia* (recapitulated in §§567–70 "revealed religion"). Here the "Son" (anthropology and christology) occupies the third moment of the triad rather than the second, and the third trinitarian moment of the Spirit stands like a kind of appendage, identified with the third section of the outer triad. What Hegel does in his later lectures is that he combines the second and third moments of the philosophical triad (nature and finite spirit) in the second moment of the trinitarian dialectic, and incorporates the third moment of the outer triad (cultus) into the third moment of the trinitarian dialectic (God's return to godself in the concrete and participatory unity of the community of the Spirit). As can be seen from his 1831 lectures, the philosophical triad of universality, particularity, and singularity is transformed into the trinitarian triad of abstract unity (universality), differentiation (particularity and finite singularity), and return (infinite singularity), or of the "Kingdom of the Father," the "Kingdom of the Son, and the "Kingdom of the Spirit." The implication of this modification is that, since the second moment of the triad is divided not into nature and finite spirit but into differentiation/estrangement and reconciliation, the "turning point" of the divine history is no longer the creation of finite spirit (the first Adam) but the incarnation and death of the Son (the second Adam).

58. *LPR*, 3:109, 225–30. For faith as a form of knowledge, see also p. 223; *LPR*, 1:387–88.

59. The most articulate formulation of this "dynamic" of salvation is found in *Enc.*, §570: "Secondly, this objective totality [the example of Jesus] is the implicit *presupposition* for the *finite* immediacy of the individual subject. For such a subject therefore it is at first an *other*, something *intuited*. But it is the intuition of *implicit truth*; and through the witness of the spirit within it the subject, because of its immediate nature, at first determines itself for itself as nought and evil. But then in accord with this example of its truth, and by means of faith in the unity, therein *implicitly* accomplished, of universal and individual essentiality, the subject is also the movement to divest itself of its immediate natural determinateness and its own will, and to merge with that example and its *implicitness* [*Ansich*] in the anguish of negativity and so recognize itself as united with essential being." See also *LPR*, 1:342–44. As John Burbidge insightfully points out, this dynamic of salvation shows that the incarnation, death, and resurrection of a singular divine individual, as a historical scandal of particularity, are indispensable to the divine idea's achievement of universal reconciliation in the community of the Spirit. Unless the example of a singular individual actually unites the two particularized extremes of universality (God) and particularity (creation), which as disjunctive alternatives are simply conjoined

by disjunctive judgment within nature and history (that is, difference or particularity is for the moment external to universality, not internal to it as in the [immanent] Trinity), other singular individuals cannot follow that example in faith. If the example is merely a myth or a fiction and not historically actual, then its narrated claim, that the disjunction created by the Fall can indeed be bridged, not only offers no assurance that the disjunction will not ultimately triumph, but could itself also be a mere wishful thinking. This is so, because, unlike the story of the Fall, which can be a myth (that is, historical Adam and Eve are not required) insofar as all finite spirits realize the disjunctive opposition in their actions, the reunion of the universal and the particular in Jesus Christ is not an action representative of reality more generally. See John W. Burbidge, "Hegel's Open Future," in *Hegel and the Tradition: Essays in Honor of H. S. Harris*, ed. Michael Baur and John Russon (Toronto: University of Toronto Press, 1997), pp. 176–78, and *Hegel on Logic and Religion: The Reasonableness of Christianity* (Albany: State University of New York Press, 1992), pp. 4–7, 132–38. Going further than Burbidge's reading, I agree with Hodgson's critique of Hegel, that although the need for a sensible presence of reconciliation in a historical person is persuasively argued by Hegel, there's no logical necessity that the savior has to be a single person and not a plurality of savior figures. Peter C. Hodgson, *Hegel and Christian Theology: A Reading of the Lectures on the Philosophy of Religion* (New York: Oxford University Press, 2005), pp. 161–62.

60. *LPR*, 3:163.
61. *LPR*, 1:116; *LPR*, 3:163–65. See also *LPR*, 3:61–62, 249–51. For Hegel's discussion of doctrine and cultic practice, see *LPR*, 3:150–53, 233–36, 333–39.
62. *LPR*, 1:250 n. 3. See also *LPR*, 3:233: "Spirit is an eternal process of self-cognition in self-consciousness, streaming out to the finite focus of finite consciousness, and then returning to what spirit actually is, a return in which *divine* self-consciousness breaks forth. The community is an eternal process of becoming." In the *Encyclopedia* chapter on absolute spirit Hegel discusses atheism, pantheism, and panentheism and carefully locates his own position in the last option: "God is only God to the extent that God knows godself; God's self-knowing is, further, a self-consciousness in humanity and humanity's knowledge *of* God, which proceeds to humanity's self-knowing *in* God" (§564R). See also *LPR*, 3:62, 170; *LPR*, 1:186–87.
63. *LPR*, 1:325.
64. See also *Enc.*, §20R. The term *übergreifen* is synonymous with what is arguably the most (in)famous term in Hegel's philosophical vocabulary, *aufheben*, usually translated "sublate." Meaning both "preserve" and "supersede" (or "encompass" and "transcend"), logically it corresponds to the notion of "determinate negation," which is a type of negation in which what is negated conditions that which negates, and in so doing leaves its "imprint" on the latter—i.e., is preserved in the latter—while being superseded. See *SL*, pp. 106–8.
65. *LPR*, 1:317–18; *Enc.*, §554. The opposite of the affirmative relation of the finite to the infinite is either the negative infinite which opposes and annihilates the finite or the affirmative finite which insists on its own subsistence independent of the infinite. See *SL*, pp. 143–50. Dale Schlitt phrases this relationship as "inclusive divine subjectivity." Dale M. Schlitt, *Divine Subjectivity: Understanding Hegel's Philosophy of Religion* (Scranton, Penn.: University of Scranton Press, 1990), p. xiv.

66. *LPR*, 1:130, 341–42; *LPR*, 3:220.
67. *LPR*, 1:84.
68. *LPR*, 3:109.
69. *LPR*, 3:138–39.
70. *LPR*, 3:135.
71. John Milbank makes a similar observation regarding Hegel, detecting in him the motif of *Chaoskampf*, but he regards it as a purely pagan motif that has nothing to do with what in his view is the orthodox Christian vision of the originally perfect peace and harmony of creation (John Milbank, *Theology and Social Theory: Beyond Secular Reason* [Oxford: Blackwell, 1990], pp. 157–60). Yet given the deep and pervasive—albeit suppressed—undercurrent of this theme present in the Christian tradition right from the book of Genesis on, as pointed out by feminist theologians, notably Catherine Keller, it is more appropriate to see this theme as a legitimate subject of intra-Christian dialogue and debate, especially in the light of the tradition's patriarchal past and present. See Catherine Keller, *Face of the Deep: A Theology of Becoming* (London: Routledge, 2003).
72. For the evaluative and ethical—and not merely theoretical—character of Hegel's view of nature, see Alison Stone, "Ethical Implications of Hegel's Philosophy of Nature," *British Journal for the History of Philosophy* 10, no. 2 (2002): 243–60.
73. Although nature prevents finite spirit from collapsing into undialectical unity with the pure rationality of the logical idea, the teleology of spirit present in nature, especially when coupled with his logical definition of nature as a realm of difference, particularity, and mutual externality, renders his thinking more anthropocentric and logocentric than it needs to be.
74. The centrality of the natural will to the rule of recognition is perhaps nowhere more evident than in Hegel's famous account of mutual recognition in *Phenomenology of Spirit* and also in the alternate account found in the Phenomenology section of the *Encyclopedia*, where he categorically rejects relations of domination among human beings. According to these accounts, the freedom of subjectivity consists in the activity of self-consciousness that achieves reconciliation with its other by finding itself and returning to itself in the latter (*PhS*, pp. 104–5; *Enc.*, §§424–25). But the act of possession, by which I as a desiring subject negate the otherness of external things and assimilate them to myself in order to satisfy my needs and desires, cannot provide me with a genuine sense of freedom for two reasons. First, the immediate satisfaction of my desire by means of external things, as in the case of direct seizure and consumption, annihilates in the moment of satisfaction the very condition of my self-certainty regarding my freedom, that is, the independence of the other whom I overcome to express my freedom. The transient nature of the certainty of my freedom in this case thus gives rise to another desire seeking another object to satisfy it, resulting in an endless alternation of desire and satisfaction (*PhS*, pp. 109; *Enc.*, §§427–28, 428A). Second, even when my satisfaction consists—as in the case of labor and signification—in transforming the other into a more-or-less enduring testimony to my freedom by "imprinting" my will on it without destroying its independent physical subsistence, its seeming independence is merely a façade, because it has acquired the content of my will as its substantial determination and has become a dependent being. As such, this mode of satisfaction raises questions as to how infinite and boundless my freedom can truly be when proven against such a dependent object,

and all the more so since the object's total submission to my interest and end fails to demonstrate that I have freed myself from my self-centered natural will and existence in deference to other ends (*PhS*, p. 119). The content of my will that the product of my labor or signification acquires as its own determination and end may well be purely subjective and particular interests of my own at odds with the interests and ends of other subjects like me, and therefore contradicting the universal and infinite aspiration of freedom as such. Consequently, in order for me to be able to prove my freedom with certainty, the other in which I attempt to find myself must be another independently existing subject who would willingly subordinate rather than oppose his own desire, interest, and activity to mine and, by doing so, affirm my will as the universal will and recognize me as the one who is truly, infinitely, and boundlessly free (*PhS*, pp. 109–10; *Enc.*, §429, 429A). Yet an interhuman relation defined by unidirectional subordination and recognition, as in the case of a master-slave relation, can neither serve as a site of genuine freedom nor sustain itself for long. First of all, in the master-slave relation the certainty of the master's freedom rests precariously on the dubious recognition given by the slave whose will has been suppressed and made dependent on the master's, and thus differs not really from the ambiguous sense of freedom gained by imprinting one's will on things. By contrast, through his—albeit forced—self-suppression and labor of inscribing his master's will on things, the slave comes eventually to rediscover himself as an implicitly independent subject who could just as well stamp his own will on things instead of his master's (*PhS*, pp. 115–19; *Enc.*, §§433A, 435, 435A; G. W. F. Hegel, *Vorlesungen über die Philosophie des Geistes: Berlin 1827/1828*, ed. Franz Hespe and Burkhard Tuschling [Hamburg: F. Meiner, 1994], pp. 171–73 [hereafter cited as *VPG*]). The "reversal" that happens here is, however, not in and of itself a sufficient condition of genuine freedom, since the emergence of the slave's self-awareness as a free subject is based solely on his formative activity and the uncertain sense of freedom accompanying it. However much he may have suppressed his natural will under the master's harsh yoke, that was merely a temporary replacement of one self-centered will (the slave's) by another self-centered will (the master's), and therefore no sure sign of his ethical self-transcendence toward what is universal (*PhS*, p. 119, *Enc.*, §§433A, 435A). Thus, even with the slave's liberation from the master, we are left only with that same inadequate sense of freedom gained by imposing one's—more than likely self-centered—will on the other, whether the other be a human being or a thing, whether the work of imprinting one's selfish will be mediated (master) or direct (slave). The only viable way of securing the freedom of the subject, then, lies in an interhuman relationship of reciprocal subordination and mutual recognition: a relationship in which two subjects knowingly and willingly submit their freedom to each other and, precisely in doing so, gain it back from each other with a certainty of one's liberation from the selfish natural will (*PhS*, pp. 111–12; *Enc.*, §436, 436R). Hegel's phenomenological account of mutual recognition is meant to show that the notion of self-determining subjectivity grounded in a stance of self-serving domination of the other is ultimately self-defeating. The institutions of mutual recognition presented in his theory of the modern state are in fact meant to be the product of a long historical struggle of humanity to come to learn that truth (*Enc.*, §§432A, 436A; *VPG*, pp. 169–71).

75. For Hegel, Africa does not even belong to this developmental history of cultures, being completely immersed in nature. G. W. F. Hegel, *Lectures on the Philosophy of World*

*History: Introduction: Reason in History*, trans. H. B. Nisbet with an introduction by Duncan Forbes (Cambridge: Cambridge University Press, 1975), pp. 173–90 (hereafter cited as *LPH*).

76. *LPH*, pp. 130, 144–45, 196–202; G. W. F. Hegel, *Lectures on the Philosophy of Religion*, ed. Peter C. Hodgson, trans. R. Brown, P. Hodgson, and J. Stewart, with the assistance of J. P. Fitzer and H. S. Harris, vol. 2, *Determinate Religion* (Berkeley: University of California Press, 1987), pp. 521–639 (hereafter cited as *LPR*, 2). In his last philosophy of religion lectures (1831) Hegel revises his position on the Oriental religions to recognize more developed spirituality in them. Here they are no longer nature religions providing immediate unity of the divine and the human, but religions in which human consciousness experiences internal ruptures (*LPR*, 2:725–36).
77. Nature religions do not worship nature or its forces and things (understood as prosaic), but rather the spiritual power hidden behind them and capable of appearing through them to manifest itself, evoking fear, presentiment, and yearning (for unity) in the minds of human beings who are not yet aware of themselves as free. See Philippe Soual, "Le Dieu inconnu de la religion de la nature chez Hegel," *Les Études philosophiques*, no. 2 (1999): 211–12.
78. For Hegel's exclusion of women from the public, represented by civil society (the sphere of particularity) and the state (the sphere of concrete universality), and his confinement of them to the ahistorical and natural immediacy of the family (which evinces a logic of domination entrenched in his logic of freedom, as I shall later argue), see Luce Irigaray, "The Eternal Irony of the Community," in *Feminist Interpretations of G. W. F. Hegel*, ed. Patricia Jagentowicz Mills (University Park: Pennsylvania State University Press, 1996), pp. 45–57, and Patricia Jagentowicz Mills, "Hegel's Antigone," *Owl of Minerva* 17, no. 2 (1986): 131–52.
79. For the exclusionary character of Hegel's social philosophy, see Raymond Plant, "Hegel on Identity and Legitimation," in *The State and Civil Society: Studies in Hegel's Philosophy*, ed. Z. A. Pelczynski (Cambridge: Cambridge University Press, 1984), pp. 239–43; Bernard Cullen, *Hegel's Social and Political Thought* (New York: St. Martin's Press, 1979), pp. 85–96. Certainly Hegel does not advocate any parochial understanding of human freedom, since for him every human being is a *Geist* and therefore inherently free. Although his account of women as confined to the family and description of non-European nations and cultures as lacking in freedom may evince the cultural prejudices he shared with his contemporaries, he never condones patriarchy, slavery, and colonialism as a matter of principle. My argument is only that in his conception of mutual recognition the underlying logic of nonmutuality and domination vis-à-vis nature makes it difficult to realize the logic of reciprocity and intersubjectivity to its fullest, universal extent as regards humanity. The erosion of the latter by the former is the theme first articulated by Theodore W. Adorno and Max Horkheimer and developed fully by Jürgen Habermas in his notion of the encroachment of the instrumental rationality of the "system" (i.e., the market and the bureaucratic state) on the intersubjective, communicative rationality of the lifeworld. See Jürgen Habermas, *Theory of Communicative Action*, trans. Thomas McCarthy, 2 vols. (Boston: Beacon Press, 1984–87).
80. This is an elaboration of the definition of freedom in terms of *bei sich selbst* (*sein*) found in Hegel's *Philosophy of Right*. G. W. F. Hegel, *Elements of the Philosophy of Right*, ed.

Allen W. Wood, trans. H. B. Nisbet (Cambridge: Cambridge University Press, 1991), §23 (hereafter cited as *PR*). See also *PR* §7A. Allen Wood phrases it as "being with oneself in an other" (*Beisichselbstsein in einem Andern*) (*PR*, p. xii).

81. I borrow the term "archeoteleological" from Cyril O'Regan. Cyril O'Regan, "Hegelian Philosophy of Religion and Eckhartian Mysticism," in *New Perspectives on Hegel's Philosophy of Religion*, ed. David Kolb (Albany: State University of New York Press, 1992), p. 124. O'Regan uses the term to refer to the "pure kataphaticism" of Hegel's "mystical" or speculative interpretation of the Christian God by means of which he attacked the Romantic Intuitionists (Jacobi, Schelling, Schleiermacher) for denying knowledge of God and betraying what he considered to be the core insight of the originary Christianity contained in Paul's preaching of Jesus Christ as the open secret of God (pp. 119–21). I think O'Regan's use of the term has a point in that, insofar as the logical idea—at the end of *SL*—is the unconditioned, fully self-determining *thought*, there is an intrinsic teleology within the divine to become fully self-determining in the sense of self-clarity and self-transparency. As a consequence, while the logical idea as self-determining thought is bound also to think and determine its other as non-ideal and non-self-determining, that is, as externality, contingency, givenness, and immediacy (see William Maker, "The Very Idea of the Idea of Nature, or Why Hegel Is Not an Idealist," in *Hegel and the Philosophy of Nature*, ed. Stephen Houlgate. [Albany: State University of New York Press, 1998], pp. 8–17), once the other is released as nature and finite spirit, the divine idea's teleology toward full self-clarity overrides its releasement of externality, contingency, and immediacy *as* externality, contingency, and immediacy. This means that the divine idea in nature and finite spirit exhibits a drive toward forming knowingly and willingly achieved—human—concrete unities which, by effectively containing nature's contingency via human action, reduce nature's immediate unities to the material out of which history is made, on the one hand, and to some essential characteristics suitable to be objects of scientific concepts, on the other.

82. Of the three forms of mediation or "syllogism" among the logical Idea, nature, and (finite) spirit, Hegel's predominant perspective, which is reflected in the order of his philosophical system, is the "natural" mediation in which nature functions only as the mean (but not the principle) by which the logical Idea achieves its embodied spirituality. What the overreaching spiritual power of Reason as genuine thinking discloses and confirms, by contrast, is the overarching presence of the same divine logical Idea in both nature and spirit—though in relatively inadequate shapes in the former—mediating between them and reconciling them to each other (*Enc.*, §§245, 245A, 246A). This represents the "logical" mediation, outlined in the last sections of *Encyclopedia* (§§575–77), in which the logical Idea is both the mean and the principle of mediation, although the second, "spiritual" mediation (in which finite spirit is the mean but not the principle of mediation) is also involved insofar as the human *recognition* of the logical idea in nature—i.e., nature's elevation to its essence—is concerned. Although the "natural" mediation has a tendency to instrumentalize nature, the other two forms of mediation provide resources for rethinking Hegel's human-centered logic of freedom. One other thing to note, in addition, is that my argument follows the "middle" Hegelians to read Hegel's triple mediation as having the logical idea as the principle of mediation throughout, while nature, spirit, and the logical idea take turns to assume the mean (the middle,

mediating position) of mediation. As Hodgson clearly shows ("Alienation and Reconciliation," 60–63), the left-wing interpreters of Hegel make either nature (naturalism and materialism) or finite spirit (humanistic subjectivism) the principle of mediation, whereas the right-wing interpreters, for whom the only principle of mediation is the logical idea, downplay the independent reality of nature and finite spirit, and reify the logical idea into an ontologically self-sufficient, transcendent realm in which nature and finite spirit participate (a panlogicist transcendent metaphysics or theistic pantheism). See also Emil L. Fackenheim, *The Religious Dimension of Hegel's Thought* (Bloomington: Indiana University Press, 1967), pp. 77–108; Georgi di Giovanni, "On the Impotence of Spirit: Profane Reflections on Hegel's Philosophy of History," in *History and System: Hegel's Philosophy of History*, ed. Robert L. Perkins (Albany: State University of New York Press, 1984), pp. 195–98. Georgi di Giovanni takes Hegel to task for the fact that, in the triple mediation of his system, although the logical Idea overreaches both nature and finite spirit, and finite spirit nature, nature qua nature exercises no overreaching function. For a more balanced system, Giovanni suggests that the mediating logic be amended to enable finite spirit to let nature *as* nature also enter the process of mediation, and not only as it has been transformed by human thought and action into the material of history and the category of thought. The way to do this, he claims, is that human beings manifest in their own actions the presence of nature as nature with all its externality and contingency, even if that would certainly entail a certain sense of natural limitation and impotence, and resist the temptation to define in a univocal sense different forms of rationality and freedom found in all aspects of experience (pp. 199–209). I think Giovanni's is a profound insight: By letting our thinking and practice shaped by the imperatives of our embodiment and our dependence on the physical and biological environment, we will be enabled to see the contingently, fragmentarily, and spontaneously achieved concrete harmonies of nature not as prefigurations of our self-present and self-determining (inter)subjectivity, but as adequate realizations of the trinitarian logic in which we as embodied creatures participate only imperfectly, owing to our will to knowledge and power. In other words, by understanding ourselves as "pre-nature," i.e., imperfectly embodied beings that still need to fulfill our telos in nature's ecological harmonies, we can let nature overreach us and in so doing raise us to our essence in the divine Idea.

83. In fact, persuasive cases have been made—mainly based on his *Lectures on the Philosophy of Religion*—for the existence of a latent typological scheme of religious and cultural differences in Hegel's system despite his unsuccessful effort to create a developmental, supersessionist narrative. See Walter Jaeschke, *Reason in Religion: The Foundations of Hegel's Philosophy of Religion*, trans. J. Michael Stewart and Peter C. Hodgson (Berkeley: University of California Press, 1990), pp. 272–87, and Peter C. Hodgson, "Logic, History, and Alternative Paradigms in Hegel's Interpretation of the Religions," *Journal of Religion* 68, no. 1 (1988): 1–20. As David Kolb reminds us, however, for such an "open" Hegelianism to succeed, the idea of determinate negation, by means of which Hegel constructs his developmental narrative, must cease to apply to history (David Kolb, "The Final Name of God," in *Hegel and the Tradition: Essays in Honor of H. S. Harris*, ed. Michael Baur and John Russon, [Toronto: University of Toronto Press, 1997], pp. 169–70).

84. *PhS*, p. 493.

### 6. *Pattern and Psychophysical Energy Are Equally Actual: The Empathetic Plurisingularity of the Great Ultimate in Nongmun's Thought*

This chapter is a heavily revised and expanded version of an essay to be published as "The Heart-Mind of the Way and the Human Heart-Mind are Non-Dual: A Reflection on the Neo-Confucian 'Panentheism' of Zhu Xi and Nongmun," in *Panentheism in the World Religions*, ed. Loriliai Biernacki and Philip Clayton (New York: Oxford University Press, forthcoming).

1. Yi I, "Dap Seong Ho-won [Reply to Seong Ho-won]," in Yi I, *Gugyeok Yulgok Jeonseo* [Complete translated works of Yulgok], ed. Hanguk jeongsin munhwa yeon-guwon jaryo josasil. 7 vols. (Gyeonggi-do Seongnam-si: Hanguk jeongsin munhwa yeon-guwon, 1984–88), III, 10.25a, p. 32 (hereafter *Jeonseo*—for citations from *Jeonseo*, I give the volume number in roman numerals, the book number and the page number in the traditional format, and then the page number in the modern pagination). For this particular phrase, I am using Michael Kalton's translation found in *The Four-Seven Debate*, p. 174.
2. Yi I, "Dap Seong Ho-won [Reply to Seong Ho-won]," in *Jeonseo*, III, 10.25a, p. 32; 20.21b, p. 30.
3. Yi I, "Dap Seong Ho-won," in *Jeonseo*, III, 10.2b, p. 21; 20.21b, p. 30. See also "Seonghak Jibyo [The essentials of the sagely learning)," in *Jeonseo*, V, 20.59b–60a, p. 40–41.
4. Yi I, "Dap Seong Ho-Won," in *Jeonseo*, III, 10.26a–b, p. 33.
5. Yi I, "Dap Seong Ho-Won," in *Jeonseo*, III, 9.39a–b, p. 19.
6. Yi I, "Dap Seong Ho-Won," in *Jeonseo*, III, 10.40a, p. 40; 10.3a, p. 21.
7. Seo Gyeong-deok, "Woligi [On original pattern and psychophysical energy]," in *Gugyeok Hwadamjip* [Collected works of Hwdam, translated], trans. Hwang Gwang-uk (Seoul: Simsan Munhwa, 2004), p. 190; "Ligiseol [Discourse on pattern and psychophysical energy]," in *Gugyeok Hwadamjip*, p. 202. Following Zhang Zai, Hwadam calls the One Psychophysical Energy also "the Great Void" (太虛 *taeheo/taixu*). See "Taeheoseol [Discourse on the Great Void]," in *Gugyeok Hwadamjip*, p. 200. I capitalize the words "One Psychophysical Energy" because Hwadam understands 一氣 (*ilgi*) as the ultimate creative ground of the cosmos, in contrast to the dominant usage of the term within the Confucian and Daoist traditions.
8. Seo Gyeong-deok, "Gwisin sasaengron [Treatise on the life and death of spirits]," *Gugyeok Hwadamjip*, p. 192.
9. Seo Gyeong-deok, "Gwisin sasaengron," *Gugyeok Hwadamjip*, p. 204. Yi I, "Dap Seong Ho-Won," in *Jeonseo*, III, 10.26a–b, p. 33; 10.37b–38a, pp. 38–39.
10. I am using Michael Kalton's translation in *The Four-Seven Debate: An Annotated Translation of the Most Famous Controversy in Korean Neo-Confucian Thought*, trans. Michael C. Kalton et al. (Albany: State University of New York Press, 1994), p. 176.
11. In fact Yulgok rejects the idea that psychophysical energy in its original condition of translucent unity and clear emptiness somehow transcends the cosmic psychophysical energy in its binary modes of receptive and active. For him, Hwadam's One Psychophysical Energy at the beginning of all thing-events is no other than the receptive psychophysical energy left over from the previous cosmic epoch. In other words, he does not accept the idea that psychophysical energy has a temporal beginning, and that what lies at the cosmic beginning is some kind of metaphysical One Psychophysical Energy

beyond *eum* and *yang* (Yi I, "Dap Bak Hwa-suk [Reply to Bak Hwa-suk]," in *Jeonseo*, III, 9.17a–b, p. 8). For Yulgok, the ground and beginning of the cosmos is pattern, that is, the Great Ultimate, whose "logic" consists in ceaseless alternations of the receptive and the active. Because the Great Ultimate is never without psychophysical energy as its "mount," there are always corresponding alternations of the receptive psychophysical energy and the active psychophysical energy. At the beginning of the cosmos, the Great Ultimate is in its receptive phase, which means that the cosmic psychophysical energy is receptive and quiescent without any activity yet emerging. Psychophysical energy in its original condition of translucent unity and clear emptiness designates this initial utter receptivity of psychophysical energy. The phrase "empty and tranquil, and without any sign," therefore, refers to the Great Ultimate in abstraction from psychophysical energy. Concretely speaking, "all figures" are always already present within the Great Ultimate, because the Great Ultimate is always with psychophysical energy in its binary modes. Yi I, "Dap Bak Hwa-suk," in *Jeonseo*, III, 9.17b–19b, pp. 8–9.

12. Yi I, "Dap Bak Hwa-suk," in *Jeonseo*, III, 9.19b–20a, pp. 9–10.
13. Yi I, "Dap Seong Ho-Won," in *Jeonseo*, III, 10.2b, p. 21. Yulgok does note that, since pattern is the "governing" principle of psychophysical energy, the production of differences can be ascribed to pattern also, not only to psychophysical energy. But he also makes it clear that without the One Pattern "mounting" psychophysical energy there would not be any production of differences.
14. Yi I, "Dap Seong Ho-Won," in *Jeonseo*, III, 10.28a, p. 34.
15. For the following discussion of the *horak* debate, I am indebted to Choe Yeong-jin Choe, "18–19 segi joseon seongnihagui simhakhwa gyeonghyang-e daehan gochal" [An examination of the tendency toward the learning of the heart-mind from eighteenth- to nineteenth-century Korean Neo-Confucianism], *Han-guk Minjok Munhwa* 33, no. 3 (2009): 339–68.
16. Im Seong-ju, "Dap Yi Baeng-nul [Reply to Yi Baeng-nul]," in Im Seong-ju (Nongmun), *Nongmunjip* [Collected works of Nongmun], ed. Minjok munhwa chujinhoe (Seoul: Gyeongin munhwasa, 2001), 5.6a, p. 91 (hereafter *Nongmunjip*—for citations from *Nongmunjip*, I give the book number and the page number in the traditional format, and then the page number in the modern pagination). See also 5.22b–23a, pp. 99–100.
17. Im Seong-ju, "Dap Gwon Saeng-gyeong (Reply to Gwon Saeng-gyeong)," in *Nongmunjip*, 9.37a, p. 191; "Dap Kim Baek-go [Reply to Kim Baek-go]," in *Nongmunjip*, 6.12b, p. 112.
18. For further analysis of Nongmun's parallel and "dipolar" construction of the pattern-psychophysical energy relation, see Son Heung-cheol, *Nongmun Im Seong-ju-ui sarmgwa cheorak* [A Study of Nongmun Im Seong-ju's life and his philosophy] (Seoul: Jisik Saneopsa, 2004), p. 443. See also Hong Jeong-geun, "Im Seong-juwa Na Heum-sun hakseorui daebijeok gochal [A comparative examination of the theories of Im Seong-ju and Na Heum-sun]," *Yugyo Sasang Yeongu* 18 (2003): 97.
19. Im Seong-ju "Nongryeo japji [Miscellaneous writings from the Deer Hut]," in *Nongmunjip*, 19.6b–7a, pp. 385–86; 19.24a–b, p. 394.
20. Im Seong-ju, "Dap Yi Baeng-nul [Reply to Yi Baeng-nul]," in *Nongmunjip*, 5.7a–b, p. 92. See also "Nongryeo japji," in *Nongmunjip*, 19.3a, p. 384; 19.6a–b, p. 385.
21. Im Seong-ju, "Nongryeo japji," in *Nongmunjip*, 19.7a–b, p. 386. See also 19.24b, p. 394; 19.4a, p. 384.

22. Zhang Zai, *Zhengmeng*, in *Zhang Zai ji* [Collected works of Zhang Zai], ed. Zhang Xichen (Beijing: Zhonghua shu ju, 1978), pp. 7, 8, 10, 66. Despite his distinction between original nature ("the nature of heaven and earth") and physical nature, Zhang Zai regards the original substance of psychophysical energy as the ontological ground of the intrinsically good human nature. Kim Hyeon, *Im Seong-juui saeng-ui cheorak* [Im Seong-ju's philosophy of life] (Seoul: Hangil Publishing, 1995), pp. 93, 209. For Nongmun's own acknowledgment of Zhang Zai's influence on him, see "Daehak (Great Learning)," in *Nongmunjip*, 16.2b, p. 328; "Nongryeo japji," in *Nongmunjip*, 19.5b–6a, p. 385. Here I capitalize the words "One Psychophysical Energy" because Zhang Zai, like Hwadam, understands 一氣 (*ilgi*) as the ultimate creative ground of the cosmos, in contrast to the dominant usage of the term within the Confucian and Daoist traditions.
23. Im Seong-ju, "Yeo Yi Baeng-nul [To Yi Baeng-nul]," *Nongmunjip*, 5.7a, p. 92.
24. Cheng Yi's elder brother.
25. Im Seong-ju, "Nongryeo japji," in *Nongmunjip*, 19.3a, p. 384; 19.6b, p. 385; 19.28a, p. 396. For Nongmun's own acknowledgment of the influence of Cheng Hao and Zhu Xi on his notion of "life-giving intention," see 10b–11a, pp. 387–88.
26. Im Seong-ju, "Nongryeo japji," in *Nongmunjip*, 19.24b, p. 394.
27. Im Seong-ju, "Nongryeo japji," in *Nongmunjip*, 19.6b, p. 385.
28. Im Seong-ju, "Nongryeo japji," in *Nongmunjip*, 19.25b, p. 395; 19.14b, p. 389; 19.7b, p. 386. See also "Cha Miho sin-gieum sampyeon [A poem appended to Miho's three songs on spiritual psychophysical energy]," in *Nongmunjip*, 26.12a, p. 549.
29. Im Seong-ju, "Nongryeo japji," in *Nongmunjip*, 19.4a, p. 384.
30. Nongmun inserts a note here: "Being so without anything making it be so refers to the so-called self-so."
31. The concept that appears in the Classic of Change as the source and origin of all life.
32. One of the eight trigrams of the Classic of Change, symbolizing heaven and the male principle in the origination of all things.
33. Im Seong-ju, "Nongryeo japji," in *Nongmunjip*, 19.1a, p. 383.
34. Im Seong-ju, "Dap Yi Baeng-nul," in *Nongmunjip*, 5.5b, p. 91.
35. Im Seong-ju, "Nongryeo japji," in *Nongmunjip*, 19.2b, p. 383. On the same page he says, "From early on I have thought about the meaning of the word 'pattern,' and come to the conclusion that its import is exhausted by the phrase 'self-so.'"
36. Im Seong-ju, "Dap Kim Baek-go," in *Nongmunjip*, 6.6b, p. 109.
37. Im Seong-ju, "Dap Kim Baek-go," in *Nongmunjip*, 6.5b–6a, p. 109.
38. Im Seong-ju, "Dap Kim Baek-go," in *Nongmunjip*, 6.5a–b, p. 109.
39. Im Seong-ju, "Nongryeo japji," in *Nongmunjip*, 19.3a–b, p. 384.
40. Im Seong-ju, "Nongryeo japji," in *Nongmunjip*, 19.3a–3b, p. 384. As is clear by now, Nongmun objects to any way of approaching pattern other than from the perspective of its union with psychophysical energy, with the proviso that the two are seen to completely correspond to each other. Hong, "Im Seong-juwa Na Heum-sun hakseorui daebijeok gochal," pp. 93–96. For the controversy surrounding the monism of psychophysical energy allegedly propounded by Nongmun, see Son, *Nongmun Im Seong-ju-ui sarmgwa cheorak*, pp. 126–28.
41. Im Seong-ju, "Nongryeo japji," in *Nongmunjip*, 19.17a, p. 391.
42. Im Seong-ju, "Nongryeo japji," in *Nongmunjip*, 19.2b, p. 383.

43. Im Seong-ju, "Nongryeo japji," in *Nongmunjip*, 19.5a, p. 385.
44. Im Seong-ju, "Nongryeo japji," in *Nongmunjip*, 19.2a, p. 383.
45. Im Seong-ju, "Dap Bak Yeong-suk [Reply to Bak Yeong-suk]," in *Nongmunjip*, 6.43a, p. 128.
46. Within parentheses are Nongmun's own comments on his text.
47. Im Seong-ju, "Dap Yi Baeng-nul," in *Nongmunjip*, 5.5b, p. 91.
48. The phrase "life-giving mandate" is my own rephrasing of Nongmun's use of the phrase "life-giving pattern" in his earlier years as a parallel—co-extensively and equally actual—concept to the life-giving intention. "Dap Min Seom-chon [Reply to Min Seom-chon]," in *Nongmunjip*, 1.13a–b, p. 14.
49. Im Seong-ju, "Yeo Yi Baeng-nul," in *Nongmunjip*, 5.8b, p. 92. Zhu Xi's original saying is found in "Da Liao Zihui [Reply to Liao Zihui]," in Zhu Xi, *Zhuzi wenji* [Collected literary works of Master Zhu], ed. Chen Junmin (Taibei: Defu wenjiao jijinhui, 2000), 5:2021: "Psychophysical energy that has already dispersed has already changed and no longer exists; but that which roots itself in pattern to emerge daily is truly vast, flood-like and infinite." (Hereafter *Wenji*—for citations from *Wenji*, I give the volume number followed by the page number.)
50. Im Seong-ju, "Dap Yi Baeng-nul," in *Nongmunjip*, 5.19a–b, p. 98.
51. Im Seong-ju, "Nongryeo japji," in *Nongmunjip*, 19.26a–b, p. 395. I use the lower case for the word "pattern" in the phrase "Heavenly pattern [天理*cheolli*]," as Nongmun's reference here is to (Heavenly) pattern in general, not the one (Heavenly) Pattern standing in contrast to many individual patterns and opposing "human desire [人欲 *inyok*]."
52. Neville suggests that the East Asian philosophical traditions have followed what he calls "the way of incipience": "This way involves taking a stand with some immanently defined state of affairs in order to refer to an ontologically more basic state in which the former was incipient. The latter state I call the ontological ground of the former. It has no character except the incipience of, or readiness to give rise to, the immanently defined state" (Robert C. Neville, *Behind the Masks of God: An Essay toward Comparative Theology* [Albany: State University of New York Press, 1991], p. 75). My use of the metaphor of incipience is different from Neville's in that the ontological ground construed as the primordial unity of indeterminate and chaotic multiplicity perhaps sounds more "determinate" than the Nevillian *nihil*.
53. Ibid., p. 76.
54. I am indebted to Catherine Keller for this understanding of ontological "depth" and creativity. See her *Face of the Deep*, p. 226.
55. Im Seong-ju, "Nongryeo japji," in *Nongmunjip*, 19.25b–26a, p. 395.
56. Im Seong-ju, "Nongryeo japji," in *Nongmunjip*, 19.5a, p. 385.
57. Choe, "18–19 segi joseon seongnihagui simhakhwa," pp. 354–56.
58. Im Seong-ju, "Dap Song Yeok-cheon [Reply to Song Yeok-cheon]," in *Nongmunjip*, 3.5a, p. 44.
59. Im Seong-ju, "Dap Gwon Saeng-gyeong," in *Nongmunjip*, 9.37a, p. 191; "Dap Kim Baek-go," in *Nongmunjip*, 6.12b, p. 112. In fact, Nongmun's main theses, "Pattern and psychophysical energy are equally actual [理氣同實 *i gi dong sil*]" and "The heart-mind and the nature completely correspond [to each other] [心性一致 *sim seong il chi*]" were

originally coined by his teacher, Yi gan, to refer to the human heart-mind in its unactivated state in which the psychophysical energy of translucent unity and clear emptiness fully resonates with the original human nature's mandate of empathy and harmony. See Choe, "18–19 segi joseon seongnihagui simhakhwa," p. 352.

60. Im Seong-ju, "Dap Yi Baeng-nul," in *Nongmunjip*, 4.22a–b, p. 73; "Dap Kim Baek-go," in *Nongmunjip*, p. 6.7a, p. 110; "Daehak [Great Learning]," in *Nongmunjip*, 16.3a, p. 329; "Nongryeo japji," in *Nongmunjip*, 19.29b–30a, p. 397.
61. For an interpretation of Toegye's philosophy as a form of idealism, see Yun Sasoon, *Critical Issues in Neo-Confucian Thought: The Philosophy of Yi T'oegye*, trans. Michael C. Kalton (Seoul: Korea University Press, 1990), p. 232. See also Jeon Duha, "Toegye-ui cheoragui haeksim [The heart of T'oegye's philosophy]," *Toegye Hakbo* 19 (December 1978): 135–38.
62. Peter C. Hodgson, *Winds of the Spirit: A Constructive Christian Theology* (Louisville, Ky.: Westminster John Knox Press, 1994), p. 365, n. 5.

## *7. The Chaosmos and the Great Ultimate: A Neo-Confucian Trinity in Conversation with Deleuze and Keller*

1. David R. Griffin, "Some Whiteheadian Comments," in *Mind in Nature: Essays on the Interface of Science and Philosophy*, ed. John B. Cobb and David Ray Griffin (Washington, D.C.: University Press of America, 1977), p. 98.
2. Robert C. Neville, *Behind the Masks of God: An Essay toward Comparative Theology* (Albany: State University of New York Press, 1991), p. 76.
3. The problem of the ontological arbitrariness and irrationality of Whitehead's metaphysical principles—such as the principle of creative advance toward novelty—has been amply criticized by Neville. Robert C. Neville, *Creativity and God: A Challenge to Process Theology* (Albany: State University of New York Press, 1995), pp. 43–44.
4. This phrase was taken from the entry on Deleuze in the *Stanford Encyclopedia of Philosophy* online. Daniel Smith and John Protevi, "Gilles Deleuze," *Stanford Encyclopedia of Philosophy* (Winter 2011), ed. Edward N. Zalta, forthcoming. http://plato.stanford.edu/archives/win2011/entries/deleuze/.
5. This is the core argument about Deleuze's "transcendental empiricism" advanced by Levi R. Bryant's *Difference and Givenness: Deleuze's Transcendental Empiricism and the Ontology of Immanence* (Evanston, Ill.: Northwestern University Press, 2008).
6. Gilles Deleuze, *Difference and Repetition*, trans. Paul Patton (New York: Columbia University Press, 1994), p. 59. See also Gilles Deleuze, *The Logic of Sense*, trans. Mark Lester with Charles Stivale, ed. Constantin V. Boundas (New York: Columbia University Press, 1990), pp. 257–58.
7. Deleuze, *Difference and Repetition*, pp. 66–67; *The Logic of Sense*, p. 253.
8. Deleuze, *Difference and Repetition*, pp. 27, 32, 40.
9. Ibid., p. 64.
10. Ibid., p. 30.
11. Ibid., p. 28.
12. Ibid., pp. 40–41. Deleuze's anti-Hegelianism is shown in his focus on the productivity of the nondialectical ("affirmative") differential forces, which Nietzsche has named "noble."

These forces affirm themselves, and in so doing differentiate themselves first, and only secondarily consider that from which they have differentiated themselves.

13. Ibid., p. 64.
14. The traditional approaches to [Leibnizian] calculus interpret differentials as infinitesimals.
15. These are the four aspects of reason as the medium of representation in terms of which difference is construed: identity in the concept, analogy in judgment, opposition of predicates, and resemblance in perception. Deleuze, *Difference and Repetition*, p. 29. Deleuze took these from Michel Foucault's analysis of classical representationalism. Manuel DeLanda, *Intensive Science and Virtual Philosophy* (London: Continuum, 2002), p. 53, n. 59.
16. Deleuze, *Difference and Repetition*, p. 171.
17. I am indebted to Manuel DeLanda for my analysis of the threefold structure of the Idea. DeLanda, *Intensive Science and Virtual Philosophy*, pp. 79–83.
18. Deleuze, *Difference and Repetition*, p. 172.
19. Ibid., p. 203.
20. For Deleuze's discussion of intensities and extensities, see ibid., pp. 244–47.
21. Ibid., p. 175. See Simon Duffy, "The Mathematics of Deleuze's Differential Logic and Metaphysics," in *Virtual Mathematics: The Logic of Difference,* ed. Simon Duffy (Manchester, UK: Clinamen Press, 2006), pp. 118–44. Singularity refers to singular points a set of which determines the topological space of a given structure. See Daniel W. Smith, "Deleuze's Theory of Sensation: Overcoming the Kantian Duality," in *Deleuze: A Critical Reader*, ed. Paul Patton (Oxford: Blackwell, 1996), p. 52, n. 16.
22. I am indebted to John Protevi for the helpful analogy of water. John Protevi, "Water," in *Rhizomes: Cultural Studies in Emerging Knowledge* 15 (Winter 2007). http://www.rhizomes.net/issue15/protevi.html.
23. DeLanda, *Intensive Science and Virtual Philosophy*, pp. 28–29.
24. Ibid., p. 81. Deleuze speaks of the "condensation" of singularities to refer to their extending themselves into "infinite series of ideal events" (*Difference and Repetition*, p. 190).
25. I am indebted to John Protevi of Louisiana State University for this helpful analogy. John Protevi, "Sports Sunday 6: The Idea of Football," *New APPS: Art, Politics, Philosophy, Science* (September 4, 2011). http://www.newappsblog.com/2011/09/sports-sunday-6-the-idea-of-football.html#more.
26. Deleuze, *Difference and Repetition*, p. 183. Further references to this book in this discussion are given by page number within parentheses in the text.
27. DeLanda, *Intensive Science and Virtual Philosophy*, p. 21.
28. Ibid.: "Individuals are signal-sign systems. All individuality is intensive, and therefore serial, stepped and communicating, comprising and affirming in itself the difference in intensities by which it is constituted. Gilbert Simondon has shown recently that individuation presupposes a prior metastable state—in other words, the existence of a 'disparateness' such as at least two orders of magnitude or two scales of heterogeneous reality between which potentials are distributed. Such a pre-individual state nevertheless does not lack singularities: the distinctive or singular points are defined by the existence and distribution of potentials. An 'objective' problematic field thus appears, determined by the distance between two heterogeneous orders. Individuation emerges like the act of solving such a problem, or—what amounts to the same thing—like the actualization of a

potential and the establishing of communication between disparates. The act of individuation consists not in suppressing the problem, but in integrating the elements of the disparateness into a state of coupling which ensures its internal resonance. The individual thus finds itself attached to a pre-individual half which is not the impersonal within it so much as the reservoir of its singularities. In all these respects, we believe that individuation is essentially intensive, and that the pre-individual field is a virtual-ideal field, made up of differential relations. Individuation is what responds to the question 'Who?', just as the Idea responds to the question 'How much?' and 'How?'"

29. Catherine Keller, "Rumors of Transcendence: The Movement, State, and Sex of 'Beyond,'" in *Transcendence and Beyond: A Postmodern Inquiry*, ed. John D. Caputo and Michael J. Scanlon (Bloomington: Indiana University Press, 2007), p. 143.
30. A slightly modified version of the title of Alphonso Lingis's book, *The Community of Those Who Have Nothing in Common* (Bloomington: Indiana University Press, 2007).
31. Gilles Deleuze, *The Fold: Leibniz and the Baroque*, trans. Tom Conley (Minneapolis: University of Minnesota Press, 1993), p. 81.
32. Deleuze, *Difference and Repetition*, p. 119. For the schizophrenia of Deleuze's God (or gods), see Tim Clark, "A Whiteheadian Chaosmos? Process Philosophy from a Deleuzean Perspective," in *Process and Difference: Between Cosmological and Poststructuralist Postmodernists*, ed. Catherine Keller and Anne Daniell (Albany: State University of New York Press, 2002), p. 204.
33. Deleuze, *Difference and Repetition*, p. 210.
34. Roland Faber, *God as the Poet of the World*, trans. Douglas W. Stott (Louisville, Ky.: Westminster John Knox Press, 2008), p. 83.
35. Deleuze, *Difference and Repetition*, p. 210.
36. Ibid., p. 43.
37. Faber, *God as the Poet of the World*, p. 82.
38. Deleuze, *Difference and Repetition*, p. 283.
39. Faber, *God as the Poet of the World*,p. 83.
40. Im Seong-ju, "Yeo Yi Baeng-nul," in Im Seong-ju (Nongmun), *Nongmunjip* [Collected works of Nongmun], ed. Minjok munhwa chujinhoe (Seoul: Gyeongin munhwasa, 2001), 5.8b, p. 92 (for citations from *Nongmunjip*, I give the book number and the page number in the traditional format, and then the page number in the modern pagination).
41. Yi I, "Yeoksu-chaek [A presentation of the regularity of change]," in Yi I, *Gugyeok Yulgok Jeonseo* [Complete translated works of Yulgok], ed. Hanguk jeongsin munhwa yeon-guwon jaryo josasil. 7 vols. (Gyeonggi-do Seongnam-si: Hanguk jeongsin munhwa yeon-guwon, 1984–88), IV, 14.48a–b, p. 15 (hereafter *Jeonseo*—for citations from *Jeonseo*, I give the volume number in roman numerals, the book number and the page number in the traditional format, and then the page number in the modern pagination). Cheng Hao's original formulation is: "The doings of High Heaven are without any sound or smell. Its substance is called Change; its pattern is called the Way; and its function is called Spirit." *Er Cheng ji*, 1:4. I thank Professor Young-Chan Ro for alerting me to Yulgok's triadic conception of the structure of the Great Ultimate, although our interpretations diverge from each other somewhat. See his *The Korean Neo-Confucianism of Yi Yulgok* (Albany: State University of New York Press, 1989), pp. 30–31.
42. Yi I, "Seonghak Jibyo [The essentials of the sagely learning]," in *Jeonseo*, V, 20.60a–b, p. 41.

43. Catherine Keller, *Face of the Deep: A Theology of Becoming* (London: Routledge, 2003), p. 189. Further references to this book in this discussion are given by page number within parentheses in the text.
44. Ibid., p. 226: "The tehomic deity remains enmeshed in the vulnerabilities and potentialities of an indeterminate creativity. As Tehom it *is* that process; as deity it is *born from and suckles* that process."
45. Neville, *Behind the Masks*, p. 75.
46. Ibid., p. 76.
47. Ibid., pp. 13–17.
48. Ibid., p. 15.
49. For a more detailed articulation of this see Robert C. Neville, *Recovery of Measure: Interpretation and Nature* (Albany: State University of New York Press, 1989), pp. 95–115.
50. See ibid., p. 125.
51. Neville, *Behind the Masks*, pp. 17–21.
52. Ibid., pp. 2, 16.
53. Robert C. Neville, "Daoist Relativism, Ethical Choice, and Normative Measure," *Journal of Chinese Philosophy* 29, no. 1 (2002): 9.
54. Ibid., pp. 9–11.
55. Keller, *Face of the Deep*, p. 226.

## *8. The Democracy of Numinous Spirits: The Panentheism of "Subaltern" Ultimate Energy in Donghak*

1. Although there exist two variants of the original Korean word used by the practitioners of Donghak for Lord Heaven, 하늘님 (*haneullim*) and 한울님 (*hanullim*), it is likely that the former is the oldest and original form. Kim Yong-hwi, "Su-un Choe Je-uui si-cheonju sasang: cheon-gwaneul jungsimeuro [Su-un Choe Je-u's notion of *Si-cheonju*: Around his view of heaven]," in *Han-gugui sasang-ga sibin*, Su-un Choe Je-u [Ten Korean thinkers: Su-un Choe Je-u], ed. Oh Mun-hwan (Seoul: Yemun seowon, 2005), p. 103 n. 1.
2. The traditional rendition of the title *Yongdam yusa* in classical Chinese is 龍潭遺詞, meaning "the songs left by Master Dragon Pond," the Dragon Pond being the dwelling place of Su-un and thus his alias. Seok-san Yun, trans., *Yongdam yusa* [Seoul: Donghaksa, 1999], pp. 257-58). I am, however, persuaded by Kim Yong-ok that the correct rendition is 龍潭諭詞, of the same phonetic value but meaning "the instructional songs from the Dragon Pond," given Su-un's original purpose of composing the songs in vernacular Korean to instruct the common people who could not read classical Chinese as the literary language of the elites. Kim Yong-ok, trans. with commentary, *Do-ol simdeuk dong-gyeong daejeon: pletharchia-ui sinsegye* [The complete scriptures of Eastern Learning as grasped by Do-ol: The new world of Pletharchia] (Seoul: Tongnamu, 2004), 1:223–25. For citations from *Dong-gyeong daejeon* and *Yongdam yusa* I am using *Cheondogyo gyeongjeon* [Cheondogyo scriptures], ed. Chondogyo jung-ang chongbu (Seoul: Cheondogyo jung-ang chongbu chulpanbu, 1988). I will give the book title followed by the verse number(s) preceded by the abbreviation v. or vv. When verse numbers are not available, I will give page numbers.
3. Neither the Korean original for Lord Heaven, 하늘님 (*haneullim*), nor its equivalent Chinese word 天主 (*cheonju*), is gendered. Here I use both "he" and "she" interchangeably,

as befitting Su-un's own explanation of the term "Lord" (*nim* or *ju*) as the honorific suffix of respect given to one's father and mother.

4. For the title 上帝 (*sangje*), see *Yongdam yusa*, "Ansimga [Songs to comfort the heart-mind]," v. 4; *Dong-gyeong daejeon*, "Podeongmun," v. 6. For the title 하늘님 (*haneullim*), see *Yongdam yusa*, "Yongdamga [Songs from the Dragon Pond]," v. 3. For the tile 天主 (*cheonju*), see *Dong-gyeong daejeon*, "Nonhangmun," vv. 3, 15.
5. *Dong-gyeong daejeon*, "Nonhangmun," v. 6.
6. Geum Jang-tae, *Gwisin-gwa jaesa* [Spirits and the ritual of ancestor veneration] (Seoul: JNC, 2009), pp. 42–53.
7. *Yongdam yusa*, "Dodeokga [Songs on way and virtue]," vv. 1, 3. For Su-un's understanding of *gwisin*, see Yong-hwi Kim, "Su-un Choe Je-uui si-cheonju sasang," pp. 118–22.
8. An Yeong-sang, "Joseon hugi sasangsa-e natanan jeoldaejawa gaeinui gwan-gye yangsang-ui ildanmyeon: Donghagui seongrihak jeok geun-georeul jungsimeuro [A cross-section of the features of the relationship between the absolute and the individual as manifest in the intellectual history of the late Joseon Dynasty: Around the Neo-Confucian basis of Donghak]," *Hanguk sasang-gwa munhwa* 33 (2006): 256–67.
9. Ibid., 244–56. For Su-un's Confucian and Neo-Confucian heritage, see Pak Gyeong-hwan, "Donghak-gwa yuhak sasang [Donghak and Confucian thought]," in *Donghak-gwa jeontong sasang* [Donghak and traditional thought], ed. Donghak hakhoe (Seoul: Mosineun saramdeul, 2005), pp. 77–96; Yun Sasoon, "Donghagui yuhakjeok seongyeok [The Confucian character of Donghak]," in *Donghak sasang-ui saero-un jomeyong* [A new illumination of Donghak thought], ed. Minjok munhwa yeon-guso (Gyeongsan-si, Gyeongsang buk-do: Yeongnam daehakgyo chulpanbu, 1998), pp. 92–108.
10. I use the lower case for the word "pattern" in the phrase "Heavenly pattern [天理 *cheolli*]," as Su-un's reference here is not to the well-known Neo-Confucian notion of the one (Heavenly) Pattern standing in contrast to many individual patterns and opposing "human desire [人欲 *inyok*]." By the words "Heavenly mandate" and "Heavenly pattern," Su-un means the mandate of Lord Heaven and the order created by Lord Heaven, respectively.
11. *Yongdam yusa*, "Gwonhakga," v. 6; *Dong-gyeong daejeon*, "Podeongmun," vv. 3–4; *Dong-gyeong daejeon*, "Sudeokmun [Writings on cultivating virtue]," v. 6.
12. *Dong-gyeong daejeon*, "Sudeokmun," v. 6. For insightful analyses of Su-un's creative retrieval of the classical Confucian worship of Heaven as a personal deity, that is, Lord on High, see Yun Sasoon, "Donghagui yuhakjeok seongyeok," pp. 103–7; Oh Mun-hwan, *Donghagui jeongchi cheorak: dodeok, saengmyeong, gwollyeok* [The political philosophy of Donghak: Morality, life, and power] (Seoul: Mosineun saramdeul, 2003), pp. 97–199. The majority of studies agree that Su-un's theism was influenced by the three religious elements (the ancient Korean indigenous worship of Heaven, the religious undercurrents of classical and Neo-Confucianism, and Roman Catholicism). See, for example, Shin Bok-ryong, *Donghak sasang-gwa gabo nongmin hyeongmyeong* [Donghak thought and the Gabo peasant revolution] (Seoul: Pyeongminsa, 1991), pp. 284–85; Choe Dong-hwi, "Dong-gyeong daejeonui jong-gyo cheorakjeogin ihae [A new religious-philosophical understanding of the complete scripture of Eastern Learning]," in *Donghak-gwa Donghak gyeongjeonui jaeinsik* [A renewed understanding of Donghak and Donghak scriptures], ed. Donghak hakhoe (Seoul: Sinseowon, 2001), pp. 37–44. There has been a

debate on whether the ancient Korean worship of Heaven constituted an earlier indigenous form of "monotheism" before the arrival of Catholic Christianity. The advocates of "Han sasang," translated as "Han-philosophy" or "Hanism," contend that the indigenous Korean spirituality and religious frame of thought before the arrival of Confucianism, Buddhism, and Daoism emphasized the unity of all, as represented by the notion of all-encompassing Heaven (Kim Sang-il, Yi Song-eun, and Oh Gang-nam, eds., *Han sasang-ui i-ron-gwa siljae* [The theory and reality of Han-philosophy] [Seoul: Jisik saneopsa, 1990]). Don Baker is critical of this argument, claiming that the emergence of monotheistic concepts of God on the Korean soil postdated the arrival of Catholic Christianity, and that the Donghak concept of Lord Heaven was the earliest case (Don Baker, *Korean Spirituality* [Honolulu: University of Hawai'i Press, 2008], p. 102). Choe Dong-hwi agrees on this point, contending that, whereas *haneunim* (meaning "Lord Heaven") worshiped by the ancient Korean religious practices was the highest god in the pantheon of many gods, Su-un's Lord Heaven was a monotheistic God ("Dong-gyeong daejeonui jong-gyo cheorakjeogin ihae," p. 37). Kim Kyoung-jae points out, however, that any discussion of the indigenous Korean worship of *haneunim* cannot be fruitful when framed by the Western dualistic categories of (radically immanent) pantheism/polytheism and (radically transcendent) theism/monotheism. Kim proposes that we use the mediating category of panentheism to understand the Donghak concept of God (Kyoung-jae Kim, *I-reum eomneun haneunim: yuilsin sinang-e daehan Kim Kyounng-jae gyosuui bon-gyeok bipan* [God without a name: The principal criticism of monotheism by Professor Kim Kyoung-jae] [Seoul: Samin, 2002], pp. 193–94, 216). I agree—given that Su-un's concept of Lord Heaven defies such binaries as polytheism and monotheism, immanence and transcendence, I believe that Kim's constructive suggestion is the way forward.

13. *Dong-gyeong daejeon*, "Jumun," p. 89.
14. *Dong-gyeong daejeon*, "Nonhangmun," v. 12.
15. Ibid.
16. 靈 (*ryeong/ling*), usually translated as "numinous," is often used interchangeably with 神 (*sin/shen*), "spiritual." Joseph A. Adler, "Varieties of Spiritual Experience: *Shen* in Neo-Confucian Discourse." In *Confucian Spirituality*, ed. Tu Wei-ming and M. E. Tucker (New York: Crossroad, 2004), 2:121–22.
17. For the Daoist (or Seondo-ist) basis of Su-un's notion of Ultimate Energy, see Shin Il-cheol, *Donghak sasang-ui ihae* (Seoul: Sahoe bipyeongsa, 1995), pp. 150–55. For the Neo-Confucian root of the notion of Ultimate Energy, see Pak Gyeong-hwan, "Donghak-gwa yuhak sasang," pp. 78–83.
18. Kim Yong-hwi, "Su-un Choe Je-uui si-cheonju sasang," pp. 112–15. Kim claims that the Ultimate Energy *is* the ultimate reality for Su-un, although in a more religious sense than the Neo-Confucian monism of psychophysical energy. Pak Gyeong-hwan makes a more direct connection between Su-un's Ultimate Energy and the neo-Confucian monism of psychophysical energy. Pak Gyeong-hwan, "Donghak-gwa yuhak sasang," pp. 78–83.
19. Adler, "Varieties of Spiritual Experience," p. 121.
20. *Yongdam yusa*, "Gyohun-ga [Songs of edifying instruction]," v. 11.
21. *Dong-gyeong daejeon*, "Nonhangmun," v. 13.
22. *Dong-gyeong daejeon*, "Jumun," p. 89.

23. *Dong-gyeong daejeon*, "Nonhangmun," v. 8.
24. For example, commenting on Zhou Dunyi's assertion that "[Of all creatures] it is human beings who attain their refinement and thus [are] most numinous," Zhu Xi says: "Because humans beings are endowed with the refinement which they alone have attained, their heart-minds are most numinous." Zhu Xi, *Tushou jie*, p. 5.
25. *Dong-gyeong daejeon*, "Nonhangmun," v. 1.
26. Kim Yong-hwi puts it succinctly in "Su-un Choe Je-uui si-cheonju sasang," p. 115, n. 24: "One could say that the anthropomorphic personification of Ultimate Energy is Lord Heaven, and that the mode of existence of Lord Heaven is Ultimate Energy."
27. See Kim Ji-ha, *Donghak iyagi* [The story of Donghak] (Seoul: Sol), pp. 33–37; *Saengmyeong* [Life] (Seoul: Sol, 1992), pp. 207–8.
28. *Dong-gyeong daejeon*, "Nonhangmun," v. 6. See also verse 14: "The Heavenly heart-mind is the human heart-mind."
29. See also *Yongdam yusa*, "Dosusa [Verses to cultivate the way]," v. 7.
30. Su-un explains the meaning of "becoming without artificial actions" as "the emergence of transformation from the midst of self-so [化出於自然之中 *hwa chureo jayeon ji jung*]." *Dong-gyeong daejeon*, "Nonhangmun": 9. In verse 7, he also summarizes the essence of his Way as "the principle of self-so [自然之理 *jayeon ji ri*]."
31. This interpretation resonates with Oh Mun-hwan's insightful reading of *si-cheonju* as the transformation of the modern—individual—subject into the cosmic self and the consequent overcoming of human alienation from both nature and the divine. Oh Mun-hwan, "'Si-cheonju' jumuneul tonghaeseo bon Su-unui in-gan-gwan [Su-un's view of human being as seen through the 'Si-cheonju' incantation]," in *Han-gugui sasang-ga sibin: Su-un Choe Je-u* [Ten Korean thinkers: Su-un Choe Je-u], ed. Oh Mun-hwan (Seoul: Yemun seowon, 2005), pp. 131–33.
32. This subversion and dismantling of the microcosm/macrocosm dualism, found in Su-un's thought, is given a succinct expression by Kim Kyoung-jae: "The word *gihwa* in the phrase *waeyu gihwa* means that Ultimate Energy, as spiritual and numinous reality, transforms the human body (as a living body) into a spiritual and numinous reality, while at the same time opening it up and organically relating it to the entire cosmic-natural realm of living bodies that surrounds it." Kyoung-jae Kim, "Su-unui si-cheonju cheheom-gwa donghagui sin-gwan [Su-un's experience of *Si-cheonju* and the Donghak view of God]," in *Han-gugui sasang-ga sibin: Su-un Choe Je-u* [Ten Korean thinkers: Su-un Choe Je-u], ed. Oh Mun-hwan (Seoul: Yemun seowon, 2005), p. 89.
33. For the Confucian notions of the superior person and the sage, see *Dong-gyeong daejeon*, "Nonhangmun," v. 13; *Yongdam yusa*, "Gyohun-ga," v. 5, 11; *Yongdam yusa*, "Gwonhakga," v. 5. The Daoist notion of the divine transcendent is found in *Yongdam yusa*, "Gyohun-ga," v. 5; *Dong-gyeong daejeon*, "Tan doyou simgeup [Lamenting the hastiness of the followers of the way]," p. 103; *Dong-gyeong daejeon*, "Gyeol [Words according to Lord Heaven's teaching]," p. 107. I am using Robert Campany's translation of the term 神仙 (*sinseon/shenxian*) as "divine transcendent." Robert Ford Campany, *To Live as Long as Heaven and Earth: A Translation and Study of Ge Hong's Traditions of Divine Transcendents* (Berkeley: University of California Press, 2002).
34. Su-un's affirmation of the traditional Confucian virtues are found in *Dong-gyeong daejeon*, "Sudeokmun," v. 9; *Yongdam yusa*, "Dodeokga," v. 4; *Yongdam yusa*, "Dosusa,"

v. 6. For Su-un's appropriation of the traditional Daoist practices, see *Dong-gyeong daejeon*, "Podeongmun," vv. 6–7; *Dong-gyeong daejeon*, "Sudeokmun," v. 8; *Yongdam yusa*, "Ansimga," vv. 5–7.

35. *Dong-gyeong daejeon*, "Nonhangmun," v. 9; *Yongdam yusa*, "Dodeokga," v. 4.
36. *Dong-gyeong daejeon*, "Nonhangmun," v. 9.
37. The alternative phrasing is found in *Dong-gyeong daejeon*, "Nonhangmun," v. 5, and "Sudeokmun," v. 9. I will not go into the text-critical debates—see Ra Myeong-jae, trans., *Cheondogyo gyeongjeon gongbuhagi* [Studying the scriptures of the religion of the heavenly way] (Seoul: Mosineun saramdeul, 2010), p. 45—favoring one or the other, as I do not see the two divergent expressions as mutually conflicting or contradictory.
38. Oh Mun-hwan makes a similar claim: rectifying psychophysical energy means recovering the original "public" nature of human beings, that is, their original unity with one another and the rest of the cosmos. Oh Mun-hwan, *Haewol Choe Si-hyeong-ui jeongchi sasang* [The political thought of Haewol Choe Si-hyeong] (Seoul: Mosineun saramdeul, 2003), p. 97.
39. *Yongdam yusa*, "Dodeokga," v. 4; *Yongdam yusa*, "Dosusa," v. 2.
40. *Yongdam yusa*, "Gyohun-ga," v. 11.
41. *Dong-gyeong daejeon*, "Jwajam [Proverbial admonitions]," p. 93.
42. *Yongdam yusa*, "Gyohun-ga," v. 11; *Dong-gyeong daejeon*, "Podeongmun," v. 7.
43. *Yongdam yusa*, "Dosusa," v. 8; *Dong-gyeong daejeon*, "Sudeokmun," v. 12; *Dong-gyeong daejeon*, "Jeon Paljeol [The first eight verses]," p. 117. See Pak Gyeong-hwan, "Donghak-gwa yuhak sasang," p. 92. According to Oh Mun-hwan, Su-un overcame the formalized rationality of the traditional neo-Confucian practice of sincerity and reverence with the believing attitude of self-cultivation encapsulated in the practice of *susim jeong-gi*. Oh Mun-hwan, *Donghagui jeongchi cheorak*, p. 109.
44. This is shown in Haewol's teaching of "Three Reverences," which I will discuss shortly.
45. Choe Dong-hwi finds a correspondence between the triad of sincerity, reverence, and trust, and the tripartite division of Su-un's commentary on *si-cheonju* into "having the numinous spirit within," "having the harmonious becoming of psychophysical energy without," and "people each know and do not leave." Choe Dong-hwi, "Dong-gyeong daejeonui jong-gyo cheorakjeogin ihae," p. 48. Although highly interesting, I think Choe's formulation does not highlight the centrality of trust as much as my pairing of both sincerity and reverence with *susim* and *jeong-gi*, respectively, and assigning of trust as the condition of possibility for that whole regimen of self-cultivative practice as such.
46. *Yongdam yusa*, "Dosusa," v. 4; *Yongdam yusa*, "Gyohun-ga," v. 11.
47. Su-un's understanding of "the Learning of the Heart-Mind" (心學 *simhak*) is, however, quite different from the tradition of 心學 (*xinxue*) championed by Lu Xiangshan and Wang Yangming in China, which identified the heart-mind with pattern and emphasized internal self-cultivation while rejecting Zhu Xi's focus on external "investigation of things." For Su-un, the heart-mind is identified with the heart-mind of Lord Heaven beyond the internal/external dichotomy. Oh Mun-hwan, *Donghagui jeongchi cheorak*, pp. 109–17; Kim Chun-seong, "Yongdam yusaui cheorakjeok gochal [Philosophical examination of *Yongdam Yusa*]," in *Donghak-gwa Donghak gyeongjeonui jaeinsik*, [A renewed understanding of Donghak and Donghak scriptures], ed, Donghak hakhoe (Seoul: Sinseowon, 2001), pp. 135–38.

48. Oh Mun-hwan, "Donghagui dodeokjeok pyeongdeung juui," in *Donghak-gwa Donghak gyeongjeonui jaeinsik*, pp. 207–8. Pak Gyeong-hwan claims that at the core of Su-un's egalitarianism lies his monism of psychophysical energy that rejects any form of ontologicaly hierarchy. Pak Gyeong-hwan, "Donghak-gwa yuhak sasang," pp. 78–89, 93–95.
49. *Dong-gyeong daejeon*, "Nonhangmun," v. 14.
50. *Yongdam yusa*, "Gyohun-ga," v. 5; *Yongdam yusa*, "Dodeokga," v. 3; *Yongdam yusa*, "Gwonhakga," v. 5; *Dong-gyeong daejeon*, "Nonhangmun," v. 17. According to Oh Mun-hwan, it is precisely the all-pervasive nature of Ultimate Energy that provides the ontological ground of the egalitarianism of *dong-gwi ilche*. Oh Mun-hwan, "Donghagui dodeokjeok pyeongdeung juui," p. 219.
51. *Yongdam yusa*, "Yongdamga," v. 3; *Yongdam yusa*, "Ansimga," vv. 4, 8; *Yongdam yusa*, "Mongjung noso mundapga [Songs about the conversations by the elderly and the young in a dream]," v. 5. 開闢 (*gaebyeok*) is the abbreviated form of 天開地闢 (*cheon-gae jibyeok*), meaning "the opening of (a new) heaven and (a new) earth."
52. Choe Si-hyeong (Haewol). *Haewol sinsa beopseol* [The sermons of Haewol, the divine teacher], in *Cheondogyo gyeongjeon* [Cheondogyo scriptures], ed. Chondogyo jung-ang chongbu (Seoul: Cheondogyo jung-ang chongbu chulpanbu, 1988), 7:9, 25:1; 7:1; 4:7. For citations from *Haewol sinsa beopseol*, I will give the chapter number followed by the verse number(s).
53. Ibid., 33:3.
54. Ibid., 7:13.
55. Ibid., 2:11; 7:4; 8:9, 12; 10:5.
56. Ibid., 7:17; 10:4.
57. Ibid., 8:12.
58. *Haewol seonsang munjip*, pp. 232–33, quoted in Choe Dong-hwi, "Haeworui jong-gyo sasang-ui daehan ihae [Understanding the religious thought of Haewol]," in *Haewol Choe Si-hyeong-gwa Donghak sasang* [Haewol Choe Si-hyeong and Donghak thought], ed. Busan yesul munhwa daehak donghak yeon-guso (Seoul: Yemun seowon, 1999), p. 83.
59. *Haewol sinsa beopseol*, 21:1–3.
60. Ibid., 24:1.
61. Ibid., 19:1.
62. Ibid., 15:8; 37:7.
63. *Yongdam yusa*, "Gwonhakga," v. 8; *Dong-gyeong daejeon*, "Nonhangmun," v. 9.
64. Oh Mun-hwan, *Donghagui jeongchi cheorak*, pp. 105–6.
65. Raimon Panikkar, *The Rhythm of Being: The Gifford Lectures* (Maryknoll, N.Y.: Orbis Books, 2010), p. 268.
66. *Dong-gyeong daejeon*, "Nonhangmun," v. 4; *Dong-gyeong daejeon*, "Podeongmun," vv. 5, 8.
67. *Haewol sinsa beopseol*, 37:7.
68. *Yongdam yusa*, "Gyohun-ga," v. 4; *Yongdam yusa*, "Mongjung noso mundapga," v. 5; *Haewol sinsa beopseol*, 37:7.
69. This story is told in Kim Ji-ha, *Saengmyeong*, pp. 188–92. I thank Professor Heup Young Kim for drawing my attention to the story and providing a helpful interpretive perspective on it. See his *Christ and the Tao* (Eugene, Ore.: Wipf & Stock, 2010), pp. 140–44.
70. Kim Ji-ha, *Saengmyeong*, p. 207.

71. Ibid., p. 190. The concept of *han* has been one of the core notions of minjung theology. According to the minjung theologian Suh Nam-dong, "*Han* is the suppressed, amassed, and condensed experience of oppression caused by mischief or misfortune so that it forms a kind of 'lump' in one's spirit." Suh Nam-dong, "Towards a Theology of *Han*," in *Minjung Theology: People as the Subjects of History*, ed. the Commission on Theological Concerns of the Christian Conference of Asia (Maryknoll, N.Y.: Orbis Books, 1983), p. 68.
72. Ibid., pp. 191–92.
73. *Yongdam yusa*, "Yongdamga," v. 3; *Dong-gyeong daejeon*, "Podeongmun," v. 6.
74. This point is also underscored by Haewol in *Haewol sinsa beopseol*, 2:12.
75. That is, befitting the meaning of the classical Chinese 主 (*ju*) of 天主 (*cheonju*).
76. Kim Ji-ha, *Donghak iyagi*, pp. 33–40; *Saengmyeong*, pp. 207–8.
77. Young, *Postcolonialism*, p. 358, quoted in Joerg Rieger, "Liberating God-Talk," p. 218.
78. See historical analysis of their revolutionary slogans and lists of demands, on the one hand, and the revolutionary governing structures, on the other hand, that they put in place in the province under their control, which subversively appropriated the Confucian ideals and institutions, see Shin Yong-ha, *Donghak nongmin hyeongmyeong-ui sahoesa*, pp. 94–163.
79. Kim Yong-hwi, "Su-un Choe Je-uui si-cheonju sasang: cheon-gwaneul jungsimeuro," p. 115, n. 4; Kyoung-jae Kim, "Su-unui si-cheonju cheheom-gwa donghagui sin-gwan," p. 87; Shin Il-cheol, *Donghak sasang-ui ihae*, p. 155.
80. Here I disagree with Kim Yong-hwi, who interprets Nongmun's thought as a monism of psychophysical energy and finds in it a point of connection with Su-un's own monism of psychophysical energy. Kim Yong-hwi, "Su-un Choe Je-uui si-cheonju sasang: cheon-gwaneul jungsimeuro," p. 118, n. 34.
81. The political philosophers Michael Hardt and Antonio Negri define multitude as such, whose other name, accordingly, is *legion*: "an internally different, multiple social subject whose constitution and action is based not on identity or unity (or much less, indifference) but on what it has in common." I will explain what they mean by "common" in the next chapter, i.e., the epilogue. Michael Hardt and Antonio Negri, *Multitude: War and Democracy in the Age of Empire* (New York: Penguin Press, 2004), p. 100.
82. Néstor Míguez, Joerg Rieger, and Jung Mo Sung, *Beyond the Spirit of Empire: Theology and Politics in a New Key* (London: SCM press, 2009), p. 161. The alternative subjectivity of the othered multitude, Míguez, Rieger, and Sung claim, "takes form in different sorts of agency, not only in the active and programmatic construction of alternatives but also in acts of protest, insubordination etc."
83. Stephen Moore, "Situating Spivak," in *Planetary Loves: Spivak, Postcoloniality, and Theology*, edited by Stephen D. Moore and Mayra Rivera (New York: Fordham University Press, 2011, p. 20.
84. Gayatri Chakravorty Spivak, *Critique of Postcolonial Reason: Toward a History of the Vanishing Present* (Cambridge, Mass.: Harvard University Press, 1999), p. 310.

## *Epilogue: The Spirit-Qi of the Multitude under the Cross of Empire*

1. Michael Hardt and Antonio Negri, *Empire* (Cambridge, Mass.: Harvard University Press, 2000), p. 164.

2. Michael Hardt and Antonio Negri, *Multitude: War and Democracy in the Age of Empire* (New York: Penguin Press, 2004), p. xii.
3. Hardt and Negri, *Empire,* pp. 309–14; *Multitude*, p. xiv.
4. Hardt and Negri, *Multitude*, p. xiv. Further references to this book in this discussion will be given by page number in parentheses in the text.
5. The examples presented by Hardt and Negri are the struggles of the Zapatista National Liberation Army in Chiapas, Mexico, the antiglobalization protests in Seattle against the World Trade Organization meetings, identity politics in the United States, among others.
6. Néstor Míguez, Joerg Rieger, and Jung Mo Sung, *Beyond the Spirit of Empire: Theology and Politics in a New Key* (London: SCM Press, 2009), p. 10. Further references to this book will be given by page number within parentheses in the text.
7. Gayatri Chakravorty Spivak, *Death of a Discipline* (New York: Columbia University Press, 2003), pp. 71–102.
8. For the following account, see Moon Dong-hwan, *Saengmyeong gongdongche-wa gihwa gyoyuk: minjug sinhakjeok ipjang-eseo* [The community of life and the education through Gihwa: From the perspective of minjung theology] (Seoul: Han-guk sinhak yeon-guso, 1997).

# BIBLIOGRAPHY


Adler, Joseph A. "Varieties of Spiritual Experience: *Shen* in Neo-Confucian Discourse." In *Confucian Spirituality*, edited by Tu Wei-ming and M. E. Tucker, 120–48. Vol. 2. New York: Crossroad, 2004.

Afkhami, Mahnaz. "Gender Apartheid and the Discourse of Relativity of Rights in Muslim Societies." In *Religious Fundamentalisms and the Human Rights of Women*, edited by Courtney W. Howland, 67–78. New York: Palgrave, 2001.

Ahn Byung-mu. *Minjung sinhak yiyagi* [Story of minjung theology]. Rev. ed. Seoul: Hanguk sinhak yeon-guso, 2005.

Aleaz, K. P. *Christian Thought through Advaita Vedanta*. Delhi: ISPCK, 1996.

Allan, Sarah. *The Way of Water and Sprouts of Virtue*. Albany: State University of New York Press, 1997.

Althaus-Reid, Marcella. *Indecent Theology: Theological Perversions in Sex, Gender, and Politics*. London: Routledge, 2000.

Ames, Roger T. *Art of Rulership: A Study of Ancient Chinese Political Thought*. Albany: State University of New York Press, 1994.

———. "The Local and Focal in Realizing a Daoist World." In *Daoism and Ecology: Ways within a Cosmic Landscape*, edited by N. J. Girardot, James Miller, and Liu Xiaogan, 266–80. Cambridge, Mass.: Center for the Study of World Religions, Harvard Divinity School, 2001.

Ames, Roger T., and David L. Hall, trans. *Daodejing "Making This Life Significant": A Philosophical Translation*. New York: Ballantine Books, 2003.

———. *Thinking from the Han: Self, Truth, and Transcendence in Chinese and Western Culture*. Albany: State University of New York Press, 1998.

An Yeong-sang. "Joseon hugi sasangsa-e natanan jeoldaejawa gaeinui gwan-gye yangsang-ui ildanmyeon: Donghagui seongrihak jeok geun-georeul jungsimeuro [A cross-section of the features of the relationship between the absolute and the individual as manifest in the intellectual history of late Joseon Dynasty: Around the Neo-Confucian basis of Donghak]," *Hanguk sasang-gwa munhwa* 33 (2006): 231–70.

Angle, Stephen C. *Sagehood: The Contemporary Significance of Neo-Confucian Philosophy*. New York: Oxford University Press, 2009.

Asad, Talal. *Genealogies of Religion: Discipline and Reasons of Power in Christianity and Islam*. Baltimore: Johns Hopkins University Press, 1993.

Bae Jong-ho. *Han-guk yuhaksa* [A history of Confucian learning in Korea]. Seoul: Yonsei daehakgyo chulpanbu, 1973.

Baker, Don. *Korean Spirituality*. Honolulu: University of Hawai'i Press, 2008.

Berman, Paul, ed. *Debating P.C.: The Controversy over Political Correctness on College Campuses*. New York: Laurel, published by Dell, 1992.

Berthold-Bond, Daniel. "Can There Be a 'Humanistic' Ecology? A Debate between Hegel and Heidegger on the Meaning of Ecological Thinking." *Social Theory and Practice* 20, no. 3 (1994): 279–309.

Berthrong, John H. *Expanding Process: Exploring Philosophical and Theological Transformations in China and the West*. Albany: State University of New York Press, 2008.

Betcher, Sharon. V. *Spirit and the Politics of Disablement*. Minneapolis: Fortress Press, 2007.

Bevans, Stephen B. *Models of Contextual Theology*. Maryknoll, N.Y.: Orbis Books, 2002.

Bhabha, Homi K. *Location of Culture*. London: Routledge, 1994.

Boff, Leonardo. *Trinity and Society*. Translated by Paul Burns. Maryknoll, N.Y.: Orbis Books, 1988.

Bokenkamp, Stephen. *Early Daoist Scriptures*. Berkeley: University of California Press, 1997.

Bracken, Joseph A. *The Divine Matrix: Creativity as Link between East and West*. Maryknoll, N.Y.: Orbis Books; Herefordshire, UK: Gracewing, 1995.

Brito, Emilio. "La Création chez Hegel et Schelling." *Revue Thomiste* 87, no. 2 (1987): 260–79.

Bryant, Levi R. *Difference and Givenness: Deleuze's Transcendental Empiricism and the Ontology of Immanence*. Evanston, Ill.: Northwestern University Press, 2008.

Burbidge, John W. *Hegel on Logic and Religion: The Reasonableness of Christianity*. Albany: State University of New York Press, 1992.

———. "Hegel's Open Future." In *Hegel and the Tradition: Essays in Honor of H. S. Harris*, edited by Michael Baur and John Russon, 176–89. Toronto: University of Toronto Press, 1997.

Calvin, John. *Institutes of Christian Religion*. Translated by Henry Beveridge. Grand Rapids, Mich.: W. B. Eerdmans, 1989.

Campany, Robert Ford. *To Live as Long as Heaven and Earth: A Translation and Study of Ge Hong's Traditions of Divine Transcendents*. Berkeley: University of California Press, 2002.

Chan, Alan K. L. *Two Visions of the Way: A Study of the Wang Pi and the Ho-shang Kung Commentaries on the Lao-Tzu*. Albany: State University of New York Press, 1990.

Chan, Wing-tsit, trans. and comp. *A Source Book in Chinese Philosophy*. Princeton, N.J.: Princeton University Press, 1963.

———, trans. *The Way of Lao Tzu (Tao-te ching)*. Indianapolis: Bobbs-Merrill, 1963.

Chen Guying, *Lao Tzu: Text Notes and Commentary*. Translated by Rhett Young and Roger T. Ames. Taibei: Chinese Materials Center, 1981.

Cheng, Chung-ying. "Chinese Metaphysics as Non-metaphysics: Confucian and Taoist Insights into the Nature of Reality." In *Understanding the Chinese Mind: The Philosophical Roots*, edited by Robert E. Allinson, 167–208. Hong Kong; New York: Oxford University Press, 1989.

———. "Reality and Divinity in Chinese Philosophy." In *A Companion to World Philosophies*, edited by Eliot Deutsch and Ron Bontekoe, 185–200. Malden, Mass.: Blackwell, 1999.

———. "The *Yi-jing* and the *Yin-Yang* Way of Thinking." In *History of Chinese Philosophy*, edited by Bo Mou, 71–106. New York: Routledge, 2009.

Cheng Hao, and Cheng Yi. *Er Cheng ji* [Collected works of the Cheng brothers]. Edited by Wang Xiaoyu. 2 vols. Beijing: Zhonghua shuju, 1981.

Chidester, David. "Anchoring Religion in the World: A Southern African History of Comparative Religion." *Religion* 26, no. 2 (1996): 141–59.

Ching, Julia. *Religious Thought of Chu Hsi*. Oxford: Oxford University Press, 2000.

Choe Dong-hwi. "Dong-gyeong daejeonui jong-gyo cheorakjeogin ihae [A new religious-philosophical understanding of the complete scripture of Eastern Learning]." In *Donghak-gwa Donghak gyeongjeonui jaeinsik* [A renewed understanding of Donghak and Donghak scriptures], edited by Donghak hakhoe, 33–48. Seoul: Sinseowon, 2001.

———. "Haeworui jong-gyo sasang-ui daehan ihae [Understanding the religious thought of Haewol]." In *Haewol Choe Si-hyeong-gwa Donghak sasang* [Haewol Choe Si-hyeong and Donghak thought], edited by Busan yesul munhwa daehak donghak yeon-guso, 71–92. Seoul: Yemun seowon, 1999.

Choe Je-u (Su-un). *Dong-gyeong daejeon* [The complete scriptures of Eastern Learning]. In *Cheondogyo gyeongjeon* [Cheondogyo scriptures]. Edited by Chondogyo jung-ang chongbu. Seoul: Cheondogyo jung-ang chongbu chulpanbu, 1988.

———. *Yongdam yusa* [The instructional songs from the Dragon Pond]. In *Cheondogyo gyeongjeon* [Cheondogyo scriptures], edited by Chondogyo jung-ang chongbu. Seoul: Cheondogyo jung-ang chongbu chulpanbu, 1988.

Choe Si-hyeong (Haewol). *Haewol sinsa beopseol* [The sermons of Haewol, the divine teacher]. In *Cheondogyo gyeongjeon* [Cheondogyo scriptures], edited by Chondogyo jung-ang chongbu. Seoul: Cheondogyo jung-ang chongbu chulpanbu, 1988.

Choe Yeong-jin. "18–19 segi joseon seongnihagui simhakhwa gyeonghyang-e daehan gochal [An examination of the tendency toward the learning of the heart-mind from 18th- to 19th-century Korean neo-Confucianism]." *Han-guk Minjok Munhwa* 33, no. 3 (2009): 339–68.

———. *Toe Yurui yigiron-gwa segye yinsik* [The theories of yi-gi relations by Toegye and Yulgok and their worldviews]. In *Toegyehak yeon-gu nonchong* [Collected essays on Toegye studies], edited by Yi Wan-je and Yun Cheon-geun, 515–27. Vol. 2. Daegu: Gyeongbuk dae hakgyo Toegye yeon-guso, 1997.

Chu Hsi. *Learning to Be a Sage: Selections from the Conversations of Master Chu, Arranged Topically*. Translated by Daniel K., Gardner. Berkeley: University of California Press, 1990.

Churchill, Ward. "White Studies: The Intellectual Imperialism of U.S. Higher Education." In *Theorizing Multiculturalism: A Guide to the Current Debate*, edited by Cynthia Willet, 334–56. Malden, Mass.: Blackwell, 1998.

Clark, Tim. "A Whiteheadian Chaosmos? Process Philosophy from a Deleuzean Perspective." In *Process and Difference: Between Cosmological and Poststructuralist Postmodernists*, edited by Catherine Keller and Anne Daniell, 191–208. Albany: State University of New York Press, 2002.

Clarke, Sathianathan. *Dalits and Christianity: Subaltern Religion and Liberation Theology in India*. Oxford: Oxford University Press, 2000.

Clayton, Philip. *Adventures of the Spirit: God, World, Divine Action*. Minneapolis: Fortress Press, 2008.

Clooney, Francis X. *Comparative Theology: Deep Learning across Religious Borders*. Chichester, UK: Wiley-Blackwell, 2010.

———. *Divine Mother, Blessed Mother: Hindu Goddesses and the Virgin Mary*. Oxford: Oxford University Press, 2005.

———. *Hindu God, Christian God: How Reason Helps Break Down the Boundaries between Religions*. Oxford: Oxford University Press, 2001.

———. "Reading the World in Christ." In *Christian Uniqueness Reconsidered: The Myth of a Pluralistic Theology of Religions*, edited by Gavin D'Costa, 63–80. Maryknoll, N.Y.: Orbis Books, 1990.

———. *Theology after Vedanta: An Experiment in Comparative Theology*. Albany: State University of New York Press, 1993.

Cobb, John B., Jr. *A Christian Natural Theology: Based on the Thought of Alfred North Whitehead*. 1965.

———. *A Christian Natural Theology: Based on the Thought of Alfred North Whitehead*. 2nd ed. Louisville, Ky.: Westminster John Knox Press, 2007.

Coe, Shoki. "Contextualizing Theology." In *Third World Theologies: Mission Trend No. 3*, edited by Gerald H. Anderson and T. F. Stansky. New York: Paulist Press; Grand Rapids, Mich.: Eerdmans, 2002.

The Commission on Theological Concerns of the Christian Conference of Asia, ed. *Minjung Theology: People as the Subjects of History*. Maryknoll, N.Y.: Orbis Books, 1983.

Coomaraswamy, Radhika. "Different but Free: Cultural Relativism and Women's Rights as Human Rights." In *Religious Fundamentalisms and the Human Rights of Women*, edited by Courtney W. Howland, 79–90. New York: Palgrave, 2001.

Costa, Ruy O. "Introduction: Inculturation, Indigenization, and Contextualization." In *One Faith, Many Cultures: Inculturation, Indigenization, and Contextualization*, edited by Ruy O. Costa, ix–xvii. Maryknoll, N.Y.: Orbis Books; Cambridge, Mass.: Boston Theological Institute, 1988.

Creel, Herrlee G. *What Is Taoism? And Other Studies in Chinese Cultural History*. Chicago: University of Chicago Press, 1970.

Cua, A. S. "Reason and Principle in Chinese Philosophy: An Interpretation of *Li*." In *A Companion to World Philosophies*, edited by E. Deutsch and R. Bontekoe, 201–13. Malden, Mass.: Blackwell, 1999.

Cullen, Bernard. *Hegel's Social and Political Thought*. New York: St. Martin's Press, 1979.

Dahlstrom, Daniel O. "Hegel's Appropriation of Kant's Account of Teleology in Nature." In *Hegel and the Philosophy of Nature*, edited by Stephen Houlgate, 167–88. Albany: State University of New York Press, 1998.

Dai Zhen, *Mengzi ziyi shu zheng* [An evidential commentary on the meanings of terms in Mencius]. In *Dai Zhen quanshu* [Complete works of Dai Zhen], edited by Zhang Dainian, 143–218. Vol. 6. Hebei: Huangshan shushe, 1995.

DeLanda, Manuel. *Intensive Science and Virtual Philosophy*. London: Continuum, 2002.

Deleuze, Gilles. *Difference and Repetition*. Translated by Paul Patton. New York: Columbia University Press, 1994.

———. *The Fold: Leibniz and the Baroque*. Translated by Tom Conley. Minneapolis: University of Minnesota Press, 1993.

———. *The Logic of Sense*. Edited by Constantin V. Boundas. Translated by Mark Lester with Charles Stivale. New York: Columbia University Press, 1990.

Di Giovanni, Georgi. "On the Impotence of Spirit: Profane Reflections on Hegel's Philosophy of History." In *History and System: Hegel's Philosophy of History*, edited by Robert L. Perkins, 195–211. Albany: State University of New York Press, 1984.

DiNoia, Joseph A. "Pluralist Theology of Religions: Pluralistic or Non-Pluralistic?" In *Christian Uniqueness Reconsidered: The Myth of a Pluralistic Theology of Religions*, edited by Gavin D'Costa, 119–34. Maryknoll, N.Y.: Orbis Books, 1990.

Drees, Martin. "Evolution and Emanation of Spirit in Hegel's Philosophy of Nature." *Bulletin of the Hegel Society of Great Britain* 26 (1992): 52–61.

Duffy, Simon. "The Mathematics of Deleuze's Differential Logic and Metaphysics." In *Virtual Mathematics: The Logic of Difference*, edited by Simon Duffy. Manchester, UK: Clinamen Press, 2006.

Faber, Roland. *God as the Poet of the World*. Translated by Douglas W. Stott. Louisville, Ky.: Westminster John Knox Press, 2008.

Fackenheim, Emil L. *The Religious Dimension of Hegel's Thought*. Bloomington: Indiana University Press, 1967.

Fanon, Frantz. *Black Skin, White Masks*. Translated by Charles Lam Markmann. New York: Grove Press, 1967.

Fitzgerald, Timothy. *The Ideology of Religious Studies*. Oxford: Oxford University Press, 2000.

Ford, Lewis. "Divine Persuasion and the Triumph of Good." In *Process Philosophy and Christian Thought*, edited by Delwin Brown, Ralph E. James Jr., and Gene Reeves. Indianapolis: Bobbs-Merrill, 1971.

Fraser, Nancy. "Recognition without Ethics?" In *Recognition and Difference*, edited by Scott Lash and Mike Featherstone, 21–42. London: Sage, 2002.

Fredericks, James L. *Faith among Faiths: Christian Theology and Non-Christian Religions*. New York: Paulist Press, 1999.

———. "A Universal Religious Experience? Comparative Theology as an Alternative to a Theology of Religions." *Horizons* 22, no. 1 (1995): 67–87.

Fulkerson, Mary McClintock. "'We Don't See Color Here': A Case Study in Ecclesial-Cultural Invention." In *Converging on Culture: Theologians in Dialogue with Cultural Analysis and Criticism*, edited by Delwin Brown, Sheila Greeve Davaney, and Kathryn Tanner, 140–57. Oxford: Oxford University Press, 2001.

Fung Yu-lan. *A History of Chinese Philosophy*. Translated by Derk Bodde. 2 vols. Princeton, N.J.: Princeton University Press, 1952–53.

Geertz, Glifford. *The Interpretation of Cultures: Selected Essays*. New York: Basic Books, 1973.

Geffré, Claude. "Double Belonging and the Originality of Christianity as a Religion." In *Many Mansions? Multiple Religious Belonging and Christian Identity*, edited by Catherine Cornille, 93–105. Maryknoll, N.Y.: Orbis Books, 2002.

Geum Jang-tae. *Gwisin-gwa jaesa* [Spirits and the ritual of ancestor veneration]. Seoul: JNC, 2009.

Girardot, N. J. *Myth and Meaning in Early Taoism: The Theme of Chaos (hun-tun)*. Berkeley: University of California Press, 1983.

Graham, Angus C. "The Ch'eng-Chu Theory of Human Nature." In *Studies in Chinese Philosophy and Philosophical Literature*. Singapore: Institute of East Asian Philosophies, 1986.

———. *Disputers of the Tao: Philosophical Argument in Ancient China*. La Salle, Ill.: Open Court, 1989.

———. *Two Chinese Philosophers: The Metaphysics of the Brothers Ch'eng*. 2nd ed. La Salle, Ill.: Open Court, 1992.

Granet, Marcel. *La pensée chinoise: La vie publique et la vie privée*. Paris: Editions Albin Michel, 1948.

Griffin, David R. "Some Whiteheadian Comments." In *Mind in Nature: Essays on the Interface of Science and Philosophy*, edited by John B. Cobb and David Ray Griffin. Washington, D.C.: University Press of America, 1977.

Griffiths, Paul J. *Problems of Religious Diversity*. Oxford: Blackwell, 2001.

———. "The Uniqueness of Christian Doctrine Defended." In *Christian Uniqueness Reconsidered: The Myth of a Pluralistic Theology of Religions*, edited by Gavin D'Costa, 154–73. Maryknoll, N.Y.: Orbis Books, 1990.

Habermas, Jürgen. *Theory of Communicative Action*. Translated by Thomas McCarthy. 2 vols. Boston: Beacon Press, 1984–87.

Hall, David L. "From Reference to Deference: Daoism and the Natural World." In *Daoism and Ecology: Ways within a Cosmic Landscape*, edited by N. J. Girardot, James Miller, and Liu Xiaogan, 245–63. Cambridge, Mass.: Center for the Study of World Religions, Harvard Divinity School, 2001.

———. *The Uncertain Phoenix: Adventures toward a Post-Cultural Sensibility*. New York: Fordham University Press, 1982.

Hansen, Chad. *A Daoist Theory of Chinese Thought: A Philosophical Interpretation*. New York: Oxford University Press, 1992.

Hardt, Michael, and Antonio Negri, *Empire*. Cambridge, Mass.: Harvard University Press, 2000.

———. *Multitude: War and Democracy in the Age of Empire*. New York: Penguin Press, 2004.

Hegel, G. W. F. *Elements of the Philosophy of Right*. Edited by Allen W. Wood. Translated by H. B. Nisbet. Cambridge: Cambridge University Press, 1991.

———. *The Encyclopedia Logic*. Translated by T. F. Garaets, W. A. Suchting, and H. S. Harris. Indianapolis: Hackett, 1991.

———. *Hegel's Philosophy of Nature*. Edited and translated by M. J. Petry. 3 vols. London: Allen and Unwin; New York: Humanities Press, 1970.

———. *Hegel's Philosophy of Mind*. Translated by William Wallace and A. V. Miller. Oxford: Clarendon Press, 1971.

———. *Hegel's Science of Logic*. Translated by A. V. Miller. Atlantic Highlands, N.J.: Humanities Press, 1969.

———. *Lectures on the Philosophy of Religion*. Edited by Peter C. Hodgson. Translated by R. Brown, P. Hodgson, and J. Stewart, with the assistance of J. P. Fitzer and H. S. Harris. 3 vols. Berkeley: University of California Press, 1984–87.

———. *Lectures on the Philosophy of Religion*. Edited by Peter C. Hodgson. Translated by R. Brown, P. Hodgson, and J. Stewart, with the assistance of H. S. Harris. One-volume edition, *The Lectures of 1827*. Berkeley: University of California Press, 1988.

———. *Lectures on the Philosophy of World History: Introduction: Reason in History*. Translated by H. B. Nisbet. Cambridge: Cambridge University Press, 1975.

———. *Phenomenology of Spirit*. Translated by A. V. Miller. Oxford: Oxford University Press, 1977.

———. *Philosophy of Subjective Spirit*. Edited and translated by M. J. Petry. 3 vols. Dordrecht: D. Reidel, 1979.

———. *Vorlesungen über die Philosophie des Geistes: Berlin 1827/1828*. Edited by Franz Hespe and Burkhard Tuschling. Hamburg: F. Meiner, 1994.

———. *Werke*. Edited by Eva Moldenhauer und Karl Markus Michel. 20 vols. Frankfurt am Main: Suhrkamp, 1969–71.

Henderson, John B. *The Development and Decline of Chinese Cosmology*. New York: Columbia University Press, 1984.

Hendrischke, Barbara. *The Scripture on Great Peace: The Taiping jing and the Beginnings of Daoism*. Berkeley: University of California Press, 2006.

Herman, Jonathan R. "Human Heart, Heavenly Heart: Mystical Dimensions of Chu Hsi's Neo-Confucianism." *Journal of the American Academy of Religion* 69, no. 1 (2001): 103–28.

Hodgson, Peter C. "Alienation and Reconciliation in Hegelian and Post-Hegelian Perspective." *Modern Theology* 2, no. 1 (1985): 43–63.

———. *G. W. F. Hegel: Theologian of the Spirit*. Minneapolis: Fortress Press, 1997.

———. *Hegel and Christian Theology: A Reading of the Lectures on the Philosophy of Religion*. Oxford: Oxford University Press, 2005.

———. "Logic, History, and Alternative Paradigms in Hegel's Interpretation of the Religions." *Journal of Religion* 68, no. 1 (1988): 1–20.

———. *Winds of the Spirit: A Constructive Christian Theology*, Louisville, Ky.: Westminster John Knox Press, 1994.

Hong Jeong-geun. "Im Seong-juwa Na Heum-sun hakseorui daebijeok gochal [A comparative examination of the theories of Im Seong-ju and Na Heum-sun]." *Yugyo Sasang Yeongu* 18 (2003): 87–116.

Honneth, Axel. "Recognition or Redistribution? Changing Perspectives on the Moral Order of Society." In *Recognition and Difference*, edited by Scott Lash and Mike Featherstone, 43–56. London: SAGE, 2002.

Hosinski, Thomas E. *Stubborn Fact and Creative Advance: An Introduction to the Metaphysics of Alfred North Whitehead*. Lanham, Md.: Rowman and Littlefield, 1993.

Ilting, Karl-Heinz. "Hegels Philosophie des Organischen." In *Hegel und Naturwissenschaften*, edited by Michael John Petry, 349–76. Stuttgart-Bad Cannstatt: Frommann-Holzboog, 1987.

Im Seong-ju (Nongmun). *Nongmunjip* [Collected works of Nongmun]. Edited by Minjok munhwa chujinhoe. Seoul: Gyeongin munhwasa, 2001.

Irigaray, Luce. "The Eternal Irony of the Community." In *Feminist Interpretations of G. W. F. Hegel*, edited byPatricia Jagentowicz Mills, 45–57. University Park: Pennsylvania State University Press, 1996.

Irwin, Dale T. "The Trinity and Socio-political Ethics." In *The Cambridge Companion to the Trinity*, edited by Peter C. Phan, 398–413. New York: Cambridge University Press, 2011.

Ivanhoe, Philip J. "The Concept of de ('Virtue') in the Laozi." In *Religious and Philosophical Aspects of the Laozi*, edited by Mark Csikszentmihalyi and Philip J. Ivanhoe, 239–57. Albany: State University of New York Press, 1999.

———, trans. *The Daodejing of Laozi*. New York: Seven Bridges Press, 2002.

Ivanhoe, Philip J., and Bryan W. Van Norden, eds. *Readings in Classical Chinese Philosophy*. 2nd ed. Indianapolis: Hackett, 2001.

Jaeschke, Walter. *Reason in Religion: The Foundations of Hegel's Philosophy of Religion*. Translated by J. Michael Stewart and Peter C. Hodgson. Berkeley: University of California Press, 1990.

Jeon Duha. "Toegye-ui cheoragui haeksim [The heart of Toegye's philosophy]." *Toegye Hakbo* 19 (December 1978): 135–70.

Johnson, Elizabeth A. *She Who Is: The Mystery of God in Feminist Theological Discourse*. New York: Crossroad, 2002.

Jones, Judith A. *Intensity: An Essay in Whiteheadian Ontology*. Nashville: Vanderbilt University Press, 1998.

Jones, Serene. "Cultural Labor and Theological Critique." In *Converging on Culture: Theologians in Dialogue with Cultural Analysis and Criticism*, edited by Delwin Brown, Sheila Greeve Davaney, and Kathryn Tanner, 158–75. Oxford: Oxford University Press, 2001.

*Juyeok* [Classic of Change from Zhou Dynasty]. Translated by Choe Won-sik. Seoul: Hyewon chulpansa, 2000.

Kaltenmark, Max. *Lao Tzu and Taoism*. Translated by Roger Greaves. Stanford: Stanford University Press, 1969.

Kalton, Michael. Introduction to *The Four-Seven Debate: An Annotated Translation of the Most Famous Controversy in Korean Neo-Confucian Thought*. Translated by Michael C. Kalton et al. Albany: State University of New York Press, 1994.

———, trans. and ed. *To Become a Sage: The Ten Diagrams on Sage Learning*, by Yi T'oegye. New York: Columbia University Press, 1988.

Kang, Namsoon. "Reconstructing *Asian* Feminist Theology: Toward a *Glocal* Feminist Theology in an Era of Neo-Empire(s)." In *Christian Theology in Asia*, edited by Sebastian C. H. Kim, 205–26. New York: Cambridge University Press, 2008.

———. "Who/What Is Asian?: A Postcolonial Theological Reading of Orientalism and Neo-Orientalism." In *Postcolonial Theologies: Divinity and Empire*, edited by Catherine Keller, Michael Nausner, and Mayra Rivera, 100–117. St. Louis: Chalice Press, 2004.

Keller, Catherine. *Face of the Deep: A Theology of Becoming*. London: Routledge, 2003.

———. *God and Power: Counter-Apocalyptic Journeys*. Minneapolis: Fortress Press, 2005.

———. "Process and Chaosmos: The Whiteheadian Fold in the Discourse of Difference." In *Process and Difference: Between Cosmological and Poststructuralist Postmodernists*, edited by Catherine Keller and Anne Daniell, 55–72. Albany: State University of New York Press, 2002.

———. "Rumors of Transcendence: The Movement, State, and Sex of 'Beyond.'" In *Transcendence and Beyond: A Postmodern Inquiry*, edited by John D. Caputo and Michael J. Scanlon, 129–50. Bloomington: Indiana University Press, 2007.

Keller, Catherine, Michael Nausner, and Mayra Rivera, eds. *Postcolonial Theologies: Divinity and Empire*. St. Louis: Chalice Press, 2004.

Kelly, J. N. D. *Early Christian Doctrines*. Rev. ed. San Francisco: Harper and Row, 1978.

Kim Chun-seong. "Yongdam yusaui cheorakjeok gochal [Philosophical examination of *Yongdam Yusa*]." In *Donghak-gwa Donghak gyeongjeonui jaeinsik* [A renewed understanding of Donghak and Donghak scriptures], edited by Donghak hakhoe, 121–44. Seoul: Sinseowon, 2001.

Kim, Heup Young. *Christ and the Tao*. Eugene, Ore.: Wipf and Stock, 2010.

Kim Hyeon. *Im Seong-juui saeng-ui cheorak* [Im Seong-ju's philosophy of life]. Seoul: Hangil Publishing, 1995.

Kim Ji-ha. *Donghak iyagi* [The story of Donghak]. Seoul: Sol, 1994.

———. *Saengmyeong* [Life]. Seoul: Sol, 1992.

Kim, Kyoung Jae. *Christianity and the Encounter of Asian Religions: Method of Correlation, Fusion of Horizons, and Paradigm Shifts in the Korean Grafting Process*. Zoetermeer: Uitgeverij Boekencentrum, 1994.

———. *I-reum eomneun haneunim: yuilsin sinang-e daehan Kim Kyoung-jae gyosuui bon-gyeok bipan* [God without a name: The principal criticism of monotheism by Professor Kim Kyoung-jae]. Seoul: Samin, 2002.

———. "Su-unui si-cheonju cheheom-gwa donghagui sin-gwan [Su-un's experience of *si-cheonju* and the Donghak view of God]." In *Han-gugui sasang-ga sibin: Su-un Choe Je-u* [Ten Korean thinkers: Su-un Choe Je-u], edited by Oh Mun-hwan, 81–102. Seoul: Yemun seowon, 2005.

Kim Sang-il, Yi Song-eun, and Oh Gang-nam, eds. *Han sasang-ui i-ron-gwa siljae* [The theory and reality of Han philosophy]. Seoul: Jisik saneopsa, 1990.

Kim, Sebastian C. H., ed. *Christian Theology in Asia*. New York: Cambridge University Press, 2008.

Kim Yong-hae. "Geurisdogyowa cheondogyoui sin-gwan bigyo [A comparison of the view of God in Christianity and the religion of the heavenly way]." In *Han-gugui sasang-ga sibin: Su-un Choe Je-u* [Ten Korean thinkers: Su-un Choe Je-u], edited by Oh Mun-hwan. Seoul: Yemun seowon, 2005.

Kim Yong-hwi. "Su-un Choe Je-uui si-cheonju sasang: cheon-gwaneul jungsimeuro [Su-un Choe Je-u's notion of *si-cheonju*: Around his view of heaven]." In *Han-gugui sasang-ga sibin: Su-un Choe Je-u* [Ten Korean thinkers: Su-un Choe Je-u], edited by Oh Mun-hwan, 103–28. Seoul: Yemun seowon, 2005.

Kim Yong-ok, trans. *Do-ol simdeuk dong-gyeong daejeon: pletharchia-ui sinsegye* [The complete scriptures of Eastern Learning as grasped by Do-ol: The new world of *pletharchia*]. Vol. 1. Seoul: Tongnamu, 2004.

King, Richard. *Orientalism and Religion: Postcolonial Theory, India, and "The Mystic East."* London: Routledge, 1999.

Kirkland, Russell. "Varieties of Taoism in Ancient China: A Preliminary Comparison of Themes in the *Nei Yeh* and Other Taoist Classics." *Taoist Resources* 7, no. 2 (1997): 73–86.

Kleeman, Terry F. *Great Perfection: Religion and Ethnicity in a Chinese Millennial Kingdom*. Honolulu: University of Hawai'i Press, 1998.

Knitter, Paul F. *Introducing Theologies of Religions*. Maryknoll, N.Y.: Orbis Books, 2002.

Kohn, Livia. "Chinese Religion." In *The Human Condition*, edited by Robert C. Neville, 21–47. Albany: State University of New York Press, 2001.

Kolb, David. "The Final Name of God." In *Hegel and the Tradition: Essays in Honor of H. S. Harris*, edited by Michael Baur and John Russon, 162–95. Toronto: University of Toronto Press, 1997.

Koyama, Kosuke. *Water Buffalo Theology*. Maryknoll, N.Y.: Orbis Books, 1974.

Kwan, Simon Shui-Man. "From Indigenization to Contextualization: A Change in Discursive Practice Rather Than a Shift in Paradigm." *Studies in World Christianity* 11, no. 2 (2005): 236–50.

Kwok, Pui-lan. *Discovering the Bible in the Non-Biblical World.* Maryknoll, N.Y.: Orbis Books, 1995.

———. *Postcolonial Imagination and Feminist Theology.* Louisville, Ky.: Westminster John Knox Press, 2005.

LaFargue, Michael. *Tao and Method: A Reasoned Approach to the Tao Te Ching.* Albany: State University of New York Press, 1994.

———, trans. *The Tao of the Tao Te Ching: A Translation and Commentary.* Albany: State University of New York Press, 1992.

Lao, Siguang. *Jung-guk cheorhaksa* [History of Chinese philosophy]. Translated by In-jae Jeong. Seoul: Tamgudang, 1987.

Lau, D. C., trans. *Tao Te Ching: A Bilingual Edition.* Hong Kong: Chinese University of Hong Kong, 2001.

Lee, Jung H. "Finely Aware and Richly Responsible: The Daoist Imperative." *Journal of the American Academy of Religion* 68, no. 3 (2000): 511–36.

Lee, Jung Young. *The Trinity in Asian Perspective.* Nashville: Abingdon Press, 1996.

Lindbeck, George A. "The Gospel's Uniqueness: Election and Untranslatability." In *The Church in a Postliberal Age*, edited by James J. Buckley, 223–52. Grand Rapids, Mich.: William B. Eerdmans, 2003.

———. *The Nature of Doctrine: Religion and Theology in a Postliberal Age.* Philadelphia: Westminster Press, 1984.

Lingis, Alphonso. *The Community of Those Who Have Nothing in Common.* Bloomington: Indiana University Press, 2007.

Liu Xiaogan. "Naturalness (Tzu-jan), the Core Value in Taoism: Its Ancient Meaning and Its Significance Today." In *Lao-tzu and the Tao-te-ching*, edited by Livia Kohn and Michael LaFargue, 211–28. Albany: State University of New York Press, 1998.

López, Alfred J. *Posts and Pasts: A Theory of Postcolonialism.* Albany: State University of New York Press, 2001.

Loy, David R. "Loving the World as Our Own Body: The Non-Dualist Ethics of Taoism, Buddhism, and Deep Ecology." In *Asian and Jungian View of Ethics*, edited by Carl B. Becker, 85–111. Westport, Conn.: Greenwood Press, 1999.

Lynn, Richard J., trans. *The Classic of Changes: A New Translation of the I Ching as Interpreted by Wang Bi.* New York: Columbia University Press, 1994.

———, trans. *The Classic of the Way and Virtue: A New Translation of the Tao-te ching of Laozi as interpreted by Wang Bi.* New York: Columbia University Press, 1999.

Maebayashi Kiyokazu, Sato Koetsu, and Kobayashi Hiroshi. *Giui bigyo munhwa* [A comparative-cultural analysis of gi]. Translated by Park Mun-hyeon and Sekine Hideyuki. Seoul: Doseo chulpan hanul, 2006.

Maker, William. "The Very Idea of the Idea of Nature, or Why Hegel Is Not an Idealist." In *Hegel and the Philosophy of Nature*, edited by Stephen Houlgate, 1–27. Albany: State University of New York Press, 1998.

Mandair, Arvind. "The Repetition of Past Imperialism: Hegel, Historical Difference, and the Theorizing of Indic Religions." *History of Religions* 44, no. 4 (2005): 277–99.

Marty, Emmanuel. *African Theology: Inculturation and Liberation.* Maryknoll, N.Y.: Orbis Books, 1993.

Mazusawa, Tomoko. *The Invention of World Religions: Or, How European Universalism Was Preserved in the Language of Pluralism.* Chicago: University of Chicago Press, 2005.

McBride, Richard. *Domesticating the Dharma: Buddhist Cults and the Hwaŏm Synthesis in Silla Korea.* Honolulu: University of Hawai'i Press, 2008.

McCutcheon, Russell, T. *Manufacturing Religion: The Discourse on Sui Generis Religion and the Politics of Nostalgia.* Oxford: Oxford University Press, 1997.

McDonnell, Killian. *The Other Hand of God: The Holy Spirit as the Universal Touch and Goal.* Collegeville, Minn.: Liturgical Press, 2003.

Mengzi. *Mengzi: With Selections from Traditional Commentaries.* Translated by Bryan W. Van Norden. Indianapolis: Hackett, 2008.

Michael, Thomas. *The Pristine Dao: Metaphysics in Early Daoist Discourse.* Albany: State University of New York Press, 2005.

Míguez, Néstor, Joerg Rieger, and Jung Mo Sung, *Beyond the Spirit of Empire: Theology and Politics in a New Key.* London: SCM Press, 2009.

Milbank, John. *Theology and Social Theory: Beyond Secular Reason.* Oxford: Blackwell, 1990.

Mills, Patricia Jagentowicz. "Hegel's Antigone." *Owl of Minerva* 17, no. 2 (1986): 131–52.

Min, Anselm K. "Dialectical Pluralism and Solidarity of Others: Towards a New Paradigm." *Journal of the American Academy of Religion* 65, no. 3 (1997): 587–604.

———. "God as the Mystery of Sharing and Shared Love: Thomas Aquinas on the Trinity." In *The Cambridge Companion to the Trinity*, edited by Peter C. Phan, 87–107. New York: Cambridge University Press, 2011.

———. *Paths to the Triune God: An Encounter between Aquinas and Recent Theologies.* Notre Dame, Ind.: University of Notre Dame Press, 2005.

———. "The Trinity and the Incarnation: Hegel and Classical Approaches." *Journal of Religion* 66, no. 2 (1986): 173–93.

Min Gyeong-bae. *Hanguk gidok gyohoesa: Hanguk minjok gyohoe hyeongseong gwajeongsa* [History of the Korean Christian Church: A history of the process of the formation of the Korean National Church]. Seoul: Yonsei daehak chulpanbu, 2007.

Moeller, Hans-Georg. *The Philosophy of the Daodejing.* New York: Columbia University Press, 2006.

Moltmann, Jürgen. *The Trinity and the Kingdom of God: The Doctrine of God.* San Francisco: Harper and Row; London: SCM Press, 1981.

Montague, George T. "The Fire in the Word: The Holy Spirit in Scripture." In *Advents of the Spirit: An Introduction to the Current Study of Pneumatology*, edited by Bradford E. Hinze and D. Lyle Dabney, 35–65. Milwaukee: Marquette University Press, 2001.

Moon Dong-hwan. *Saengmyeong gongdongche-wa gihwa gyoyuk: Minjung sinhakjeok ipjang-eseo* [The community of life and the education through *gihwa*: From the perspective of minjung theology]. Seoul: Han-guk sinhak yeon-guso, 1997.

Moore, Stephen. "Situating Spivak." In *Planetary Loves: Spivak, Postcoloniality, and Theology*, edited by Stephen D. Moore and Mayra Rivera, 15–30. New York: Fordham University Press, 2011.

Moore, Stephen D., and Fernando F. Segovia, eds. *Postcolonial Biblical Criticism: Interdisciplinary Intersections.* London: T & T Clark, 2005.

Morris, Brian. "Taoism, Confucianism, and the Chinese Self." *International Journal of Moral and Social Studies* 8, no. 3 (1993): 273–96.

Mou Zhongjian. "Laozi's Discourse on the Way and Its Significance Today." *Contemporary Chinese Thought* 30, no. 1 (1998): 75–79.

*Nanhua zhenjing*. In *Zhonghua daozang*. Edited by Jiyu Zhang. Vol. 13. Beijing: Huaxia chubanshe, 2004.

Needham, Joseph. *Science and Civilization in China*. Vol. 2, *History of Scientific Thought*. Cambridge: Cambridge University Press, 1956.

Neville, Robert C. *Behind the Masks of God: An Essay toward Comparative Theology*. Albany: State University of New York Press, 1991.

———. *Boston Confucianism: Portable Tradition in the Late-Modern World*. Albany: State University of New York Press, 2000.

———. *Creativity and God: A Challenge to Process Theology*. Albany: State University of New York Press, 1995.

———. "Daoist Relativism, Ethical Choice, and Normative Measure." *Journal of Chinese Philosophy* 29, no. 1 (2002): 5–20.

———. *Recovery of Measure: Interpretation and Nature*. Albany: State University of New York Press, 1989.

Nicholson, Hugh. "Comparative Theology after Liberalism." *Modern Theology* 23, no. 2 (2007): 229–51.

Nirmal, Arvind P., ed. *A Reader in Dalit Theology*. Madras: Gurukul Theological Seminary, 1990.

Nuyen, A. T. "Naming the Unnameable: The Being of the *Tao*." *Journal of Chinese Philosophy* 22, no. 4 (1995): 487–97.

Oh Mun-hwan. "Donghagui dodeokjeok pyeongdeung juui." In *Donghak-gwa Donghak gyeongjeonui jaeinsik* [A renewed understanding of Donghak and Donghak scriptures], edited by Donghak hakhoe, 205–22. Seoul: Sinseowon, 2001.

———. *Donghagui jeongchi cheorak: dodeok, saengmyeong, gwollyeok* [The political philosophy of Donghak: Morality, life, and power]. Seoul: Mosineun saramdeul, 2003.

———. *Haewol Choe Si-hyeong-ui jeongchi sasang* [The political thought of Haewol Choe Si-hyeong]. Seoul: Mosineun saramdeul, 2003.

———. "'Si-cheonju' jumuneul tonghaeseo bon Su-unui in-gan-gwan [Su-un's view of human being as seen through the 'Si-cheonju' incantation]." In *Han-gugui sasang-ga sibin: Su-un Choe Je-u* [Ten Korean thinkers: Su-un Choe Je-u], edited by Oh Mun-hwan, 129–54. Seoul: Yemun seowon, 2005.

O'Leary, Joseph S. *Religious Pluralism and Christian Truth*. Edinburgh: Edinburgh University Press, 1996.

O'Regan, Cyril. "Hegelian Philosophy of Religion and Eckhartian Mysticism." In *New Perspectives on Hegel's Philosophy of Religion*, edited by David Kolb, 109–29. Albany: State University of New York Press, 1992.

———. *The Heterodox Hegel*. Albany: State University of New York Press, 1994.

Panikkar, Raimon. *The Intrareligious Dialogue*. New York: Paulist Press, 1978.

———. *The Rhythm of Being: The Gifford Lectures*. Maryknoll, N.Y.: Orbis Books, 2010.

Paper, Jordan. *The Spirits Are Drunk: Comparative Approaches to Chinese Religion*. Albany: State University of New York Press, 1995.

Pak Gyeong-hwan. "Donghak-gwa yuhak sasang [Donghak and Confucian thought]." In *Donghak-gwa jeontong sasang* [Donghak and traditional thought], edited by Donghak hakhoe, 71–96. Seoul: Mosineun saramdeul, 2005.

Park Sung-bae. *Toegye sasang-ui jong-gyojeok seong-gyeok* [The religious aspects of Toegye's thought]. In *Toegyehak yeon-gu nonchong* [Collected essays on Toegye studies], edited by Song Hwi-chil and Shin Gwi-hyeon, 9:247–58. Daegu: Gyeongbuk daehakgyo Toegye yeon-guso, 1997.

Parkes, Graham. "The Place of the Human in Nature: Paradigms of Ecological Thinking, East and West." In *Is There a Human Nature?* edited by Leroy S. Rowner, 149–71. Notre Dame, Ind.: University of Notre Dame Press, 1997.

Phan, Peter C. *Christianity with an Asian Face: Asian American Theology in the Making.* Maryknoll, N.Y.: Orbis Books, 2003.

———. *In Our Own Tongues: Perspectives from Asia on Mission and Inculturation.* Maryknoll, N.Y.: Orbis Books, 2003.

Plant, Raymond. "Hegel on Identity and Legitimation." In *The State and Civil Society: Studies in Hegel's Philosophy*, edited by Z. A. Pelczynski, 239–43. Cambridge: Cambridge University Press, 1984.

Protevi, John. "Sports Sunday 6: the Idea of Football." In *New APPS: Art, Politics, Philosophy, Science* (September 4, 2011). http://www.newappsblog.com/2011/09/sports-sunday-6-the-idea-of-football.html#more.

———. "Water." In *Rhizomes: Cultural Studies in Emerging Knowledge.* 15 (Winter 2007). http://www.rhizomes.net/issue15/protevi.html.

Puett, Michael. *The Ambivalence of Creation: Debates concerning Innovation and Artifice in Early China.* Stanford: Stanford University Press, 2001.

———. *To Become a God: Cosmology, Sacrifice, and Self-Divinization in Early China.* Cambridge, Mass.: Harvard University Asia Center for the Harvard-Yenching Institute, 2002.

Pyo Yeong-sam. *Donghak 1: Su-unui sarmgwa sang-gak* [The life and thought of Su-un]. Seoul: Tongnamu, 2004.

———. *Donghak 2: Haweorui gonan yeokjeong* [Haewol's life course of hardship and suffering]. Seoul: Tongnamu, 2005.

Ra Myeong-jae, trans. *Cheondogyo gyeongjeon gongbuhagi* [Studying the scriptures of the religion of the heavenly way]. Seoul: Mosineun saramdeul, 2010.

Race, Alan. *Christians and Religious Pluralism: Patterns in the Christian Theology of Religions.* Maryknoll, N.Y.: Orbis Books, 1982.

Rambo, Shelly. *Spirit and Trauma: A Theology of Remaining.* Louisville, Ky.: Westminster John Knox Press, 2010.

Reilly, Thomas H. *The Taiping Heavenly Kingdom: Rebellion and the Blasphemy of Empire.* Seattle: University of Washington Press, 2004.

Rieger, Joerg. *Christ and Empire: From Paul to Postcolonial Times.* Minneapolis: Fortress Press, 2007.

———. "Liberating God-Talk: Postcolonialism and the Challenge of the Margins." In *Postcolonial Theologies: Divinity and Empire*, edited by Catherine Keller, Michael Nausner, and Mayra Rivera, 204–20. St. Louis: Chalice Press, 2004.

Rivera, Mayra. *The Touch of Transcendence: A Postcolonial Theology of God.* Louisville, Ky.: Westminster John Knox Press, 2007.

Ro, Young-Chan. *The Korean Neo-Confucianism of Yi Yulgok*. Albany: State University of New York Press, 1989.

Roberts, Michelle Voss. "Gendering Comparative Theology." In *The New Comparative Theology: Interreligious Insights from the Next Generation*, edited by Francis X. Clooney, 109–28. London: T & T Clark, 2010.

Robertson, Roland. "Glocalization: Time-Space and Homogeneity-Heterogeneity." In *Global Modernities,* edited by Mike Featherstone, Scott Lash, and Roland Robertson, 25–44. London: Sage, 1995.

Robinet, Isabelle. "The Diverse Interpretations of the Laozi." In *Religious and Philosophical Aspects of the Laozi,* edited by Mark Csikszentmihalyi and Philip J. Ivanhoe, 129–59. Albany: State University of New York Press, 1999.

———. *Taoism: Growth of a Religion*. Translated by Phyllis Brooks. Stanford: Stanford University Press, 1997.

Rosenlee, Li-Hsiang Lisa. *Confucianism and Women: A Philosophical Interpretation*. Albany: State University of New York Press, 2006.

Roth, Harold D. "The Laozi in the Context of Early Daoist Mystical Praxis." In *Religious and Philosophical Aspects of the Laozi,* edited by Mark Csikszentmihalyi and Philip J. Ivanhoe, 59–96. Albany: State University of New York Press, 1999.

———. *Original Tao: Inward Training (Nei-yeh) and the Foundations of Taoist Mysticism.* New York: Columbia University Press, 1999.

Ryu Dong-sik. *Hanguk sinhagui gwangmaek* [The mineral vein of Korean theology]. Seoul: Dasan Geulbang, 2003.

Said, Edward W. *Orientalism*. New York: Vintage Books, 1978.

Sayuki-Tiemeier,Tracy. "Comparative Theology as a Theology of Liberation." In *The New Comparative Theology: Interreligious Insights from the Next Generation*, edited by Francis X. Clooney, 129–50. London: T & T Clark, 2010.

Schlitt, Dale M. *Divine Subjectivity: Understanding Hegel's Philosophy of Religion*. Scranton, Penn.: University of Scranton Press, 1990.

Schneider, Laurel C. *Beyond Monotheism: A Theology of Multiplicity*. London: Routledge, 2009.

Schreiter, Robert J. *Constructing Local Theologies*. Maryknoll, N.Y.: Orbis Books, 1985.

———. *The New Catholicity: Theology between the Global and the Local.* Maryknoll, N.Y.: Orbis Books, 1997.

Schwartz, Benjamin. "The Thought of the Tao-te-ching." In *Lao-tzu and the Tao-te-ching,* edited by Livia Kohn and Michael LaFargue, 189–211. Albany: State University of New York Press, 1998.

———. *The World of Thought in Ancient China*. Cambridge, Mass.: Belknap Press of Harvard University Press, 1985.

Sedgwick, Sally S. "Hegel's Treatment of Transcendental Apperception in Kant." *Owl of Minerva* 23, no. 2 (1992): 151–63.

Seo Gyeong-deok (Hwadam). *Gugyeok Hwadamjip* [Collected works of Hwadam, translated]. Translated by Hwang Gwang-uk. Seoul: Simsan Munhwa, 2004.

Shenk, Wilbert R. "The Missionary Encounter with Culture since the Seventeenth Century." In *Appropriate Christianity*, edited by Charles H. Kraft, 35–48. Pasadena, Calif.: William Carey Library, 2005.

Shin Bok-ryong. *Donghak sasang-gwa gabo nongmin hyeongmyeong* [Donghak thought and the Gabo peasant revolution]. Seoul: Pyeongminsa, 1991.

Shin Il-cheol. *Donghak sasang-ui ihae*. Seoul: Sahoe bipyeongsa, 1995.

Shin Yong-ha. *Donghak nongmin hyeongmyeong-ui sahoesa* [Social history of the Donghak peasant revolutionary movement]. Seoul: Jisik saneopsa, 2005.

Singer, Michael. "Relativism, Culture, Religion, and Identity." In *Religious Fundamentalisms and the Human Rights of Women*, edited by Courtney W. Howland, 45–54. New York: Palgrave, 2001.

Sivin, Nathan. "State, Cosmos, and Body in the Last Three Centuries B.C." *Harvard Journal of Asiatic Studies* 55, no. 1 (1995): 5–37.

Slingerland, Edward. "Effortless Action: The Chinese Spiritual Ideal of Wu-Wei." *Journal of the American Academy of Religion* 68, no. 2 (2000): 293–328.

———. *Effortless Action: Wu-wei as Conceptual Metaphor and Spiritual Ideal in Early China*. Oxford: Oxford University Press, 2003.

Smith, Daniel W. "Deleuze's Theory of Sensation: Overcoming the Kantian Duality." In *Deleuze: A Critical Reader*, edited by Paul Patton, 29–56. Oxford: Blackwell, 1996.

Smith, Daniel, and John Protevi. "Gilles Deleuze." In *The Stanford Encyclopedia of Philosophy* (Winter 2011 edition). Edited by Edward N. Zalta. Forthcoming. http://plato.stanford.edu/archives/win2011/entries/deleuze.

Son Heung-cheol. *Nongmun Im Seong-juui sarmgwa cheorak* [A study of Nongmun Im Seong-ju's life and his philosophy]. Seoul: Jisik Saneopsa, 2004.

Song, C. S. *Third-Eye Theology: Theology in Formation in Asian Settings*. Maryknoll, N.Y.: Orbis Books, 1979.

Soual, Philippe. "Le Dieu inconnu de la religion de la nature chez Hegel." *Les Études philosophiques*, no. 2 (1999): 201–21.

Spence, Jonathan. *God's Chinese Son: The Taiping Heavenly Kingdom of Hong Xiuquan*. New York: W. W. Norton, 1996.

Spivak, Gayatri Chakravorty. *A Critique of Postcolonial Reason: Toward a History of the Vanishing Present*. Cambridge, Mass.: Harvard University Press, 1999.

———. *Death of a Discipline*. New York: Columbia University Press, 2003.

———. *Outside in the Teaching Machine*. New York: Routledge, 1993.

———. "Subaltern Studies: Deconstructing Historiography." In *The Spivak Reader*, edited by Donna Landry and Gerald Maclean, 214–21. New York: Routledge, 1996.

———. "Translator's Preface and Afterword to Mahasweta Devi, *Imaginary Maps*." In *The Spivak Reader*, edited by Donna Landry and Gerald Maclean, 267–86. New York: Routledge, 1996.

Stone, Alison. "Ethical Implications of Hegel's Philosophy of Nature." *British Journal for the History of Philosophy* 10, no. 2 (2002): 243–60.

Suchocki, Marjorie Hewitt. *The End of Evil: Process Eschatology in Historical Context*. Albany: State University of New York Press, 1988.

Suh, David Kwang-sun. *The Korean Minjung in Christ*. Hong Kong: Christian Conference of Asia, 1991.

Sugirtharajah, R. S. *The Bible and the Third World: Precolonial, Colonial, and Postcolonial Encounters*. Cambridge: Cambridge University Press, 2001.

Sugirtharajah, Sharada. *Imagining Hinduism: A Postcolonial Perspective*. London: Routledge, 2003.

Suh Nam-dong. "Towards a Theology of *Han*." In *Minjung Theology: People as the Subjects of History*, edited by the Commission on Theological Concerns of the Christian Conference of Asia, 55–69. Maryknoll, N.Y.: Orbis Books, 1983.

Tanner, Kathryn. *Theory of Culture: A New Agenda for Theology*. Minneapolis: Fortress Press, 1997.

Tateno Masami. "A Philosophical Analysis of the Laozi from an Ontological Perspective." In *Religious and Philosophical Aspects of the Laozi*, edited by Mark Csikszentmihalyi and Philip J. Ivanhoe, 175–86. Albany: State University of New York Press, 1999.

Taylor, Charles. *Hegel*. Cambridge: Cambridge University Press, 1975.

———. "The Politics of Recognition." In *Multiculturalism: Examining the Politics of Recognition*, edited and introduced by Amy Gutmann, 25–74. Princeton, N.J.: Princeton University Press, 1994.

Thangaraj, M. Thomas. *The Crucified Guru: An Experiment in Cross-Cultural Christology*. Nashville: Abingdon Press, 1994.

Thatamanil, John J. "Comparative Theology after 'Religion.'" In *Planetary Loves: Spivak, Postcoloniality, and Theology*, edited by Stephen D. Moore and Mayra Rivera, 238–57. New York: Fordham University Press, 2011.

———. "God as Ground, Contingency, and Relation: Trinitarian Polydoxy and Religious Diversity." In *Polydoxy: Theology of Multiplicity and Relation*, edited by Catherine Keller and Laurel C. Schneider, 238–57. London: Routledge, 2010.

Thompson, David M. "Introduction: Mapping Asian Christianity in the Context of World Christianity." In *Christian Theology in Asia*, edited by Sebastian C. H. Kim, 3–21. New York: Cambridge University Press, 2008.

Thomson, Iain. "Ontotheology? Understanding Heidegger's *Destruktion* of Metaphysics." *International Journal of Philosophical Studies* 8, no. 3 (2009): 297–327.

Tomoeda Ryutaro. "Yi T'oegye and Chu Hsi: Differences in Their Theories of Principle and Material Force." In *The Rise of Neo-Confucianism in Korea*, edited by Wm. Theodore de Bary and JaHyun Kim Haboush, 243–60. New York: Columbia University Press, 1985.

Tracy, David. *The Analogical Imagination: Christian Theology and the Culture of Pluralism*. New York: Crossroad, 1981.

Tu Wei-ming. *Confucian Thought: Selfhood as Creative Transformation*. Albany: State University of New York Press, 1985.

———. "T'oegye's Creative Interpretation of Chu Hsi's Philosophy of Principle." *Korea Journal* 22, no. 2 (1982): 12.

Tucker, Mary Evelyn. "The Philosophy of Ch'i as an Ecological Cosmology." In *Confucianism and Ecology*, edited by Mary Evelyn Tucker and John Berthrong, 187–207. Cambridge, Mass.: Harvard University Center for the Study of World Religions, 1998.

Wagner, Rudolf G. *A Chinese Reading of the Daodejing: Wang Bi's Commentary on the Laozi with Critical Text and Translation*. Albany: State University of New York Press, 2003.

Waley, Arthur. *The Way and Its Power: A Study of the Tao Tê Ching and Its Place in Chinese Thought*. London: George Allen and Unwin; New York: Macmillan, 1934.

Wallace, Mark I. *Finding God in the Singing River: Christianity, Spirit, Nature*. Minneapolis: Fortress Press, 2005.

———. *Fragments of the Spirit: Nature, Violence, and the Renewal of Creation*. New York: Continuum, 1996.

Wallack, F. Bradford. *The Epochal Nature of Process in Whitehead's Metaphysics*. Albany: State University of New York Press, 1980.

Wawrytko, Sandra A. "The Problem of the Problem of Evil: A Taoist Response." In *The Problem of Evil: An Intercultural Exploration*, edited by Sandra A. Wawrytko, 21–39. Amsterdam: Rodopi, 2000.

Weber, Max, *The Religion of China: Confucianism and Taoism*. Translated and edited by Hans H. Gerth. Glencoe, Ill.: Free Press, 1951.

Whitehead, Alfred North. *Adventures of Ideas*. New York: Free Press, 1967.

———. *Process and Reality: Corrected Edition*. Edited by David Ray Griffin and Donald W. Sherburne. New York: Free Press, 1978.

Yi Hwang (Toegye). *Toegye Jeonseo* [Complete works of Toegye]. Edited by Toegyehak chongseo pyeon-gan wiwonhoe. 17 vols. Seoul: Toegyehak yeon-guwon, 1989–94.

Yi I. *Gugyeok Yulgok Jeonseo* [Complete translated works of Yulgok]. Edited by Han-guk jeongsin munhwa yeon-guwon jaryo josasil. 7 vols. Gyeonggi-do Seongnam-si: Han-guk jeongsin munhwa yeon-guwon, 1984–1988.

Yi Seok-myeong, trans. *Noja dodeokgyeong hasang-gong jang-gu* [The Heshang Gong commentary to Laozi's Daodejing]. Seoul: Somyeong chulpansa, 2005.

Yoon Sung-bum. *Gidokgyowa hanguk sasang* [Christianity and Korean thought]. Seoul: Daehan gidokgyo seohoe, 1964.

Young, Robert J. C. *Postcolonialism: An Historical Introduction*. Oxford: Blackwell, 2001.

Yuasa Yasuo. *Momgwa uju* [The universe and the body]. Translated by Yi Jeong-bae and Yi Han-yeong. Seoul: Jisik saneopsa, 2004.

Yun Sasoon. *Critical Issues in Neo-Confucian Thought: The Philosophy of Yi T'oegye*. Translated by Michael C. Kalton. Seoul: Korea University Press, 1990.

———. "Donghagui yuhakjeok seongyeok [The Confucian character of Donghak]." In *Donghak sasang-ui saero-un jomeyong* [A new illumination of Donghak thought], edited by Minjok munhwa yeon-guso, 92–108. Gyeongsan-si, Gyeongsang buk-do: Yeongnam daehakgyo chulpanbu, 1998.

Yun Seok-san, trans. *Yongdam yusa*, by Choe Je-u. Seoul: Donghaksa, 1999.

Zhang Liwen. *Giui cheorak* [A philosophy of gi]. Translated by Kim Gyo-bin. Seoul: Yemun seowon, 2004.

Zhang Zai. *Zhengmeng* [Correcting the ignorant]. In *Zhang Zai ji* [Collected works of Zhang Zai], edited by Zhang Xichen. Beijing: Zhonghua shuju, 1978.

*Zhouyi zhengyi* [Correct meaning of the Classic of Change of the Zhou Dynasty]. Vol. 1 of *Shisan jing zhushu* [Commentaries and subcommenatries to the thirteen classics]. Edited by Ma Xinmin and Li Xueqin. Beijing: Beijing daxue chubanshe, 2000.

Zhu Xi. *Daehak·Jungyong jang-gu* [Collected commentaries on the Great Learning and the Doctrine of the Mean]. Rev. ed. Translated with commentary by Seong Baek-hyo. Seoul: Jeontong munhwa yeon-guhoe, 2006.

———. *Maengja jipju* [Collected commentaries on Mencius]. Translated with commentary by Seong Baek-hyo. Seoul: Jeontong munhwa yeon-guhoe, 1991.

———. *Non-eo jipju* [Collected commentaries on the Analects]. Translated with commentary by Seong Baek-hyo. Rev. and exp. ed. Seoul: Jeontong munhwa yeon-guhoe, 2006.

———. *Taiji tushou jie* [Commentary on the Explanation of the Diagram of the Great Ultimate]. In *Zhou Dunyi ji* [Collected works of Zhou Dunyi], edited by Chen Keming. Beijing: Zhonghua shuju, 1990.

———. *Zhuzi quanshu* [Complete works of Master Zhu]. Edited by Zhu Jieren et al. 27 vols. Shanghai: Shanghai guji chubanshe; Hefei: Anhui jiaoyu chubanshe, 2010.

———. *Zhuzi wenji* [Collected literary works of Master Zhu]. Edited by Chen Junmin. 10 vols. Taibei: Defu wenjiao jijinhui, 2000.

———. *Zhuzi yulei* [Conversations of Master Zhu, arranged topically]. Edited by Li Jingde and Wang Xingxian. 8 vols. Beijing: Zhonghua shuju, 1986.

Ziporyn, Brook. *The Penumbra Unbound: The Neo-Taoist Philosophy of Guo Xiang*. Albany: State University of New York Press, 2003.

Zizioulas, John D. *Being as Communion: Studies in Personhood and the Church*. Crestwood, N.Y.: St. Vladimir's Seminary Press, 1985.

# INDEX